A Reader's Guide
to the Short Stories of

MARK TWAIN

*A
Reference
Publication
in
Literature*

A Reader's Guide
to the Short Stories of
MARK TWAIN

James D. Wilson

G.K.HALL &CO.
70 LINCOLN STREET, BOSTON, MASS.

Library of Congress Cataloging-in-Publication Data

Wilson, James D. (James Darrell), 1946–
    A reader's guide to the short stories of Mark Twain.

    (A Reference publication in literature)
    Includes index.
    1. Twain, Mark, 1835–1910—Criticism and interpretation.   2. Twain,
Mark, 1835–1910—Bibliography.
I. Title.   II. Series.
PS1338.W5   1987   813'.4   86-29578
ISBN 0-8161-8721-5

This publication is printed on permanent / durable acid-free paper
MANUFACTURED IN THE UNITED STATES OF AMERICA

Contents

The Author

James D. Wilson is professor of English at the University of Southwestern Louisiana in Lafayette. Previously he taught at Georgia State University in Atlanta, where he served as editor of *Studies in the Literary Imagination* (1973–84). His publications include *The Romantic Heroic Ideal* (Baton Rouge: Louisiana State University Press, 1982) and more than a score of articles on nineteenth-century American literature and English and European romanticism. In addition he has edited three collections of essays: *American Realism: The Problem of Form* (1984); *Tradition and Revolution in Colonial American Literature* (1976); and, with Lilian R. Furst, *The Anti-Hero: His Emergence and Transformations* (1976). His studies of Mark Twain have appeared in such journals as the *Southern Review, Texas Studies in Literature and Language,* the *South Atlantic Review,* and the *Canadian Review of American Studies.* During the 1980–81 academic year, Professor Wilson served as Fulbright Senior Lecturer in American Literature at the University of Milan, Italy.

Preface

Never a formalist, Mark Twain wrote relatively few short stories that would satisfy strict application of genre requirements. Lines of demarcation between invention and reminiscence, fact and fiction, sketch or anecdote and story, are indistinctly drawn, and the author himself showed little disposition either to classify his work according to standardly accepted genres or to confine his comic genius within the rigid structural patterns those genres impose. As a result Mark Twain's accomplishments in the short story have not received the critical attention afforded other American masters in the genre like Poe, Hawthorne, or James. Granted, "Jim Smiley and His Jumping Frog," "Jim Baker's Blue Jay Yarn," and "The Man That Corrupted Hadleyburg" are acknowledged masterpieces, frequently anthologized and familiar to virtually every student of American literature. But the vast majority of his short narratives has received scant critical attention and is known only to professional scholars.

In the selection of material covered in this critical introduction to Mark Twain's short stories I have tried to be inclusive rather than exclusive. The sixty-five stories chosen for analysis span the length of Mark Twain's career as professional writer, show the diverse range of his genius, and reflect the themes and methods characteristic of his longer, more familiar works. Included are burlesques of popular literary forms, extended anecdotes or jokes adapted from oral tales, domestic farces, philosophical fables, science fiction, and sentimental pieces written in old age. All are self-contained short fictional narratives, under fifty pages in length, and essentially complete. A few of the pieces were published as short stories in magazines or miscellaneous collections of tales and sketches; many were written initially for newspapers and subsequently gathered in book form; some were intended as chapters in travel books but deleted and published separately; some appeared initially as chapters in *Roughing It, A Tramp Abroad, Life on the Mississippi,* or *Following the Equator,* then extracted and published as independent short stories by later editors; a few were published posthumously.

Charles Neider's edition of *The Complete Short Stories of Mark Twain* served as a basic guide in determining my selection of stories to be included, since it is to date the only available comprehensive anthology of Mark Twain's short fiction. I have added a few stories to Neider's list, primarily early burlesques like "Aurelia's Unfortunate Young Man" and "Lucretia Smith's Soldier," and several stories published for the first time after Neider's 1957 edition. I have also deleted a few exceedingly brief pieces, such as "Hunting the Deceitful Turkey," "Playing Courier," and "Science vs. Luck," that are really more sketches or essays than stories and have received virtually no scholarly commentary. The most notable deletion is *The Mysterious Stranger,* which presents enormous textual difficulties and is, even in its fragmentary form, more a novella than a short story; the corrupt text printed in the Neider edition runs to seventy-seven pages. The student who wishes to include *The Mysterious Stranger* in a study of Mark Twain's short fiction should begin with the Iowa-California edition of *Mark Twain's Mysterious Stranger Manuscripts,* edited by William M. Gibson (Berkeley and Los Angeles: University of California Press, 1969) and Sholom Kahn, *Mark Twain's Mysterious Stranger: A Study of the Manuscript Texts* (Columbia: University of Missouri Press, 1979).

A Reader's Guide to the Short Stories of Mark Twain offers a critical introduction to each of sixty-five stories. The format follows that established in Lea Newman's pioneering guide to Hawthorne's short fiction (Boston: G. K. Hall, 1982). As a general rule, each chapter focuses on an individual short story, and stories appear in alphabetical order. In some instances, however, I have grouped several related stories in a single chapter to minimize repetition or to avoid excessively short chapters devoted to stories that have received little scholarly attention. An appendix lists the stories in chronological order according to year of initial publication.

Each chapter is subdivided into five sections. The first details the publication history of each story—when and where it first appeared in print, subsequent reprintings during the author's lifetime, significant revisions, and the most reliable texts currently available to the general reader. For information in this section I am greatly indebted to Merle Johnson's *Bibliography of the Works of Mark Twain,* rev. ed. (New York: Harper & Brothers, 1935), to Albert Paine's *Mark Twain: A Biography,* 4 vols. (New York: Harper & Brothers, 1912), to Everett Emerson's *The Authentic Mark Twain: A Literary Biography of Samuel L. Clemens* (Philadelphia: University of Pennsylvania Press, 1984), and to the excellent introductions and textual commentaries in the Iowa-California edition of *The Works of Mark Twain,* specifically *Early Tales & Sketches,* vol. 2 *(1864–1865), Roughing It,* and *Mark Twain's Fables of Man.*

The second section of each chapter provides historical and biographical background information relevant to the story's composition—when and where each story was written, biographical and cultural forces that influenced its composition, and sources from Mark Twain's reading and/ or personal experience that inspired the tale. The third section places the story in context, drawing appropriate parallels in theme, style, and method to other Mark Twain works. The fourth section offers a critical synopsis of the story, focusing on its distinguishing characteristics; it also summarizes relevant scholarly commentary, assesses the story's critical standing, and highlights points of critical controversy. Each chapter concludes with a comprehensive bibliography of materials germane to a study of the story or stories under consideration. The reader should note that the primary source for the story treated in a given chapter is marked by an asterisk (*) before the item in the chapter's primary bibliography. The book is thus intended to serve a dual function: to provide an introduction and guide for the general reader to stories with which he or she may not be familiar; and to assist the specialist by bringing together in cohesive form a review of all scholarship directly germane to a particular story.

The comprehensive chapter bibliographies are designed to indicate my specific indebtedness in preparing this reference guide and to direct the student or scholar who wishes to investigate a particular story more thoroughly. Such a format necessitates repetition. Certain scholarly books are cited throughout the guide as they are indispensable to any study of Mark Twain's work: Albert B. Paine's 1912 biography; Everett Emerson's detailed study of his literary career; landmark investigations of his comic methods by Pascal Covici, Jr., Henry Nash Smith, and James M. Cox; studies of his early work in the West by Ivan Benson and Edgar Branch; Howard Baetzhold's meticulous analysis of literary sources in *Mark Twain and John Bull: The British Connection;* and the evaluations of the accomplishments of the last decade of Mark Twain's life by Hamlin Hill and William Macnaughton. Equally indispensable to my work were certain reference tools that I did not have occasion to mention in the individual bibliographies: the Merle Johnson bibliography, Alan Gribben's two-volume *Mark Twain's Library: A Reconstruction* (Boston: G. K. Hall, 1980), and Thomas A. Tenney's comprehensive annotated bibliography, *Mark Twain: A Reference Guide* (Boston: G. K. Hall, 1977) together with his annual supplements in *American Literary Realism.* I would also like to acknowledge my indebtedness to my wife and colleague, Mary Ann Wilson, who read my manuscript carefully and offered invaluable encouragement and suggestions for its improvement at every stage of its preparation.

Aurelia's Unfortunate Young Man

Publication History

The story first appeared in print 22 October 1864 in the San Francisco *Californian*, bearing the title "Whereas" and introduced by a mock personal essay about "Love's Bakery." Mark Twain made several revisions on the newspaper clipping for inclusion in his first book. Evidence indicates that at the time of these revisions he intended to retain the "Love's Bakery" portion of the original version. His publisher, however, shortened the sketch by deleting the introductory essay and retitled it "Aurelia's Unfortunate Young Man" (*Celebrated Jumping Frog* 20–25). The authorized British edition, published by George Routledge and Sons (1872) incorporates minor authorial revisions detailed by Branch and Hirst (*Works* 597–604). The two authorized American editions of Mark Twain sketches (1874; 1875) reprint the Routledge text. The Iowa-California edition of *The Works of Mark Twain* includes a text based on the original publication in the *Californian*.

Circumstances of Composition, Sources, and Influences

This sketch is one of Mark Twain's "freshest and most original" early pieces. Like much of his California journalism, "Aurelia's Unfortunate Young Man" assumes the burlesque form in vogue at the time and directs its satire at one of the most fashionable targets of San Francisco's literary bohemians: the conventions of sentimental romantic fiction (Emerson 24, 30–31). The opening account of "Love's Bakery," which, Mark Twain writes, serves "as a peculiarly fitting introductory to a story of love and misfortune," mimics the polite familiar essay form established by Oliver Goldsmith, Washington Irving, and Charles Lamb. The subsequent story of Aurelia's love for her "unfortunate young man" employs black comedy as a means of satirizing the genre of sentimental romance. Its frame—Mark Twain responding to a letter from the unknown young woman of San José—burlesques the popular newspaper column of advice to correspondents (*Works* 86–87). Rogers reports that in its use of the burlesque form and in its control of language—alliterative sentences, puns, marked prose rhythms—the story shows evidence of the author's debt to Charles Henry Webb, editor of the *Californian* who later in New York (1867) published Mark Twain's first book (20–23).

Relationship to Other Mark Twain Works

Branch cites "Aurelia's Unfortunate Young Man" as an example of Mark Twain's tendency during this early journalistic period to begin with a humorous idea and then play it for all the comic effect he can wring from it (117–18). Mark Twain also burlesqued letters from the lovelorn seeking advice from newspaper columnists in "Answers to Correspondents," a weekly feature in the *Californian* during June-July 1865 (*Works* 86). In its attack on sentimental romantic fiction, the story bears affinities to "Lucretia Smith's Soldier" (1864) and "Story of the Bad Little Boy" (1865)— "condensed novels" that satirize genteel sensitivities and romantic expectations. Mark Twain wrote to William Dean Howells (23 August 1876) that although he had "heard of readers convulsing audiences" in oral renditions of the sketch, he failed to see the basis of its lasting appeal: if there was "anything really funny in the piece, the author is not aware of it" (*Mark Twain-Howells Letters* 147). Yet in *Adventures of Huckleberry Finn* (1885), Mark Twain returns to a variation on the same theme in Huck's delightful deadpan account of Emmeline Grangerford's ridiculously outlandish graveyard verse and morbid drawings.

Critical Studies

Scholars have virtually ignored this comic sketch, other than to point out its purpose—to satirize "romantic love stories" (Branch, *Literary Apprenticeship*, 117–18; Emerson 24, 30–33)—or to mention briefly its essential form, the burlesque (Rogers 20–23; *Works* 86–87). Yet intrinsically the story has qualities that give it some distinction among Mark Twain's early fiction.

A key to the story's comic success lies in the author's delicate control of point of view and understated language. Like Huck Finn in his account of Emmeline Grangerford, Mark Twain is the outsider who in relating the "story of love and misfortune" (90) never betrays the awareness that what he recounts is absurd. The object of Aurelia's faithful affections, Williamson Breckenridge Caruthers, proves indeed a most trying and ill-fated young man. A bout with a virulent strain of smallpox leaves his face "pitted like a waffle-mould" (91). The day before his scheduled wedding, Caruthers stumbles into an open well while watching an ascending balloon and breaks a leg, which consequently is removed "above the knee." The "premature discharge of a Fourth-of-July cannon" costs him one arm, and three months later "a carding-machine" wrenches out the other (91). As the rescheduled wedding day approaches, Caruthers falls victim to erysipelas, losing sight in one eye. Subsequently he breaks his remaining leg—it too is amputated—and is the only man scalped by a raiding party of Owens River Indians. Emphasis in the story, however, falls on what Emerson calls "Aurelia's inner life" (24), for "deeply grieved to see her lover passing from her piecemeal," Aurelia must contend with the "field of her affections . . . growing more and more circumscribed everyday" (91–92). Possessing "a generous spirit which did her credit," Aurelia is in a quandary: "she still loves what is left" of her lover (92), but her parents oppose the match because the couple's financial prospects seem dim indeed.

As advisor to the lovelorn, Mark Twain too faces a most delicate situation, one that "involves the life-long happiness of a woman, and that of nearly two-thirds of a man" (92). His ostensibly practical advice—delivered deadpan as "a mere suggestion in the case"—is as outlandish as the situation of the man "whose extraordinary instincts were against him": Aurelia, if she can "afford the expense," should "furnish her mutilated lover with wooden arms and wooden legs, and a glass eye and a wig, and give him another show" (93). If he survives three months, she should then marry him, for even in the likely event that "his infernal propensity for damaging himself every time he sees a good opportunity" finishes him, "the wooden legs and such other valuables as he may possess, revert to the widow" (93).

The relationship of the introductory frame essay on "Love's Bakery" to the account of Aurelia's dilemma with her ill-fated young man adds a dimension of complexity to the original story absent in subsequent abridged versions. The diction of the opening paragraph serves to establish the character of the columnist, whose position as advisor to romantic young lovers positions him as the defender of genteel sympathies. The sight of a mere window sign occasions "the sensation of mingled astonishment, gladness, hope, doubt, anxiety, and balmy, blissful emotion that suffused my being and quivered in a succession of streaky thrills down my backbone" (88). In the midst of urban San Francisco, the presence of "a place devoted to the high and holy employment of instilling the passion of love into the human heart" fosters the tantalizing conceit that one can engineer human happiness, can "take a couple of hopeful hearts in the rough, and work them up, with spices and shortening and sweetening enough to last for a lifetime, and turn them out well kneaded together, baked to a turn, and ready for matrimony" (89). Such hopes implicitly buttress all those who extend advice to correspondents, for in serving as mentors to those who seek the bliss of romantic love, columnists "invade the very realms of the immortal, and presume to guide and control the great passions, the unpalpable essences, that have hitherto dwelt in the secret chambers of the soul" (88).

Unfortunately the grim reality of life shatters the fanciful expectations of those who presume to engineer happiness. Aurelia and Caruthers, "victims of an accumulation of distressing circumstances," render absurd the assumption that "by some mysterious magic, by some strange and awful invention, the divine emotion was to be confined within set bounds and limits, controlled, weighed, measured, and doled out to God's creatures in quantities and qualities to suit the purchaser, like vulgar beer and candles!" (90). The original version of the story provides an arena in which the sentimental illusions of genteel romance must confront reality, the specific case that illuminates the false assumptions and gross ineffectuality of "Love's Bakery." Committed to upholding the illusions of genteel romance, the columnist is trapped when confronted with an actual situation that renders those illusions blatantly inappropriate. His "delicate" response is wonderfully ambiguous, for while it sustains the genteel ideal of love faithful to the end, it deflates the absurd sentimentality with the practical observation about the widow's inheritance.

Bibliography

PRIMARY

The Celebrated Jumping Frog of Calaveras County, and Other Sketches. Edited by John Paul. New York: Charles Henry Webb, 1867.

Mark Twain-Howells Letters: The Correspondence of Samuel L. Clemens and William Dean Howells, 1872–1910. Vol. 1. Edited by Henry Nash Smith and William M. Gibson. Cambridge, Mass.: Harvard University Press, 1960.

Mark Twain's Sketches. Selected and Revised by the Author. London: George Routledge & Sons, 1872.

Mark Twain's Sketches, New and Old. Now First Published in Complete Form. Hartford and Chicago: American Publishing Co., 1875.

Mark Twain's Sketches, Number One. Authorized Edition. New York: American News Co., 1874.

The Works of Mark Twain: Early Tales & Sketches. Vol. 2 (1864–1865). Edited by Edgar M. Branch and Robert H. Hirst. Vol. 15 of the Iowa-California edition of *The Works of Mark Twain.* Berkeley and Los Angeles: University of California Press, 1981.

SECONDARY

Branch, Edgar M. *The Literary Apprenticeship of Mark Twain, With Selections from His Apprentice Writing.* Urbana: University of Illinois Press, 1950.

Emerson, Everett. *The Authentic Mark Twain: A Literary Biography of Samuel L. Clemens.* Philadelphia: University of Pennsylvania Press, 1984.

Rogers, Franklin R. *Mark Twain's Burlesque Patterns.* Dallas: Southern Methodist University Press, 1960.

2

The Belated Russian Passport

Publication History

The story was first published in *Harper's Weekly*, 6 December 1902. Book publication came the following year in *My Debut as a Literary Person*.

Circumstances of Composition, Sources, and Influences

Mark Twain wrote "The Belated Russian Passport" while living at York Harbor, Maine, in the summer of 1902. Most of his attention that summer went to his wife, Olivia, whose health was rapidly deteriorating. His literary interests focused primarily on plans for a new Huckleberry Finn-Tom Sawyer book although, as Macnaughton reports, nothing survives from this project save a few notebook entries (186–89). Two other fragments, "Tom Sawyer's Conspiracy" and "Which Was It?," also date to this period; both are aborted fictional attempts to depict the plight of the freed slave. "The Belated Russian Passport" is lighter fare and reflects his belief "that topical and contemporaneous materials were the right ones for current publication" (Hill 49). Mark Twain read the story to William Dean Howells, who later in a letter refers to its "goat's tail ending" (Paine 1177).

Relationship to Other Mark Twain Works

Baldanza reads the story as a satire on bureaucracy and as such links it to "The Man Who Put Up at Gadsby's" (1880) and "Facts in the Great Beef Contract" (1876) (99). The satirical elements assume minor importance in the story, however, for it is a neatly crafted but intellectually light piece designed primarily for entertainment. Like "A Medieval Romance" (1870) and "A Story without End" (from *Following the Equator* [1897]), "The Belated Russian Passport" leads its protagonist into a seemingly impossible dilemma. Unlike the first two stories, which abandon the hero to a tragic or embarrassing fate because the author cannot devise a way out, "The Belated Russian Passport" employs an O. Henry, or "goat's tail," ending—a sudden comic twist—that rescues poor Parrish from seemingly inevitable exile to Siberia. The combination of the hero's timid nature, implacable governmental regulations, and circumstance seems to move toward pathos; however, the tone throughout is mildly comic, dissipating any deep reader concern and preparing for the surprise conclusion.

Critical Studies

"The Belated Russian Passport" has received very little scholarly attention. Ferguson calls it "a mere skit" (292), and Emerson claims the story "put Mark Twain's talents to no good purpose" (243). Paine is a bit more enthusiastic when he labels it "a strong, intensely interesting story," but he laments that Mark Twain allowed the piece to dissipate into "a joke . . . altogether unimportant, and on the whole disappointing" (1177).

Actually the story is a competent if undistinguished piece of commercial fiction, well paced and mildly entertaining even if void of any significant intellectual substance. It details the catastrophic adventure of a homesick American youth, Alfred Parrish, traveling in Europe. "Girlish and timorous" by nature, Parrish is cajoled by a pompous and domineering American army major into visiting Saint Petersburg before returning home. Though the proposal runs counter to his instinct and better judgment, Parrish is powerless before his "brisk and businesslike" elder who "seemed to exude energy." Parrish surrenders his rail tickets to Paris and all his money to the fast-talking stranger, who then books passage to Russia. Real danger lurks when the Russian consul is out of town and the office clerk refuses to issue a required visa; the major convinces Parrish to leave his passport behind, on the expectation that the visa will be approved and forwarded to Saint Petersburg with the passport on the next day's mail train. This he does, even though the penalty for traveling in Russia without a passport is "ten years in Siberia."

Events then rush toward the apparently inevitable ruin of the timorous Parrish. Once smuggled into Russia, Parrish finds that his major's "connections" prove illusory—though "the major's eloquence and the boy's misery" do manage to coax a twenty-four-hour reprieve from a Russian prince: "If the passport is not here then, don't come near me; it's Siberia without hope of pardon" (417). An accident involving the mail train seems to spell certain doom, but the major sees a ray of hope; they will secure a new passport at the American embassy in Saint Petersburg, which consists "of a room and a half on the ninth floor, ... a minister or an ambassador with a brakeman's salary, a secretary of legation who sells matches and mends crockery for a living, a hired girl for interpreter and general utility, pictures of the American liners, a chromo of the reigning President, a desk, three chairs, kerosene-lamp, a cat, a clock, and a cuspidor with the motto,

'In God We Trust' " (420). All seems lost when they learn that the minister is on vacation, and the secretary refuses to cooperate because "there's no way in the world to identify" the pathetic boy. Then, just as Parrish's doom seems certain, the O. Henry ending comes to the rescue. The secretary, hearing the boy's name, begins nonchalantly to question him. The questioning grows more insistent, until finally it turns out that the secretary had once lived in a Connecticut rooming house with Parrish's family and had in fact painted a picture that the boy's clergyman father, in an unguarded moment, had labeled "the hell-firedest nightmare he ever struck!" The secretary thus can identify Parrish and issue the passport. Parrish is saved by his memories of home and his father's honest, if injudiciously vocal, bit of art criticism: " 'Oh, come to my arms, my poor rescued boy,' cried the Major, 'We will always be grateful to God that He made this artist—if He did' " (423).

Bibliography

PRIMARY

The Complete Short Stories of Mark Twain. Now Collected for the First Time. Edited by Charles Neider. Garden City, N.Y.: Hanover House, 1957.

My Debut as a Literary Person with Other Essays and Stories. Hartford: American Publishing Co., 1903.

SECONDARY

Baldanza, Frank. *Mark Twain: An Introduction and Interpretation*. New York: Holt, Rinehart & Winston, 1961.

Emerson, Everett. *The Authentic Mark Twain: A Literary Biography of Samuel L. Clemens*. Philadelphia: University of Pennsylvania Press, 1984.

Ferguson, Delancey. *Mark Twain: Man and Legend*. Indianapolis: Bobbs-Merrill, 1943.

Hill, Hamlin. *Mark Twain: God's Fool*. New York: Harper & Row, 1973.

Macnaughton, William R. *Mark Twain's Last Years as a Writer*. Columbia: University of Missouri Press, 1979.

Paine, Albert B. *Mark Twain: A Biography*. Vol. 3. New York: Harper & Brothers, 1912.

3

The Californian's Tale

Publication History

Mark Twain wrote "The Californian's Tale" in late summer, 1892, and promptly sent it to his agent Fred Hall for placement. Before Hall could get it in print, Mark Twain sent a copy of the story to Arthur Stedman, who published it in an 1893 volume entitled *The First Book of the Authors Club, Liber Scriptorum* (Emerson 188). The story is collected in the 1906 Harper and Brothers edition of *The $30,000 Bequest and Other Stories*.

Circumstances of Composition, Sources, and Influences

Having just completed an extended jaunt through Switzerland and Italy, Mark Twain settled for the summer 1892 in Bad Nauheim, Germany. He was apparently in quite good spirits, for he had learned from two local physicians that Olivia's health problems were not as severe as he had feared. He wrote to his brother Orion: "the bath physicians say positively that Livy has no heart disease but has only weakness of the heart muscles and will soon be well again. That was worth going to Europe to find out" (Paine 950–51). This good news freed him to devote his energies to his writing; moreover, the expenses of European travel impressed upon him the necessity of earning a living with his pen. That summer he began *Tom Sawyer Abroad* (1894) and *Pudd'nhead Wilson* (1894) in addition to completing five stories and nine essays. In October, after settling in at the Villa Viviani in Florence, he began *Personal Recollections of Joan of Arc* (1896) (Paine 957; Emerson 188).

The germ of "The Californian's Tale" actually dates back to Mark Twain's sojourn with Jim Gillis in the Tuolumne country at Angel's Camp during the winter 1864–65 (Benson 127). DeVoto reports that Mark Twain had been deeply impressed by the aging miners he encountered in the saloons there, "a dwindling race" of "melancholy men who had failed to find gold and could not bear to go home" and "who declined through eccentricity to madness" (169). The broken spirit of these pathetic men certainly inspired his portrait of the husband and his "grizzled, stranded pioneer" friends Tom, Joe, and Charley (269). While at Angel's Camp, Mark Twain had jotted down notes that later formed the basis of his story (Bellamy 145), and in 1882 he recorded in his notebook a rough plot outline that he elaborated in his story a decade later (Emerson 188).

Mark Twain's longstanding concern with Olivia's health perhaps explains why he delayed so long in writing "The Californian's Tale." The good news he received—that she had no heart disease and would get better—perhaps freed him in the summer 1892 to return to the story of a man's lingering affection for his wife, who had been dead nineteen years. That he treats the story sentimentally should come as no surprise; he had, after all, confronted the possibility of Livy's death for more than a decade, and during the composition of the story he fretted over rumors of a cholera epidemic in Hamburg (Paine 952).

Relationship to Other Mark Twain Works

Throughout most of his career, Mark Twain launched a sustained attack upon sentimentality. Prime examples are his "condensed novels"— "Aurelia's Unfortunate Young Man" (1864), "Lucretia Smith's Soldier" (1864), "Story of the Bad Little Boy" (1865)—in which he ridiculed the sentimental conventions of popular fiction and dramatized the radical discrepancy between genteel expectations and harsh reality. As in the Emmeline Grangerford section of *Huckleberry Finn* (1885), burlesque and parody are the tools of his comic deflation that render absurd a sentimental, escapist approach to life's inherent tragedies. During the last fifteen years of his life, the attacks on sentimentality continued: sometimes explicitly, in the form of bitter diatribes that exploded comfortable myths regarding humanity's "special" place in a providentially ordered universe (e.g., *The Mysterious Stranger* [1916]); sometimes ironically, in narratives that lay bare a universally depraved human nature (*Pudd'nhead Wilson*, "The Man That Corrupted Hadleyburg" [1899], "The $30,000 Bequest" [1904]).

Stone points out, however, that in his late writings Mark Twain reveals a dual personality, becoming not only "the sardonic satirist" but also a "soft-hearted man of feeling" (169–70). "The Californian's Tale" belongs to a group of stories and fragments that manifests the very sentimentality he characteristically ridiculed in his earlier fiction and essays. The group includes such maudlin pieces as *Joan of Arc*, "Was It Heaven? or Hell?" (1902), "The Death Disk" (1901), "A Dog's Tale" (1903), and "A Horse's Tale" (1906). All suffer aesthetically from the author's failure to establish ironic detachment from his subject (Baldanza 101; Bellamy 370).

The evocation of the California mining camps and their memorable, even haunting, inhabitants links "The Californian's Tale" to such early stories as "Jim Smiley and His Jumping Frog" (1865) and "Jim Baker's Blue Jay Yarn" (1880). This story, however, is humorless and lacks the narrative sophistication of the earlier California tales. Despite the title, Mark Twain tells the story, not the vernacular protagonist. Moreover, there is neither dramatic irony nor distance established between Mark Twain the author and either Mark Twain the character, or the reader: we learn the details of the plot only as Mark Twain does, and his response to the principals involved governs our own.

Critical Studies

Those few scholars who give any attention to "The Californian's Tale" uniformly lament its sentimentality (Bellamy 324; DeVoto 169; Emerson 244). The story, however, does have redeeming features. Rhode calls attention to the author's skillful control of setting: "The Californian's Tale" is "the single example of a short story in which the reader's eye is actually trained on the landscape, and in which a scene is maintained long enough to make any real impression" (91–92). The plot is carefully crafted with little superfluous commentary, and the O. Henry twist at the end catches the reader by surprise even though it is consistent with the elegiac tone established at the outset. The trick ending actually mitigates the tragedy. The discovery that the absent bride has been dead nineteen years and that what we have witnessed is an annual ritual—a communal charade that sustains the husband by keeping alive the memory of his beloved and hope for her potential return—deflects the focus from what would have been a catastrophically tragic recognition scene. The emphasis falls instead on the pathetic husband's moving love for his bride and the remarkable camaraderie that provides community among the "living dead men—pride-smitten poor fellows, grizzled and old at forty, whose secret thoughts were made all of regrets and longings . . . regrets for their wasted lives, and longings to be out of the struggle and done with it all" (266).

Typically Mark Twain's fiction employs irony and burlesque to undercut sentimental illusions that render impossible any honest or authentic human intercourse. In "The Californian's Tale," however, illusion proves beneficial, for it makes bearable an otherwise bleak existence. Tuttleville, a "lovely region, woodsy, balmy, delicious," had once been "populous"; now, however, it is a virtual ghost town: "the people had vanished and the charming paradise was a solitude" (266). In the midst of this desolation sits a "cosy little rose-clad" cottage—an oasis that is well kept, nicely furnished, feminine. The cottage, of course, is part of the charade; but it is also a breath of life to which gravitate the "grizzled, stranded pioneers"— at first twenty-seven of them "without counting the girls," now only three.

The illusion sustains life, occasions human affection and meaningful community, in the face of a reality that threatens their extinction. In short, the story testifies to the remarkable resilience of the human spirit.

Bibliography

PRIMARY

*The Complete Short Stories of Mark Twain. Now Collected for the First Time. Edited by Charles Neider. Garden City, N.Y.: Hanover House, 1957.

The $30,000 Bequest and Other Stories. New York: Harper & Brothers, 1906.

SECONDARY

Baldanza, Frank. Mark Twain: An Introduction and Interpretation. New York: Holt, Rinehart & Winston, 1961.

Bellamy, Gladys C. Mark Twain as a Literary Artist. Norman: University of Oklahoma Press, 1950.

Benson, Ivan. Mark Twain's Western Years. Stanford, Calif.: Stanford University Press, 1938.

DeVoto, Bernard. Mark Twain's America. Boston: Little, Brown, 1932.

Emerson, Everett. The Authentic Mark Twain: A Literary Biography of Samuel L. Clemens. Philadelphia: University of Pennsylvania Press, 1984.

Paine, Albert B. Mark Twain: A Biography. Vol. 3. New York: Harper & Brothers, 1912.

Rhode, Robert D. Setting in the American Short Story of Local Color, 1865–1900. The Hague: Mouton, 1975.

Stone, Albert E., Jr. The Innocent Eye: Childhood in Mark Twain's Imagination. New Haven: Yale University Press, 1961.

4

Cannibalism in the Cars

Publication History

The story appeared originally in the November 1868 issue of the *Broadway,* an English journal that was essentially a house organ for George Routledge and Sons, later to become Mark Twain's authorized British publisher. Routledge reprinted the story in its 1872 collection of Mark Twain sketches. Clemens and Bliss subsequently included it in the authorized American collected edition.

Circumstances of Composition, Sources, and Influences

"Cannibalism in the Cars" was written shortly after Mark Twain's return to the United States from his excursion to Europe and the Holy Land aboard the *Quaker City,* during a period (1867–69), Steinbrink contends, when "the basic terms of accommodation between writer and persona were at least provisionally established" (300). Although he completed an extended and exhausting lecture tour of the Northeast and Midwest and worked diligently at revising the *Alta California* travel letters into *Innocents Abroad* (1869), Mark Twain feared his career had grown stagnant. He wrote in a 4 June 1869 letter to his mother and sister: "In twelve months (or rather I believe it is fourteen) I have earned just *eighty dollars* by my pen—two little magazine & one newspaper letter—altogether the idlest, laziest 14 months I ever spent in my life" (Emerson 55–56).

The relative lack of productivity during the period resulted from two related phenomena: a) most of Mark Twain's energies focused on his courtship of Olivia Langdon—"I have had really *no* inclination to anything but court Livy," he wrote in the 4 June letter—and b) ashamed of his reputation and achievement as a "mere" humorist, Mark Twain desperately wanted to establish himself as a respectable man-of-letters, to change the course his career seemed to be following. In a letter to Mrs. Fairbanks, thanking her for persuading her husband to print his Christmas Eve 1868 nativity letter in a Cleveland, Ohio, newspaper, Mark Twain adds that Livy "wants me to thank you from her heart . . . & she wants a copy of the paper— poor girl, anybody who could convince her that I was not a humorist would secure her eternal gratitude! She thinks a humorist is something perfectly awful" (*Mark Twain to Fairbanks* 63). Brooks sees the revisions in the *Alta* letters to make them suitable for book publication as part of a general pattern in Mark Twain's career at the time, a pathetic attempt to please and soothe the mundane pieties of those—especially Olivia Langdon and Mrs. Fairbanks—whom he thought representative of the dominant culture (147). Steinbrink more or less concurs with Brooks: the attempt to "reform" his career under the spell of Olivia led to his temporary "alienation from the imaginative resources embodied in Mark Twain" (311). So complete was his repudiation of his past achievement that Mark Twain, in a 31 December 1868 letter, begged Livy: "*Don't* read a word of that jumping frog book, Livy—*don't*. I hate to hear that infamous volume mentioned. I would be glad to know that every copy of it was burned, & gone forever. I'll never write another like it" (*Love Letters* 41).

Fortunately Mark Twain's actions did not adhere to the sentiments of the letter to Livy. The "Jumping Frog" book proved highly successful, both the 1867 Webb text (see Primary Bibliography, Chap. 1) and numerous pirated reprintings of it in England. Mark Twain supervised authorized reissues of most of its sketches in 1872, 1874, and 1875. But clearly at the time, Mark Twain wanted his writing to take a more serious turn: humorists, he thought, wanted only to make the public laugh; "he was determined," Steinbrink writes, "to make it think and feel as well" (310). In its political satire and moral implications (that human nature is inherently selfish), "Cannibalism in the Cars" reflects this new dimension to Mark Twain's comic sketches.

Sloane reports (93, n. 10) that Artemus Ward, while in London in 1866, provided an analogue for the story. The analogue is printed by Aaron Watson in "Artemus Ward and Mark Twain," *The Savage Club* (London: Fisher Unwin, 1907), 120–22. Political satire had long been a favorite genre of American humorists, dating back to pre–Revolutionary War times; most of it, however, had been the work of conservatives casting a critical eye on the social and political foibles of an emergent democracy. Despite the elevated, sophisticated tone that Mark Twain learned to cultivate under the influence of San Francisco's bohemian literary colony in the early 1860s, his "Jumping Frog" story and travel letters to the *Alta* had earned him a reputation as the exponent of a typically American egalitarian point of view. Increasingly, however, his writing, as in "Cannibalism in the Cars," considered the ambiguities of American political and moral life (Sloane 85).

Branch provides a full discussion of sources for "Cannibalism in the Cars," as he uses the story as an illustration of the author's creative method. The central source, Branch suggests, is an article that appeared in Orion's newspaper, the *Muscatine Tri-Weekly Journal* (9 February 1855), entitled "Three Hundred People in a Snow Bank." It reports of a train loaded with a contingent of Illinois legislators and their families that becomes snow-bound for days; to avoid starvation, the group had to eat dogs. "Cannibalism in the Cars" builds upon this remembered newspaper story incorporating bits and pieces of recollected personal experience. Directly germane, Branch points out, are Mark Twain's recent and direct experience of politics in the nation's capital and earlier in frontier Nevada, his several rail trips across Illinois and in particular a long overnight journey on a passenger train through a menacing snowstorm in March 1867, "and his observation of human behavior in varied unfriendly environments that placed a premium upon survival at any cost." The fact that five of the characters in the story bear the names of Mark Twain's good friends—Howland, Bowen, Van Nostrand, Slote, and Charley Langdon—and that most of the others are named for people Mark Twain had known in Washington, Nevada, or Hannibal, lends an air of verisimilitude to this grotesque tale of "man's ineradicable competitive violence" (585–91).

Relationship to Other Mark Twain Works

The macabre humor and extravagant effect of "Cannibalism in the Cars" link it to "The Invalid's Story" (1882) and "The Great Prize Fight," (1863) pieces that arise from what Bellamy calls "the primitive humor of cruelty" (123; Baldanza 101). In "Riley—Newspaper Correspondent," published in the *Galaxy,* November 1870, Mark Twain reduced the story to a one-line joke: "a grand human barbeque in honor of [the cannibal flag], in which it was noticed that the better a man liked a friend the better he enjoyed him" (Sloane 93, n. 10). As political satire or legislative burlesque, however, the story is actually a polished culmination of a series of newspaper parodies Mark Twain had written during the preceding year: a burlesque of governmental rhetoric in the Saint Louis *Republican,* March 1867; an attack on P. T. Barnum's candidacy for U.S. Congress, "How Are the Mighty Fallen!" in the 9 April 1867 *Alta California* and a variant, "Barnum's First Speech in Congress," published in the New York *Evening Express,* 5 March 1867; and numerous newspaper burlesques on the question of women's suffrage published during 1867–68. Although its comic diction and frame structure make "Cannibalism in the Cars" more generalized than these earlier related pieces, the political cynicism characteristic of them all foreshadows *The Gilded Age* (1873) and Pap's diatribe against the "gov'ment" in *Huckleberry Finn* (1885) (Sloane 84–90).

In its use of the frame—Mark Twain listening to a "member of Congress" relate the gruesome story—"Cannibalism in the Cars" recalls "Jim Smiley and His Jumping Frog" (1865). Both combine a storyteller who employs digression and deadpan delivery with a fantastic burlesque rooted in contemporary American life. The fact that we are auditors to a narrated story rather than witnesses to the event renders the whole a "fantasy" whose ultimate subject is the ethics governing any corporate body. Although at the conclusion of the tale Mark Twain "felt inexpressibly relieved to know that I had only been listening to the harmless vagaries of a madman instead of the genuine experiences of a bloodthirsty cannibal" (383), the naturalistic theme of the tale remains clear: in times of crisis even the most civilized of people will revert to savagery to protect their interests. As Sloane points out, later episodes in Mark Twain's longer works depend precisely on this method: "they are applicable as philosophical experience even though the reader knows they are unreal" (94–95).

Critical Studies

Despite the fact that in its announcement of *Sketches, New and Old* the New York *Tribune* (21 September 1875) singled out "Cannibalism in the Cars" with "The Jumping Frog" and "the erudite papers on 'Political Economy' " as "productions by which Mr. Clemens has become famous in the scientific world" (Hill 95), the story has received very little scholarly attention. In assessing the impact of *Sketches, New and Old,* Paine argued in 1912 that with the exception of "The Jumping Frog" and "A True Story" (1874) the volume contains little of enduring value: "There is no reason to suppose that any of its contents will escape oblivion. The greater number of the sketches [including "Cannibalism in the Cars"] . . . would better have been allowed to die" (441). With the exception of Bellamy, who briefly examines the story in terms of Stephen Leacock's *Humor: The Theory and Technique,* noting the "disharmony between a thing and its setting, between its present and its usual accompaniment" (123–24), only Sloane and Branch have given "Cannibalism in the Cars" more than cursory mention. The latter, however, calls the story "a brilliant tour de force that successfully blends grim insights, macabre humor, and hilarious political satire into a skillfully structured, powerful statement" (585).

The unobtrusive frame to the story does little more than to establish its fable qualities, for there is minimal interaction between Mark Twain and the tale's eventual narrator, "a mild, benevolent-looking gentleman" with a thorough knowledge of "the ins and outs of political life at the Capital," who sits next to him on the train from Terre Haute to Saint Louis. A conversation between two men nearby seems to trigger the narrator's memory, and he offers to reveal to Mark Twain "a secret chapter of my life—a chapter that has never been referred to by me since its events transpired" (371). The uninterrupted story he tells to the stunned auditor resembles Hawthorne's account of Goodman Brown's rendezvous in the forest or the Ancient Mariner's adventure on the "painted ocean"; it is a fantastic—even surrealistic—fable with gruesome moral and political implications that remain even after Mark Twain's ostensibly reassuring discovery that he had "been listening to the harmless vagaries of a madman."

The story concerns a party of twenty-four men aboard a train from Washington to Chicago who become stranded in a snowstorm. Their initially jovial mood turns to gloom as they confront the "cheerless prospect" of an indifferent nature: "not a living thing visible anywhere, not a human habitation; nothing but a vast white desert" (374). Alienated from all vestiges of civilization and faced with imminent starvation, the men resort to cannibalism. They mask their barbarism, however, by clinging to the polite rules of parliamentary procedure to govern the selection of their meals. A series of legislative episodes highlights the satire: the men caucus, call the legislative body to order in emergency session, make committee assignments and file reports, motions, and amendments; make nominations, entertain resignations; conduct debates and hold elections (Branch 591). The humor of the story depends upon Mark Twain's comic diction, the ludicrous disjunction of parliamentary rhetoric, and the grotesque situation to which it is applied: "some little caucussing followed" the nomination of prospective dinners; "this decision created considerable dissatisfaction among the friends of Mr. Ferguson, the defeated candidate"; "on the sixth [ballot], Mr. Harris was elected, all voting for him but himself." Underneath the ironic rhetoric lies the inescapable conclusion that we all are governed by self-interest and expediency. No one offers himself as a willing sacrifice to the welfare of the communal whole; rather, all are subject to the laws of survival, using parliamentary skills at their disposal to jockey for position at the expense of less accomplished members of the party. Even friendship poses no obstacle when survival is the issue. The narrator confesses: "I liked Harris. He might have been better done, perhaps, but I am free to say that no man ever agreed with me better than Harris, or afforded me so large a degree of satisfaction" (380).

Though the story exposes the selfish and brutal nature of all people, its immediate target, Sloane contends, is an egalitarian concept of government based on false assumptions about human nature. Unlike the more specifically focused newspaper burlesques that preceded it, this story is a "finished" work of art whose masterful handling of irony and comic diction furnishes "the deadpan pose essential to a burlesque of democratic formuli" (93–95). This macabre, chilling tale strips the civilized veneer from democratic men, as it shows how they satiate their " 'savage hunger' by utilizing the civilities and refinements of civilization" (Branch 591).

Bibliography

PRIMARY

The Love Letters of Mark Twain. Edited by Dixon Wecter. New York: Harper & Brothers, 1947.

Mark Twain to Mrs. Fairbanks. Edited by Dixon Wecter. San Marino, Calif.: Huntington Library, 1949.

Mark Twain's Sketches. Selected and Revised by the Author. London: George Routledge & Sons, 1872.

*Mark Twain's Sketches, New and Old. Now First Published in Complete Form. Hartford and Chicago: American Publishing Co., 1875.

SECONDARY

Baldanza, Frank. *Mark Twain: An Introduction and Interpretation.* New York: Holt, Rinehart & Winston, 1961.

Bellamy, Gladys C. *Mark Twain as a Literary Artist.* Norman: University of Oklahoma Press, 1950.

Branch, Edgar M. "Mark Twain: Newspaper Reading and the Writer's Creativity." *Nineteenth-Century Fiction* 37 (March 1983): 576–603.

Brooks, Van Wyck. *The Ordeal of Mark Twain.* 1920. Rev. ed. New York: E. P. Dutton, 1933.

Emerson, Everett. *The Authentic Mark Twain: A Literary Biography of Samuel L. Clemens.* Philadelphia: University of Pennsylvania Press, 1984.

Hill, Hamlin. *Mark Twain and Elisha Bliss.* Columbia: University of Missouri Press, 1964.

Paine, Albert B. *Mark Twain: A Biography.* Vol. 2. New York: Harper & Brothers, 1912.

Sloane, David E. E. *Mark Twain as a Literary Comedian.* Baton Rouge: Louisiana State University Press, 1979.

Steinbrink, Jeffrey. "How Mark Twain Survived Sam Clemens' Reformation." *American Literature* 55 (October 1983): 299–315.

5

The Canvasser's Tale

Publication History

Mark Twain published "The Canvasser's Tale" in the *Atlantic Monthly*, December 1876. Under the title, "The Echo That Didn't Answer," the story was reprinted in the *Beeton's Christmas Annual* (London: 1877). The first book publication in the United States came in 1878, *Punch, Brothers, Punch!* Subsequently the story was collected in the Harper and Brothers edition of *Tom Sawyer Abroad*.

Circumstances of Composition, Sources, and Influences

Mark Twain spent the summer of 1876 in Elmira, New York, in relative tranquility. He had begun *Huckleberry Finn* (1885) as a sequel to the recently published *Adventures of Tom Sawyer* (1876), but put the manuscript aside after completing about a hundred pages: "I like it only tolerably well," he wrote to William Dean Howells (Paine 577–79). He also began preparations to write *The Prince and the Pauper* (1882), closely examining "ancient English books with the purpose of saturating myself with archaic English"; the work with language, Blair contends, colored the "archaic and highfalutin" diction of "The Canvasser's Tale," which was the only work Mark Twain completed for publication that summer (93).

Although "The Canvasser's Tale" is, as Paine writes, "a burlesque of no special distinction" (578), it was written with some care. According to Bellamy, Mark Twain revealed to Howells that he had initially intended to make Uncle Ithuriel a collector of caves "and afterwards of echoes, but perceived that the element of absurdity . . . was so nearly identical as to amount to a repetition of an idea." Such comment, Bellamy argues, demonstrates that the author worked carefully and methodically to achieve a "wild and absurd" end (135).

Relationship to Other Mark Twain Works

"The Canvasser's Tale" is an extravagant burlesque of human eccentricities that depends upon hyperbole for its comic effect. The situation is ridiculously implausible but the satiric insight into human vanity and obsession is nevertheless realistic. In tone and method the story resembles "The Loves of Alonzo Fitz Clarence and Rosannah Ethelton" (1878), which likewise turns upon an outrageous situation (a long-distance telephone love affair) and employs inflated language to satirize sentimental illusion and pretension.

Baldanza links the story to "Playing Courier" (1891) and "Political Economy" (1870), for all three satirize the good-natured, absentminded male "at a hilarious disadvantage." The best of Mark Twain's stories in this vein are the three McWilliams stories (written in the late 1870s and early 1880s), domestic farces that burlesque the daily frustrations of genteel married life. Like "Political Economy" and "My Watch" (1870), "The Canvasser's Tale" concerns itself, in part, with what Baldanza calls "life's little exasperations as embodied in sales persons" (99). Mark Twain interrupts the canvasser as he makes the transition from his tale to his sales pitch with a litany of his frustrations at the hands of other peddlers: "My friend, I have not had a moment's respite from canvassers this day. I have bought a sewing-machine which I did not want; I have bought a map which is mistaken in all its details; I have bought a clock which will not go; I have bought a moth poison which the moths prefer to any other beverage; I have bought no end of useless inventions, and now I have had enough of this foolishness" (126). The same theme is developed more fully, and more effectively, in "The McWilliamses and the Burglar Alarm" (1882).

In a couple of its minor details, the story bears tangential relationship to two of Mark Twain's more substantial works. Like *Innocents Abroad* (1869), the story satirizes the American's emulation of European customs. It is the canvasser who inspires his uncle's obsession with collecting useless objects (first cowbells, then brickbats, "flint hatchets and other implements of Primeval Man," "Aztec inscriptions and stuffed whales," and finally the intangible "echoes"), and the canvasser, in turn, had gotten the idea from his travels abroad: "In those far lands I reveled in the ambrosial food that fructifies the soul, the mind, the heart. But of all things, that which most appealed to my inborn esthetic taste was the prevailing custom there, among the rich, of making collections of elegant and costly rarities, dainty *objects de vertu,* and in an evil hour I tried to uplift my uncle Ithuriel to a plane of sympathy with this exquisite enjoyment" (122). There is also a variation of the joke that dooms David Wilson to the status of "pudd'nhead" in Mark Twain's 1894 novel: his casual remark that if he owned half of a dog whose barking disturbed the peace he would kill his half. In "The Canvasser's Tale," Uncle Ithuriel owns but "one-half of the king echo of the universe": he is able to buy only the east hill; the west hill, necessary of course to reverberate an echo across "the swale between" that "was the dividing line," is owned by another collector who steadfastly refuses to sell.

Frustrated that he can possess only one-half of the echo, the rival collector maliciously decides to remove his hill: "My uncle remonstrated with him, but the man said, 'I own one end of this echo; I choose to kill my end; you must take care of your own end yourself' " (125).

Critical Studies

The story begins with a brief frame in which Mark Twain introduces a "poor, sad-eyed stranger" whose "decayed-gentility clothes" suggest that he has for some reason fallen from previous prosperity to his present dissolute condition. Despite his normal aversion to canvassers, Mark Twain listens—"all attention and sympathy" (122)—to his tale, which, told in first person, explains his story and serves as a prelude to the sales pitch that completes the frame at the end.

The tale is a double-barreled one. The major focus falls on the uncle's adventures as a collector, a rather common dissipation of the idle rich: "He began to neglect his great pork business; presently he wholly retired and turned an elegant leisure into a rabid search for curious things" (123). A series of frustrating experiences culminates in his disappointment over not being able to obtain "an Aztec inscription from the Cundurango regions of Central America that made all former specimens insignificant," an experience that turned his "coal-black hair . . . white as snow in a single night" (123). Vowing to collect only objects "no other man was collecting," Ithuriel then begins amassing echoes, a hobby that eventually depletes his $5 million fortune. The second "barrel" of the story concerns the canvasser and his ill-fated love for the "noble Celestine," the daughter of an English earl who is willing for his daughter to marry the young American because "it was known that I was sole heir to an uncle held to be worth five millions of dollars" (124). When the uncle dies and it is learned that his money is gone and his sole legacy to his nephew only "a vast collection of echoes," all heavily mortgaged, the earl of course cancels the impending wedding. Devastated, Celestine dies within a year, and the poor canvasser is left to peddle his echoes.

The main plot of "The Canvasser's Tale" burlesques the dissipation and foolishness of the idle rich who fall prey to impractical obsessions for lack of anything else meaningful in their lives. The subplot is a parody of sentimental romance fiction, akin to "Lucretia Smith's Soldier" (1864) or "The Esquimau Maiden's Romance" (1893). The frame, which does little except furnish an occasion for the tale, is in tone similar to such domestic farces as "The McWilliamses and the Burglar Alarm"; it chronicles Mark Twain's vulnerability to sentimentality and petty harassment. After threatening the canvasser with a gun, he succumbs to his "sad, sweet smile" and at the "end of an intolerable hour" buys "two double-barreled echoes in good condition." In an act of good faith, the canvasser "threw in another" echo, one that "was not salable because it only spoke German" (126).

Bibliography

PRIMARY

The Complete Short Stories of Mark Twain. Now Collected for the First Time. Edited by Charles Neider. Garden City, N.Y.: Hanover House, 1957.

Punch, Brothers, Punch! and Other Sketches. New York: Slote, Woodman & Co., 1878.

Tom Sawyer Abroad, Tom Sawyer, Detective, and Other Stories, Etc. Etc. New York: Harper & Brothers, 1896.

SECONDARY

Baldanza, Frank. *Mark Twain: An Introduction and Interpretation*. New York: Holt, Rinehart & Winston, 1961.

Bellamy, Gladys C. *Mark Twain as a Literary Artist*. Norman: University of Oklahoma Press, 1950.

Blair, Walter. *Mark Twain & Huck Finn*. Berkeley and Los Angeles: University of California Press, 1962.

Paine, Albert B. *Mark Twain: A Biography*. Vol. 2. New York: Harper & Brothers, 1912.

6

Cecil Rhodes and the Shark
The Joke That Made Ed's Fortune
A Story without End

Publication History

These three stories are part of *Following the Equator* (1897); they were written specifically for that book and never published independently during Mark Twain's lifetime. Prepared as a subscription book and heavily edited by the author, his wife, and two publishers, *Following the Equator* is the last in a series of travel books. Preliminary titles—"Another Innocent Abroad," "The Latest Innocent Abroad," "The Surviving Innocent Abroad"—and the title of the British edition, *More Tramps Abroad,* clearly suggest that Mark Twain envisioned *Following the Equator* to be a sequel to his earlier work in the genre. Emerson reports that the book proved both profitable and popular: Mark Twain received 12.5 percent royalties on the American edition and a ten-thousand-dollar advance; the book sold well in England, and in the United States more than twenty-eight thousand copies sold in the first five months after its November 1897 release (204–9). Income from book sales and from the lecture tour that spawned it enabled Mark Twain to struggle clear of debt by January 1898 (Macnaughton 20).

In his introduction to *The Complete Short Stories of Mark Twain,* editor Charles Neider reveals that the inspiration for his collection of Mark Twain's stories came from his discovery of the author's peculiar "habit of inserting yarns of pure fiction in a non-fictional work, yarns tossed in just because they were good ones which he had in his head at the time" (xiii). "Cecil Rhodes and the Shark," "The Joke That Made Ed's Fortune," and "A Story without End" are three such "yarns" from *Following the Equator,* a book, Baldanza notes, that is composed of "commercial statistics, and other measurements indulged in simply for the love of figures; tall tales; sketches of queer travelers and natives; scenic descriptions; catalogues of flora, fauna, and climate; and reforming diatribes" (64). Because "strictly speaking . . . these yarns don't belong in the books which house them," Neider extracted them from their original context, supplied titles, and published them as independent short stories in his 1957 collection.

Circumstances of Composition, Sources, and Influences

In July 1895 Mark Twain launched a tour that was to take him around the globe. He wrote to H. H. Rogers in February 1895 that the purpose of the voyage was recreational, "to get Mrs. Clemens and myself away from the phantoms and out of the nervous strain for a few months" (*Mark Twain's Correspondence* 126). The major motivation, however, was financial, for he hoped to forestall bankruptcy with money generated from an extended lecture tour that entailed more than a hundred public performances in a year's time. The tour took Mark Twain to Australia for five weeks, to New Zealand for five weeks, to India for two months, to South Africa for two and a half months, then to England, where he hoped his daughters Jean and Susy would join him and Olivia while he put together a book based on his recent travels. Unfortunately Susy proved too ill to travel, and in fact she died of spinal meningitis on 18 August 1896. Devastated by his daughter's death, Mark Twain submerged himself in his work on *Following the Equator:* "I work all the days, and trouble vanishes away when I use that magic" (DeVoto 109). The book was important to him for, as Emerson writes, "he needed to believe he could live again after the loss of both his daughter Susy and his dreams of wealth" (207–9). Upon completing *Following the Equator* Mark Twain wrote to Frank Bliss that he would not trade it for any of his earlier books (Macnaughton 19).

Following the Equator is the most personal and direct of Mark Twain's travel books. DeVoto claims that it is also the "dullest" (110). Certainly it is the bleakest in outlook; as Salomon writes, "the ideal of civilization that Twain has so confidently held up in his early travel books, in *Following the Equator* is everywhere exposed as a sham and a delusion" (195). The various narrative poses that served to distance the author from his material in the earlier travel books appear less frequently in *Following the Equator,* and as a result the book is, Long writes, more "a storehouse of Mark's mature judgments than anything else" (228). The style, structure, and content of the book, Baetzhold contends, show the influence of the English essayist Macaulay, while Mark Twain's "skill in adapting materials drawn from actual experience and observation" and his "paternalistic concern for the 'lesser breeds without the Law'" recall one of his favorite authors, Rudyard Kipling (187–89).

Of the three stories considered here, however, only "Cecil Rhodes and the Shark" bears any significant relationship to the author's recent extended tour. Mark Twain's investigations had led him to believe that Rhodes had engineered the Jameson Raid in South Africa (December-January, 1895–96) to provoke British intervention and eventual annexation of the Transvaal; moreover, Rhodes had done so "not out of patriotism but for personal gain" (Baetzhold 185). While set in the 1870s and ostensibly unrelated to the Jameson Raid, the story nevertheless exposes Rhodes as an opportunist who prospers on the misfortune of others. It is a naturalistic tale that calls into question "the white man's notion that he is less savage than the other savages" (Baetzhold 182–83).

Relationship to Other Mark Twain Works

In general, *Following the Equator* reflects the pessimism characteristic of Mark Twain's writing during the last decade of his life (Baldanza 63–67). As Salomon writes, it is "a discursive series of impressions, anecdotes, and experiences" that emphasizes humans' "eternal corruption" (195). "Cecil Rhodes and the Shark," however, is the only one of the three stories considered here that is consistent with the decidedly naturalistic vision of Mark Twain's later life. On a general level the story reveals, as Rhodes confesses, that "everything is transitory in this world" (337); humans and shark are both predators in a Darwinistic struggle for survival. More particularly the story satirizes the machinations of Cecil Rhodes, whose ingenuity, self-confidence, and ruthless activity make him the beneficiary of this predatory cycle. The story is thus related to Mark Twain's "Affeland," an unpublished beast fable from the late 1890s that uses animals to satirize Rhodes's imperialistic adventurism (Baetzhold 190).

The other two stories hark back to the author's earlier work. "A Story without End" is akin to "A Medieval Romance"; like the 1870 *Express* piece, this "storiette" is a hoax on the reader: it leads the sympathetically portrayed protagonist into an impossible dilemma, then abandons him and challenges the reader to devise an appropriate ending (Covici 144; Baldanza 100). "The Joke That Made Ed's Fortune" likewise involves a hoax, this one perpetrated by fellow dockworkers at the expense of the naive protagonist Ed Jackson. A practical joke designed to embarrass the obscure wharfboat clerk, the hoax backfires and in the end occasions his fortune. The theme of nostalgia relates the story to the author's fictional evocations of his childhood on the banks of the Mississippi: *Tom Sawyer* (1876), *Huckleberry Finn* (1885), *Life on the Mississippi* (1883), etc. Commodore Vanderbilt aids Ed Jackson because the imaginary letter of introduction he unwittingly brings evokes memories of an irrecoverable past; though the letter is fraudulent and the events it recounts purely fictional, the artifice has the semblance of truth and strikes a responsive chord in the aging tycoon's heart: "I know it happened—I can *feel* it! and lord, how it warms my heart, and brings back my lost youth" (339).

Critical Studies

The first three sentences of "Cecil Rhodes and the Shark" establish that "the shark is the swiftest fish that swims" and "roams far and wide in the oceans, and visits the shores of all of them . . . in the course of his restless excursions" (332). The remainder of the initial expository paragraph shifts abruptly to introduce a "tale" about a young man newly arrived in Australia in 1870—destitute, hungry, and unemployed—who in cleaning "an unusually large shark" he has caught discovers information that will make his fortune. The tale itself consists almost entirely of dialogue, first between the young stranger—Cecil Rhodes—and the old fisherman who loans him his line, then between the suddenly self-assured Rhodes and "the richest wool-broker in Sydney." It depends for its effect on withheld information; the reader learns simultaneously with the wool-broker the secret information gathered from the entrails of the fleet predator: a sheet of the London *Times* reporting that France has declared war on Germany. The information is precious because it is but ten days old. Since it normally takes fifty days for news from Europe to reach Australia by boat, the young man is the only person in the country to know of the war. Rhodes hence corners the wool market, on borrowed funds, knowing the price will skyrocket as soon as news of the war reaches the colony.

Rhodes is daring, confident, cunning—a "remarkable" man. He is also a vicious one. The wool-broker tells Rhodes that there is "something that's born in you and oozes out of you" (334); like the shark, his predatory habits are natural or innate. As the title and the abrupt juxtaposition of shark and protagonist in the first paragraph suggest, there is kinship between the man and the beast. Both feed on hapless victims by instinct. The wool-broker classifies people into three groups: "Commonplace Men, Remarkable Men, and Lunatics" (337). In an evolutionary struggle for survival, the "Remarkable Men" like Rhodes rise to eminence and fortune; the others feed their insatiable appetites.

"The Joke That Made Ed's Fortune" is a testimony to the power of art. Gullible Ed Jackson, having saved his money for a trip to New York from Memphis, is given a fraudulent letter of introduction to Commodore Vanderbilt by pranksters who expect the letter to cause Jackson great humiliation. The letter, however, is a work of art, "bringing in names of imaginary comrades, and detailing all sorts of wild and absurd and, of course, wholly imaginary school boy pranks and adventures, but putting them into lively and telling shape" (338). The illusion of truth, which is art, proves more convincing than any mundane recording of actual fact. The letter moves the aging and lonely Vanderbilt, convinces him that the fictional events truly transpired, that the imaginary people were a vital part of his past. The "joke" is the consummate art form: it brings joy to "the tired spirit of a hard-worked man" (339) and wealth to its creators and purveyor.

"A Story without End" is little more than a game, a challenge from author to reader to devise an ending for a "storiette" that has frustrated all previous attempts to draw an aesthetically satisfying conclusion: "Any ordinary man will find that the story's strength is in its middle, and that there is apparently no way to transfer it to the close, where of course it ought to be" (343). Unlike "A Medieval Romance" (1870), which offers readers no prior warning that they are being led into a trap, "A Story without End" states its structural difficulties at the outset and then challenges the reader to reconcile those difficulties. The tale is essentially burlesque. Thirty-one-year-old John Brown, the "good, gentle, bashful, timid . . . superintendent of the Presbyterian Sunday-School," who "could always be counted upon for help when it was needed, and for bashfulness both when it was needed, and when it wasn't" (343), finds himself in an impossible dilemma. After an implausible but carefully delineated chain of events, Brown is seated without any pants on in a wagon surrounded by five very proper Christian women, including the girl he loves and her skeptical mother. His potential embarrassment concealed by a lap robe, Brown momentarily appears to have escaped from the situation undetected; but when circumstances demand that he surrender the robe for the comfort of the ladies, he is caught "on account of Brown's character—great generosity and kindliness, but complicated with unusual shyness and diffidence, particularly in the presence of ladies" (348).

The author claims that this is one tale that cannot be ended satisfactorily. Only a "happy ending" will do: "the finish must find Brown in high credit with the ladies, his behavior without blemish, his modesty unwounded, his character for self-sacrifice maintained." But such a conclusion seems impossible. "Brown's shyness would not allow him to give up the lap-robe" and when asked to explain his refusal, "his shyness would not allow him to tell the truth, and lack of invention and practice would find him incapable of contriving a lie that would wash" (343). Covici argues that as in "A Medieval Romance" the problem lies in inherent deficiencies of the form. The reader's interest in the protagonist "has been built up through the romance-pattern of the tale," but the pattern proves "illegitimate," for "it cannot possibly fit the facts of life as the central character experiences them" (144).

Bibliography

PRIMARY

The Complete Short Stories of Mark Twain. Now Collected for the First Time. Edited by Charles Neider. Garden City. N.Y.: Hanover House, 1957.

Following the Equator. Hartford: American Publishing Co., 1897.

Mark Twain's Correspondence with Henry Huttleston Rogers, 1893–1909. Edited by Lewis Leary. Berkeley and Los Angeles: University of California Press, 1969.

SECONDARY

Baetzhold, Howard G. *Mark Twain and John Bull: The British Connection.* Bloomington: Indiana University Press, 1970.

Baldanza, Frank. *Mark Twain: An Introduction and Interpretation.* New York: Holt, Rinehart & Winston, 1961.

Covici, Pascal, Jr. *Mark Twain's Humor: The Image of a World.* Dallas: Southern Methodist University Press, 1962.

DeVoto, Bernard. *Mark Twain at Work.* Cambridge, Mass.: Harvard University Press, 1942.

Emerson, Everett. *The Authentic Mark Twain: A Literary Biography of Samuel L. Clemens.* Philadelphia: University of Pennsylvania Press, 1984.

Long, E. Hudson. *Mark Twain Handbook.* New York: Hendricks House, 1957.

Macnaughton, William R. *Mark Twain's Last Years as a Writer.* Columbia: University of Missouri Press, 1979.

Salomon, Roger B. *Twain and the Image of History.* New Haven: Yale University Press, 1961.

7

A Curious Experience

Publication History

"A Curious Experience" appeared first in *Century Magazine,* November 1881, then was reprinted in *The Stolen White Elephant Etc.* volume the following year.

Circumstances of Composition, Sources, and Influences

Mark Twain wrote "A Curious Experience" in spring 1881, following the completion of *A Tramp Abroad* (1880) and *The Prince and the Pauper* (1882). The period was, according to Emerson, a particularly stagnant one in Mark Twain's aesthetic development. Most of the author's time went into his investments, most of which were unsuccessful and as a result emotionally taxing; his literary activity centered on editing collections of his previous work, such as a "Cyclopedia of Humor," which he hoped would return a quick profit for little original effort. At the suggestion of William Dean Howells, Mark Twain began in March to write a burlesque etiquette book, but abandoned the project after completing about a hundred manuscript pages. He also left unfinished a burlesque of *Hamlet.* "A Curious Experience," sold to *Century Magazine* in May, was, Paine reports, "the most notable of the few completed manuscripts of this period" (705). The completion of this rather pedestrian story, Emerson concludes, shows only that "Mark Twain was for the moment barren of original ideas, except bad ones" (115).

Mark Twain made no claim of originality for this story, for he begins with an acknowledgment that he is simply rehearsing, "as nearly as I can recall it" (163), a true story told him by a major in the U.S. Army. He then allows the major to tell the story, in first-person narration, as a recollection of a "curious experience" that befell him as commanding officer at Fort Trumbull during the winter 1862–63. The story concludes with an authorial note that assures the reader of its accuracy: Mark Twain has shown the completed manuscript to the major, who acknowledges that "you have got the main facts of the history right, and have set them down just about as they occurred" (186). The result, Emerson writes, is a "wholly unoriginal" piece, a retelling, "without much personality or art, of a Civil War story that had been told to him" (115).

Despite Mark Twain's unequivocal denial of originality, one irate reader of *Century Magazine* complained in a letter to "a New York publication" that the story struck him "as strangely familiar, and I soon recognized the story as a true one, told me in the summer of 1878 by an officer of the United States artillery"; the reader rather testily concludes, "Did Mr. Twain expect the public to credit this narrative to his clever brain?" (Paine 719–20). Outraged by the public attack, Mark Twain responded in a private letter to the editor that he had indeed identified his source and had made no claims of originality: "Your correspondent is not stupid, I judge, but purely and simply malicious. He knew there was not the shadow of a suggestion, from the beginning to the end of 'A Curious Episode,' that the story was an *invention*" (Paine 720).

Relationship to Other Mark Twain Works

Mark Twain had, of course, used stories told to him by others as inspiration for his own work (e.g., Ben Coon's yarn and "Jim Smiley and His Jumping Frog" [1865]); usually, however, he transforms the bare source yarn into a marvelously original creation, enriched by a sophisticated control of the elements of fiction. Why in "A Curious Experience" is he satisfied with a slavish devotion to his source? One reason, no doubt, was the pressing financial need for quick magazine publication; another is that the story is the product of a particularly fallow period in his life. Yet the story does dramatize themes common in his more original work. Long points out that the portrait of "a boy so completely confused by the cheap romance of dime novels that the world of imagination blinded him to the real" accords well with Mark Twain's sustained disparagement of romanticism, particularly the Sir Walter Scott variety, which the author believed evaded reality and clouded moral judgment (258). Relevant here is Mark Twain's infamous charge that Scott was responsible for the Civil War, and his scathing indictment of genteel romantic chivalry in the Shepherdson-Grangerford and Sherburn-Boggs episodes of *Huckleberry Finn* (1885). Fantasy games may be an innocuous expression of a child's fertile imagination, as Tom Sawyer's raid on the "A-rabs and the Elephants" (in reality a Sunday school class picnic) demonstrates; however, when they govern behavior in a more serious adult context—the Shepherdson-Grangerford feud, for example, or Tom's games with Jim's quest for freedom—they are neither cute nor innocuous but rather pose serious threat to the moral basis of civilized life. Robert Wicklow's attempts to enact the fantasies of dime novels in the adult world of war—however innocently conceived—prove more than "a curious experience": "he made trouble enough for us, and just no end of humiliation. You see, on account of him we had fifteen or twenty people under arrest and confinement in the fort, with sentinels before their doors" (186). Innocent people suffer profound injustice because of his "play."

Mark Twain returns to a variation on the same theme in "The $30,000 Bequest" (1904), when again a couple's fantasy daydreams stunt moral development, blind them to compassion and human needs, and ruin their marriage.

Critical Studies

"A Curious Experience" has received no critical discussion, nor does it particularly merit any. The fact that Mark Twain stays close to his source and adds virtually no aesthetic embellishment renders the story intrinsically banal and inappropriate as an index to the author's artistic method. Baldanza rather vaguely relates the story to "The Death Disk" (1901), for both are, he claims, "belabored and ineffective historical romances" (100).

Whatever effect the story achieves depends upon its ability to generate suspense, or arouse the reader's curiosity. Who is Robert Wicklow, how much truth is there in what he reveals about his past, what explains his "curious" behavior? As readers we learn about Wicklow only what the major reveals and as he reveals it. There are no clues to explain his action or to cast doubt that he may not in fact be the Confederate spy everyone comes to assume he is. Finally the reader is the victim of a hoax, but it is perpetrated neither by the narrator nor by Wicklow, really, but by the "curious" nature of the boy's psychological difficulties, which are revealed in summary fashion at the story's end: "a ravenous devourer of dime novels and sensation-story papers," he is a child who escapes reality into a world of imaginative "dark mysteries and gaudy heroisms" (185). As the major concludes, "he lived in a gorgeous, mysterious, romantic world during those few stirring days, and I think it was *real* to him, and that he enjoyed it clear down to the bottom of his heart" (186).

The unimaginative approach to its subject renders the story inconsequential fiction. Perhaps the problem is point of view: from the major's perspective, the whole affair is merely a "curious experience" that contains, for Mark Twain, the seeds of a homiletic lesson: the consequences of fantasy approaches to adult life. Never do we see Wicklow from the inside nor share his "colored" view of reality. Had the story been told from Wicklow's perspective, it would have offered more opportunity for imaginative art and intrinsic interest. But it would also have required more original work than Mark Twain was willing to give it in the spring of 1881.

Bibliography

PRIMARY

*The Complete Short Stories of Mark Twain. Now Collected for the First Time. Edited by Charles Neider. Garden City, N.Y.: Hanover House, 1957.

The Stolen White Elephant Etc. Boston: James R. Osgood, 1882.

SECONDARY

Baldanza, Frank. Mark Twain: An Introduction and Interpretation. New York: Holt, Rinehart & Winston, 1961.

Emerson, Everett. The Authentic Mark Twain: A Literary Biography of Samuel L. Clemens. Philadelphia: University of Pennsylvania Press, 1984.

Long, E. Hudson. Mark Twain Handbook. New York: Hendricks House, 1957.

Paine, Albert B. Mark Twain: A Biography. Vol. 2. New York: Harper & Brothers, 1912.

8

A Day at Niagara
Journalism in Tennessee
A Ghost Story
A Curious Dream

Publication History

These four stories are among the fifty or so sketches and tales Mark Twain wrote for the Buffalo *Express* in 1869–70. "A Day at Niagara" appeared 21 August 1869; "Journalism in Tennessee," 4 September 1869; "A Ghost Story by the Witness," 15 January 1870; "A Curious Dream," in the editions of 30 April and 7 May 1870. The first of these stories was reprinted twice in 1872, in *Practical Jokes* and *One Hundred Choice Selections,* under the title "Mark Twain at Niagara Falls." "Journalism in Tennessee" appeared in a British collection of Mark Twain sketches published by Hotten in 1871. "A Curious Dream" was published separately in pamphlet form in 1872, and collected in 1873 in *Book for an Hour.* All four are included in the 1875 authorized edition of *Mark Twain Sketches, New and Old;* in this collection the "Niagara" story bears the title, "A Visit to Niagara," and "A Ghost Story by the Witness" simply "A Ghost Story."

In the Neider edition of *The Complete Short Stories* the editor mistakenly dates "A Ghost Story" to 1888, apparently confusing it with Mark Twain's sketch of the same title that appeared in *Werner's Readings and Recitations* (New York: 1888); the later story is actually "The Golden Arm," included later in "How to Tell a Story."

Circumstances of Composition, Sources, and Influences

During the period 1868–69, Mark Twain devoted most of his time to revising the *Alta* letters for *Innocents Abroad* (1869), traveling on lecture tour through New York, Pennsylvania, and Ohio, and courting Olivia Langdon. In his early thirties, hoping to marry into a genteel, upper middle-class family, Mark Twain sought to establish a career as a respectable man-of-letters. Despite having finished his first book, Mark Twain still considered himself a journalist and was anxious to secure a meaningful post: "I want to get located in life," he confessed to Olivia in May 1869 (Emerson 56). Mrs. Fairbanks secured for him an opportunity to join the staff of the Cleveland *Herald,* but Mark Twain declined the offer because it was just "*another* apprenticeship—another one, to the tail end of a foolish life *made up* of apprenticeships." Instead he purchased one-third interest in the Buffalo *Express* with money loaned him by his prospective father-in-law, Jervis Langdon (Emerson 56–57).

Mark Twain began his work as associate editor with enthusiasm and lofty ideals. Much of his personal writing for the newspaper continued in the burlesque tradition of his California and Nevada journalism. "A Day at Niagara," for example, shows the influence of Bret Harte and Charles Henry Webb, masters of literary parody whose work and personal encouragement helped to shape much of Mark Twain's apprentice writing (Rogers 19). Yet Mark Twain believed that his responsibilities as journalist involved more than providing light entertainment. In San Francisco, as early as 1865, he had lamented the failure of local newspapers to live up to their public responsibility to expose corruption and work for social justice. Ideally, he wrote in 1905, the mission of the journalist is "to disseminate truth; to eradicate error; to educate, refine, and elevate the tone of public morals and manners, and make all men more gentle, more virtuous, more charitable, and in all ways better, and holier, and happier" (Branch 154–55). Such commitment has its dangers, of course, as he demonstrates in "Journalism in Tennessee," for the unvarnished truth often incites an audience to angry and at times violent reprisal. But the completely "de-Southernized" Mark Twain was willing to run that risk; a staunch Republican, with profound sympathy for the oppressed, Mark Twain supplemented his numerous anecdotes in the *Express* with a series of "fearless, scathing, terrific" editorials on public issues (Paine 398–402). His fiction, too, turned its attention to serious themes. Although "Journalism in Tennessee" is, as Paine notes, "one of his wilder burlesques" (402), it also voices Mark Twain's "belief in the power of the press" and by indirection praises the journalist who remains loyal to his civic responsibility (Bellamy 92). "A Ghost Story" calls attention to a public hoax of the time, simultaneous exhibitions of a petrified man, the "Cardiff Giant," in Albany and in New York City: "A fact. The original fraud was ingeniously and fraudfully duplicated, and exhibited in New York as the 'only genuine' Cardiff Giant (to the unspeakable disgust of the owners of the real colossus) at the very same time that the latter was drawing crowds at a museum in Albany" (*Complete Short Stories* 248). "A Curious Dream" likewise directs its satire towards a social issue, as it exposes those cities that permit graveyards to fall into ruin and disarray; the story, Paine reports, "made a lasting impression on his Buffalo readers" and inspired a movement for reform (402; Long 167). The burlesque proved a popular form for American humorists in the 1860s and 1870s, for it enabled them to highlight the radical disparity between lofty political idealism and often grim social realities. As Sloane writes, "Mark Twain was if anything more sharply focused on the ethical dimensions of comedy than his counterparts" (146–47).

Relationship to Other Mark Twain Works

All four of these stories are in the burlesque mode that Rogers shows dominated Mark Twain's fiction from 1863 to 1871. Twenty-three of the fifty-one short items Mark Twain published during this "apprentice" period are essentially burlesques (19). "A Day at Niagara" parodies the fiction of James Fenimore Cooper, with specific attention to his sentimental portrayal of Indians (Branch 284). It thus anticipates the later essay "Fenimore Cooper's Literary Offenses." Although "Journalism in Tennessee" is based loosely on Mark Twain's experiences working with the Hannibal, Missouri, newspaper in 1850–51 (Long 102 n.), it too is full of the hyperbole characteristic of the burlesque. Baldanza links the story to "How I Edited an Agricultural Paper Once" (1870) as an example of Mark Twain's "nearly hysterical exaggerated 'tall-tale' humor" (99). "A Curious Dream" Baldanza relates to "A Ghost Story," for both are parodies of graveyard fiction (100). These tales of reanimated corpses belong to a group of morbid but humorous writings that, Gribben contends, reflect "a diabolically conjoined existence of antithetical beauty and ugliness, mirth and tears, elation and remorse, security and terror" (198). Some of the same conventions and techniques Mark Twain will employ later in the Injun Joe sections of *Tom Sawyer* (1876).

Critical Studies

"A Day at Niagara" is a story of disillusionment, a satiric deflation of romantic expectations. Mark Twain is the tourist, as in *Innocents Abroad*, who discovers the much celebrated resort to be less than it is reputed to be. Opportunities for fishing seem to abound—indeed they "are not surpassed in the country"—but unfortunately "the fish do not bite anywhere" (16). To view the magnificent falls close up one "can descend a staircase here a hundred and fifty feet down, and stand at the edge of the water"; however, "after you have done it, you will wonder why you did it" (17). Or one can amuse oneself by watching the other tourists: "papa and momma, Johnny and Bub and Sis, or a couple of country cousins, all smiling vacantly, . . . all looming up their awe-inspiring imbecility before the snubbed and diminished presentment of that majestic presence" of the falls (17).

Mark Twain's greatest disappointment, however, results from his encounter with the "Indians" who seem to be everywhere at Niagara. Inspired by Cooperesque "tales and legends and romances," Mark Twain stands in awe of the "Red Man": "I love to read of his inspired sagacity, and his love of the wild free life of mountain and forest, and his general nobility of character, and his stately metaphorical manner of speech, and his chivalrous love for the dusky maiden, and the picturesque pomp of his dress and accoutrements" (19). Actual experience, however, shatters romantic expectations. The "noble Son of the Forest" turns out to be "Dennis Hooligan, that ye'd be takin' for a dirty Injin." The "gentle daughter of the aborigines in fringed and beaded buckskin" who "had just carved out a wooden chief that had a strong family resemblance to a clothespin" is in fact one "Biddy Malone" (19). The "Indians" at Niagara are all from "Limerick"! Eastern, commercial imitations of America's western grandeur ring hollow to the American who comes to see them through his own eyes.

"Journalism in Tennessee" is a story of initiation, full of comic mayhem, innocuous violence in the vein of Sennett slapstick. On advice of his physician, the fledgling journalist Mark Twain takes a post in Tennessee as associate editor of the *Morning Glory and Johnson County War-Whoop*. The polite, genteel, noncommittal language of his initial journalistic effort draws the ire of the crusty chief editor: "Do you suppose my subscribers are going to stand such gruel as that?" (28). The seasoned veteran proceeds to give Mark Twain a lesson in frontier journalism, thoroughly revising the novitiate's work until it is "peppery and to the point." In the midst of the lesson, someone shoots into the office; the editor promptly draws a revolver from his belt and wounds the would-be assailant who, disconcerted, returns fire and shoots the innocent Mark Twain. Then follows a series of madcap encounters with various and sundry desperadoes who had been offended by the paper's uncompromising language and public accusations. Mark Twain bears the brunt of the violence and soon realizes that temperamentally he is ill suited to the excitement of a career in frontier journalism: "I think maybe I might write to suit you after a while. . . . But, to speak the plain truth, that sort of energy of expression has its inconveniences, and a man is liable to interruption. . . . Vigorous writing is calculated to elevate the public, no doubt, but then I do not like to attract so much attention as it calls forth" (31). He resigns from the paper and retreats to the security of the local hospital. It is safer, to quote Emily Dickinson, "to tell the truth, but tell it slant." But the hero of the story is the uncompromising chief editor, who tells Mark Twain, "mush-and-milk journalism gives me the fan-tods" (29).

"A Ghost Story" is a first-person narrative that carefully builds up an atmosphere of terror, then dispels the tension with burlesque. As soon as the narrator discovers that the spirit haunting him in the "special twilight" is in fact "the majestic Cardiff Giant," he relaxes: "Never a lonely outcast was so glad to welcome company as I was to greet the friendly giant" (247). After the lumbering ghost smashes all the furniture in the room trying to find a comfortable seat, he reveals that he is "the spirit of the Petrified Man that lies across the street there in the museum" (248). He must haunt those in the neighborhood to get people to put his remains back in the ground where they belong: "I can have no rest, no peace, till they have given that poor body burial again" (248). The joke falls on the poor spirit, as the narrator tells the ghost, "you have been haunting a *plaster cast* of yourself—the real Cardiff Giant is in Albany!" (248). The spirit is devastated: "The Petrified Man has sold everybody else, and now the mean fraud had ended by selling its own ghost." He departs, dejected, but takes with him the narrator's "red blanket and my bathtub" (249).

"A Curious Dream" is a dream vision containing a moral, the narrator suggests, but no "poetry." After the establishment of mood and setting—midnight, with "no human sound in the air, not even a footstep"—the story consists of a dialogue between Mark Twain and "John Baxter Copmanhurst," deceased. Ghosts are roaming the streets at night, dissatisfied with the condition of their graves: "Look at this shroud—rags. Look at this gravestone, all battered up. Look at that disgraceful old coffin. . . . My pride is hurt, and my comfort is impaired—destroyed" (33). The dialogue form allows the dead to have their say, to articulate the dreadful and calloused "neglect of one's posterity": "My grandson lives in a stately house built with money made by these old hands of mine, and I sleep in a neglected grave with invading vermin that gnaw my shroud to build them nests withal!" (34–35). The purpose of this fiction "containing a moral" is serious: to prick the conscience of a community and thereby occasion reform. The appeal of this "ghost" story is not to fear but to guilt.

Bibliography

PRIMARY

The Complete Short Stories of Mark Twain. Now Collected for the First Time. Edited by Charles Neider. Garden City, N.Y.: Hanover House, 1957.

Eye Openers: Good Things, Immensely Funny Sayings & Stories That Will Bring a Smile upon the Gruffest Countenance. London: John Camden Hotten, 1871.

Mark Twain's Sketches, New and Old. Now First Published in Complete Form. Hartford and Chicago: American Publishing Co., 1875.

SECONDARY

Baldanza, Frank. *Mark Twain: An Introduction and Interpretation*. New York: Holt, Rinehart & Winston, 1961.

Bellamy, Gladys C. *Mark Twain as a Literary Artist*. Norman: University of Oklahoma Press, 1950.

Branch, Edgar M. *The Literary Apprenticeship of Mark Twain*. Urbana: University of Illinois Press, 1950.

Emerson, Everett. *The Authentic Mark Twain: A Literary Biography of Samuel L. Clemens*. Philadelphia: University of Pennsylvania Press, 1984.

Gribben, Alan. "Those Other Thematic Patterns in Mark Twain's Writing." *Studies in American Fiction* 13 (Autumn 1985): 185–200.

Long, E. Hudson. *Mark Twain Handbook*. New York: Hendricks House, 1957.

Paine, Albert B. *Mark Twain: A Biography*. Vol. 2. New York: Harper & Brothers, 1912.

Rogers, Franklin R. *Mark Twain's Burlesque Patterns*. Dallas: Southern Methodist University Press, 1960.

Sloane, David E. E. "Mark Twain's Comedy: The 1870s." *Studies in American Humor* 2 (January 1976): 146–56.

9

The Death Disk

Publication History

"The Death Disk" first appeared in the December 1901 issue of *Harper's Magazine*. Almost immediately Mark Twain adapted the story to dramatic form and presented it at Carnegie Hall in early winter 1902 (Paine 1194). The story was published in Germany in the *A Double-Barreled Detective Story* volume (Tauchnitz: 1902), then in the United States the following year in *My Debut as a Literary Person*.

Circumstances of Composition, Sources, and Influences

Mark Twain claimed that he worked twelve years on "The Death Disk," even though it was "the shortest story I ever wrote" (Bellamy 370). The source for the story is Carlyle's five-volume edition of *Cromwell's Letters and Speeches,* which Mark Twain read in May 1883 (Baetzhold 87). In a subsequent notebook entry, the author noted the account in Carlyle's edition of a young girl who is required to determine the death of some rebellious soldiers in the Roundhead army, and in a 20 December 1883 letter to William Dean Howells, Mark Twain described his projected play version of the incident he had read "in Carlyle's Cromwell a year ago" (*Mark Twain-Howells Letters* 455–58). The plans for a dramatic tragedy were abandoned, however, until October 1899 when, while living in London, Mark Twain resuscitated the project and turned it into a short story (Macnaughton 175–76). Emerson writes that "The Death Disk" is among "some slight but publishable pieces that show that his disdain for writing for money was not complete" (231).

Relationship to Other Mark Twain Works

Mark Twain wrote "The Death Disk" at the same time he was at work on drafts of *The Mysterious Stranger* (1916). Radically different in tone, these two works signal Mark Twain's dual poses as artist at the turn of the century: the dominant pose controlling such works as *The Mysterious Stranger, What Is Man?* (1906), "Little Bessie" (written 1908–09), and

"The Victims" (ca. 1902), is that of sardonic satirist; there is at the same time, however, the undercurrent pose of the grandfatherly Victorian gentleman, the "soft-hearted man of feeling," that surfaces in maudlin pieces like "The Death Disk," "A Dog's Tale" (1903), and "A Horse's Tale" (1906) (Stone 170). Cox notes that these three stories, "all more or less nauseating shorter fiction following the lines of *Joan of Arc*," feature young, innocent, courageous girls as heroines whose exploits are described in "the same unctuous tone of the Sieur Louis De Conte" (265). Abby Mayfair thus joins the ranks of Joan of Arc, Cathy Alison ("A Horse's Tale"), Eve (in "Eve's Diary" [1905]), and the heroine of "Marjorie Fleming, the Wonder Child" (1909), a gallery of sentimental, asexual girls—loosely modeled on his daughter Susy—who testify to what Stone calls the "power and beauty of girlhood" (232).

The "power and beauty" fails to surface, however, because of the maudlin sentimentality. Bellamy laments the "patheticism" of the melodramatic "Death Disk," and points to the revealing contrast of the "mawkish" scene between Abby and her father, and the "honest simplicity" of Jim's account in *Huckleberry Finn* (1885) of his young daughter's illness and subsequent deafness (370).

Critical Studies

Although Mark Twain apparently was captivated by this story, thinking about various ways to adapt it off and on for almost twenty years, the final product is an aesthetic failure. Like "A Curious Experience" (1881), it is, Baldanza writes, "a belabored and ineffective historical romance" (100). Characters are the conventional stereotypes of Victorian melodrama; the plot—though supposedly based on an historical occurrence—is contrived and implausible; and the theme rings hollow in a story more suitable for children than adults.

The story opens with a note of foreboding: "The winter evening was come, and outside were storm and darkness." A young officer in Cromwell's army and his wife, in "a melancholy silence," await impending doom. But they must summon their courage, feign a cheerful air in front of their seven-year-old daughter, Abby, and place their hope in Providence: "And we will accept what is appointed for us, and bear it in patience, as knowing that whatsoever He doeth is done is righteousness and meant in kindness—" (391). The reference to Providence serves to sustain the reader through a series of events seemingly programmed for the young officer's death. Abby, a Wordsworthian child who in her courage, naiveté, and self-righteousness becomes "a quite impossible creature" (Wagenknecht 150), is the agent of Providence who unwittingly condemns her father to death, then secures his release. Cromwell closes the story marveling at the girl's role in executing God's providential intervention: "God be thanked for the saving accident of that unthinking promise; and you, inspired by Him, for reminding me of my forgotten pledge, O incomparable child!" (399).

"The Death Disk" breaks into two related parts. The first centers on an intimate family gathering at nightfall, when Abby demands that her doting father tell her a "dreadful" bedtime story, because "Nurse says people don't always have gay times" (392). The father then explains his plight in a story Abby recognizes as true, though she does not identify her father as one of the unfortunate colonels facing execution for heroism that "exceeded their orders" (393). The first part closes as Cromwell's soldiers arrive to carry Colonel Mayfair off to the Tower of London for execution the next morning.

The second part opens as the three condemned men stand before Cromwell, awaiting what seems to be their inevitable doom. Dramatic irony creates overwrought pathos. The reader knows the situation; Abby does not. Infatuated with the charming child brought in off the street, Cromwell asks her to give one of the three discs—two white, one red—to each of the three condemned men. Of course he is unaware that one of the men is her father; she is unaware that the man to whom she gives the "prettiest" disc, the red one, will die. Inexorably she gives the red one to her father, creating the necessity of her heroic defiance of the general and the intervention of divine Providence to avoid a catastrophic conclusion.

Bibliography

PRIMARY

The Complete Short Stories of Mark Twain. Now Collected for the First Time. Edited by Charles Neider. Garden City, N.Y.: Hanover House, 1957.

Mark Twain-Howells Letters: The Literary Correspondence of Samuel L. Clemens and William Dean Howells, 1872–1910. Edited by Henry Nash Smith and William M. Gibson. Vol. 2. Cambridge, Mass.: Harvard University Press, 1960.

My Debut as a Literary Person with Other Essays and Stories. Hartford: American Publishing Co., 1903.

SECONDARY

Baetzhold, Howard G. *Mark Twain & John Bull: The British Connection.* Bloomington: Indiana University Press, 1970.

Baldanza, Frank. *Mark Twain: An Introduction and Interpretation.* New York: Holt, Rinehart & Winston, 1961.

Bellamy, Gladys C. *Mark Twain as a Literary Artist*. Norman: University of Oklahoma Press, 1950.

Cox, James M. *Mark Twain: The Fate of Humor*. Princeton, N.J.: Princeton University Press, 1966.

Emerson, Everett. *The Authentic Mark Twain: A Literary Biography of Samuel L. Clemens*. Philadelphia: University of Pennsylvania Press, 1984.

Macnaughton, William R. *Mark Twain's Last Years as a Writer*. Columbia: University of Missouri Press, 1979.

Paine, Albert B. *Mark Twain: A Biography*. Vol. 3. New York: Harper & Brothers, 1912.

Stone, Albert E., Jr. *The Innocent Eye: Childhood in Mark Twain's Imagination*. New Haven: Yale University Press, 1961.

Wagenknecht, Edward. *Mark Twain: The Man and His Work*. New Haven: Yale University Press, 1935.

10

A Dog's Tale
A Horse's Tale

Publication History

"A Dog's Tale" first appeared in the Christmas number of *Harper's Magazine*, December 1903. The National Anti-Vivisectionist Society of Great Britain, much impressed with the piece, asked the publishers for permission to distribute a pamphlet reprint for purposes of propaganda. Harper and Brothers supplied three thousand such pamphlets for distribution in London in 1904 (Blanck 617). In September 1904 Harper and Brothers released a deluxe clothbound book with illustrations by W. T. Smedley. The story is reprinted in *The $30,000 Bequest and Other Stories* (1906).

The last story published during Mark Twain's lifetime, "A Horse's Tale" appeared in two installments of *Harper's Magazine* during August and September 1906. The seventeen-thousand-word tale was published the following year by Harper and Brothers as an illustrated book. The actress Minnie Maddern Fiske, who had requested the story and was immensely pleased with it, promised to have it published and distributed in Spain, but there is no evidence that she did so (Emerson 260–61; Paine 1245).

Circumstances of Composition, Sources, and Influences

Mark Twain wrote very little during the summer of 1903. In residence at Quarry Farm near Elmira, New York, he tended to business ventures and prepared for the family's move to Florence, Italy, in autumn, a move designed to improve Olivia's health. While at the farm Mark Twain did find time to write the sentimental "A Dog's Tale" for daughter Jean, who was an outspoken opponent of vivisection (Emerson 244).

The summer of 1905 proved an especially trying time for Mark Twain. His twenty-five-thousand-dollar investment in Plasmon had proved disastrous and he was full of bitterness against Henry Betters, who he thought had swindled him; moreover, his family was literally disintegrating. Olivia's death in 1904 had left him emotionally devastated and the remaining family full of recriminations: Clara, her own health failing, avoided her father, in part because she held him responsible for her mother's death; Mark

Twain in turn resented Jean, the daughter whose epilepsy he blamed for Olivia's death. An emergency appendectomy in May 1905 provided a convenient excuse for Clara to remain in New York apart from her father and sister who had retreated to Dublin, New Hampshire, for the summer. Somehow the appendicitis had affected Clara's vocal chords, and her slow recovery aggravated her father's despair. Jean's chronic condition also worsened, and the general hysteria and suspected alcoholism of her nurse and Mark Twain's secretary, Isabel Lyon, did little to alleviate the tension and despair of the household (Hill 93–110).

The author took refuge from his loneliness with an Aeolian orchestrelle, an elaborate player piano that evoked bittersweet nostalgic reflections of happier family times, before the death of Susy almost a decade earlier (Ferguson 301). His mood vacillated from bitterness and rage over personal, social, and cosmic injustices to sentimental effusions of tender emotion, usually connected with childhood innocence and courageous virtue. Such vacillation is apparent in the several writing projects on which he worked simultaneously during the summer of 1905: *The Mysterious Stranger*, "Three Thousand Years among the Microbes," revision of "Adam's Diary," and "A Horse's Tale" (Kaplan 573). As Stone writes, "If the pendulum of despair swung Twain in *The Mysterious Stranger* close to Melville's mood of *The Confidence Man*, the opposite swing brought him back into the neighborhood of Frances Hodgson Burnett" (250).

Campbell notes that "A Dog's Tale" is in the tradition of Aesop's fables, which include an account of a dog wrongfully punished after rescuing his master's child (43–49). A more immediate influence comes from Robert Browning, whose poetry Mark Twain greatly admired and often read aloud to audiences in his home. Gribben contends that in 1905 Mark Twain tried consciously to emulate Browning's monologues in "King Leopold's Soliloquy" and "The Czar's Soliloquy," but his indignation made it impossible for him to capture the English poet's characteristic subtlety (87–103). The specific source for "A Dog's Tale" is Browning's poem "Tray," a poem about a loyal old dog who after saving a drowning child risks his life a second time to retrieve the child's doll. The speaker in the poem proposes to buy the dog so that "By vivisection, at expense/ Of half a hour and eighteenpence,/ How brain secretes dog's soul, we'll see!" As Baetzhold points out, Mark Twain's story expands Browning's poem and intensifies its attack on science; but because Mark Twain lacks Browning's detachment, and "allowed his own emotions to intrude too blatantly," his tale "approaches the maudlin" (292–93).

"A Horse's Tale" was composed at the request of Minnie Maddern Fiske, who wrote to Mark Twain in September 1905 asking his assistance in her campaign to put an end to bullfighting in Spain. Mark Twain's writings and many public performances both in the United States and in

Europe had made him an international celebrity, and his antivivisectionist story, "A Dog's Tale," led Mrs. Fiske to believe he might be sympathetic to her cause. Moreover, earlier that year Mark Twain's daughter Jean had published in *Harper's Weekly* (April 1905) a piece on the cruelty of check-reins and martingales entitled "A Word for the Horses" (Stone 252–53; Emerson 260–61). Mrs. Fiske's request carried specific instructions: she wanted "a story of an old horse that is finally given over to the bull-ring," something parallel to his dog story that would expose the barbaric cruelty of the Spanish national sport (Paine 1245–46).

Mark Twain promptly agreed to Mrs. Fiske's request, although he cautioned that he "may not get it to suit me, in which case it will go in the fire" (Paine 1246). But the story did indeed "suit" him; in a 7 October 1906 letter to his business agent F. A. Duneka, Mark Twain revealed that he was "deeply interested" in the project and "dead to everything else" during its composition. The reason for his compelling devotion to the piece, however, had less to do with the ostensible occasion than with the direction the story took during its evolution: "the heroine is my daughter, Susy, whom we lost. It was not intentional—it was a good while before I found it out" (*Mark Twain's Letters* 779). Drawing upon his idealized memories of Susy in his portrait of Cathy Alison, Mark Twain surrendered to the sentimentality that he had so virulently condemned in his earlier burlesque sketches, creating a story, Emerson contends, that "might well have been written as the basis for a Shirley Temple movie" (261). He read the story aloud to audiences in his home, the elaborate orchestrelle sounding the bugle calls at appropriate moments. Isabel Lyon reinforced the sentimental pathos of the occasion, becoming, Hill reports, "uncontrollable in her appreciation and enthusiasm" (113). Unquestionably the story assumed unmerited significance to the aging, distraught Mark Twain, and he gave lengthy directions concerning the illustrations for the 1907 volume.

Relationship to Other Mark Twain Works

Maudlin sentimentality becomes increasingly characteristic of Mark Twain's fiction in the author's late life. Emerson links "A Dog's Tale" with "The Californian's Tale" (1893) and "Was It Heaven? or Hell?" (1902): the three show that "the one time archfoe of sentimentalism had drifted over the enemy's camp" (244). Cox compares the story with "A Horse's Tale" and "The Death Disk" (1901)—"all more or less nauseating shorter fiction following the lines of *Joan of Arc*" (265). Both "A Dog's Tale" and "A Horse's Tale" are written to oppose barbaric abuses of innocence—vivisection in the former, bullfighting in the latter—and both rely on pathos to generate reader protest.

"A Horse's Tale" has a dual focus for its unabashed sentimentality: the fate of Soldier Boy, the old horse who serves as narrator for a significant portion of the story; and Cathy Alison, the young girl modeled on Mark Twain's daughter Susy, who perishes with her horse in the bullring. It is thus a story about both animals and children. Mark Twain, of course, had written numerous tales about both. The use of animals in "A Dog's Tale" and "A Horse's Tale," however, contrasts markedly with their use in earlier pieces like "Jim Smiley and His Jumping Frog" (1865), "Some Learned Fables for Good Old Boys and Girls" (1875), "Dick Baker and His Cat" (from *Roughing It* [1872]), and "Jim Baker's Blue Jay Yarn" (from *A Tramp Abroad* [1880]). The earlier, successful animal stories delight with their sardonic wit. Like Swift, Mark Twain debunks pomposity through a process of reduction that magnifies the absurdity of certain patterns of human behavior. There is little sentimental identification with the animals; rather, they are simply vehicles for the author's ironic, satiric observations about human nature. In "A Dog's Tale" and "A Horse's Tale," both narrated from an animal's point of view, humanization of animals serves to illuminate the vicious nature of the men who abuse them. The dog and the horse are more loyal, more courageous, more sensitive, more loving—in short, more human—than their masters. These stories are much less satisfying or successful than the earlier animal fictions in large part because they are requested object lessons—written specifically to expose the evils of vivisection and bullfighting—and are victims of Mark Twain's inability to establish ironic detachment from subjects that aroused his ire (Baldanza 101; Brashear 234).

As a story about children, "A Horse's Tale" is at the end of a series of stories about young, pubescent girls that appeared during the last fifteen years of Mark Twain's life. Earlier in his career, of course, Mark Twain had used children with considerable aesthetic effect: the fate of the Shepherdson and Grangerford children and Huck's response to the Bricksville mob in *Huckleberry Finn* (1885) form a powerful indictment of antebellum life along the river; likewise, in *A Connecticut Yankee in King Arthur's Court* (1889) children are used to heighten the effect of the barbaric, socially sanctioned cruelties of feudal Britain. In *A Connecticut Yankee,* however, the two conflicting components of what Stone calls Mark Twain's split personality—"the sardonic satirist and the soft-hearted man of feeling"—begin to separate (169–170). The former surfaces in the bleak pessimism of *The Mysterious Stranger* (1916), "The Man That Corrupted Hadleyburg" (1899), and *What Is Man?* (1906); the latter controls the tone of such sentimental pieces as "The Death Disk," "A Dog's Tale," "Marjorie Fleming, the Wonder Child," "Eve's Diary," and "A Horse's Tale"— all dominated by girls who in their innocence, purity, and victimization at the hands of a patriarchal social order recall the heroine of *Personal Recollections of Joan of Arc* (1896).

Stone (230) and Cox (265) argue that the saccharine narratives concerning young girls were written to "assuage grief" over the death of Susy. Certainly they offer an alternative perspective to the chronic misanthropy and incessant rage against cosmic injustices that are characteristic of the author's final vision. Doomed though they may be, the young maidens of his later fiction manifest qualities of courage, faith, virtue, and devotion that testify to Mark Twain's desire to believe in what Stone calls "the potential dignity of the human condition" (231). But they also reflect the deep-seated emotional difficulties that led Mark Twain in later life to surround himself with pubescent female admirers: the fifteen-year-old Gertrude Natkin, his "dream grandchild" whom he admonished in 1906, "Don't get any older—I can't have it. Stay always just as you are" (Hill 127–28); Helen Allen, with whom Hill suggests the aging author behaved improperly, causing concern to her parents and occasioning his hasty departure from Bermuda in April 1910 (259–61); and the "Angel Fish," a group of school-age girls whose sole function, Cox reports, "was to cast their doting gazes upon the club's founder and chief member" (265).

Critical Studies

Although unabashedly sentimental, "A Dog's Tale" has drawn qualified praise from some quarters. Baetzhold calls it "a moving story, and a powerful indictment of cruelty to animals" (293). Wagenknecht claims "there is no tenderer dog story in literature" (153). Herzberg calls attention to its less obvious but serious themes, which include "the misuse of language" as social weapon, "the cold-bloodedness of science and the evils of slavery" (20).

The story opens with the dog's first-person reminiscence of its mother, a collie with "a fondness" for large words that she uses to impress "them all, from pocket-pup to mastiff." Despite her "rather vain and frivolous character," she proves an excellent mother because "she taught us not by words only, but by example, and that is the best way and the surest and the most lasting" (489–90). The dog's mother thus stands in ironic contrast to the girl's father: his fine words laud his pet's reason and courage in rescuing his infant daughter from a nursery fire and he disputes his empirically minded friends who insist the animal's behavior is purely instinctual; but in sacrificing the dog's pup to vivisection to settle an abstract argument, his actions—or "example"—belie his vocal sentiments. A further ironic contrast surfaces when the dog, well trained by its mother to "do our duties without repining, take our life as we might find it, live it for the good of others, and never mind the results," is pleased to have saved the girl from the fire—despite the personal danger and subsequent abuse it receives—because it sympathizes with the bereavement the father would have felt had the dog not acted: "Why, what would life be without my puppy!" (494). The father, however, proves not to have been so well trained, for he callously sacrifices the dog's puppy without any parallel regard for the mother's feelings.

The major point of the story is its attack on "frosty" science, particularly the barbaric practice of vivisection. The scientists operate on the puppy not to save its life or ease its discomfort, but simply to discover whether a certain brain injury will cause blindness. They learn that it will, and as the tortured pup dies painfully, scientists proclaim a boon to "suffering humanity" as a result of their experimentation. The actual "benefit" of the experiment is of course open to question. But there is no question of the emotional trauma experienced by the pup's heroic mother who, after witnessing the pup's bloody carcass, slowly starves herself to death.

Mark Twain scholars are virtually unanimous in their condemnation of "A Horse's Tale," an awkward, rambling narrative that as Long contends "added no more to his [Mark Twain's] reputation than it hindered bullfighting" (240). Although the story may exemplify the eighteenth-century concept of "nature's social union" (Wagenknecht 65; Brashear 234), its sentimentality and abrupt, bloody conclusion are, as Emerson writes, "distinctly overdone" (261). Not since his early days as a Nevada journalist had Mark Twain shown so little control of his materials or such lack of self-discipline in his treatment of theme (Hill 114); as a result, the story's serious themes fall victim to the author's failure to structure them within a credible and aesthetically satisfying context.

Major problems result from the story's split focus and unctuous tone. "A Horse's Tale" is in part a story told by a horse—Soldier Boy, Buffalo Bill's trusted and faithful mount—and in part a story about a horse—his memories of past glories, his relationship to the idolized Cathy Alison, nine-year-old niece of the commanding general at Fort Paxton, and his gruesome demise in a Spanish bullring. But the story is only in part a horse's tale, for the focus shifts to Cathy Alison to the point that we as readers almost lose sight of Soldier Boy until the end, when the two are united in bloody death. As narrator, Soldier Boy is ineffective, for his rank sentimentality renders him incapable of detached commentary or ironic observation; he is, to say the least, "an awkward successor to Simon Wheeler, Huck Finn, Louis de Conte, and Theodor Fischer" (Stone 253). Gibson argues that Soldier Boy's dialogue testifies to Mark Twain's love of nonsense language, à la Lewis Carroll (15); more often, however, his language is stilted to the point of parody. Other narrators are hardly more successful, for they too engage in sentimental homage to Cathy, making her "an American St. Joan"; General Alison's death-scene speech, Stone contends, reverberates "with pathos carried almost to the point of travesty" (256).

Bibliography

PRIMARY

The Complete Short Stories of Mark Twain. Now Collected for the First Time. Edited by Charles Neider. Garden City, N.Y.: Hanover House, 1957.

A Dog's Tale. Illustrated by G. T. Smedley. New York: Harper & Brothers, 1904.

A Horse's Tale. New York: Harper & Brothers, 1907.

Mark Twain's Letters. Edited by A. B. Paine. Vol. 2. New York: Harper & Brothers, 1917.

The $30,000 Bequest and Other Stories. New York: Harper & Brothers, 1906.

SECONDARY

Baetzhold, Howard G. *Mark Twain and John Bull: The British Connection*. Bloomington: Indiana University Press, 1970.

Baldanza, Frank. *Mark Twain: An Introduction and Interpretation*. New York: Holt, Rinehart & Winston, 1961.

Blanck, Jacob. "BAL Addendum 3479: Twain's 'A Dog's Tale.' " *Publications of the Bibliographical Society of America* 62 (1968):617.

Brashear, Minnie. *Mark Twain: Son of Missouri*. Chapel Hill: University of North Carolina Press, 1934.

Campbell, Killis. "From Aesop to Mark Twain." *Sewanee Review* 19 (January 1911):43–49.

Cox, James M. *Mark Twain: The Fate of Humor*. Princeton, N.J.: Princeton University Press, 1966.

Emerson, Everett. *The Authentic Mark Twain: A Literary Biography of Samuel L. Clemens*. Philadelphia: University of Pennsylvania Press, 1984.

Ferguson, Delancey. *Mark Twain: Man and Legend*. Indianapolis: Bobbs-Merrill, 1943.

Gibson, William M. *The Art of Mark Twain*. New York: Oxford University Press, 1976.

Gribben, Alan. " 'A Splendor of Stars and Suns': Mark Twain as Reader of Browning's Poems." *Browning Institute Studies* 6 (1978):87–103.

Herzberg, Gay. " 'A Dog's Tale': An Expanded View." *Mark Twain Journal* 19, no. 1 (1977–78):20.

Hill, Hamlin. *Mark Twain: God's Fool*. New York: Harper & Row, 1973.

Kaplan, Justin. *Mr. Clemens and Mark Twain*. New York: Simon & Schuster, 1966.

Long, E. Hudson. *Mark Twain Handbook*. New York: Hendricks House, 1957.

Paine, Albert B. *Mark Twain: A Biography*. Vol. 3. New York: Harper & Brothers, 1912.

Stone, Albert B., Jr. *The Innocent Eye: Childhood in Mark Twain's Imagination*. New Haven: Yale University Press, 1961.

Wagenknecht, Edward. *Mark Twain: The Man and His Work*. New Haven: Yale University Press, 1935.

11

A Double-Barreled Detective Story

Publication History

Mark Twain wrote "A Double-Barreled Detective Story" over a six-day period in late summer 1901 and sent it immediately to *Harper's Magazine*, where it appeared in two installments in early 1902. When the story appeared collected in book form by Harper and Brothers later the same year, Mark Twain inserted several letters from readers of the magazine version who questioned his reference to the "solitary esophagus" in the descriptive passage that opens chapter 4. Macnaughton contends that in doing so Mark Twain called attention to the burlesque intention of both the specific passage in question and the piece as a whole (172–73). The story appears in the Author's National Edition of *The Writings of Mark Twain* (1907–18) and is reprinted in Neider's edition of Mark Twain's short stories.

Circumstances of Composition, Sources, and Influences

Mark Twain wrote "A Double-Barreled Detective Story" during the summer of 1901 while he and his family lived in a log cabin at Saranac Lake in New York (Long 233). During the same summer he wrote the essay "The United States of Lyncherdom" and laid plans to complete a book on the history of lynching in the United States—plans he abandoned for fear of alienating his southern audience (Kaplan 364–65). Macnaughton conjectures that Mark Twain's research for the book on lynching tempted him to move his story—with its melodramatic opening involving the abuse of southern womanhood—toward a climactic lynching scene (168).

The direct inspiration for the story, however, came from the detective fiction of Arthur Conan Doyle, whose vastly popular *A Study in Scarlet* (1887) his friend Joe Twichell had loaned to Mark Twain several years earlier. Although the popularity of Doyle's fiction in the United States perhaps inspired Mark Twain to employ detectives and courtroom revelations in much of his fiction during the 1890s (e.g., *Pudd'nhead Wilson* [1894], *Personal Recollections of Joan of Arc* [1896], *Tom Sawyer, Detective*

[1896]), he generally disparaged the genre. In a June 1896 notebook entry, Mark Twain wrote: "What a curious thing a 'detective' story is. And was there ever one that the author needn't be ashamed of, except 'The Murders of the Rue Morgue'?" (Baetzhold 299). In a letter to Twichell, Mark Twain described "A Double-Barreled Detective Story" as a "condensed novel" designed to satirize Doyle's "pompous sentimental 'extraordinary man' with his cheap & ineffectual ingenuities" (Emerson 239). Doyle's famous detective, Sherlock Holmes, appears in Mark Twain's story, and both his assumed expertise and the public's gullible adulation of him fall victim to the author's satire (Gribben 155). The melodramatic crime that opens "A Double-Barreled Detective Story," as well as Archy's peculiar gift of a bloodhound's scent, may have been inspired by the first installment of *The Hound of the Baskervilles* (Baetzhold 302).

The primary object of Mark Twain's extended burlesque, however, is *A Study in Scarlet*. The most acclaimed section of Mark Twain's story, the nature description with its reference to the "solitary esophagus," parallels Doyle's effusive description of Utah's "great alkali plain" in the middle of his 1887 novella. Although Doyle sees a region of "desolation and silence" while Mark Twain portrays the West as a natural paradise where "everywhere brooded stillness, serenity, and the peace of God" (436), the latter consciously parodies "this section of the Doyle story almost exactly" (Kraus 12). Baetzhold (299–304) and Ritunnano (10–14) offer detailed analyses of other specific and extensive parallels—in structure, plot, and characterization—between the two stories that leave little doubt of a genetic relationship. Mark Twain's elaborate burlesque of his source material follows "a clear satiric pattern," Ritunnano writes: "The ultimate effect of his alteration is a satire of the naive idealism of the assumptions underlying Conan Doyle's story" (11).

Cooper suggests another possible source for the "solitary esophagus" passage, a novel by Walter Besant and James Rice entitled *The Seamy Side, a Story* published in London in 1880. Cooper bases his argument on verbal echoes, particularly a reference to "the lilacs and laburnums" (85–87). The burlesque techniques Mark Twain employs in this passage may well have been learned from Charles Henry Webb, who influenced Mark Twain greatly during his early days as a San Francisco journalist. Rogers points specifically to "the consciously inappropriate use of technical terms and foreign expressions" that provide much of the burlesque humor in Mark Twain's parody of purple prose that opens chapter 4. The allusion to the "esophagus" echoes Webb's burlesque passage in *St. Tivel'mo* (1867), with its reference to the "chirurgeons who have passed beyond the stormy esophagus of science" (Rogers 24). Both Mark Twain and Webb perpetrate their hoaxes through language, using what Covici terms "the hoax of language"; the principal effect, in both instances, is "to jolt the reader" (148).

Relationship to Other Mark Twain Works

"A Double-Barreled Detective Story" belongs to a series of stories and novellas that involved crime detection. Courtroom revelations figure prominently in *Pudd'nhead Wilson, Tom Sawyer, Detective,* and "The Chronicle of Young Satan" (1916); trial scenes or public revelations of guilt play significant roles in *Joan of Arc,* and "The Man That Corrupted Hadleyburg" (1899) as well. But as Baetzhold points out, Mark Twain "evidently looked upon detectives and detective fiction with mixed emotions" (298). In the late 1870s he twice turned his satiric eye and burlesque tools to the operations of Allan Pinkerton and his agents: in "Cap'n Simon Wheeler, the Amateur Detective" (1877), and "The Stolen White Elephant" (1882) (Emerson 201–2; Smith 181). To William Dean Howells, Mark Twain wrote that he had burlesqued the detective business "very extravagantly . . . if it *is* possible to burlesque that business extravagantly" (*Mark Twain-Howells Letters* 246).

In a sense, "A Double-Barreled Detective Story" assimilates the materials that had governed Mark Twain's fiction throughout his career. The particular mode of burlesque, the condensed novel, links the story to earlier literary parodies like "Aurelia's Unfortunate Young Man" (1864) and "Lucretia Smith's Soldier" (1864); again, the principal targets of satire are sentimentality and the romantic expectations of genteel readers. The parody of purple prose recalls the "Love's Bakery" segment of the former and the effusive opening of the latter. The spoof of English detective fiction is in line with Mark Twain's burlesque of European manners and cultural artifacts in *Innocents Abroad* (1869), while the focus on Archy, the exceptional lad, is in the tradition of his boy stories like *Tom Sawyer* (1876), *Huckleberry Finn* (1885), and *The Mysterious Stranger* (1916). The setting in the colorful world of the western mining camps calls to mind *Roughing It* (1872), "Jim Smiley and His Jumping Frog" (1865), and "Jim Baker's Blue Jay Yarn" (1880), and the parody of the yokels' fascination with the English celebrity (Holmes) recalls the gullibility of simple Arkansas folks before the chicanery of the duke and the dauphin in *Huckleberry Finn.* As he does with the Shepherdson-Grangerford feud in that novel, Mark Twain subjects the southern revenge code to ridicule, and in the manner of Sherburn's defiance of the Bricksville yokels, he again dramatizes a confrontation between the lynch mob and the single courageous spokesman for order. Archy's comment, "How blind and unreasoning and arbitrary are some of the laws of nature—the most of them, in fact!" (430), is the major theme of most of Mark Twain's writing during the last decade of his life. In fact, Hill contends that the only redeeming feature of this "extravagant mixture of literary parody, melodrama, and low burlesque" is that "Mark Twain managed for the last time to complete a substantial work of fiction which embodied elements of the major themes of his career" (31–32).

Critical Studies

The melodramatic excesses and structural obscurities of "A Double-Barreled Detective Story" arise from its form: it is a burlesque, inspired by a particular source, of Conan Doyle's detective fiction and of his "extraordinary man" Sherlock Holmes; and, more generally, it is a parody of formula writing and reader response to it. Hence if Mark Twain's story is "execrable fiction, certainly one of the worst tales ever foisted upon his public" (Macnaughton 169), it is so intentionally. As Macnaughton points out, exaggeration of defects is crucial to any successful burlesque or parody: "if the disparity between the original and the burlesque itself is not great, then it is sometimes almost impossible to decide whether the writer wishes to be taken seriously or to be laughed at" (169–70).

Several critics, however, argue that even as parody the story is radically flawed. The direct attack on Holmes, Baetzhold maintains, is so bald as to lose comic effectiveness, and the farcical excesses throughout undermine the satire (302). Emerson agrees that the story lacks subtlety and control. The burlesque features are so exaggerated and the structure so diffuse that readers are left thoroughly confused unless they have recently read the objects of Mark Twain's burlesque attack; intrinsically it "is probably the worst story that Mark Twain ever wrote" (238–39).

Ferguson points out that Mark Twain's story is structured rather like *Pudd'nhead Wilson* in that it conflates "two mutually contradictory themes": it is both a grim revenge tragedy and a parody of Sherlock Holmes. The crucial difference between this story and the 1894 novel, Ferguson argues, is that "Mark Twain did not realize what he had done and consequently did not separate them in a drastic revision" (286). Kraus and Ritunnano, however, dispute the allegation that Mark Twain could not control the structure of "A Double-Barreled Detective Story," for each sees it as a carefully orchestrated burlesque of its source *A Study in Scarlet*. Both Mark Twain's story and Doyle's novella are "double-barreled." Whereas Doyle allows Holmes to solve the crime in barrel one and then in barrel two explains the revenge motive that justifies the crime in the first place, Mark Twain reverses the process: we see first Jacob Fuller's motivation, his heinous abuse and humiliation of his young bride, and her son Archy's dogged determination to bring his father to justice; then we see the farcical pursuit, detective work of Holmes, and eventual unraveling of the case at the end.

The structural reversal signals thematic reversals as well. In Doyle's story the human "bloodhound" is the culprit Jefferson Hope who, in his monomaniacal pursuit to avenge the humiliation and cruel abuse of his betrothed by two American desperadoes, becomes a moral agent; his murder of Drebber, who had coerced the girl to marry him, and Strangerson, who had killed her father, is noble and justified. Archy, the "bloodhound" of Mark Twain's story, is neither so noble nor so effective: his pursuit of his father is forced on him by his mother, and he never accomplishes his mission; instead of being the agent of moral justice, Archy is the source of a great deal of havoc in his bungling pursuit of the wrong man. Ritunnano points out that even the loose, rambling structure of "A Double-Barreled Detective Story" mocks its source to highlight profound philosophical differences between the two late nineteenth-century writers. Whereas "nothing is superfluous" in Doyle's "neatly arranged plot" that "imposes order on human events," Mark Twain's tale "is a series of accidents." In Doyle's ordered world Providence reigns to insure justice; Archy's attempts to establish justice are farcically ineffective. For Mark Twain, "life is not so neat as fiction nor is it so nice" (14).

One reason that Mark Twain's story seems so overdone and diffuse to contemporary readers is that the attention to the twin objects of burlesque ridicule—melodrama and detective fiction—renders the whole disjointed. To Mark Twain, however, the two are intertwined: the problem with detective fiction is that it is too melodramatic, formulaic, implausible, and sentimental in its assumption of a providential order governing human destinies. But his attacks on the two genres are not clearly interrelated in the story. He parodies melodrama in the first three chapters—the first barrel—then burlesques detective fiction in the second barrel.

The first "barrel" opens with a gruesome crime that sets the stage for a melodramatic revenge tragedy. Jacob Fuller, "of an old but unconsidered family," woos a nineteen-year-old girl, who "is intense, high strung, romantic, immeasurably proud of her Cavalier blood," and "so passionate in her love for" Fuller that she "braved her father's displeasure" to marry her lover. Fuller, however, is so angered by his haughty father-in-law's verbal attacks on his character and motives that he takes revenge by humiliating and abusing his bride, inflicting "all the humiliations, all the insults, all the miseries that [his] diligent and inventive mind . . . could contrive." Unable to break his bride's spirit through three months of such ghastly treatment, Fuller plans his ultimate humiliation: "he said, with a dark significance in his manner, 'I have tried all things but one'—and waited for her reply. 'Try that,' she said, and curled her lip in mockery" (424). At midnight he ties his pregnant wife to a tree on a public road, gags her and whips her across the face with a cowhide lash, sets his bloodhounds loose on her to rip her clothes off, and leaves her naked to be discovered by passersby at dawn. All of this proves more than the aristocratic father can bear. Fuller's revenge is completed as the old man "wasted away, day by day, and even his daughter rejoiced when death relieved him" (425). The young woman's quest for revenge, however, has just begun. Her son Archy, with "no playmates and no comrade, and no teacher but the mother," has the peculiar "gift of the bloodhound"—no doubt the legacy of his father's ultimate treachery. Convinced that "God has appointed the way," the mother unleashes her son on his fugitive father: "you will make of him another Wandering Jew; . . . you shall shadow him, cling to him, persecute him, till you break his heart" (428).

Throughout the first three chapters the focus is on melodramatic excess. Fuller's degradation of his bride, replete with the sexually titillating suggestion of bestiality, provides the occasion for revenge. The formulaic description and dialogue, the exaggerated postures assumed by the protagonists, the suggestiveness of Fuller's ultimate crime—"I have tried all things but one"—all, Macnaughton writes, are "archetypically melodramatic" (171). Mark Twain deflates the melodrama, however, with the ludicrous account of Archy's "peculiar" gift, discovered as he sniffs the postman's trail along a sidewalk and applied errantly in pursuit of the wrong man to Mexico. Archy discovers upon his return to Silver Gulch that his real prey has vanished and that he, rather than his father, has become the "Wandering Jew."

The second "barrel" shifts the tone from melodrama to farce as it burlesques the formulae and conventions of detective fiction. The setting is October 1900 in Hope Canon, "a silver-mining camp away down in the Esmeralda region" (439). Archy Stillman is yet around, having lost the trail of the wrong man he had been pursuing to apologize for inconveniencing him. Otherwise a whole new cast of characters appears on the scene: Flint Buckner, "a sour creature, unsociable" with an unknown past; Fetlock Jones, a sixteen-year-old English lad who works with Buckner, is abused by him, and plots his murder; Ferguson, the Wells Fargo man, who considers Buckner "a blight on this society"; and Sherlock Holmes, the "extraordinary man" who turns out to be Fetlock's uncle but whose sudden appearance in California is left unexplained. When an explosion kills Buckner and Holmes deduces what the reader already knows—that it is no accident—another detective quest begins. Holmes accuses the wrong man of Buckner's murder, but Archy comes to the rescue with the discovery that it is Fetlock who is guilty. Fetlock manages to escape from jail, however, to the delight of both the townspeople and the reader. The two "barrels" fuse at the end with the revelation that Buckner was actually Jacob Fuller. Ironically, the father suffers not at all from Archy's dogged pursuit; in fact, it is Archy who brings his murderer to justice—though he, too, finally escapes.

The transition between these two radically disjointed narratives is a paragraph that opens chapter 4 describing "a crisp and spicy morning in early October" when "the lilacs and laburnums, lit with the glory-fires of autumn, hung burning and flashing in the upper air" (436). Ferguson points to this paragraph—a parody of "the sappy nature descriptions of the late Victorian novelists"—as the brilliant triumph in an otherwise dismal work of fiction (286). Mark Twain further fragments the structure of the story by including several letters he had received concerning the paragraph and its reference to the mysterious "solitary esophagus." What delights him is the fact that his parody almost worked to deceive a public receptive to such saccharine prose. He responds to one letter: "Nothing in the paragraph disturbed him but that one word. It shows that that paragraph was most ably constructed for the deception it was intended to put upon the reader. It was my intention that it should read plausibly, and it is now plain that it does" (*Complete Short Stories* 437). Mark Twain also reprints an editorial that appeared in a New York newspaper (10 April 1902) that praises "A Double-Barreled Detective Story" as "the most elaborate of burlesques on detective fiction, with striking melodramatic passages in which it is difficult to detect the deception, so ably it is done" (438). Such authorial intrusions prepare readers for the burlesque that follows, and orient them towards the melodrama that precedes, lest they be deceived into thinking Mark Twain is serious and hence as wretched a storyteller as those whose work he parodies.

Bibliography

PRIMARY

The Complete Short Stories of Mark Twain. Now Collected for the First Time. Edited by Charles Neider. Garden City, N.Y.: Hanover House, 1957.

A Double-Barreled Detective Story. New York: Harper & Brothers, 1902.

Mark Twain-Howells Letters: The Correspondence of Samuel L. Clemens and William Dean Howells, 1872–1910. Edited by Henry Nash Smith and William M. Gibson. Vol. 1. Cambridge, Mass.: Harvard University Press, 1960.

The Writings of Mark Twain. Author's National Edition. Harper & Brothers Edition. Vol. 23. New York: P. F. Collier & Son, 1907.

SECONDARY

Baetzhold, Howard G. *Mark Twain and John Bull: The British Connection.* Bloomington: Indiana University Press, 1970.

Cooper, Lane. "Mark Twain's Lilacs and Laburnums." *Modern Language Notes* 47 (February 1932):85–87.

Covici, Pascal, Jr. *Mark Twain's Humor: The Image of a World.* Dallas: Southern Methodist University Press, 1962.

Emerson, Everett. *The Authentic Mark Twain: A Literary Biography of Samuel L. Clemens.* Philadelphia: University of Pennsylvania Press, 1984.

Ferguson, Delancey. *Mark Twain: Man and Legend.* Indianapolis: Bobbs-Merrill, 1943.

Gribben, Alan. "Stolen from Books, Tho' Credit Given': Mark Twain's Use of Literary Sources." *MOSAIC* 12 (1979):149–55.

Hill, Hamlin. *Mark Twain: God's Fool.* New York: Harper & Row, 1973.

Kaplan, Justin. *Mr. Clemens and Mark Twain.* New York: Simon & Schuster, 1966.

Kraus, W. Keith. "Mark Twain's 'A Double-Barreled Detective Story': A Source for the Solitary Oesophagus." *Mark Twain Journal* 16, no. 3 (Summer 1972):10–12.

Long, E. Hudson. *Mark Twain Handbook.* New York: Hendricks House, 1957.

Macnaughton, William C. *Mark Twain's Last Years as a Writer.* Columbia: University of Missouri Press, 1979.

Ritunnano, Jeanne. "Mark Twain vs. Arthur Conan Doyle on Detective Fiction." *Mark Twain Journal* 16, no. 1 (Winter 1971–72):10–14.

Rogers, Franklin R. *Mark Twain's Burlesque Patterns.* Dallas: Southern Methodist University Press, 1960.

Smith, Henry Nash. *Mark Twain: The Development of a Writer.* Cambridge, Mass.: Harvard University Press, 1962.

12

A Dying Man's Confession
The Professor's Yarn
A Burning Brand

Publication History

These three stories are among the interpolated short narratives Mark
Twain added to *Life on the Mississippi* in an attempt to pad the manuscript
for purposes of the subscription trade. Although the first two were written
in the 1870s, all three appear in print for the first time in *Life on the
Mississippi,* published in 1883 by James R. Osgood. "A Dying Man's
Confession" appears in chapters 31–32, "The Professor's Yarn" in chapter
36, and "A Burning Brand" in chapter 52. In his edition of *The Complete
Short Stories of Mark Twain,* Charles Neider reprints each as an independent short fiction.

Circumstances of Composition, Sources, and Influences

Life on the Mississippi began as a series of articles published in the
Atlantic Monthly, January–August 1875. The series, called "Old Times on
the Mississippi," details Mark Twain's memories of his experiences as a
cub pilot on the river and is essentially idyllic in its evocation of a lost era:
"a choice tapping of Clemens' creative memory," Baldanza explains, "clearly
and consecutively organized on the progressive difficulties of learning to
pilot a large steamboat" (48). On 10 April 1882 Mark Twain signed a
contract with Osgood to produce a subscription book about Mississippi
river lore and promised to have the completed manuscript ready by 1 October 1882. His intention was to appropriate the *Atlantic* articles for the
first half of the book (actually they appear in chaps. 4–17), then to fill out
the second half with new material garnered from a return visit to the river.
On 17 April, accompanied by Osgood and a stenographer named Roswell
Phillips, Mark Twain boarded a train to Saint Louis and from there traveled by steamboat downriver to New Orleans, where he met with George
Washington Cable and Joel Chandler Harris. From New Orleans, Mark

Twain cruised the length of the river to Saint Paul, Minnesota, stopping for a few days in Hannibal in route (Blair 285–87; Emerson 123).

The month-long trip, however, yielded less material for the new project than Mark Twain had expected. The subscription trade demanded a large book, and upon his return to Quarry Farm in New York Mark Twain not only found the 1 October deadline impossible to satisfy but, as he confessed to William Dean Howells, he felt hard-pressed to fill out "this now apparently interminable book" (Paine 742). Kaplan reports that Mark Twain padded his manuscript with extensive quotations from other travel writers and borrowed from *Huckleberry Finn* (1885), which he was writing at the same time (381–82). He also incorporated several digressionary tales and sketches for, as Hill writes, "he believed he had perfected a formula for writing a travel book that made the sketches an integral part" (55–57). Among the digressionary sketches are these three stories, which are related to other material in *Life on the Mississippi* "only by virtue of their appropriateness to the setting" (Rogers 90). "The Professor's Yarn," for example, was left over from material Mark Twain had discarded in writing *A Tramp Abroad* (1880); apologizing for the digression, he confesses, "I insert it in this place merely because it is a good story, not because it belongs here—for it doesn't" (304).

Relationship to Other Mark Twain Works

The three stories are linked most closely to Mark Twain's early western tall tales and anecdotes, many of which work on the principle of deceit (Miller 48) and, as DeVoto writes, reflect "the frontier's desire to burlesque and caricature itself" (243). Like "The Dandy Frightening a Squatter" (1852) and "Jim Smiley and His Jumping Frog" (1865), "The Professor's Yarn" tells of a con-man who is himself unexpectedly conned or victimized by his reckless self-confidence. In this case "three professional gamblers . . . rough, repulsive fellows" ruthlessly plan to take advantage of Mr. John Backus, who "from his clothes and his looks" appears to be "a grazier or farmer from the backwoods of some Western state—doubtless Ohio." Backus plays his part perfectly, feigning "drunken gravity" and betting foolishly against experienced and treacherous men; as it turns out Backus is in complete control, revealing after he wins the hand with four aces, "I'm a professional gambler myself, and I've been laying for you duffers all this voyage" (312). The would-be swindlers are swindled by a confidence man more deceitful and proficient than they.

Again as in "Jim Smiley and His Jumping Frog," Mark Twain is auditor in the tale; he simply repeats "a story which I picked up on board the boat last night" from a fellow "passenger—a college professor" (304). In its structure and in the crucial relationship of narrator to tale, "The Professor's Yarn" resembles Huck Finn's account of the drunk who emerges from the crowd at a circus to ride a wild horse. Huck fully expects the drunken intruder to be killed and feels sympathy for him, never in his naiveté suspecting he might be part of a prearranged act. The drunk, of course, strips off several layers of clothing and masters the wild beast—to the delight and surprise of Huck and the gullible audience. Similarly in "The Professor's Yarn," the narrator believes Backus's ploy, and his point of view governs our own expectations: "I could not bear the scene, so I wandered forward and tried to interest myself in the sea and the voices of the wind. But no, my uneasy spirit kept dragging me back at quarter-hour intervals, and always I saw Backus drinking the wine—fairly and squarely, and the others throwing theirs away. It was the painfulest night I ever spent" (310). The gambler's triumph over his seedy foes reverses expectations of both narrator and reader. This O. Henry style ending, Baldanza notes, derives from Mark Twain's "lecture-platform technique" (50), a method that governs many of his early tall tales.

A pattern similar to that of "The Professor's Yarn" operates in "A Dying Man's Confession." Again Mark Twain is essentially an auditor as he repeats to his two traveling companions a tale told him in Germany by the emaciated and dying Karl Ritter. A Gothic story "of revenge, detective ratiocination, and terror in the Poe vein" (Baldanza 50), Ritter's confession builds up expectations that are shattered by an ironic reversal at the end: he learns to his horror that he had by mistake murdered not the villain who slaughtered his wife and child but the one bandit who had tried to spare their lives. The frame that surrounds the Ritter narrative likewise employs the surprise, ironic ending. Before dying, Ritter revealed to Mark Twain the location of ten thousand dollars hidden away in Napoleon, Arkansas, and asked that he retrieve the money and send it to Adam Kruger, the son of the man he had mistakenly slain. The conclusion of the story becomes what Goldstien calls "a humorous parable of greed" (42), for Mark Twain and his companions debate what to do with the prospective treasure. Progressively they assign to themselves larger and larger shares and allocate to Kruger proportionally smaller amounts on the pretext of sparing him the misery and corruption wealth inevitably brings; finally they decide to keep all the money themselves and to send only a "chromo" to the appointed heir. Their greed and the treacherous plot it spawns are thwarted, however, by the discovery that "There *ain't* any Napoleon any more. Hasn't been for years and years. The Arkansas River burst through it, tore it to rags, and emptied it into the Mississippi" (285). The ending to the story, Goldstien writes, reinforces "the opposition between the river-god and the money-god" that Lionel Trilling sees at the center of *Huckleberry Finn* (42).

Ferguson calls the story "melodramatic blather" (214) and Goldstien claims it "serves no function" in *Life on the Mississippi* (42), but whatever its intrinsic merit "A Dying Man's Confession" shares affinities with other Mark Twain works of the same period. The grotesque Gothic elements, specifically the death-watch scenes, recall the Muff Potter and Injun Joe episodes in *Tom Sawyer* (1876); they are, Baldanza writes, "a sign of Mark Twain's preoccupation with more lurid aspects of death and putrefaction" (50). Similar elements govern "Cannibalism in the Cars" (1868) and "The Invalid's Story" (1882). As detective fiction, with its specific reliance on the new science of fingerprinting and the ironic consequences it engenders, the story anticipates *Pudd'nhead Wilson* (1894).

"A Burning Brand" is a story of an elaborate hoax involving a letter supposedly written by "an ex-thief and ex-vagabond of the lowest origin and basest rearing, a man all stained with crime and steeped in ignorance" to one Charles Williams. Harvard graduate and son of a New England clergyman, Williams is a convicted burglar who, in prison and apparently suffering from consumption, "put his old life behind him and became a Christian." The letter, written in "thieves argot," details the moving regeneration of the "man all stained with crime" (416) occasioned by his daily encounter with Williams in prison. As it is circulated throughout the community, the letter causes quite a stir: clergymen read it from the pulpit to emotionally charged congregations and plans are devised to give the letter worldwide circulation. Sentimental Christians are quick to see the letter as moving testimony to the redemptive power of grace, despite the cautionary observation of Charles Dudley Warner "that it is too neat, and compact, and fluent, and nicely put together for an ignorant person, an unpracticed hand" (422). Only at the end do we learn that the letter is "a pure swindle," "the confoundedest, brazenist, ingenuousest piece of fraud and humbuggery" (421). A "gifted rascal," Williams wrote the letter and had it mailed to himself in prison, knowing it would be confiscated and read by prison officials and lead, he hoped, to concerted public pressure for his premature release. Williams remains, the prison chaplain reports, "a dissolute, cunning prodigal" (424).

The story thus employs the surprise-ending reversal of carefully nurtured expectations characteristic of "The Professor's Yarn" and "A Dying Man's Confession." Baldanza notes that this form, which Mark Twain "undoubtedly developed to handle legendary material," is here "applied to actual experience" and is indicative of the author's fictional method: "no matter whether an account is legendary material supported circumstantially [e.g., 'A Dying Man's Confession'] or actual experience elaborated with legend [e.g., 'A Burning Brand'], it is always drawn from the never-never land between fact and fiction, the region presided over by Twain's inimitable genius" (51). The hoax serves throughout Mark Twain's career as a particularly rich fictional device, governing such early journalistic sketches as "The Petrified Man" (1862), short stories like "Legend of the Capitoline Venus" (1869), "The $30,000 Bequest" (1904), and "The Man That Corrupted Hadleyburg" (1899), and assuming a prominent role in novels like *Tom Sawyer, Huckleberry Finn, A Connecticut Yankee,* and *Pudd'nhead Wilson.* The satiric exposure of sentimental Christianity and its susceptibility to fraudulent manipulation appears as a source of comic delight in *Huckleberry Finn* as, for example, in Judge Thatcher's attempted reformation of Pap.

Critical Studies

Critical discussion of these three stories has focused on the appropriateness of their placement in *Life on the Mississippi.* The volume falls into two parts: the first twenty chapters—4–17 drawn from the "Old Times on the Mississippi" articles—provide an historical framework that elevates the river and its meticulously detailed milieu to mythic status and nostalgically chronicles the author's experiences as a cub pilot during a colorful but vanished era; the second part is a loosely structured travelogue account of the mature author's 1882 return to the river, padded with digressionary observations and "blissfully irrelevant yarns" (Baldanza 50). Critics are virtually unanimous in their judgment that the quality of the book deteriorates sharply after chapter 20. Paine sets the tone of such critical commentary: "It is the difference between the labor of love and duty; between art and industry, literature and journalism" (Paine 746).

DeVoto, however, argues that the two parts of *Life on the Mississippi* are more intricately interrelated than most scholars have been willing to grant. Although most commentators have "found the realism of the belated second part hard to reconcile with the idyllic first part," the whole of the book delineates a consistent cosmos, a world where "everything that chicanery, sabotage, bribery, and malfeasance could devise was part of the commonplace mechanism of the trade." The three short stories discussed here are "part of that picture" (106–9). Backus and Charles Williams are among the "steady procession of con-men" that people Mark Twain's mythic landscape (Miller 48).

Bibliography

PRIMARY

The Complete Short Stories of Mark Twain. Now Collected for the First Time. Edited by Charles Neider. Garden City, N.Y.: Hanover House, 1957.

Life on the Mississippi. Boston: James R. Osgood, 1883.

Life on the Mississippi. Introduction by J. W. Rankin. Harper's Modern Classics. New York: Harper & Brothers, 1923.

SECONDARY

Baldanza, Frank. *Mark Twain: An Introduction and Interpretation*. New York: Holt, Rinehart & Winston, 1961.

Blair, Walter. *Mark Twain & Huck Finn*. Berkeley and Los Angeles: University of California Press, 1962.

DeVoto, Bernard. *Mark Twain's America*. Boston: Little, Brown, 1932.

Emerson, Everett. *The Authentic Mark Twain: A Literary Biography of Samuel Langhorne Clemens*. Philadelphia: University of Pennsylvania Press, 1984.

Ferguson, Delancey. *Mark Twain: Man and Legend*. Indianapolis: Bobbs-Merrill, 1943.

Goldstien, Neal L. "Mark Twain's Money Problems." *Bucknell Review* 19 (Spring 1971):37–55.

Hill, Hamlin. *Mark Twain and Elisha Bliss*. Columbia: University of Missouri Press, 1964.

Kaplan, Justin. *Mr. Clemens and Mark Twain*. New York: Simon & Schuster, 1966.

Miller, Robert Keith. *Mark Twain*. New York: Frederick Ungar, 1983.

Paine, Albert B. *Mark Twain: A Biography*. Vol. 2. New York: Harper & Brothers, 1912.

Rogers, Franklin R. *Mark Twain's Burlesque Patterns*. Dallas: Southern Methodist University Press, 1960.

13

Edward Mills and George Benton: A Tale

Publication History

The story first appeared in the August 1880 issue of the *Atlantic Monthly*. Book publication did not come until 1906.

Circumstances of Composition, Sources, and Influences

Mark Twain scholarship has turned up very little regarding "Edward Mills and George Benton: A Tale." It was written in early summer 1880, while Mark Twain, in Hartford, was finishing up *A Tramp Abroad* (1880) and at work on *The Prince and the Pauper* (1882). Howells published the story in the August issue of the *Atlantic* and, as Paine reports, the story received warm endorsement from laity and clergy who praised its attack on sentimental, misdirected social zeal "which manifested itself in making heroes of spectacular criminals" (674). The subject matter of this essentially humorless moral tale reflects its author's attempt to write serious fiction that addressed pressing social issues. No one has discovered a source for the story or suggested any specific influence on its composition. One might see it as a repudiation of romantic concepts of childrearing and an attack on popular, sentimental children's literature that reinforced those concepts.

Relationship to Other Mark Twain Works

Although Wagenknecht compares the story to "Luck" (1891) in its emphasis on the fortuitous element in worldly success (111), "Edward Mills and George Benton" is cut from the same cloth as Mark Twain's earlier burlesques of sentimental fiction for children, specifically "Story of the Bad Little Boy" (1865) and "Story of the Good Little Boy Who Did Not Prosper" (1870). Like its predecessors, the story pointedly undercuts the Protestant ethic in its demonstration that virtue, clean living, and hard work do not necessarily spell success; rather, the realities of nineteenth-century American life favor those unscrupulous enough to manipulate to personal advantage the misguided social zeal and jejune sentimentality of fellow citizens. Virtue and honesty are character weaknesses in a capitalistic society whose citizens, in their misguided exercise of Christian charity, waste their energies and resources on the hopeless reprobate.

"Edward Mills and George Benton" anticipates *Pudd'nhead Wilson* (1894) in its study of "twins" who develop opposite personalities as a result of environmental conditioning. Mills and Benton are "distantly related to each other—seventh cousins," both orphaned while babes and raised together by a childless couple, the Brants. Like Tom Driscoll and Chambers they are opposite in behavior and disposition, and the exploitation of the docile, sweet child by the aggressive, mean-spirited one is encouraged by a social order blind to the consequences of its action: "Baby Mills was a comfort to everybody about him. When he wanted candy and could not have it, he listened to reason, and contented himself without it. When Baby Benton wanted candy, he cried for it until he got it. Baby Mills took care of his toys; Baby Benton always destroyed his in a very brief time, and then made himself so insistently disagreeable that, in order to have peace in the house, little Edward was persuaded to yield up his playthings to him" (144). Every advantage goes to the bad George: he gets the lion's share of his guardians' attention; he inherits all of their property at their death, "because he 'needed it' "; he wins Mary, "a sweet and kindly spirited girl," who though she loves Edward marries George, because he "began to haunt her," and "her high and holy duty" dictates that she wed "poor George" to "reform him"; he gets the attention and financial assistance of the town whose citizens were "drowned in happy tears over the re-restoration of the poor beast and struggling victim of the fatal bowl." The diligent, virtuous Edward, on the other hand, "died out of public knowledge and interest" (146). The more advantages and indulgences granted George, the more of a reprobate he becomes; the more Edward is abused, ignored, and cheated, the more diligent and honest he is. As in *Pudd'nhead Wilson*, the effects of such environmental conditioning manifest themselves in a cowardly murder when George slays Edward during a bank robbery.

Critical Studies

"Edward Mills and George Benton" is a humorless moral tale that satirizes several aspects of nineteenth-century American culture. One is the Protestant ethic, the belief that virtue, religious devotion, and hard work insure success in a capitalistic society governed by the laws of divine Providence. The children learn their guardians' motto—"Be pure, honest, sober, industrious, and considerate of others, and success in life is assured"—even before they master the Lord's Prayer: "it was painted over the nursery door, and was about the first thing they learned to read" (144). Experience shatters such facile optimism, however, for the child who lives by the ethic perishes in oblivion and leaves no substantial legacy to his heirs. The inscription on his tombstone serves as an ironic reminder that the Protestant ethic proves hollow delusion: "Be pure, honest, sober, industrious, considerate, and you will never—" (148). The fate of the other child parodies the biblical account of the prodigal son. The reprobate George, whose wayward habits earn the solicitude of the entire community, ends by killing his foster brother in a tawdry bank robbery and goes to the gallows.

The primary target of satiric attack, however, is the community's response to the two protagonists, its sentimental misapplication of Christian charity (Budd 70). In ignoring Edward and wasting its energy and resources on George, the community disregards any concept of justice and insanely elevates the worthless reprobate to a position of esteem. George becomes the darling of the "Ladies' Temperance Refuge," and is "so popular at home, and so trusted—during his sober intervals—that he was enabled to use the name of a principal citizen [i.e., forgery], and get a large sum of money at the bank" (147). Sympathetic public pressure holds his prison sentence to two years and secures a pardon for George in less than half that time. Even the prison sentence serves George's interests, for he thus becomes the pet of the "Prisoner's Friend Society," which greets him at the prison door "with a situation and a comfortable salary," after it had rejected a plea for help from the struggling but honest Edward. Even after George is convicted of Edward's murder, the community springs to his defense: the governor is "besieged with petitions for commutation or pardon" brought "by tearful young girls; by sorrowful old maids; by deputations of pathetic widows; by shoals of impressive orphans" (148). The governor, however, holds fast and sends George to the gallows—but not before reports of his religious conversion spark another outpouring of public sentiment. But communal efforts on behalf of the murdered Edward are ineffectual. In appreciation of his "fidelity and heroism" and to alleviate the suffering of his family, "all of the banks in the land" raise a grand total of five hundred dollars—"an average of nearly three-eighths of a cent for each bank in the Union." Other "appreciative people," ignoring the "stringent circumstances" of the victim's family, raise forty-two thousand dollars to build "a Memorial Church."

Bibliography

PRIMARY

The Complete Short Stories of Mark Twain. Now Collected for the First Time. Edited by Charles Neider. Garden City, N.Y.: Hanover House, 1957.

The $30,000 Bequest and Other Stories. New York: Harper & Brothers, 1906.

SECONDARY

Budd, Louis J. *Mark Twain: Social Philosopher*. Bloomington: Indiana University Press, 1962.

Paine, Albert B. *Mark Twain: A Biography*. Vol. 2. New York: Harper & Brothers, 1912.

Wagenknecht, Edward. *Mark Twain: The Man and His Work*. New Haven: Yale University Press, 1935.

14

The Esquimau Maiden's Romance

Publication History

This story was published in late 1893 in *Cosmopolitan Magazine,* whose editor, John Brisben Walker, had offered Mark Twain five thousand dollars for twelve stories for the magazine. This one earned him eight hundred dollars, which the author used to cover living expenses in New York while there temporarily, looking after his rapidly deteriorating business interests (Emerson 189). The story was reprinted in the 1900 *Hadleyburg* volume.

Circumstances of Composition, Sources, and Influences

"The Esquimau Maiden's Romance" was written for money and shows the strain of hasty composition. The spring and summer of 1893 brought severe financial pressures to Mark Twain's household, enforcing "economies hitherto undreamed of" (Paine 966). The family was living in Europe, at the Villa Viviani near Florence, then in Germany for the summer; Susy, her health failing, left for Paris to receive expert medical attention. Mark Twain had to make two trips to the United States to look after his sagging business ventures, the Paige typesetter and the Webster Publishing Company. Concern about money, even fear of total financial collapse, sapped creative energies. Manuscript pages from the period show marginal notations of amounts owed creditors, household expenses, income possibilities, etc. Mark Twain wrote to Fred Hall on 6 August 1893: "I have been overwrought & unsettled in mind by apprehensions, & that is a thing that is not helpable when one is in a strange land & sees his resources melt down to a two months' supply & can't see any sure daylight beyond" (Paine 967). Olivia reported that Mark Twain often arose from his bed in the middle of the night and paced the floor in his distress. When he could find energy and time to write he tried to market for immediate return; in addition to the pieces for *Cosmopolitan,* the magazine he hoped might merge with Webster to solve one of his major financial problems, Mark Twain published *Pudd'nhead Wilson* serially in the *Century* and *Tom Sawyer Abroad* in the *St. Nicholas* (Paine 967).

Relationship to Other Mark Twain Works

"The Esquimau Maiden's Romance" recalls "The Loves of Alonzo Fitz Clarence and Rosannah Ethelton" (1878) and "Aurelia's Unfortunate Young Man" (1864), for it is in large measure a burlesque of the conventional romantic love story (Baldanza 100). The central situation—a young Eskimo princess loses her lover because he is falsely accused of stealing one of her father's fishhooks—is intrinsically as ridiculous as the long-distance telephone affair of Alonzo and Rosannah or the incredible ill fortune of Aurelia's bumbling young man that results in his gradual dismemberment.

Yet as Emerson points out, in this 1893 "romance" Mark Twain "has trouble deciding whether the story is sentimental or satiric" (189). A serious theme underpins the burlesque plot: that of money and its corrupting impact upon a simple society. The bereaved princess laments: "Our tribe was once plain, simple folk, and content with the bone fishhooks of their fathers; now they are eaten up with avarice and would sacrifice every sentiment of honor and honesty to possess themselves of the debasing iron fishhooks of the foreigner" (302). Her observation foreshadows Mark Twain's treatment of the same theme in "The Man That Corrupted Hadleyburg" (1899) and "The $30,000 Bequest" (1904): money destroys innocence and genuine human affection. Like many of the stories, fables, and parables of this period of acute financial pressures, "The Esquimau Maiden's Romance," Geismar contends, is "concerned with the meaning of money as romance, fairy tale, delusion, disease, and nightmare" (199).

Critical Studies

"The Esquimau Maiden's Romance" is essentially two interwoven stories. The first is the "romance" itself, Lasca's account of her ill-fated love. After the beautiful Arctic maiden attracts the man of her dreams, her fabulously wealthy father ostentatiously showers her with his twenty-two iron fishhooks—the token of his vast riches. When one of the fishhooks is discovered missing, the community executes the innocent lover on suspicion of theft. After his death Lasca, while giving her hair its annual brushing, discovers the missing hook embedded in her locks. Obviously a parody of conventional romance fiction, the preposterous story gains some poignancy from its effect on the bereaved maiden.

The dominant story of "The Esquimau Maiden's Romance," however, is not the simple account of the girl's unfortunate history but the frame that encloses it: the interaction and dialogue between Mark Twain—the representative of the dominant culture—and the maiden, unequaled among the many girls who feed "at her father's hospitable trough" (294). Humor in the story results from the incongruity between the two realms, a radical disparity signaled by the language of the opening paragraphs. Mark Twain introduces Lasca: "She had been absently scraping blubber-grease from her cheeks with a small bone-knife and transferring it to her fur sleeve, while she watched the Aurora Borealis swing its flaming streamers out of the sky and wash the lonely snow-plain and the templed icebergs with the rich hues of the prism, a spectacle of almost intolerable splendor and beauty" (294). The incongruity between the image of the girl "scraping blubber-grease from her cheeks" and the narrator's genteel description of the splendid Aurora Borealis prepares us for profound cultural differences. Lasca is "a beautiful creature," Mark Twain reports, at least "from the Esquimau point of view. Others would have thought her a trifle over-plump. . . . The beauty of her face at least was apparent; but her figure had to be taken on trust" (294). He accompanies her on a fishing trip, "but not in her perilous boat"; careful to keep a safe distance, he confesses, "I merely followed along on the ice and watched her strike her game with her fatally accurate spear." Later he accompanies her on a bear hunt, "but turned back before the finish, because at bottom I am afraid of bears" (295).

Contrast governs this story, which focuses on radically different ideas of wealth. The furs Lasca's father accumulates—of vast value in Mark Twain's world—"were not the kind of things that ranked as riches with her people." Household accoutrements likewise reflect cultural differences: "not even the richest man in the city of New York has two slop-tubs in his drawing-room" (296). From his cross-cultural experiences Mark Twain draws a lucrative lesson: "Since a hundred million dollars in New York and twenty-two fish-hooks on the border of the Arctic Circle represent the same financial supremacy, a man in straitened circumstances is a fool to stay in New York when he can buy ten cents' worth of fish-hooks and emigrate" (307).

"The Esquimau Maiden's Romance" is thus both a parody of the conventional love story and a burlesque of traditional concepts of wealth. Unity is provided, Covici argues, by the romance form, which "takes the reader on a conducted tour from the safety and respectability of the fireside out into the no-man's land of political, metaphysical, or sexual exploration" and then returns us to everyday reality (127). The alien world of the Arctic north and the fantastic, even absurd, tale of Lasca's ill-fated love yield satiric insights into any culture that values material wealth over human affection.

Bibliography

PRIMARY

The Complete Short Stories of Mark Twain. Now Collected for the First Time. Edited by Charles Neider. Garden City, N.Y.: Hanover House, 1957.

The Man That Corrupted Hadleyburg and Other Stories and Essays. New York: Harper & Brothers, 1900.

SECONDARY

Baldanza, Frank. *Mark Twain: An Introduction and Interpretation.* New York: Holt, Rinehart & Winston, 1961.

Covici, Pascal, Jr. *Mark Twain's Humor: The Image of a World.* Dallas: Southern Methodist University Press, 1962.

Emerson, Everett. *The Authentic Mark Twain: A Literary Biography of Samuel L. Clemens.* Philadelphia: University of Pennsylvania Press, 1984.

Geismar, Maxwell. *Mark Twain: An American Prophet.* Boston: Houghton Mifflin, 1970.

Paine, Albert B. *Mark Twain: A Biography.* Vol. 3. New York: Harper & Brothers, 1912.

15

Experience of the McWilliamses with Membranous Croup
Mrs. McWilliams and the Lightning
The McWilliamses and the Burglar Alarm

Publication History

"Experience of the McWilliamses with Membranous Croup," written in 1875, appeared in *Mark Twain's Sketches, New and Old*, published by Elisha Bliss in the same year. In 1882 Mark Twain asked James R. Osgood, his publisher at the time, to consult with William Dean Howells and put together a volume of short sketches garnered from the files of the *Atlantic Monthly* and the stock of unpublished pieces Mark Twain had assembled. Mark Twain had no role in the selection or ordering of contents of the resulting book, *The Stolen White Elephant Etc.*, which reprinted the contents of *Punch, Brothers, Punch!* (1878) with a number of new sketches including "Mrs. McWilliams and the Lightning" (written in 1880) and "The McWilliamses and the Burglar Alarm" (written in 1882) (Emerson 4). The latter story appears in the 1882 *Harper's Magazine*, Christmas issue, and the former is reprinted in *Merry Tales*, published by Webster and Company in 1891. All three are collected in the thirty-seven volume Stormfield Edition of *The Writings of Mark Twain*, published by Harper and Brothers (1922–29), which is the basis for the Neider text.

Circumstances of Composition, Sources, and Influences

Written between 1875–82, these three stories reflect the author's domestic life in Hartford: "just as Howells liked to entangle his characters in elevators and talking machines and parlor cars and sleeping cars, so Samuel Clemens of Hartford drew laughs from his and Olivia's involvements with burglar alarms and telephones" (Gibson 80). The critical consensus is that Mortimer and Caroline (or Evangeline) McWilliams are thinly disguised portraits of Mark Twain and his wife Livy, showing as Baldanza claims "the patient, rational male at the mercy of a beloved but distraught wife's feminine intuitions and fears" (99). The "oblique look at life in the Clemens household" is amusing and gently satiric but, as Emerson argues, it may also "be read as the author's subtle revenge" (88).

Mark Twain scholars in general have shown very little sympathy or patience with him during what one might call the "domestic" phase of his life. Busy with the practical challenges of establishing a marriage, family, household, and a solid financial base, Mark Twain in mid-life seems disturbingly too much like the rest of us. Emerson reports that during the period 1880–82, when both "Mrs. McWilliams and the Lightning" and "The McWilliamses and the Burglar Alarm" were written, the author was essentially unproductive, "devoting much of his time to investments, mostly bad, and editing books . . . not writing them" (118). He was also making and spending a great deal of money; in 1881 he grossed nearly two hundred fifty thousand dollars from book sales, lecture tours, etc., and spent more than a hundred thousand, much of it on poor investments and his house and adjacent land in Connecticut. His harshest critic, Van Wyck Brooks, argues that "Mark Twain was not simply living the bourgeois life now; he had adopted all the values and ideals of the bourgeoisie" (137). Such bourgeois values, Brooks would have us believe, were largely the result of Olivia's emasculating influence and posed a serious threat to his creative energies. When Mortimer McWilliams confesses, "Whenever I want a thing, and Mrs. McWilliams wants another thing, and we decide upon the thing that Mrs. McWilliams wants—as we always do—she calls that a compromise" (193), the temptation may well be to see the Mark Twain-Olivia relationship lurking in the background. But Mortimer and his wife, or Mark Twain and his, are hardly the only parents to suffer from an overzealous albeit unnecessary concern for a sick child's health in the night, or to endure the frustrations of a mechanical system that never seems to work properly. Mark Twain concludes "Experience of the McWilliamses with Membranous Croup" with the ironic comment, "Very few married men have such an experience as McWilliams's, and so the author of this book thought that maybe the novelty of it would give it a passing interest to the reader" (104). Howells notes that the story reads "like an abuse of confidence to every husband and father" (103). Indeed, although the inspiration for the McWilliams stories may derive from Mark Twain's personal domestic life, their appeal arises from their universal applicability; as Covici writes, "We read into Mr. McWilliams' fate our own ineffectual protests against life's irrationalities, and smile wryly at ourselves as well as at Mortimer" (47).

Relationship to Other Mark Twain Works

Baldanza links the three McWilliams stories to the "Diaries" of Adam and Eve; in their depiction of the battle of the sexes, the two diaries and three stories form a unified body of work that proves Mark Twain "to be an accomplished humorist in the delicate and mild area of domestic ironies" (128). The domestic focus of the McWilliams stories, however—the fact that Mortimer and his wife are "refined people in a refined society" (Gibson 82)—offers a "striking contrast" to those sketches that endorse the values of the West and have come to be regarded as more typical of the artist's work. Emerson mentions specifically the radical difference in tone between "Experience of the McWilliamses with Membranous Croup" and "Some Learned Fables for Good Old Boys and Girls," both of which appear in the 1875 collection of Mark Twain sketches (88). Covici too compares the McWilliams stories with earlier "western" efforts, noting that while Mortimer McWilliams is another of the eccentric narrators that had become standard in the western author's comic repertoire, "the subtle artistry of the McWilliams narratives" testifies to Mark Twain's surer control of technique and point of view. In the Thomas Jefferson Snodgrass letters (1856–57), for example, the author is so heavy-handed in his ridicule of his character's boorishness that he makes it difficult for one to sympathize with the vulgar country yokel loose in a baffling urban environment. This "sledgehammer technique" dissipates in the McWilliams stories, however, because Mark Twain has learned "to subordinate the demands of social commentary to the artistry of characterization" and hence achieves "a central rather than a confused effect" (45–46).

Critical Studies

Each of the three stories opens with an identical frame, Mark Twain traveling by train with Mortimer McWilliams, "a pleasant New York gentleman" who relates a recent domestic experience. The first sketch involves the farcical adventures of Mortimer and his wife Caroline as they pass a sleepless night fretting because "a slight cough" by daughter Penelope during evening prayers convinces Caroline that the dreaded killer "membranous croup" threatens the life of both Penelope and her infant sibling. Mrs. McWilliams worries that the baby sleeps too comfortably, that "he seems to breathe so *regularly*," that the room at seventy degrees "is too warm" but with the heat shut down is too cold. News that the summoned physician "was ill and confined to his bed" convinces Mrs. McWilliams that Providence has intervened to punish the family because "we have not been living as we ought" (101). A farcical evening passes with the poor, henpecked Mortimer roused out of bed continuously by his distraught wife to stoke the fire and apply medicines to the child; in her absurd phobias, Caroline is convinced the girl will not last the night. The arrival of the "poor sick" doctor and the news that Penelope suffers not from "membranous croup" overjoys Mortimer. Having been given pieces of pine stick to chew because Caroline had heard that the turpentine in the wood "is good for weak back and the kidneys" (99), the girl had simply "got some little slivers in her throat." Caroline, however, is less thrilled with the discovery that her worry had been for naught: "she turned away in disdain and left the room" (104).

The second sketch, "Mrs. McWilliams and the Lightning," rehearses the ludicrous adventures in the McWilliams household the night Mortimer's wife—Evangeline—awakens him from a deep sleep to upbraid him for his calloused disregard of "such an awful storm going on." She promptly blames him for the lightning and censures his careless violation of folk injunctions regarding appropriate behavior during a storm which, coupled with his improper language, she is certain will bring destruction to the family. To the accusation that the violent thunderstorm comes as a direct result of Mortimer's neglect of his evening prayers—he had "got to trying to cipher out how much twelve times thirteen is" and overlooked his customary duty—Mr. McWilliams protests gently, "I don't think it's fair for you to make so much of it, anyway, seeing it happens so seldom; I haven't missed before since I brought on that earthquake, four years ago." But such ironic rejoinders to Evangeline's phobias are of little avail; she calls him to read from a book in German containing directions for his preservation during a storm. Mortimer's inability to translate the instructions into comprehensible English leads him to take preposterous precautions. Concluding that the text advises that "it is dangerous not to ring the church bells during a thunderstorm," and having no church bells handy, Mortimer takes the dinner bell, mounts a chair in the middle of the room, and clangs "that dreadful bell a matter of seven or eight minutes." The clamor soon draws a crowd of curious neighbors who, peering "wildly at my nightdress and my warlike accoutrements," manage to abate their gleeful laughter to explain that the "lightning" and thunder are actually the flash and roar of cannon fire celebrating Garfield's nomination for the presidency (158). In deadpan manner, Mortimer ironically concludes his tale with the observation, "Yes, Mr. Twain, as I was saying in the beginning . . . the rules for preserving people against lightning are so excellent and so innumerable that the most incomprehensible thing in the world to me is how anybody ever manages to get struck" (159).

"The McWilliamses and the Burglar Alarm," the last and perhaps funniest story in the series, documents Mortimer's reasons for not going "one single cent on burglar alarms." "With but ill-controlled emotion," Mortimer explains that having finished his new home with "a little cash left over, on account of the plumbers not knowing it," Mrs. McWilliams decides the family must have a burglar alarm (193). The family's misadventures with the alarm system demonstrate human vulnerability to mechanical devices that seem beyond control. The expensive system works like a magnet to attract burglars. Soon after it is installed Mortimer is awakened early one morning by smoke emanating, he soon discovers, from an intruder's pipe. The burglar apologizes for not triggering the first-floor alarm system, but explains that he did not know one was present because he had entered through a second-story window. Appalled by so glaring a defect in his security system, Mortimer promptly summons the salesman from New York to install three-hundred-dollar alarms on each of the other two floors of the house. Yet another problem surfaces, however, when the family cook initiates the alarm as she enters the kitchen door each morning at 5:00 A.M.: "the first effect of that frightful gong is to hurl you across the house, and slam you against the wall, and then curl you up, and squirm you like a spider against the stove lid" (195). To preserve the sanity of the house, the McWilliamses again summon the New York salesman, who adjusts the system so that the alarm could be disconnected before the kitchen door is opened. Unfortunately, the system falls prey to human error and ingenuity: the butler becomes confused and habitually disconnects the alarm in early evening and switches it on again at dawn, just in time for the cook to enter and set the whole house astir again; moreover, with the alarm shut down at night, a whole band of burglars takes refuge from the police in the various unoccupied bedrooms, judging "that the detectives would never think of a tribe of burglars taking sanctuary in a house notoriously protected by the most imposing and elaborate burglar alarm in America" (195). Again the New York technician is summoned. This time he rigs the system so that it shuts down when the kitchen door is opened, but then, of course, the burglars merely enter the house through the kitchen. The result: "For months we couldn't have any company. Not a spare bed in the house; all occupied by burglars" (196).

False alarms next plague the McWilliams household, one of them resulting in an exchange of gunfire between Mortimer and his coachman that leaves a nurse crippled and removes Mortimer's "back hair." After "three or four hundred false alarms" (196), McWilliams systematically disconnects the whole system, room by room. Burglars then enter the house and steal the alarm, "ripped it out, tooth and nail; . . . they took a hundred and fifty miles of copper wire; they just cleaned her out, bag and baggage" (197). Not to be defeated, Mortimer installs at "prodigious" expense another alarm system, governed this time by a "patent clock." The clock, however, proves perverse, turning the alarm on during the day and off at night. With Mrs. McWilliams's "full consent," Mortimer "took the whole thing out and traded it off for a dog, and shot the dog" (198). His experiences have taught him, Mortimer concludes, that "those things are made solely in the interest of the burglars" (198).

Within a tightly confined domestic circumference, the McWilliams sto-

ries effectively combine gentle irony and farcical, almost slapstick, esca-
pades to render vividly and comically the foibles and frustrations of the
nation's growing middle class. Their central technique is comic exaggeration of a common human frustration to the point that it ceases to irritate
or confound and instead amuses and delights. The dilemmas with which
Mortimer must contend are those that in some degree plague us all, but
few of us face them in such extremes; his trials hence make our own seem
more manageable, defuse our anxiety by reassuring us that in our petty
tribulations we are members of a larger community of men and women
who are reminded daily of their common vulnerability and humanity.

Habegger argues that the McWilliams stories highlight "a dialectic
between female propriety and masculine freedom" and that, since the husband is invariably the one with good sense, the stories are essentially sexist
in orientation (888). Certainly Mortimer is "one of the most appealing
henpecked husbands of all time" (Covici 46), but his unbroken spirit, self-
awareness, and sense of humor afford him critical distance from his potentially humiliating misadventures. The key to Mortimer's appeal as character
and the effect of his narrative lies in Mark Twain's use of first-person point
of view. Third-person narration, Covici points out, would render Mortimer
an object for scorn or pity. Yet in telling his own story with irony and
deadpan humor, Mortimer earns our respect as "a self aware human being,"
one with no delusions either about himself or the baffling and trivial world
with which he must contend (45–47).

Bibliography

PRIMARY

*The Complete Short Stories of Mark Twain. Now Collected for the First Time. Edited by
    Charles Neider. Garden City, N.Y.: Hanover House, 1957.

Mark Twain's Sketches, New and Old. Now First Published in Complete Form. Hartford and
    Chicago: American Publishing Co., 1875.

The Stolen White Elephant Etc. Boston: James R. Osgood, 1882.

SECONDARY

Anderson, Frederick, and Hamlin Hill. "How Samuel Clemens Became Mark Twain's Pub-
    lisher: A Study of the James R. Osgood Contracts." Proof 2 (1972):117–43.

Baldanza, Frank. Mark Twain: An Introduction and Interpretation. New York: Holt, Rine-
    hart & Winston, 1961.

Brooks, Van Wyck. The Ordeal of Mark Twain. 1920. Rev. ed. New York: E. P. Dutton,
    1933.

Covici, Pascal, Jr. *Mark Twain's Humor: The Image of a World.* Dallas: Southern Methodist University Press, 1962.

Emerson, Everett. *The Authentic Mark Twain: A Literary Biography of Samuel L. Clemens.* Philadelphia: University of Pennsylvania Press, 1984.

Gibson, William M. *The Art of Mark Twain.* New York: Oxford University Press, 1976.

Habegger, Alfred. "Nineteenth Century American Humor: Easygoing Males, Anxious Ladies, and Penelope Lapham." *PMLA* 91 (October 1976):884–97.

Howells, William Dean. *My Mark Twain: Reminiscences and Criticism.* New York: Harper & Brothers, 1910.

16

Extracts from Captain Stormfield's Visit to Heaven

Publication History

Although written over a period of almost forty years, "Extracts from Captain Stormfield's Visit to Heaven" was first published in two installments in the December 1907 and January 1908 issues of *Harper's Magazine*. Funds from the project provided the loggia for Mark Twain's Redding, Connecticut, home, which he christened "Stormfield" (Emerson 114). The two magazine installments were collected as a Christmas gift book published by Harper and Brothers in October 1909; released just six months prior to the author's death, this was the last of Mark Twain's books published during his lifetime.

The never completed "Captain Stormfield's Visit to Heaven" actually exists in three versions (Gibson 83): a manuscript written in the early 1870s, supplemented with later additions and notebook entries, some of which remain unpublished; the "Extracts" that Mark Twain edited himself and chose to publish after his wife's death, first in *Harper's Magazine* and then as the Christmas gift book; and a 1952 version, assembled and edited by Dixon Wecter in *Report from Paradise,* that includes two introductory chapters deleted from the originally published "Extracts" and prefatory editorial discussion of other excised passages and revisions. The Wecter text is generally considered the standard scholarly edition. Another text, with added materials from the notebooks, is included in a 1970 book edited by Ray Browne.

The text used here is the 1909 book, the last published form that Mark Twain controlled and edited. Although apparently fragmentary, the "Extracts" has aesthetic integrity (Emerson 113). Cox calls Mark Twain's decision to present his story not as a completed work nor even as an unfinished fragment but as a deliberate extraction of publishable passages from otherwise forbidden materials "the decisive fact of form in Captain Stormfield's adventure" (291–92).

Circumstances of Composition, Sources, and Influences

Because Mark Twain worked on "Captain Stormfield's Visit to Heaven" off and on for most of his career, it is difficult to place the work at any specific place in his canon. A western sketch he wrote in 1863 detailing his adventures among the "Spiritualists"—one of whom he questions about life in the hereafter—foreshadows the "Visit to Heaven" (Bellamy 368), but the seed for the story is an account of a dream he heard from Captain Ned Wakeman on a voyage from the Isthmus of Nicaragua to San Francisco in the spring of 1868. At the time Mark Twain wrote to the Chicago *Republican* merely that "the old gentleman told us his remarkable dream" (Emerson 48). In a 1906 autobiographical dictation, Mark Twain recalls that he kept Wakeman's tale "in my mind and a month or two later I put it on paper—this was the first quarter of 1868, I think" (*Report from Paradise*, ed. Wecter, xii). Wecter reports, however, that the stationery and ink of the earliest surviving draft date the original composition in the early 1870s. In this early draft, the hero bears the name "Cap'n Hurricane Jones," the character of an 1877 sketch in "Rambling Notes of an Idle Excursion"; but this name is methodically crossed out and "Stormfield" substituted for it. The reference to the Rev. T. DeWitt Talmage, pastor of the Central Presbyterian Church in Brooklyn, also dates the manuscript to the early 1870s, since Mark Twain attacked Talmage in the *Galaxy* in 1870—and continued to satirize him throughout the decade—for having said from the pulpit that the stench of working men in his congregation offended his genteel sensibilities. We know that Mark Twain returned to the manuscript in 1873, when he showed it to William Dean Howells, who encouraged its publication. Mark Twain's wife, however, objected to the unconventional portrayal of heaven and feared that the tale's ridicule of traditional Christian concepts might be deemed blasphemous. The author deferred to Olivia's wishes and left the piece unpublished. A letter to his brother Orion reveals Mark Twain's sensitivity to his wife's criticism in its insistence that he never intends to appear blasphemous in his writings: "Neither Howells nor I believe in hell or the divinity of the Savior, but no matter, the Savior is none the less a sacred Personage, and a man should have no desire or disposition to refer to him lightly, profanely, or otherwise than with the profoundest reverence" (*Report from Paradise*, ed. Wecter, xii–xviii).

Although he placed "Captain Stormfield" aside, Mark Twain never entirely forgot it and steadfastly refused to destroy it. Captain Wheeler relates a dream in *Cap'n Simon Wheeler, Amateur Detective* (1877) that is an abbreviated version of "Captain Stormfield's Visit," and a notebook sketch of August 1880 reveals that Mark Twain continued to plan additional episodes. This particular one reveals reservations about a democratic heaven: at first delighted that paradise is free of social barriers, Stormfield becomes disenchanted when a Negro, a Fiji Islander, an Eskimo, and assorted politicians, vagrants, and other pariahs presume on his good will, raid his table, and address him familiarly as "Brother Stormfield" (Baetzhold 65–66). Mark Twain aborts this episode, however, perhaps because it undercuts his satire of the pompous elitist Talmage. He returned to the story again in the fall of 1881, and apparently completed all but the two voyage chapters written in 1901, only to decide once again that because of Olivia's objections he could never publish it (Gibson 89). But in the early 1890s, his thoughts drifted back to the story again as he toys with the idea of replacing Stormfield with Simon Wheeler (Cox 291). After a public reading of the story at a dinner party in New York in 1894, Mark Twain wrote to Olivia that "it is a raging pity that that book has never been printed" (Emerson 273). In October 1902 he wrote to his business agent, Frank Whitmore, requesting the return of the "Stormfield" manuscript for additional work (Macnaughton 186).

Olivia's death in 1903 apparently gave Mark Twain the freedom to publish "Captain Stormfield." Actually the period immediately following his wife's death until the publication of *What Is Man?* (late 1906) proved remarkably fertile for Mark Twain, despite many frustrations and intense psychological pressures. Not only did he have to reconcile himself to Olivia's death and cope with his own role in aggravating her condition, but he had to mollify its effect on his two surviving daughters and cope with their own health problems, especially the epilepsy of Jean that had become severe and threatening by late 1906. Moreover, he was worried about investment difficulties, literary contracts, and his own health and advanced age. Perhaps more than anything else, Olivia's death left him feeling utterly alone in an alien universe, acutely aware of his own mortality. But he continued to write: short pieces for *Harper's;* stories on demand, such as "A Horse's Tale" (1906); polemical works like "The Czar's Soliloquy" (1905) and "King Leopold's Soliloquy" (written 1905) and fables about war and political issues such as "The War Prayer" (written 1905; published 1923) and "The Fable of the Bees" (written 1905); longer, and ultimately unfinished manuscripts—"Three Thousand Years among the Microbes" (written 1905), "The Refuge of the Derelicts" (written 1905–6; published 1972); autobiographical dictations, chapters of "No. 44, The Mysterious Stranger" (written 1905; published 1969), and the extended philosophical essay *What Is Man?* (1906). Mark Twain submitted "Captain Stormfield's Visit to Heaven" to *Harper's* first in 1905, only to have it rejected by Colonel Harvey because he thought it, ironically, "too damn godly for a secular paper like the magazine" (Hill 119). The frantic pace that Mark Twain maintained during the period testifies, Macnaughton writes, to his "strong, persistent drive to answer large questions and to confront mammoth problems before his death" (203).

The central source for "Captain Stormfield's Visit to Heaven" is Ned Wakeman, the seasoned ship captain whose account of his "remarkable dream" inspired the story and whose character shaped Mark Twain's conception of Captain Stormfield (Allen 145). Mark Twain was apparently greatly charmed by Wakeman, whom he describes in his notebook as a "portly, hearty, jolly, boisterous, good-natured old sailor" who "never swears, except in the privacy of his own quarters, with a friend or so, & then his feats of blasphemy are calculated to fill the hearer with awe & admiration" (Emerson 36). Possessing what Wecter calls "the damned-up communicativeness of a lonely way-faring man," Wakeman delighted the young aspiring writer with his yarns and good humor and subsequently became a favorite character in Mark Twain's fiction (*Report from Paradise* x; Baldanza 55–56). He first appears as Captain Waxman in the *Alta* letters written in 1867 but not collected until 1940 as *Mark Twain's Travels with Mr. Brown*. Later he appears as Captain Ned Blakely in *Roughing It* (1872) and as Captain Hurricane Jones of "Rambling Notes of an Idle Excursion" (1877) (Gibson 83). Browne offers a detailed discussion of the relationship of Mark Twain and Ned Wakeman, suggesting that the young writer saw in the seasoned veteran an incarnation of his "boyhood idol" Horace Bixby (320–29).

Another influence on "Captain Stormfield's Visit to Heaven" was an 1868 novel by Elizabeth Stuart Phelps entitled *The Gates Ajar,* a popular best-seller that offered a "saccharine and sentimental" vision of paradise (*Report from Paradise,* ed. Wecter, xiii; Wagenknecht 43). Mark Twain writes in his *Autobiography* that the "Extracts" was intended to be "a burlesque of *The Gates Ajar,* a book which had imagined a mean little ten-cent heaven about the size of Rhode Island—a heaven large enough to accommodate about a tenth of one percent of the Christian billions who had died in the past nineteen centuries" (*Autobiography* 277). Rogers, however, claims that this burlesque dimension vanishes in later revisions (31–32), though the concept of the immensity of the heavens remains central to Mark Twain's story. The real influence of Phelps's novel was that it stimulated key events and concepts (Gibson 85). In a detailed comparison of the two works, Rees notes that Mark Twain not only satirizes Phelps's novel but appropriates several major ideas from her: that traditional notions of heaven are absurd; that unending prayer and singing of psalms is an incredibly boring way to pass eternity; that heaven offers people the opportunity to do what makes them happy and to devote their time to ventures for which they are ideally suited; that the justice of heaven brings acclaim to those unheralded on earth; and that the intellect and senses are heightened in paradise (197–202).

Relationship to Other Mark Twain Works

"Captain Stormfield's Visit to Heaven" reflects Mark Twain's long-standing fascination with cosmology and the nature of afterlife as well as his ridicule of traditional, sentimental theological concepts and hypocritical or absurd Christian practices. Having inherited from his agnostic father and Presbyterian mother a skeptical cast of mind coupled with a command of the Christian mythology taught in the Hannibal, Missouri, Sunday school, Mark Twain found Wakeman's dream full of fictional possibilities. If, as Wecter observes, Mark Twain did not actually believe in heaven, he "was powerfully attracted to it—if for no other purpose than to explode the orthodoxies of those who claimed it as their monopoly" (*Report from Paradise* xiii). Satire of the smug complacency of nominal Christians figures largely in *Innocents Abroad, Huckleberry Finn* (1885), "The Man That Corrupted Hadleyburg" (1899), and "The War Prayer"; burlesque of Sunday school nonsense and sentimental theology appears in a wide range of his fiction, from *Tom Sawyer* and "Story of the Good Little Boy" in the 1870s to *The Mysterious Stranger* (1916) and *Letters from the Earth* (written 1909; published 1962), the latter serving, in many ways, as a serious continuation of the Stormfield story (Hill 246). Most specifically, "Captain Stormfield's Visit" is related to an 1894 sketch entitled "The Late Reverend Sam Jones's Reception into Heaven" (also known as "A Singular Episode"): in this sketch, also suppressed by Olivia, the highly disreputable protagonist fraudulently gains admission to the genteel circles of heaven by exchanging tickets with the slumbering archbishop of Canterbury on a train bound for New Jerusalem and Sheol (Emerson 178).

As a character, Stormfield belongs to the long line of vernacular narrators who seem to dominate much of Mark Twain's best fiction. His rambling style of narration and vernacular prejudices link him to Simon Wheeler (Emerson 264); in fact, at one point Mark Twain flirted with the idea of substituting Wheeler for Stormfield in the story. But as Cox points out, the brash, reckless, and assertive Stormfield with his fantasy and racy slang is more akin to the Connecticut Yankee Hank Morgan than he is to the deadpan Wheeler (291). His innocence, his preconceptions shaped by a genteel society that ostracizes him, and his first-person account in vernacular language of his eye-opening experiences link Stormfield to Huck Finn.

This story, like *Huckleberry Finn* and, indeed, many of Mark Twain's novels and short tales, is a story of initiation, focusing on an essentially innocent hero who moves between two worlds. The usual pattern in Mark Twain's fiction traces the innocent as he moves from an ignorant and basically free condition in a simplified world into a darker, more civilized world where he learns that innocence is an illusion and paradise irrevocably lost. In "Captain Stormfield's Visit," as in *Roughing It* (1872), the protagonist reverses this pattern, moving instead from repression to freedom, from civilization to nature. Hence, as Spengemann notes, the story becomes "an account of a denitiation narrated in the vernacular by the innocent himself" and, if we accept that the story was written in the early 1870s, it significantly foreshadows Mark Twain's method in *Huckleberry Finn*. Stormfield is the first of the author's innocent protagonists to tell his own story in his own language (3, 15, 26–28).

In its apparent fragmentation, "Captain Stormfield's Visit" resembles "Adam's Diary" (1893) and "Eve's Diary" (1905), for in effect it is actually a completed form (Cox 292). It is more balanced and more aesthetically satisfying than other fragments of the later years because it manages to provide a vision of what Bellamy calls "the twofold aspect of life." Like *Huckleberry Finn*, the story shows both the ideal and its aberration (372–74). Because he sets the story in heaven, Mark Twain can effectively manage the contrast between Stormfield's misinformed earthly expectations on the one hand, and the revelations of a genuinely wonderful cosmic order on the other (Cox 292). In other works characteristic of the last decade of his life, Mark Twain typically fails to achieve aesthetic distance; as a result, he either "stood before what he disliked and 'pounded it to pulp,' or he enveloped his material in a sentimental glow" (Bellamy 374). Here the tone is more subdued, more controlled, and the result is aesthetically satisfying fiction: "nearly the most perfect thing he has ever written," Gaines argues, for while subjecting orthodox traditions to "the light of common sense," Mark Twain maintains sympathy "with the human longing that lies behind every article of the old literal faith" (223–25).

Critical Studies

"Extracts from Captain Stormfield's Visit to Heaven" is a delightful comic satire of traditional beliefs about the nature of the afterlife. Stormfield's initial experiences reveal the immensity of space and shatter all notions of an earth-centered universe as well as the self-centered theological concepts such notions foster. Whizzing through space at an average speed of more than "a million miles a minute," Stormfield travels for thirty years before arriving at last at the gates of heaven, or one of them, for there are many to handle the traffic from the countless worlds the Savior has redeemed. The clerks at the gate are unfamiliar with the solar system from which Stormfield comes, let alone his particular "world"; on the vast map of the universe, a map "as big as Rhode Island," a clerk with a microscope finally locates the planet earth, which "is called the Wart" (23–24). The portion of paradise given to the billions from earth, Stormfield learns, is a rather insignificant border territory. At the outset Mark Twain thus deflates what Wecter terms the "absurd cosmic egotism of man" (*Report from Paradise* xiii–iv; Baldanza 131).

The story depends for its effect in large part on the nature of its narrator, a forthright, irrepressible character who speaks in an authentic, colloquial slang and who, Emerson notes, suggests the literary personality of the author (113). The two introductory chapters deleted from the "Extracts" but restored in the 1952 Wecter text treat Stormfield's death, the beginning of his journey into the hereafter, and encounters with various people—e.g., Solomon Goldstein, the former slave Sam—that serve to strip away accumulated prejudices and reveal the hero's capacity for empathy. Stormfield is essentially an innocent who, like Huck Finn, operates under illusions gained from a genteel society that alienates him; he, like Huck, thinks he is going to hell (Spengemann 28) and is most at ease among companions who are likewise exiled from polite, white Christian society.

Equipped with the sentimental and absurd preconceptions of conventional Christians, Stormfield must be reeducated before he can avail himself of the multifold joys of heaven, "a glowing, beautiful, bewitching country" (14). The first-person narrative technique enforces reader identification as we too learn simultaneously with the hero the true nature of paradise. The story consists largely of dialogues between Stormfield and his heavenly informants, Sam Bartlett and Sandy McWilliams, who patiently answer his questions, point out the irrationality of Stormfield's preconceptions, and introduce him to a heaven that is in fact a complete reversal of conventional expectations (Gibson 89). Stormfield learns, for example, that the traditional accoutrements of the departed—the harp, angels' wings, wreath, halo, hymnbook, and palm branch—are in fact impediments that are requested by naive newcomers but quickly discarded when they discover "that sort of thing wouldn't make a heaven—at least not a heaven that a sane man could stand a week and remain sane" (40–41). Bartlett explains to Stormfield, "Singing hymns and waving palm branches through all eternity is pretty when you hear about it in the pulpit, but it's as poor a way to put in valuable time as a body could contrive. It would just make a heaven of warbling ignoramuses, don't you see?" (40–41). Indeed, heaven is a place not of rest and idle dissipation but of work—meaningful activity that allows people to use their true talents: "It's the same here as it is on earth—you've got to earn a thing, square and honest, before you enjoy it. . . . You can choose your own occupation, and all the powers of heaven will be put forth to help you make a success of it, if you do your level best. The shoemaker on earth that had the soul of a poet in him won't have to make shoes here" (42–43).

Other preconceptions are similarly shattered in heaven. Stormfield, like most of us, assumes that there is no pain or suffering in heaven. But he learns there is plenty of both, only they are transitory; pain and suffering are necessary to happiness, the contrast that renders it meaningful and valuable. He also learns that the reunion of loved ones is not always joyful, at least not initially, because the aspirations of the individuals concerned frequently lead them in such different directions that they have little left in common. But at least in heaven there is time to "get adjusted by and by" (58; Bellamy 370). Another egotistical notion that proves false is the democratic assumption of the pious that they will be equal to the prophets and the patriarchs, have immediate and free access to Adam, Moses, or Jacob, and be able to embrace Abraham and weep on his shoulders. Sandy explains, however, that heaven is no republic: "There are ranks, here. There are viceroys, princes, governors, sub-governors, sub-sub-governors, and a hundred orders of nobility, grading along down from grand-ducal archangels, stage by stage, till the general level is struck" (81–82). Indeed, if Abraham, Isaac, and Jacob permitted the sixty thousand who arrive from earth each day to kiss and weep on them, "they would be tired out and wet as muskrats all the time." No, Sandy concludes, "there are limits to the privileges of the elect, even in heaven" (73).

If "Captain Stormfield's Visit to Heaven" is primarily a satire of our facile expectations of paradise, it is also, as Emerson notes, "a thoughtful exploration of the human condition" (113). The inhabitants of heaven, for example, are allowed to choose any age they wish to be, and most in their vanity want to be young again. The dead soon discover, however, the "awkward diffident, sentimental immaturities of nineteen," and most come eventually to settle at the age "where [their] mind was last at its best, for there's where [their] enjoyment is best, and [their] ways most set and established" (51). The great joy of heaven is its justice, which insures that all are free to follow their talent and natural inclination and to receive proper recognition. Prophets are highest in heaven's natural aristocracy and include among their ranks "heathens" like Mohamet, Zoroaster, "and a knife-grinder from ancient Egypt," and poets like Shakespeare and Homer who must, however, take their place behind "a common tailor from Tennessee, by the name of Billings" [McClary], and "a horse-doctor named Sakka, from Afghanistan" (86), whose poetic talents were superior but unappreciated on earth. In heaven people get what they deserve, and that, finally, is what they want.

The technique of allowing accessory characters like Sam Bartlett and Sandy McWilliams to explain heaven to the passive Stormfield, exposing the inaccuracy of his preconceived notions, generally gives the story a static quality. This "rather mechanical use of reliable commentators," Spengemann writes, "is one of the story's main drawbacks" because it threatens to relegate the vernacular Stormfield to a secondary role, a foil to occasion exposition (27). Spengemann's point is well taken: long sections of the story resemble lectures; too few of Stormfield's discoveries result from dramatic situations or human interaction. The story is most delightful when it narrates a humorous situation, such as the opening encounter between Stormfield and the bemused gatekeeper who cannot identify his place of origin. Another such situation is Sandy's account of his visit to the English corner of heaven where, lonely and desperate for conversation, he tries to engage residents in meaningful discussion. But unfortunately they cannot understand one another: "I had some talk with one Langland and a man by the name of Chaucer—old-time poets—but it was no use, I couldn't understand them and they couldn't quite understand me. I have had letters from them since, but it is such broken English I can't make it out" (108). This section is successful in large part because Sandy here assumes a vernacular role rather like that of Stormfield.

Bibliography

PRIMARY

The Autobiography of Mark Twain. Edited by Charles Neider. New York: Harper & Row, 1959.

"Captain Stormfield's Visit to Heaven." *Report from Paradise*. Edited by Dixon Wecter. New York: Harper & Brothers, 1952.

*Extracts from Captain Stormfield's Visit to Heaven. New York: Harper & Brothers, 1909.

Mark Twain's Quarrel with Heaven: "Captain Stormfield's Visit to Heaven" and Other Sketches. Edited by Ray B. Browne. New Haven: College and University Press, 1970.

SECONDARY

Allen, Jerry. *The Adventures of Mark Twain*. Boston: Little, Brown, 1954.

Baetzhold, Howard G. *Mark Twain and John Bull: The British Connection*. Bloomington: Indiana University Press, 1970.

Baldanza, Frank. *Mark Twain: An Introduction and Interpretation*. New York: Holt, Rinehart & Winston, 1961.

Bellamy, Gladys C. *Mark Twain as a Literary Artist*. Norman: University of Oklahoma Press, 1950.

Browne, Ray B. "Mark Twain and Captain Wakeman." *American Literature* 33 (November 1961):320–29.

Cox, James M. *Mark Twain: The Fate of Humor*. Princeton, N.J.: Princeton University Press, 1966.

Emerson, Everett. *The Authentic Mark Twain: A Literary Biography of Samuel L. Clemens*. Philadelphia: University of Pennsylvania Press, 1984.

Gaines, Clarence H. "Mark Twain *the* Humorist." *Book News Monthly* 28 (April 1910):583–88. Reprint in *Critical Essays on Mark Twain*, edited by Louis J. Budd, 221–25. Boston: G. K. Hall, 1982.

Gibson, William M. *The Art of Mark Twain*. New York: Oxford University Press, 1976.

Hill, Hamlin. *Mark Twain: God's Fool.* New York: Harper & Row, 1973.

Macnaughton, William R. *Mark Twain's Last Years as a Writer.* Columbia: University of Missouri Press, 1979.

McClary, Ben Harris. "Melville, Twain, and the 'Legendary Tennessee Poet.'" *Tennessee Folklore Society Bulletin* 29 (September 1963):63–64.

Rees, Robert A. "*Captain Stormfield's Visit to Heaven* and *The Gates Ajar.*" *English Language Notes* 7 (March 1970):197–202.

Rogers, Franklin R., ed. *Mark Twain's Satires and Burlesques.* Berkeley and Los Angeles: University of California Press, 1967.

Spengemann, William C. *Mark Twain and the Backwoods Angel: The Matter of Innocence in the Works of Samuel L. Clemens.* Kent, Ohio: Kent State University Press, 1966.

Wagenknecht, Edward. *Mark Twain: The Man and His Work.* New Haven: Yale University Press, 1935.

17

Extracts from Adam's Diary
Eve's Diary

Publication History

"Extracts from Adam's Diary" first appeared as Mark Twain's contribution to *The Niagara Book* (1893), with the title, "The Earliest Authentic Mention of Niagara Falls. Extracts from Adam's Diary. Translated from the Original Ms. By Mark Twain." The story is included in the British edition of *Tom Sawyer, Detective* (1897), with some 750 words deleted, including all mention of Niagara Falls (Emerson 189–90). Harper and Brothers published the text of the story as it had appeared in *The Niagara Book* as a separate book in 1904. In summer 1905 Mark Twain revised "Extracts from Adam's Diary" to make it more clearly a companion piece to "Eve's Diary," which he was writing at the same time. But the story as it appears in *The $30,000 Bequest and Other Stories* (1906) is essentially the same as the 1893 Niagara version.

"Eve's Diary" was an original contribution to the Christmas issue of *Harper's Magazine*, December 1905. William Dean Howells and Henry Alden included the story in a 1906 collection entitled *Their Husbands' Wives*. The story also appears in *The $30,000 Bequest* volume. Later in 1906 Harper and Brothers published it as a separate book; this version of the story adds the new material Mark Twain had written in July 1905 for "Adam's Diary" as a brief italicized interjection entitled "Extract from Adam's Diary."

"Eve's Diary" and the 1904 book version of "Extracts from Adam's Diary" are collected together in a 1931 volume, *The Private Lives of Adam and Eve*. Charles Neider likewise groups them together as "The Diary of Adam and Eve" in his *Complete Short Stories of Mark Twain*, and uses as his text the book versions of each story.

Circumstances of Composition, Sources, and Influences

Mark Twain completed a draft of "Extracts from Adam's Diary" sometime prior to the spring of 1893, when he received a request from friends Charles and Irving Underhill for a humorous piece on Niagara Falls to be included in a souvenir book for the 1893 World's Fair to be held in Buffalo, New York. Initially he turned down the request because he did not have anything appropriate on hand nor the time to produce a fresh contribution. He soon realized, however, that he could modify the "Adam's Diary" manuscript by placing Eden at Niagara and so sent the Underhills the revised story in mid-April 1893 (Emerson 258–59). At first both Mark Twain and Olivia were pleased with the piece (Ensor 45–46), but when Mark Twain returned to it in July 1905 he was disappointed. A request from F. A. Duneka for contributions to *Harper's Magazine* lured Mark Twain from his work on *The Mysterious Stranger* (1916) to write "Eve's Diary." At the same time he reread the Adam piece, judged it "not litera-ture" because of its connection to the 1893 Buffalo exposition, and refash-ioned it to make it a companion story to his new work. He deleted some seven hundred words, added five new manuscript pages, and in a letter to Duneka, pronounced it "dam good—sixty times as good as it was" (Emer-son 258). Mark Twain's intention was to publish the revised "Extracts from Adam's Diary" with "Eve's Diary" in the Christmas 1905 issue of *Harper's* (Hill 112). But Duneka did not comply with his intentions. Even in the 1906 collection, *The $30,000 Bequest and Other Stories,* Harper and Brothers merely reprinted its 1904 text. The five new pages of "Adam's Diary" were not published until the 1906 book version of "Eve's Diary."

The major literary influence on the two stories is the Bible. Brashear points out that no American writer "used Bible stories as mythology to the extent Mark Twain has" (208). Brodwin contends that the whole series of Adamic diaries reflects Mark Twain's longstanding obsession with the book of Genesis, "the story of the fall and its characters" (51). In his compre-hensive study of Mark Twain's use of the Bible, Ensor notes 295 references to Genesis in Mark Twain's work, 76 of them specifically to Adam—and his listing is admittedly incomplete (110 n.5). The "Extracts from Adam's Diary," Ensor argues, grows out of Mark Twain's personal identification with the Adam story; by 1895 he had come to view his family's life in Hartford during the 1870s and 1880s in the same manner as he viewed his childhood in Hannibal—both were essentially paradises lost (43).

The fact that the man is "a fool and a tool in contact with the woman," Henry Adams notes, shows that the point of view of Mark Twain's diaries "is unconsciously the same as that of the twelfth-century mystery and of Milton" (326–27). The dynamics of the Adam-Eve relationship in the two stories recalls Milton's *Paradise Lost,* not so much because Eve is the temp-tress responsible for the Fall but because of her role as humanizing agent. As Harris writes, Eve "represents the acquisition of truly human emotions and an escape from the paralysis of solitude" (127). For Mark Twain, as for Milton, the Fall is fortunate. But the theological focus differs. For Mil-ton the Fall permits the full extent of God's love and mercy to make itself evident; for Mark Twain, the emphasis falls on the human relationship, Adam's discovery that Eve's "companionship is necessary for his happiness." Eve has the beneficent power "to coax the man out of himself, to make him aware that his is not the only consciousness in existence" (Harris 124–27).

Mark Twain's diaries are to some extent burlesques of their literary sources. Baldanza contends that because Mark Twain did not hold the Bible to be divinely inspired, he had no reluctance to burlesque its stories. He transforms the Genesis story into a "domestic comedy" in "Extracts from Adam's Diary": the protagonist is "the lone male who is pestered and harried by the unwelcomed attentions of the busybody female" (127–28). Brodwin sees the diaries as "theological folk stories" that "employ many of the techniques and forms of the Southwestern American humor Twain knew and brought to perfection: exaggeration, linguistic distortion, slang, puns, and above all, the tall-tale, the kind of story that makes fantasy real and the real fantastic" (50–52).

"Eve's Diary" is heavily colored by one biographical fact of profound significance: the death of Mark Twain's wife Olivia. The 1905 story is, according to Hill, "a eulogy to Olivia" (112). Paine is even more explicit on this point: the Eve story "in the widest and most reverential sense, from the first word to the last, conveys his love, his worship, and his tenderness for the one he had laid away" (1225). Adam's final comment about Eve— "Wherever she was, *there* was Eden"—serves, Emerson contends, as the author's moving epitaph for Olivia (258). The implication of Adam's statement, that without Eve Eden would vanish—poignantly underscores the despair of the aging author who must now face the vicissitudes of life alone.

Relationship to Other Mark Twain Works

"Extracts from Adam's Diary" and "Eve's Diary" form part of a group of works Brodwin calls Mark Twain's "Adamic Diaries." The others include "That Day in Eden" and "Eve Speaks," both written around 1900 and published posthumously in *Europe and Elsewhere* (1923), and "Papers from the Adam Family" and "Eve's Autobiography" (written about 1905–6), both published for the first time in DeVoto's edition of *Letters from the Earth* (1962). The two stories published during Mark Twain's lifetime are essentially comic and, Brodwin writes, treat the Fall "paradoxically in an Horatian life-affirming way"; the works published posthumously, on the other hand, turn to "bitter, Juvenalian satire" in their focus on what Brodwin calls the "humor of the absurd" (50–51). Macnaughton argues that because they were written for a specific audience, "Extracts from Adam's Diary" and "Eve's Diary" lack the complexity and pathos of the posthumous diaries (219). Certainly they differ in tone, for as Ensor maintains, Mark Twain's purpose in the posthumously published pieces "was not comedy but a serious attack on either God or the Bible, or both" (56).

The tone of "Extracts from Adam's Diary" and "Eve's Diary" is both comic and sentimental. In their emphasis on domestic adjustment, human foibles, and comic misunderstanding the Adam and Eve diaries recall the McWilliams stories written in the late 1870s and early 1880s. Baldanza contends that as a "veiled presentation of Clemens' domestic life" the diaries testify to the author's achievement in "the delicate and mild area of domestic ironies" (128). The sentimentality of "Eve's Diary" links it to *Personal Recollections of Joan of Arc* (1896), "A Horse's Tale" (1906), "The Death Disk" (1901), and "Marjorie Fleming, the Wonder Child" (1909)—all works written in the last fifteen years of the author's life that celebrate what Stone calls "the power and beauty of girlhood" (232). Hill, however, claims that "Eve's Diary" is superior to his other stories about pubescent girls; it is more graceful, sympathetic, and perceptive than "A Horse's Tale"—Mark Twain's "eulogy to Susy"—and its comic irony, a result of Eve's "delightful naiveté," prevents the maudlin excesses of the other sentimental pieces (114; Emerson 258).

Cox focuses on the narrative form of the diaries, linking them to "Captain Stormfield's Visit to Heaven." The extract form frees Mark Twain from the general rules governing narrative fiction, but the "apparent fragmentation" of these "Extracts" becomes in itself a complete form even as it intimates there is more, perhaps scandalous, material to come (292).

Critical Studies

The romantic emphasis of the diaries, their scenes of comic domestic bickering and adjustment, and the gentle liberties taken with the biblical source did not please all readers. An anonymous reviewer for the *Spectator* complained in 1897 that "Extracts from Adam's Diary" shows a lack of both taste and skill, "is too far-fetched, grotesque in fact, and the humor by no means rich," and admonished the author "to leave such subjects alone" (89). Most readers, however, are moved by what Harris sees as Mark Twain's "delineation of the ideal woman" (123).

Certainly Mark Twain emends his biblical source. Central episodes in Genesis receive little attention in these two stories. God's command not to eat the fruit of the Tree of Knowledge, the temptation scene, the Fall itself, Cain's murder of Abel—all are neglected. "Adam's Diary" makes no mention of God at all; Eve refers to God on two or three occasions, but simply as "the Giver of it all." The extract form of the diaries enables Mark Twain to gloss over matters of theological import and to focus instead on the developing relationship of the protagonists. "Extracts from Adam's Diary" opens shortly after the arrival of Eve—she is "the new creature"—and continues through the Fall to a time some ten years after the birth of Abel. "Eve's Diary" follows essentially the same time frame; indeed Eve uses "Adam's diary as her unwitting text" (Ensor 49). The first man and woman are, Macnaughton writes, "scientists whose major pleasure in life comes from exploring their magnificent environment" (220).

And, one might add, exploring each other, for the diaries chart their discovery of the redemptive power of human love. For Adam, the Fall proves fortunate because it occasions his full discovery of Eve. Convinced by his mate that it was the chestnut—one of his jokes—that led to the Fall, Adam blesses that "chestnut that brought us near together and taught me to know the goodness of her heart and the sweetness of her spirit!" (280). His final comment—"Wheresoever she was, *there* was Eden" (294)—suggests that Eve, or the human love she manifests, is the indispensable component of any paradise. As Hill points out, Eve too is "willing to sacrifice her prelapsarian innocence for her love of her husband" (113–14). "The Garden is lost," she muses, "but I have found *him,* and am content" (292). Eve prays that she and Adam might die together or, if that is impossible, that she die first; life without her mate, she realizes, is no life at all. Mark Twain, Brodwin writes, transmutes "Eve into the Eternal Feminine, all love derived from her" (57). "I am the First Wife," Eve reflects, "and in the last wife I shall be repeated" (294).

The humanization of Adam through his discovery of Eve is according to Harris the central theme of the two stories. At the outset Adam is totally self-absorbed, and his primitive control of language testifies to an underdeveloped aesthetic imagination. To him the created universe is merely a collection of objects designed for his own practical benefit. Eve too is an object, an "it," until she teaches him the words "she" and "we"—and the concepts those words represent; she is an annonyance Adam wishes "would but go by herself and not talk" (*Complete Short Stories* 274). In short, Harris writes, Adam's Eden is "a solipsistic universe in which any voice from outside offends the privacy of his dream" (126). But Eve, whose greatest horror is utter loneliness, shatters Adam's solipsistic dream, forces him to "cease imagining that he is alone and include her in his psychic landscape." The destruction of Adam's self-absorbed dream coincides with the Fall; the loss of Eden makes him human. Adam's increasing sophistication with language reflects his broadened vision of the world occasioned by Eve's devotion and love, the "truly human emotions" that free him from the edenic "paralysis of solitude" (Harris 127). The objects of this world appear intrinsically beautiful to his awakened aesthetic imagination, and the loss of his solipsistic dream—Eden—becomes inconsequential. Far more devastating is the loss of Eve.

In his penetrating study of the humor in the Adamic diaries, Brodwin focuses not on the relationship of Adam and Eve but on the Fall as the "central event" in Mark Twain's "theology of the comic." Humor in the diaries, Brodwin writes, derives from "contradiction, absurdity, and incongruity, the principle of irony triumphant"; it "functions as a theological sign of man's fall but at the same time enables him to deal with that pathetic state" (49). In Mark Twain's version of Genesis, the Fall results from Eve's compassion and Adam's humor. Eve willingly brings death into the world not because she is motivated by vanity or pride but because in her naive sympathy for God's creatures she believes death necessary to provide appropriate food for carnivores. When subsequently Eve blames Adam for the Fall, he realizes that his "chestnut"—"meaning an aged and moldy joke" (276)—was likewise responsible: "Alas, I am indeed to blame." But if the "chestnut" caused the Fall, it is also the agent of redemption, for it is the "blessed" chestnut, Adam confesses later, "that has brought us together" (280). Hence, Brodwin concludes, "Eve's compassion and Adam's humor, twin ideas that at best reflect man's celebratory, healing qualities, have caused the fall, caused the exile and at the same time created the means by which man is able to face that exile" (55). The ironic absurdity of life is that human values such as compassion, love, humor "would find no place in the 'real' world if they were not needed to cope with a Divine Nature which has no place for them; indeed, makes them the very causes of the fall" (57).

Bibliography

PRIMARY

*The Complete Short Stories of Mark Twain. Now Collected for the First Time. Edited by Charles Neider. Garden City, N.Y.: Hanover House, 1957.

Eve's Diary. New York: Harper & Brothers, 1906.

Extracts from Adam's Diary. New York: Harper & Brothers, 1904.

The Niagara Book. Buffalo, N.Y.: Underhill & Nichols, 1893.

The Private Lives of Adam and Eve. New York: Harper & Brothers, 1931.

The $30,000 Bequest and Other Stories. New York: Harper & Brothers, 1906.

Their Husband's Wives. Edited by William Dean Howells and Henry Mills Alden. New York: Harper & Brothers, 1906.

Tom Sawyer, Detective. London: Chatto & Windus, 1897.

SECONDARY

Adams, Henry. Letters of Henry Adams (1892–1918). Edited by W. C. Ford. Boston: Houghton Mifflin, 1938.

Baldanza, Frank. *Mark Twain: An Introduction and Interpretation.* New York: Holt, Rinehart & Winston, 1961.

Brashear, Minnie. *Mark Twain: Son of Missouri.* Chapel Hill: University of North Carolina Press, 1934.

Brodwin, Stanley. "The Humor of the Absurd: Mark Twain's Adamic Diaries." *Criticism* 14 (1972):49–64.

Cox, James M. *Mark Twain: The Fate of Humor.* Princeton; N.J.: Princeton University Press, 1966.

Emerson, Everett. *The Authentic Mark Twain: A Literary Biography of Samuel L. Clemens.* Philadelphia: University of Pennsylvania Press, 1984.

Ensor, Allison. *Mark Twain and the Bible.* Lexington: University Press of Kentucky, 1969.

Harris, Susan K. *Mark Twain's Escape from Time: A Study of Patterns and Images.* Columbia: University of Missouri Press, 1982.

Hill, Hamlin. *Mark Twain: God's Fool.* New York: Harper & Row, 1973.

Macnaughton, William R. *Mark Twain's Last Years as a Writer.* Columbia: University of Missouri Press, 1979.

Paine, Albert B. *Mark Twain: A Biography.* Vol. 3. New York: Harper & Brothers, 1912.

Review of "Adam's Diary." *Spectator,* 17 July 1897, 89.

Stone, Albert E., Jr. *The Innocent Eye: Childhood in Mark Twain's Imagination.* New Haven: Yale University Press, 1961.

18

Facts concerning the Recent Carnival of Crime in Connecticut

Publication History

Although Covici reports that "Facts concerning the Recent Carnival of Crime in Connecticut" was written in 1875 (202), Emerson is more likely correct in dating its composition in January 1876 (90). Mark Twain read the story to the Monday Evening Club of Hartford on 24 January 1876 (Cox 167). Joe Twichell remembered the story delivered that evening as "serious in its intent though vastly funny and splendidly, brilliantly read" (Kaplan 295). The story first appeared in print in the *Atlantic Monthly* of June 1876 and in book form with "A True Story" the following year. James R. Osgood included it with other pieces from the *Atlantic* in the *Stolen White Elephant* volume of 1882.

Circumstances of Composition, Sources, and Influences

Mark Twain wrote "Carnival of Crime" in two days but, he informed William Dean Howells, he spent three more "trimming, altering, and working at it" (Bellamy 135). Inspired by his recent reading of W. E. H. Lecky's *History of European Morals from Augustine to Charlemagne* (1869), Mark Twain revealed that he wanted to explore "an exasperating metaphysical question . . . in the disguise of a literary extravaganza" (Emerson 90–91; Bellamy 135). The "question" had to do with the origin and function of conscience. Lecky, who agreed with those who held that conscience was an "original faculty" arising from an innate sense of good and evil, attacked the utilitarian position that conscience was simply an "association of ideas" imposed by social convention and consistent with a pleasure/pain principle of morality. Since conscience proves a source of pain far more often than it does pleasure, Lecky argued that the utilitarian who holds pleasure to be the sole end of life would be best served by its elimination. Baetzhold contends that "Carnival of Crime" follows "Lecky's discussion almost exactly" (58). Mark Twain wrote in an 1897 notebook entry that his story "was an attempt to account for our seeming *duality*—the presence in us of *another person;* not a slave of ours, but wholly free and independent, and with a character distinctly its own" (Harris 142–43). The destruction of that other "person"—conscience—produces "Bliss, unalloyed bliss" (*Great Short Works* 128).

The idea of the doppelgänger or double as a projection of conscience is of course common in nineteenth-century literature. Emerson suggests a possible reference to the well-known story by E. E. Hale, "The Man without a Country" (1863), whose hero is hounded by self-inflicted mental agony (221). Actually the story bears closer affinities to Edgar Allan Poe's story "William Wilson." Although there is no external confirmation of direct influence, the stories are remarkably similar: in each, the double resembles the protagonist in features and voice; no one sees the double save the protagonist; the double's "business" and pleasure is to censure the protagonist for his bad habits, dissipation, immorality, and secret sins; and, finally, the double falls victim to the protagonist's rage. The themes of the two stories, however, differ radically. Wilson's murder of his conscience insures his own demise; Mark Twain's elimination of the hideous dwarf is a liberation. Poe's story is a Gothic tale of terror; Mark Twain's story, though it has Gothic elements, is finally comic.

Although Mark Twain makes a feeble attempt to distinguish the narrator of his story from himself (e.g., the narrator is a father of sons), scholars have contended that the major influences on the "Carnival of Crime" are autobiographical. Gibson sees the story as an "unusually frank—and effective—use of the author's own experiences." Aunt Mary, who from "atop" her "pedestal" pleads to no avail that the narrator "quit [his] pernicious [smoking] habit," may be inspired by Mark Twain's wife Olivia (182). Her name, however, suggests Mrs. Mary Fairbanks, the genteel Cleveland, Ohio, socialite who had served as a kind of surrogate mother to Mark Twain during the *Quaker City* voyage and subsequently, during the process of writing *Innocents Abroad* (1896), had encouraged him to tone down the blasphemy of the original *Alta* letters. The dishonest "publisher who once stole some sketches of mine for a 'series' of his" (*Great Short Works* 126) is probably an allusion to W. F. Gill, who had appropriated Mark Twain's name without permission for one of the *Treasure Trove Series* (Gibson 182).

More significant than these allusions to real models is the general treatment of conscience. As Baldanza writes, Mark Twain had an "easily aroused sense of guilt that took upon itself the Herculean burdens of remorse" (11). In his *Autobiography* he reports that even as a child he perceived accidents and catastrophes in Hannibal as the result of divine intervention to teach him moral lessons and encourage his renovation. Indeed, throughout his life Mark Twain labored under self-imposed remorse for accidents or developments he could not control: the death of his infant son from pneumonia; Olivia's sagging health and eventual death, as well as her apparent loss of religious faith; Susy's death from meningitis. The reference in the story to the narrator's betrayal of his younger brother who "always lovingly trusted in you with a fidelity that your manifold treacheries were not able to shake" (117) recalls Mark Twain's profound guilt over the steamboat accident that claimed his brother Henry's life. The "Carnival of Crime" becomes, Kaplan concludes, a means for Mark Twain "to explore the roots of his black depression" (*Mr. Clemens* 300).

In dramatizing his triumph over a nagging conscience, "Carnival" is also a celebration of Mark Twain's freedom from the restraints imposed by the bourgeois, domestic life he was forced to live in Hartford (Geismar 55). Geismar and Emerson, among others, point to Mark Twain's fear of waning creativity during the mid-1870s, when the pressures of conforming to genteel standards of conduct constrained his more natural frontier voice and rebellious temperament. In this story, Mark Twain is a victim both of his own self-imposed guilt and the confining social strictures of polite society, represented by Aunt Mary. His murder of his dwarf conscience and ensuing liberation suggests, Emerson writes, that Mark Twain "is not ready to submit to the discipline of the social demands being made of him without protest" (91).

Relationship to Other Mark Twain Works

"Carnival of Crime" marks a significant advance, Miller argues, from Mark Twain's humor in "Jim Smiley and His Jumping Frog" (1865). In that story we find an "uncritical acceptance of local mores," but in "Carnival" Mark Twain begins "to take issue with values his contemporaries held sacred" (164–65). Miller, however, overstates the case; certainly *Innocents Abroad*, or early sketches like "Lucretia Smith's Soldier" (1864), "Aurelia's Unfortunate Young Man" (1864), and "Story of the Bad Little Boy" (1865) burlesque or satirize sacred communal values. "Carnival of Crime" assumes major importance in Mark Twain's fiction in that it foreshadows the concern with conscience, guilt, and moral responsibility that comes to dominate the author's later writings.

Several scholars, for example, have noted the similarities between Aunt Mary in "Carnival" and Aunt Polly in *Tom Sawyer* (1876) (Geismar 52; Gibson 182; Johnson 72–73). Harris treats the story in light of Mark Twain's depiction of women generally in his fiction. She points out that in "Carnival," as in his novels about children (e.g., *Tom Sawyer* and *Huckleberry Finn* [1885]), the woman fails in her attempt to reform the protagonist because her "moral largess is a disguise for authoritarian prowess" that affords his own meager conscience no opportunity for legitimate moral growth. Aunt Mary, Aunt Polly, and Miss Watson share an inflexible will and preoccupation with essentially irrelevant matters of social decorum that obscure a more crucial moral lesson: the need to sacrifice personal desires to communal welfare (142–43).

Baldanza sees "Carnival" as a foreshadowing of Mark Twain's treatment of superstition and guilt in *Tom Sawyer,* related phenomena rooted in fear and ignorance: superstition leads one to impose "a magic cause and effect relationship" in the hopes of placating exterior forces; guilt, on the other hand, is a manifestation of a deeper fear—terror in the face of incomprehensible internal forces one cannot control or channel into constructive directions (107). The narrator of "Carnival" objectifies his fear in the form of the dwarf conscience and slays it, thereby achieving liberation from debilitating social restrictions. A more extended battle with conscience shapes the central conflict of *Huckleberry Finn.* The objective embodiment this time is the letter Huck drafts revealing Jim's identity and satisfying a conscience that has been shaped by genteel slaveholding society. Huck too slays his conscience with his surrender to what he ironically perceives to be his natural depravity: "All right, then, I'll *go* to hell" (Emerson 138; Blues 22–23).

The "Carnival of Crime" anticipates a series of later writings concerned with what Gibson calls "the anatomy and physiology of the mental personality" (185). Of especial relevance here are *Pudd'nhead Wilson* (1894), "The Man That Corrupted Hadleyburg" (1899), and *The Mysterious Stranger* (1916)—all, like "Carnival," part of the "dark line of surrealistic parables" Geismar sees as characteristic of Mark Twain's later fiction (52). Covici mentions that the punitive role of conscience in "Carnival of Crime" anticipates the function of Burgess in "Hadleyburg": "Spurned by the town, by those who try to deny the dual nature of humanity, he rises to hold the town to strict account—which is exactly what the town unknowingly wants" (202). That Burgess enjoys his task of awakening the townspeople to full awareness of their limitations, that it is his intention to inflict pain, accords well with the perception of his role voiced by the narrator's conscience in "Carnival of Crime": " 'We do it simply because it is 'business.' It is our trade. The *purpose* of it is to improve the man, but *we* are merely disinterested agents. . . . We *do* crowd the orders a trifle. . . . We enjoy it" (121). Gibson mentions the parallel between the conscience of "Carnival" and the punitive role of the "moral sense" in "The Chronicle of Young Satan," one of the several *Mysterious Stranger* manuscripts (185).

Covici develops the relationship between "Carnival" and *The Mysterious Stranger* in substantial detail. The parallel he draws, however, is not between the conscience and the "moral sense" but between the conscience of "Carnival" and Philip Traum: Traum is, Covici argues, "a projection of the human conscience, the accusing superego of the damned human race."

Just as Traum is fully aware that people are foolish to accept personal responsibility for their actions yet blames them anyway, so Mark Twain's conscience in "Carnival" gleefully inflicts suffering no matter what his victim does: "between the devil and the conscience there is little to choose" (235–37).

Critical Studies

"Facts concerning the Recent Carnival of Crime in Connecticut" is a farce, comic in tone, that in its concern with ungovernable forces in the subconscious mind becomes, as Howells noted, "an impassioned study of the human conscience," a "powerful allegory" that Hawthorne or Bunyan "might have been proud to imagine" (Bellamy 135). Like Conrad's "Secret Sharer" or Dostoevski's "Double," the story centers upon the middle-aged narrator's confrontation with his conscience (Emerson 91). Conscience in the story assumes two rather distinct forms: the narrator's perennial nemesis Aunt Mary, a sweet and well-meaning woman who embodies the genteel mores of polite society; and a gnarled dwarf covered with "a fuzzy, greenish mold," who in his "devilish glee" assumes as "my *business*—and my joy—to make you repent of *every*thing you do" (122; Blues 22–23). The latter proves the more formidable of the two adversaries. Although "unsubstantial, just as other spirits are," the grotesque creature "seemed to bear a sort of remote and ill-defined resemblance to" the narrator as he objectifies his internal fears and insecurities. The story dramatizes the narrator's dialogue with his censuring conscience and his eventual triumph over its debilitating effects as he bolts past his aunt, strangles the dwarf, tears him "to shreds and fragments," and casts "the bleeding rubbish into the fire," leaving the narrator "a man whose life-conflict is done, whose soul is at peace; a man whose heart is dead to sorrow, dead to suffering, dead to remorse; a man *without a conscience!*" (128).

The story then comes to an abrupt conclusion as the narrator rehearses the "carnival of crime" made possible by the elimination of his conscience. In "bliss, unalloyed bliss" he embarks on a two-week binge in which he murders thirty-eight people "on account of ancient grudges," burns a house that obstructs his view, and swindles "a widow and some orphans out of their last cow, which is a very good one, though not thoroughbred" (128). The intrinsically horrible nature of his crimes would seem to justify the earlier restraints imposed by conscience and hence undercut the apparent theme of the story. Yet the playful context, "archly melodramatic" language, and comic hyperbole throughout diffuses what is potentially a horrifying Gothic tale (Miller 162–64). Gibson points out that Mark Twain's narrator is no Raskolnikov; the anticlimactic ordering of his crimes "and the business jargon and flat prose of the last paragraph set firmly the key of burlesque" (181).

The dark undercurrents of the story, Kaplan reports, puzzled Mark Twain's public who, expecting him "to be a funny man only," were frustrated by the moralistic tone, the examination and rejection of community values, and the exploration of his inner psyche offered in "Carnival of Crime" (*Mr. Clemens* 296). Though they assume burlesque form, Mark Twain's basic concerns in this story, Gibson argues, anticipate Freud and may be stated in Freudian terms: the narrator assumes the role of the ego, tormented by his Aunt Mary who, as a representative of parents and other authority figures as a "vehicle of tradition," shapes the superego; the id, "invisible in the unconscious" through most of the story, explodes in "the compulsively demonic behavior of the narrator-ego at the end" (183).

Geismar, on the other hand, writes disdainfully of the "orthodox Freudians" who "shake their head sadly and commiserate ad nauseam over poor Sam Clemens' burden of sin and guilt." Geismar prefers to see the story "in Rankian cultural terms." "Carnival of Crime" dramatizes the hero's "liberation" from the debilitating restraints imposed by his culture, his repudiation of conventional patterns of moral, decorous behavior, and his consequent achievement of the self-fulfillment indispensable to the artist. "This was Sam Clemens exorcising his Puritan past," Geismar concludes (54).

Bibliography

PRIMARY

Great Short Works of Mark Twain. Edited by Justin Kaplan. New York: Harper & Row, 1967.

The Stolen White Elephant Etc. Boston: James R. Osgood, 1882.

A True Story and The Recent Carnival of Crime. Boston: James R. Osgood, 1887.

SECONDARY

Baetzhold, Howard G. *Mark Twain and John Bull: The British Connection*. Bloomington: Indiana University Press, 1970.

Baldanza, Frank. *Mark Twain: An Introduction and Interpretation*. New York: Holt, Rinehart & Winston, 1961.

Bellamy, Gladys C. *Mark Twain as a Literary Artist*. Norman: University of Oklahoma Press, 1950.

Blues, Thomas. *Mark Twain and the Community*. Lexington: University Press of Kentucky, 1970.

Covici, Pascal, Jr. *Mark Twain's Humor: The Image of a World.* Dallas: Southern Methodist University Press, 1962.

Cox, James M. *Mark Twain: The Fate of Humor.* Princeton, N.J.: Princeton University Press, 1966.

Emerson, Everett. *The Authentic Mark Twain: A Literary Biography of Samuel L. Clemens.* Philadelphia: University of Pennsylvania Press, 1984.

Geismar, Maxwell. *Mark Twain: An American Prophet.* Boston: Houghton Mifflin, 1970.

Gibson, William M. *The Art of Mark Twain.* New York: Oxford University Press, 1976.

Harris, Susan K. *Mark Twain's Escape from Time: A Study of Pattern and Images.* Columbia: University of Missouri Press, 1982.

Johnson, James L. *Mark Twain and the Limits of Power: Emerson's God in Ruins.* Knoxville: University of Tennessee Press, 1982.

Kaplan, Justin. *Mr. Clemens and Mark Twain.* New York: Simon & Schuster, 1966.

Miller, Robert Keith. *Mark Twain.* New York: Frederick Ungar, 1983.

Paine, Albert B. *Mark Twain: A Biography.* Vol. 2. New York: Harper & Brothers, 1912.

19

The Facts in the Case of the Great Beef Contract
How I Edited an Agricultural Paper Once

Publication History

"The Facts in the Case of the Great Beef Contract" (1870) was the first of Mark Twain's contributions to his "Memoranda" section of the *Galaxy* (Paine 404). The story subsequently appeared in the American News Company edition of *Mark Twain's Sketches,* published in 1874. Another of Mark Twain's eighty-seven pieces written for the *Galaxy* between March 1870 and March 1871, "How I Edited an Agricultural Paper Once" appeared in the July 1870 issue. First book publication was in the 1875 edition of *Sketches, New and Old.*

Circumstances of Composition, Sources, and Influences

Shortly after his marriage to Olivia Langdon (2 February 1870), Mark Twain began writing a series of essays, sketches, and stories for the *Galaxy,* a monthly magazine edited by Francis P. Church. Already associate editor of the Buffalo *Express* and a regular contributor to its pages, Mark Twain sought a more prestigious outlet for his creative work. He wrote to Elisha Bliss in March 1870: "I consider the magazine because it will give me an opening for higher class writing, stuff which I hate to shovel into a daily newspaper" (Kaplan 183–84). Mark Twain's agreement with Church required that he supply ten pages of printed copy a month for a regular section of the magazine entitled, "Memoranda." His stipend was twenty-four hundred dollars a year. During the period March 1870 to March 1871 he wrote some eighty-seven sketches, essays, and stories for the *Galaxy.* Much of this material is ephemeral; ten of the pieces were reprinted in *Sketches, New and Old.* Emerson writes that the work for the *Galaxy* represents "no new development in the writer's career but rather a continuation of the sketch-writing he had begun in the West" (58–60).

Relationship to Other Mark Twain Works

Sloane reports that in the late 1860s and early 1870s, Mark Twain created "a new genre which is best described as semi-fiction: a naive persona embroiders an exaggerated burlesque on the real 'facts' of cosmopolitan travel and thereby develops his 'American' skeptical vision" (149). Though neither of these two stories is really concerned with travel, they are both "semi-fiction," exaggerated fictional elaborations of past experiences designed to entertain an audience. "How I Edited an Agricultural Paper Once," Long writes, is "just pure fun, devoid of seriousness" (168); Paine calls it "an excellent example of Mark Twain's more extravagant style of humor" (407).

In tone and style the two stories are akin to the burlesque sketches characteristic of Mark Twain's California and Nevada journalism. Working under the influence of Bret Harte and Charles Henry Webb, Mark Twain had developed an identifiable formula for writing based on comic hyperbole; his sketches, Bellamy writes, were "a product of calculated detail and conscious elaboration . . . formlessness and comic verbosity were his goals" (122). These two stories, however, signal an advance in Mark Twain's development as a literary comedian, for he shows in them a sure control of structure. The stories build toward a climax, as successive episodes and details grow increasingly comic: "Mark Twain employs both the surprise ending and the progressive form in which the ending is foreseen. . . . The reader's sense of humor is excited almost as much by the anticipation as by the final arrival of the climax" (122).

Critical Studies

"The Facts in the Case of the Great Beef Contract" is a satire on governmental bureaucracy, similar in theme to "The Man Who Put Up at Gadsby's" (1880). The announced purpose of the narrative is to explain the narrator's role in settling accounts pertaining to an agreement between a John Wilson Mackenzie, deceased, and the U.S. government "to furnish to General Sherman the sum of thirty barrels of beef"—a "matter which has so exercised the public mind, engendered so much ill-feeling, and so filled the newspapers of both continents with distorted statements and extravagant comments" (40).

The story consists of two parts. The first traces the progress of Mackenzie in a futile quest to locate Sherman, a quest that takes him along the trail of Sherman's march through Georgia to the sea, to the Near East, then to the American Great Plains where, within four miles of Sherman's headquarters, "he was tomahawked and scalped, and the Indians got the beef"— all except one barrel, which Sherman's troops seized in a subsequent attack. The second part narrates the frustrating attempts of Mackenzie's heirs to collect from the government the contract price for the beef (three thousand dollars) and traveling expenses, which totaled almost six times the value of the beef. Eventually the contract falls to Mark Twain, who arduously makes his way through a maze of governmental agencies before learning at last that he is eligible for payment on only the one barrel of beef that actually reached Sherman's troops, and then only if he can identify the Indian who scalped Mackenzie. From his experience Mark Twain learns "that if a man lives long enough he can trace a thing through the Circumlocution Office of Washington and find out, after much labor and trouble and delay, that which he could have found out on the first day if the business of the Circumlocution Office were as ingeniously systematized as it would be if it were a great private mercantile institution" (45).

"How I Edited an Agricultural Paper Once" is a satire on journalism. Burlesque in form, it relates Mark Twain's brief experience as editor of an agricultural paper, a temporary post he assumed with "misgivings" because the salary is attractive and he wants to assist the regular editor who is off on holiday. The problem is that he knows absolutely nothing about agriculture. His editorial columns—full of advice, such as "Turnips should never be pulled, it injures them. It is much better to send a boy up and let him shake the tree"—occasion a stir in the community among the farmers who fail to appreciate his "figurative" language. The editor returns, dismayed at the commotion in the community and concerned about the reputation of his paper: "if you had made the acquiring of ignorance the study of your life, you could not have graduated with higher honor than you could to-day. . . . Why didn't you *tell* me you didn't know anything about agriculture?" (49).

The story reaches its climax in a lengthy concluding paragraph, in which Mark Twain defends himself and in the process lambasts the profession:

> I tell you I have been in the editorial business going on fourteen years, and it is the first time I ever heard of a man's having to know anything in order to edit a newspaper. . . . Who write the dramatic critiques for the second-rate papers? Why, a parcel of promoted shoemakers and apprentice apothecaries, who know just as much about good acting as I do about good farming and no more. Who review the books? People who never wrote one. . . . I have been through it from Alpha to Omaha, and I tell you that the less a man knows the bigger the noise he makes and the higher the salary he commands. (49–50)

Ultimately, he argues, the paper is best served by an editor who knows nothing of his subject: "I said I could make your paper of interest to all classes—and I have. I said I could run your circulation up to twenty thousand copies, and if I had had two more weeks I'd have done it. And I'd have given you the best class of readers that ever an agricultural paper had—not a farmer in it" (50). The tirade undercuts, of course, conventional notions of the function of a newspaper, but it is, at the same time, an implicit defense of the kind of journalism that established Mark Twain's reputation.

Bibliography

PRIMARY

The Complete Short Stories of Mark Twain. Now Collected for the First Time. Edited by Charles Neider. Garden City, N.Y.: Hanover House, 1957.

Mark Twain's Sketches, New and Old. Now First Published in Complete Form. Hartford and Chicago: American Publishing Co., 1875.

Mark Twain's Sketches. *Number One*. Authorized Edition. New York: American News Co., 1874.

SECONDARY

Bellamy, Gladys C. *Mark Twain as a Literary Artist*. Norman: University of Oklahoma Press, 1950.

Emerson, Everett. *The Authentic Mark Twain: A Literary Biography of Samuel L. Clemens*. Philadelphia: University of Pennsylvania Press, 1984.

Kaplan, Justin. *Mr. Clemens and Mark Twain*. New York: Simon & Schuster, 1966.

Long, E. Hudson. *Mark Twain Handbook*. New York: Hendricks House, 1957.

Paine, Albert B. *Mark Twain: A Biography*. Vol. 2. New York: Harper & Brothers, 1912.

Sloane, David E. E. "Mark Twain's Comedy: The 1870s." *Studies in American Humor* 2 (January 1976):146–56.

20

The Facts in the Great Landslide Case
Buck Fanshaw's Funeral
A Trial
Jim Blaine and His Grandfather's Ram
Dick Baker and His Cat

Publication History

These five stories are among what Beidler calls the "self-sustaining narratives" in Mark Twain's 1872 travel book, *Roughing It* (43). Three of the pieces saw print for the first time in the 1872 volume: "Buck Fanshaw's Funeral" (chap. 47), "A Trial" (chap. 50), "Jim Blaine and His Grandfather's Ram" (chap. 53). The other two underwent a somewhat slower process of evolution. "The Facts in the Great Landslide Case" (chap. 34) is Mark Twain's 20 August 1863 letter to the San Francisco *Call*, entitled "A Rich Decision"; this letter is reprinted by A. E. Hutchinson in the 1952 *Twainian*. An expanded version of the *Call* letter, entitled "The Facts in the Great Landslide Case," appeared in the Buffalo *Express* 2 April 1870. This sketch is only slightly revised for inclusion in *Roughing It*, where the plaintiff's name is changed from Dick Sides to Dick Hyde. The earliest version of "Dick Baker and His Cat," entitled "Remarkable Sagacity of a Cat," appeared in an 1865 issue of the *Californian* (*Roughing It*, ed. Rogers and Baender, 533–35). Mark Twain used the story again as one of his "Around the World Letters" in the *Express*, 18 December 1869, and modified it only slightly for *Roughing It* (chap. 61).

All five have appeared as independent short stories in various collections of Mark Twain's fiction: "Landslide Case" in *Great Short Works* (1967); "Fanshaw's Funeral" in *Complete Short Stories* (1957) and *Mark Twain's Library of Humor* (1906); "A Trial" in *Complete Short Stories;* "Jim Blaine" in *Complete Short Stories* and *Great Short Works;* and "Dick Baker" in *Choice Humorous Works* (1873 and 1877); *Complete Short Stories* (where it is entitled "Tom Quartz"), *Mark Twain's Library of Humor,* and *Selections from American Humor* (1888). A greatly modified version of "Jim Blaine," which the author prepared for platform readings in 1884, is reprinted in *Mark Twain in Eruption* (1940). Both Hollenbach (303–12) and Covici (52–58) analyze and compare the written and oral versions of the tale.

Circumstances of Composition, Sources, and Influences

Paine reports that it was Elisha Bliss who suggested the subject for *Roughing It* during a visit to the household of Mark Twain in July 1870 (2:420). Actually Mark Twain had already begun work on the topic, having written six pieces about Nevada and California for his "Around the World" series of letters in the *Express* from 16 October 1869 to 22 January 1870. Most of this material later resurfaced in *Roughing It*. In early January 1870 Mark Twain told Mrs. Fairbanks that he planned to write a book during the coming summer, and in late February he wrote to his family in Saint Louis asking that they forward to him the files of his *Territorial Enterprise* articles. He also began work on a play that included such Nevada characters as Scotty Briggs and Buck Fanshaw, but he abandoned the project, presumably to turn his attention to a book about his adventures in the American West that would serve as a companion volume to his enormously successful *Innocents Abroad* (1869). In any event, he wrote to Mrs. Fairbanks in May 1870 that his publishers were pressuring him for another book and, he mused, "I doubt if I could do better than rub up old Pacific memories & put them between covers along with some eloquent pictures" (Emerson 62). He signed a contract with Bliss on 15 July 1870 to complete an unspecified book by the end of the year, and that same day wrote to his brother Orion asking that he prod his memory of their journey to Nevada in 1861. Specifically he wanted "a memorandum of the route we took. . . . Do you remember any of the scenes, names, incidents or adventures of the coach trip?—for I remember next to *nothing* about the matter" (Hill 40–58).

The writing of *Roughing It* did not proceed as smoothly as Mark Twain had hoped. The subscription trade demanded a large book—he had promised Bliss some two hundred forty thousand words—but unlike *Innocents Abroad* where the original *Alta* letters provided a first draft, this time there was little prepared material with which to work: a few letters to the *Territorial Enterprise*, some Nevada correspondence to the Keokuk, Iowa, *Gate City*, and the Saint Louis *Missouri Democrat* (the former being, Rogers claims, "one of the most extensive single sources for *Roughing It*" ([*Pattern*, ed. Rogers, vii]), the six *Express* pieces, and the Sandwich Island letters that he eventually used to fill out the ending of the book. Major portions of the new book would have to come from his memory of people and places experienced, events witnessed, and tales heard almost a decade earlier in the West. More than time separated the author from his earlier life in the mining camps; to Mark Twain—married, expecting his first child, and settled in the East—Nevada and California had become, as Fender observes, "a comically distanced field of adventure" (752). To recreate that vanished era, Mark Twain needed time to concentrate, to reminisce, and to reflect. Unfortunately, domestic crises intervened to frustrate his concentration: Jervis Langdon, his father-in-law, died in August 1870, some six months after Mark Twain's marriage to Olivia; a house guest fell ill and died in their home; his wife, plagued with poor health through most of the year, gave birth prematurely to their first child in November. Dissatisfied both with Buffalo and his work with the *Express,* Mark Twain sold his interest in the newspaper at a loss of ten thousand dollars and by spring 1871 had settled in Elmira, New York. There, spurred by the promise of 7.5 percent royalties—the largest "ever paid on a subscription book in this country"—he turned all his attention to his literary project: "I am writing with a red-hot interest," Mark Twain wrote to Bliss. "Nothing bothers me or gets my attention—I don't think of anything but the book. . . . I find myself so thoroughly interested in my work, now (a thing I have not experienced for months) that I can't bear to lose a single moment of the inspiration" (Bellamy 269–70; Emerson 62–66). A two-month visit from his old friend and former Nevada editor Joe Goodman (April–May 1871) stimulated Mark Twain's memories and creative imagination, offered a retreat from the pressing concerns and confinement of respectable eastern domesticity, and gave direction to the manuscript—which Mark Twain completed in August 1871.

Like Mark Twain's other travel books, *Roughing It* defies genre classification. The first twenty chapters or so resemble a novel, a *Bildungsroman;* they focus on the hero's maturation during his first-hand encounter with the American West. As Benson writes, "Here on the Comstock Lode, robustly conscious of the great drama of the frontier, Mark Twain was born" (65). The second half of the book, which critics such as Smith (61–67) and Fender (755–56) consider inferior to the first, consists largely of a series of anecdotes, tall tales, and local color descriptions; focus shifts from the psychological development of the tenderfoot to a more objective delineation of his environment (Spengemann 19–21). Towers contends that the shift reflects Mark Twain's disillusionment with the deceptive "lazy freedom and spontaneous democracy of the camp world" that serve to mask a reality of "violence, disorder, repression and death" (7–12). The five stories considered here belong to this second half of the book, which one critic contends is "a splendid anthology of anecdotes and tales" (Gibson 48). Mark Twain, as character, assumes a significant role in only one, "Jim Blaine." Yet all five are part of what Geismar calls "a classical account of a frontier society" and play an integral role in "an altogether new literary form: the prose epic of travel, or the American picaresque" (21–22). In *Roughing It* Mark Twain attempts to reconstruct the story of his own maturation in the West, for his life in Nevada and California had been crucial to his personal and aesthetic development, providing, Fender notes, a "style of living as well as writing" (740); at the same time, he wants to recapture a fleeting phase of American history, refashion a cosmos far different from the civilization circumscribing his conventional life in the East (Gibson 53). The five stories, as unrelated as they may seem to the chronicle of the tenderfoot's maturation, are thus nevertheless integral to what Beidler calls "a self-validating mode of literary perception": Mark Twain's attempt "to fashion his own artistic synthesis between the truth of personal observation and some larger context of abstract value and meaning" (34–35).

The general source or inspiration for each of the five stories is Mark Twain's memory of his experiences in the West. The mining country was, as Mark Twain wrote to his mother shortly after his arrival in Carson City in 1861, "fabulously rich in gold, silver, copper, lead, coal, iron . . . thieves, murderers, desperadoes, ladies, children, lawyers, Christians, Indians, Chinamen, Spaniards, gamblers, sharpers, cayotes (pronounced ki-yo-ties), poets, preachers, and jackass rabbits. I overheard a gentleman say, the other day, that it was 'the d——dest country under the sun,' and that comprehensive conception I fully subscribe to" (Paine 1:175). Actual events, real people, tall tales, and regional folklore from "the d——dest country under the sun" surely fueled Mark Twain's aesthetic imagination, but whether they provided specific sources for any of the five tales is a matter of conjecture. Mack suggests that one of them, "Landslide Case," has a factual basis: Buncombe, she argues, is modeled on Benjamin Bunker, attorney general for Nevada from 1861 to 1863, who resigned his post as a result of his humiliation in a landslide hoax perpetrated by two local ranchers, Dick Sides and Tom Rust (143–48). Indeed, in the first version of the sketch, published in the *Call*, Mark Twain identifies Bunker by name and dates the episode in 1861. Yet even this original anecdote, Smith reports, "has a distinctive air of the tall tale about it," and the expanded version in *Roughing It* "is essentially a piece of fiction" (59–60). Rogers and Baender dispute Mack's contention altogether, noting that the record shows that President Lincoln removed Bunker from office for incompetence and that "no such hoax is mentioned in contemporary writings" (*Roughing It*, 580–81).

Sources for the other four stories are even more mercurial. In manner and method of telling a tale, Jim Blaine resembles the marvelous raconteurs who entertained Mark Twain around the fire in Gillis's cabin on Jackass Hill or in the saloon at nearby Angel's Camp—specifically Jim Gillis, or Ben Coon, the "solemn, fat-witted person, who dozed by the stove, or told slow, endless stories, without point or application" (Paine 1:271). In the cabin on Jackass Hill where he stayed with Gillis during the winter 1864–65, Mark Twain met Dick Stoker and his cat Tom Quartz. In Hawaii Mark Twain met a Mr. Rising, the inspiration for "the fragile, gentle, spiriteul new fledgling" minister of "Fanshaw's Funeral" (Paine 1:214–15); Mark Twain implies in *Roughing It* that he had heard the story directly from the clergyman involved, but Baldwin reports that no specific source for the tale has surfaced (16). Like Captain "Hurricane" Jones of "Some Rambling Notes of an Idle Excursion" and Captain Stormfield, Ned Blakely of "A Trial" is modeled on Edgar Wakeman, the colorful sea captain Mark Twain encountered on his voyage from San Francisco to Nicaragua in 1865. But the *Roughing It* story of Ned Blakely, "although in character," is probably imaginary for, as Rogers and Baender report, Wakeman made no mention of it in his autobiography (*Roughing It* 592). Benson, Fatout, and Mack all provide detailed biographical discussion of Mark Twain's western adventures; the evidence suggests, however, that while specific experiences and people stimulated Mark Twain's imagination, the five stories considered here are all independent fiction.

The primary literary influence on *Roughing It* in general and these stories in particular comes from southwestern humor. Lynn offers the most comprehensive study of this tradition and its influence on Mark Twain's fictional method. Smith notes a major shift in narrative point of view in the second half of *Roughing It* to which the five stories considered here belong: the narrator who speaks through these stories "is the man who had written the newspaper stories pasted in the scrapbooks that lay on Mark Twain's desk"; the resulting narrative pose is frequently that common to southwestern humorists, the aloof, self-controlled gentleman who "identifies himself with the responsible citizens of Virginia City as against the propertyless miners and prospectors." Specifically Smith argues that in "Fanshaw's Funeral" there is noticeable distance sustained between the vernacular Scotty and the narrator Mark Twain. The latter, like the gentleman narrator of most fiction in the school of southwestern humor, becomes "fully identified with the point of view of an upper class that considers itself to be custodian of the official values." Mark Twain obviously enjoys Scotty's "short-haired slang," but it is, Smith contends, "the pleasure of an A. B. Longstreet in the dialect of his Georgia crackers" (61–63; Gerber 297). Rachal suggests a more specific influence from southwestern humor on "Fanshaw's Funeral," a chapter in Johnson Jones Hooper's *Adventures of Captain Simon Suggs*. The chapter "Simon Plays the Snatch Game" includes a verbal exchange between Simon and his father, the Reverend Jed'diah Suggs; as in the dialogue between Scotty Briggs and the minister, humor results from their "mutual failure to communicate" and in each case the clergyman is baffled by the "card metaphor" underlying the vernacular protagonists's language (10–11).

Fender agrees with Smith that in these sections of *Roughing It* Mark

Twain loses control, oscillating between being a "spokesman for the official culture" and burlesquing it. The contrast drawn between eastern gentility and the savagery of the western frontier that underlies much of this fiction is a distinguishing feature not only of the southwestern humorists but also of the Washoe Wits, cultured gentlemen like Dan De Quille who used their pen to burlesque law, politics, and customs of the primitive West (752–55).

Another literary influence comes from the popular stage. Smith contends that these stories suffer because such characters as Ned Blakely and Scotty Briggs are essentially stereotypes lifted directly from contemporary melodrama. The word "stalwart," Smith reports, is used to describe both Blakely and Briggs, as well as Jim Blaine; the term serves as "a shorthand designation for the formula by which crude, impulsive strength could be transformed from a threat to established values into a means of defending them" (66–67).

Relationship to Other Mark Twain Works

"Landslide Case" revolves around a hoax, a central feature in Mark Twain's fiction from the early journalistic sketch "The Petrified Man" (1862) to such later stories as "The $30,000 Bequest" (1904) and "The Man That Corrupted Hadleyburg" (1899) (Covici 143–205). In this case the hoax is not literary but structural: both narrator and reader know from the outset that the pompous, self-important Buncombe is the victim of a "practical joke." All the characters are aware of the hoax too, save Buncombe, "an impatient and irascible man": "At the end of two months the fact that he had been played upon with a joke had managed to bore itself, like another Hoosac Tunnel, through the solid adamant of his understanding" (229). In Mark Twain's later fiction, e.g., *Huckleberry Finn* (1885), "The Man That Corrupted Hadleyburg" and *The Mysterious Stranger* (1916), the hoax serves as a device to expose social and cosmic ironies and hence reinforces a serious theme; in this story, it is essentially a vehicle for the humorous deflation of the pompous tenderfoot who looks with disdain on the frontier locals he deems "fools." The story thus resembles "The Dandy Frightening the Squatter" (1852) or "Jim Smiley and His Jumping Frog" (1865) in that it chronicles the humiliation of the easterner at the hands of "the older citizens of a new territory" who "look down upon the rest of the world with a calm, benevolent compassion, as long as it keeps out of the way— when it gets in the way they snub it" (*Roughing It*, ed. Rogers and Baender, 224).

The central figure in the hoax is ex-Governor Roop, the judge who presides over the trial. Assuming the role of the deadpan native humorist,

Roop resembles Simon Wheeler: he wears "upon his face a solemnity so awe-inspiring that some of his fellow-conspirators had misgivings that maybe he had not comprehended, after all, that this was merely a joke" (226). Just as Wheeler toys with and, in his own way, victimizes the easterner Mark Twain, so Roop, Smith writes, "destroys the pretensions of the traditional culture by producing a solemn exaggeration of the rhetoric in which its most cherished values are clothed" (59–60).

A major part of the fun in this story thus results from its language. Buncombe's courtroom manner is reminiscent of Mark Twain's burlesque of Representative Sterns's oratory in a letter to the *Enterprise,* 5 December 1863 (*Mark Twain of the Enterprise* 92–95): Buncombe "pounded the table, he banged the law-books, he shouted, and roared, and howled, he quoted from everything and everybody, poetry, sarcasm, statistics, history, pathos, bathos, blasphemy, and wound up with a grand war-whoop for free speech, freedom of the press, free schools, the Glorious Bird of America and the principles of eternal justice!" (227). Roop, in turn, delivers his decision in language that, as Smith points out, burlesques both "the pomposity of the law and the cant of a decadent Calvinist orthodoxy." The effect of the whole, Smith concludes, is to ridicule "the effrontery of self-appointed spokesmen who arrogate to themselves the function of interpreting [divine] decrees to ordinary mortals" (59–60).

"Fanshaw's Funeral" is among Mark Twain's western stories and sketches that depend for their humorous effect on language to convey fundamental conflicts in perspective or point of view. An early antecedent is "The Case of Smith vs. Jones," published 26 June 1864 in the San Francisco *Golden Era* (Bellamy 143; Emerson 21). In this sketch a judge listens impatiently to the vernacular testimony of two witnesses to a fight; each contradicts the other and does so in language the genteel judge finds difficult to decipher. The judge appears ridiculous in his formal request that the untutored witnesses "refrain from the embellishments of metaphor and allegory as far as possible" (*Works* 16), but no more so than the minister who suggests to Scotty Briggs, "Would it not expedite matters if you restricted yourself to categorical statements of fact unencumbered with obstructing accumulations of metaphor and allegory?" (*Roughing It,* ed. Rogers and Baender, 300). The villians in each instance are metaphor and allegory; their usual purpose, of course, is to clarify, to make familiar a situation or abstract concept by explaining it in terms more readily accessible to one's audience. The judge and the minister are outsiders here, for their limited genteel background insulates them from the shared experiences of the communities they serve. As a result, true communication is impossible.

The crucial role of language to denote differences in moral and cultural perspective links "Fanshaw's Funeral" to "Jim Blaine." Both stories, Beidler writes, "turn on a single preoccupation, a preoccupation, not surprisingly, with the nature of expression as a crucial denominator of experiential meaning and value. They all depict . . . the problematic character of a world in which the ability to make meaning clearly or to understand the meanings made by others stands in urgent, essential relation to wisdom" (45–47). Baldwin notes that the play with language in "Fanshaw's Funeral" anticipates Mark Twain's similar use of language in *Huckleberry Finn* (17). Again, difficulties in communication reflect discrepancies in values or perspective. Miss Watson's genteel exegesis of biblical principles and stories Huck finds inapplicable to his daily life (e.g., Moses and the Bulrushers). When Huck translates these principles and stories into his own vernacular language, Miss Watson—like the judge in "Case of Smith vs. Jones" or the minister in "Fanshaw's Funeral"—is frustrated and puzzled, dismissing him as a fool. Nothing is communicated between them because they do not speak the same language. Later Huck ironically finds himself in the position of defending polite biblical exegesis in his debate with Jim over the wisdom of Solomon. Jim fails to see the "point," Huck insists; that is, he cannot grasp the metaphoric dimensions of the story. But in translating the story into terms he can understand very well, Jim argues that the "real pint is down deeper": no man is wise who will sacrifice an innocent life to settle a dispute. Frustrated by their inability to communicate, Huck responds just as Miss Watson had earlier with him or the judge with the two vernacular witnesses: he dismisses Jim with the condescending reflection, "You can't learn a nigger to argue."

Covici points out that Scotty Briggs's "poker vocabulary" is a common element in Mark Twain's fiction, denoting the westerner in many of his earlier sketches; not until "Fanshaw's Funeral," however, is the card terminology used to provide specific insight into character. Covici compares this story with "The $30,000 Bequest" in their use of "poker vocabulary," noting that the latter involves a far more sophisticated use of metaphor to reveal theme. In "Fanshaw's Funeral" Mark Twain provides "an exhibition of language for its own sake," though it does at the same time reinforce the dichotomy of East and West (21–24).

Like "Jim Smiley and His Jumping Frog" and the Whittier birthday address, "Fanshaw's Funeral" dramatizes through language the confrontation of East and West, a confrontation that reflects Mark Twain's dual role as eastern gentleman and "sage-brush bohemian." When at the conclusion of the story Mark Twain reveals that it had been his "large privilege . . . to hear [Scotty] tell the beautiful story of Joseph and his brethern" in slang-riddled vernacular language, we might recall that Mark Twain too had "retold" the story of Joseph in his own language but deleted it from *Innocents Abroad* for fear it would offend genteel eastern tastes.

"A Trial" is part of Mark Twain's ongoing attack on the criminal justice system in America. Benson points out that crime conditions in frontier Nevada inspired Mark Twain's protest against the American jury system, which "rewarded ignorance, stupidity and perjury" and as a result made a mockery of justice (74). Budd reports that Mark Twain had been outraged over a trial in 1870 that had established a precedent for the insanity plea as a defense in capital crimes and had responded with two letters of protest to the Buffalo *Express* ("The New Crime," 16 April 1870; "Our Precious Lunatic," 14 May 1870) and one to the *Galaxy* ("Unburlesqueable Things," July 1870). The insanity plea was, in Mark Twain's view, a "legal dodge that interfered with the state's main job—the punishment of thieves and murderers" (Budd 47). Germane here, Gibson argues, is the original dedication of *Roughing It: "TO THE LATE CAIN THIS BOOK IS DEDICATED . . .* in that it was his misfortune to live in a dark age that knew not the beneficent insanity plea" (Gibson 38). The story follows an account in *Roughing It* of the raw violence that characteristically undermined justice in the West, leaving it to the "long-tailed heroes of the revolver"; Mark Twain, however, has little patience with the more civilized alternative, for he confesses in "A Trial" that he wishes "to tamper with the jury law to put a premium on intelligence and character, and close the jury box against idiots, blacklegs, and people who do not read newspapers" (Gibson 38–39). In calmly taking the matter of justice into his own hands, Blakely anticipates Colonel Sherburn in *Huckleberry Finn,* the cool aristocrat who shoots the insolent Boggs down in the street and defies the ignorant, cowardly mob to attempt reprisal.

"Jim Blaine" opens with a frame very much like that of "Jim Smiley and His Jumping Frog." The "boys" pique Mark Twain's interest with their repeated insistence that he "ought to get one Jim Blaine to tell me the stirring story of his grandfather's old ram." They caution him, however, that Blaine will tell the story only when "comfortably and sociably drunk" (344). Hence as character, Mark Twain must await impatiently for the right opportunity: "he was often moderately but never satisfactorily drunk. I never watched a man's condition with such absorbing interest, such solicitude; I never so pined to see a man uncompromisingly drunk before" (344). Once Blaine is appropriately intoxicated and seated comfortably by the fire, Mark Twain—and by extension, the reader—becomes the eager auditor. In the end, Mark Twain again realizes that he has been the butt of a practical joke: "The tears were running down the boys' cheeks—they were suffocating with suppressed laughter—and had been from the start. . . . I perceived that I was 'sold' " (348). This "creation of an intermediary character and the careful selection of framework 'facts,' " Covici writes, "are as much a part of Twain's examination of oral humor as vernacular and western 'experience' themselves" (58).

As in "The Jumping Frog" emphasis falls not so much on the tale as on the manner of its telling; indeed, "the mention of the ram in the first sentence was as far as any man had ever heard him get, concerning it" (348). Covici points out that Blaine's story captures "the quality of mind implicit in the form of frontier oral narration," for Blaine, like Simon Wheeler, digresses endlessly, gives equal emphasis to each distinct facet of the tale, fails "to discriminate between the important and the trivial" (58). Jim Blaine's rambling monologue serves as the perfect example of the narrative technique outlined in Mark Twain's essay "How to Tell a Story." "The humorous story," Mark Twain writes, "may be spun out to great length, and may wander around as it pleases, and arrive nowhere in particular" (*Great Short Works* 182). Despite the attention given to establishing a frame that makes both Mark Twain and the reader the butt of the joke, "Jim Blaine" delights us primarily in Blaine's deadpan digressionary anecdotes and character sketches. As Hollenbach writes, "paradoxically, the very elements in his [Mark Twain] work that suggest lack of artistry, the uncontrolled ebullitions of a great improvisor, may be signs of a very conscious, painstaking, artistic effort" (305). Feinstein notes that "Jim Blaine" not only "anticipates stream-of-consciousness portraiture" but reflects Mark Twain's thinking that form "is ideally the externalization of an author's thinking . . . personal, informal, digressive" (160–63).

"Dick Baker" provides another of Mark Twain's portraits of California miners. Baker, "slenderly educated, slouchily dressed, and clay-soiled," is, like the inhabitants of the delapidated community of "The Californian's Tale" (1893), "another of those victims of eighteen years of unrequited toil and blighted hopes" (390). He too lives largely in the past. Possessing a heart of "finer metal than any gold his shovel ever brought to light," Baker habitually retreats from current problems into reminiscences of better days in "Dead-Horse Gulch" and his attachment to "the remarkablest cat *I* ever see" (390). His exaggerated and largely sentimental "tribute to the firmness of his humble friend of other days," Mark Twain confesses, "will always be a vivid memory with me" (393).

The story of the cat Tom Quartz is like "Jim Blaine" and "The Jumping Frog" essentially an oral tale, one that uses language to distinguish the local miners from the more genteel Mark Twain, who remains an outsider. As narrator, Mark Twain describes Dick Baker and then allows him to tell his anecdote in his own voice. Hence we as readers become auditors to a tale told in vernacular language that serves to characterize Baker and the class of miners he represents. Dick Baker's "muscular idiom," like Scotty Briggs's slang, represents, Budd contends, "the supreme achievement of Twain's personal democracy—the sinewy vernacular that controls the choicest passages of *Roughing It*" (46–47). The tale, however, lacks the sophistication and richness of either "Jim Blaine" or "The Jumping Frog" in large part because Mark Twain as character occupies an essentially insignificant role. There is no practical joke here, no tension between East and West. "Dick Baker" is, however, rather typical of the stories that comprise the second half of *Roughing It,* a series of anecdotes and tall tales that concentrate on what Spengemann calls "the eccentric and ebullient personalities, the freedom and excitement of the place" in an attempt "to capture a regional flavor" (21).

Critical Studies

Many of the stories and sketches of *Roughing It* revolve around the general theme of victimization and humiliation though, as Emerson points out, "the victim is seldom hurt for long, and the tone is good-natured, compassionate, seldom hostile or sadistic" (67). "Landslide Case" is a prime example of such a story as it chronicles the humiliation of the arrogant General Buncombe, newly appointed U.S. attorney to the Nevada Territory, who falls prey to a practical joke orchestrated by virtually the entire community.

Mark Twain sets the stage for the elaborate hoax with an initial discussion of severe landslides in the Carson, Eagle, and Washoe valleys: "the reader cannot know what a landslide is," he claims, "unless he has lived in that country and seen the whole side of a mountain taken off some fine morning and deposited in the valley" (224). The brief preliminary mention of the catastrophic landslides characteristic of the region establishes one part of the necessary framework for Buncombe's credulity.

The other part necessary to make the hoax successful is supplied by Buncombe: vanity. Because he "considered himself a lawyer of parts, and he very much wanted an opportunity to manifest it" (224), Buncombe is prime for debunking. He accepts Dick Hyde's incredible story without question, since it confirms his opinion of the western yokels fate has forced him to serve: "He said he had suspected before that the people of that territory were fools, and now he knew it" (226). Convinced that "victory was just as certain as if the conflict were already over," Buncombe enters the courtroom confident that "good strong testimony, a great speech," and his superior command of the law will carry the case (226).

But Buncombe's vanity has blinded him to the fact that he is the victim of a hoax, the pompous outsider humiliated through the concerted effort of the locals he deems fools. Ex-Governor Roop, a conspirator in the hoax who presides over the trial, rules against Buncombe: "Gentlemen, it ill becomes us, worms as we are, to meddle with the decrees of Heaven. It is plain to me that Heaven, in its inscrutable wisdom, has seen fit to move this defendant's ranch for a purpose. We are but creatures, and we must submit. . . . Gentlemen, it is the verdict of this court that the plaintiff, Richard Hyde, has been deprived of his ranch by the visitation of God!"

(228). Buncombe, "frantic with indignation," remains blind to the fact that he had been taken; it takes two months for that fact "to bore itself . . . through the solid adamant of his understanding." East and West collide and as in "The Dandy Frightening the Squatter" the arrogant gentleman discovers to his chagrin that the yokels are not the fools he thinks them to be.

"Fanshaw's Funeral" is in many ways a tall tale, built on hyperbole and replete with stereotypical, albeit memorable, characters. A "representative citizen," keeper of a "sumptuous saloon," Buck Fanshaw suffers an heroic death, one as violent as the life he lived: "in the delirium of a wasting typhoid fever, [he] had taken arsenic, shot himself through the body, cut his throat, and jumped out of a four-story window and broken his neck" (297). His passing is mourned "especially in the vast bottom-stratum of society"; the "sad and tearful" jury of his peers decides that Buck's death was no suicide but was instead brought on "by the visitation of God" (297). The responsibility for funeral arrangements falls to Scotty Briggs, "a stalwart rough" with "a warm heart, and a strong love for his friends" (298).

Conflict in the story arises when Scotty attempts to discuss plans for the funeral with the town minister, "a fragile, gentle, spirituel new fledgling from an Eastern theological seminary, and as yet unacquainted with the ways of the mines" (298). The conflict of East and West, as Covici points out, is in this story a conflict of language (23). Scotty speaks the "slang of Nevada," which, the narrator informs us, was "the richest and the most infinitely varied and copious that had ever existed anywhere in the world" (298); the bemused minister invariably responds in the genteel language appropriate to his eastern seminary education. To Scotty's initial inquiry "Are you the duck that runs the gospel-mill next door?" the minister replies, "I am the shepherd in charge of the flock whose fold is next door. . . . The spiritual adviser of the little company of believers whose sanctuary adjoins these premises" (299). Scotty is thoroughly befuddled by the minister's linguistic circumlocutions: "You ruther hold over me, pard. I reckon I can't call that hand. Ante and pass the buck" (299). The exchange reveals, however, that the differences between the eastern minister and the Virginia City "roughs" Scotty represents are more than linguistic, for neither Briggs nor Fanshaw is part of the "little company of believers."

Throughout their conversation Scotty resorts to poker metaphors to express his failure to comprehend. When, for example, the minister questions Fanshaw's religious affiliation—"Was he, or rather had he ever been connected with any organization sequestered from secular concerns and devoted to self-sacrifice in the interests of morality?"—Scotty responds, "you're most too many for me, you know. . . . Every time you draw, you fill; but I don't seem to have any luck. Let's have a new deal" (303). Covici argues that this recurrent "poker terminology" accomplishes several objectives. Not only does it give local color to the tale but through "the metaphoric equation of chips and cards with words" it draws attention to the crucial subsidiary plot line—the inability of the representatives of East and West to communicate. Moreover, the poker vocabulary defines Scotty's character and thus prepares for his "conversion" at the end; never does the westerner try to bluff, for he readily admits his opponent's ability to "draw and fill" and acknowledges that his own "hand" is woefully inadequate (24).

The confrontation of East and West is finally resolved, with no compromise of integrity on either side. Both men want desperately to communicate and make every effort to do so, and neither is disparaged (Baldwin 17). Scotty tells the minister, "You've treated me like a gentleman, pard, and I ain't the man to hurt your feelings intentional. I think you're white. I think you're a square man, pard. I like you" (304). Scotty succeeds in his mission, getting from the minister all "the obsequies" that " 'the boys' could desire": "such a marvel of funeral pomp had never been seen in Virginia" (304). The minister's patience, example, and good will also bring him a significant victory, for Scotty "achieved the distinction of becoming the only convert to religion that was ever gathered from the Virginia roughs" (305). Yet Scotty enters the domain of genteel Christian faith with his integrity intact: his conversion "did not warp his generosity or diminish his courage" (305). He brings with him his vernacular slang—the language that defines him—and as a Sunday school teacher "talked to his pioneer small-fry in a language they understood" (305). Their "consuming interest" in his fractured biblical stories, "riddled with slang," "showed that they were as unconscious as he was that any violence was being done to the sacred proprieties!" (305).

Although Smith criticizes the story because Scotty "conforms too closely to the stereotype to be interesting," and laments the narrator's identification with the minister's perspective (62–63), his is clearly a minority position. Other scholars celebrate "Fanshaw's Funeral," claiming that it is, as Baldwin writes, "an early case of Twain's better artistry," a story that successfully counterpoints regional differences for comic effect (17). Gibson agrees that the story is "finely wrought" and, like Covici, praises Mark Twain's creation of Scotty Briggs—a memorable, fully developed vernacular character (51; Covici 22).

"A Trial" explores the problem of justice in a primitive social order. Set in the lawless Chincha Islands, where "there were no courts and no officers; there was no government," the story is "a scrap of history" (Gibson 38–39) that chronicles Captain Ned Blakely's steadfast commitment to absolute, sure, and swift justice in the face of a bureaucracy he fears will thwart it.

The plot is straightforward. The captain, who is given the pseudonym Blakely ("that name will answer as well as any other fictitious one"), is especially fond of a Negro mate who "was his pet" (318). While ashore, the mate is ruthlessly murdered by one Bill Noakes, "a bully" who "had created a small reign of terror there" (319). None of the six witnesses to the crime is especially anxious to hold Noakes accountable for his actions. Blakely, "furious for justice," decides to take matters into his own hands: he arrests Noakes and plans to execute him immediately, without trial. The other six captains, witnesses to the crime, are horrified that Blakely would assume such responsibility and forego customary civilized procedures. Blakely, however, is a man who "hated trifling conventionalities," and by nature distrusts the legal system: he "steadfastly believed that the first and last aim and object of the law and lawyers was to defeat justice" (321). Hence he sees no reason for the formality of a trial: "What do I want to try him for, if he killed the nigger?" Reluctantly, however, Blakely agrees to a trial, though it is quite obvious he has no intention of allowing this formality to deter his resolute plans for quick justice: he enters the court-room "leading the prisoner with one hand and carrying a Bible and a rope in the other." When his "searching eye" detects that the jury includes two of Noakes's friends, he promptly intervenes to insure nothing will go amiss: "Now you vote right, do you hear?" he "confidentially" cautions the two, "or else there'll be a double-barreled inquest here when this trial's off, and your remainders will go home in a couple of baskets" (322). Thus chastened, the jury convicts Noakes and appoints a sheriff "to do the hanging." Blakely, however, will have none of that; he resolutely takes Noakes out of the courtroom and promptly hangs him with his own rope. He does delay the execution long enough to read four chapters of the Bible, selected at random, then tells Noakes, "There's few that would have took the pains with you that I have" (323).

Mark Twain's obvious admiration for Captain Blakely defuses any questions regarding the morality or appropriateness of the frontier justice administered by the "stalwart, warm-hearted, eagle-eyed veteran . . . a rough, honest creature, full of pluck and just as full of hard-headed sim-plicity, too" (318). Blakely's zealous, albeit primitive, administration of retributive justice, Spengemann writes, testifies to Mark Twain's "faith in the individual's ability to do right without recourse to legal codes" (21–22). Gibson argues that the positioning of the story in *Roughing It* is im-portant, because Mark Twain's sympathy for Blakely's actions and atti-tudes should be seen in the context of the author's exposé of " 'blood and carnage,' of murder condoned, and of the non-functioning jury law in the West" (51). Although the story of Ned Blakely takes place in the remote, anarchic Chincha Islands, its implications extend to the American West;

we are told at the story's conclusion that Blakely's actions make him greatly admired in California, which "had a population then that 'inflicted' justice after a fashion that was simplicity and primitiveness itself" (324).

Blakely's moral courage and sterling character, coupled with Noakes's obvious villainy and unequivocal guilt, mute serious moral questions. The story comes perilously close to a defense for lynching, though Mark Twain skirts that dilemma since Blakely does indeed consent to a trial and Noakes is convicted by a jury of his peers. Yet Blakely engineers the trial and is prepared to administer a hanging regardless of its outcome. The question is, in its simplest terms, whether civilized and constitutional safeguards of individual rights and human dignity should be allowed to take precedence over moral justice. Noakes deserves hanging; whether the interests of a civilized society are best served by the abrogation of due process that seems at times to thwart moral justice is more dubious. To Mark Twain, at least in this story, due process is a means not an end; justice is the end, and if the means interfere with that end, then they cease to be sacrosanct.

"Jim Blaine" is one of a series of episodes in which Mark Twain as character is the tenderfoot taken in by a peculiarly western brand of humor (Gerber 301; Rosen 191); it is, through the frame, a story of initiation as the "boys" introduce the unsuspecting but receptive outsider to the master storyteller Jim Blaine. Of course, the story is rich in local color, for Blaine's rambling monologue provides comic insight into the economic and social life of the Nevada mining community (Covici 58). Yet "Jim Blaine" delights primarily because of its intrinsic quality. If the object of *Roughing It* is, as Mark Twain claims, "rather to help the resting reader while away an hour than afflict him with metaphysics, or goad him with science" (*Roughing It*, ed. Rogers and Baender), then the "incomparably funny" "Jim Blaine" (Baldanza 45) is perhaps the author's supreme achievement.

Blaine, who sits "upon any empty powder-keg, with a clay pipe in one hand and the other raised to command silence," dominates the scene. There is little "point" to his tale; as Covici points out, "clause follows co-ordinate clause with the tacit assumption that no one particular fact is worth more than any other" (58). There is no rising action, no conflict, no resolution. Rosen, however, sees "a certain underlying logic" tying together Blaine's seemingly disparate anecdotes, for most of them play upon the theme of illusion and deception: the borrowed eye, leg, and hair of Miss Wagner; the feigned death of Robbins to cheat Jacobs out of money and coffin; "the illusory comfort of religion" assumed by Mrs. Wheeler as she provides a funeral and burial for the carpet into which her husband has been woven, or the mistaken notion held by those who believe missionaries "et up by the savages" had in fact converted them. All reinforce the per-vading theme of *Roughing It*, that truth is best perceived by a "skeptical state of mind" (192–93). If Blaine's narrative has no destination, the journey itself is replete with richly comic compensations in Blaine's unforgettable "cameos" (Baldanza 45). There is, for example, Miss Jefferson, a "poor old filly" who would loan her glass eye "to old Miss Wagner, that hadn't any, to receive company in":

> it warn't big enough, and when Miss Wagner warn't noticing, it would get twisted around in the socket, and look up, maybe, or out to one side, and every which way, while t'other one was looking as straight ahead as a spy-glass. . . . She tried packing it in raw cotton, but it wouldn't work, somehow—the cotton would get loose and stick out. . . . She was always dropping it out, and turning up her old deadlight on the company empty. . . . So somebody would have to hunch her and say, 'Your game eye has fetched loose, Miss Wagner, dear'—and then all of them would have to sit and wait till she jammed it in again—wrong side before, as a general thing, and green as a bird's egg. (345)

Smith complains that in such digressionary episodes Mark Twain lets the story get out of hand "by turning [it] into wild slapstick" (68). Indeed the account of Miss Wagner and her borrowed glass eye or the dispute between Robbins and Jacobs over an extravagant coffin is slapstick. But slapstick is the essence of "Jim Blaine," and nowhere in American fiction is it handled with more skill.

There are elements of slapstick in "Dick Baker" as well, but they are assimilated into what is finally an essentially nostalgic evocation of a vanished era. The description of the cat left sleeping "on the gunny-sack" while the miners dynamite quartz rock that had "got so hard that we had to put in a blast" is farcical: "In 'bout a minute we seen a puff of smoke bust up out of the hole, 'n' then everything let go with an awful crash, 'n' about four million tons of rocks 'n' dirt 'n' smoke 'n' splinters shot up 'bout a mile an' a half into the air, an' by George, right in the dead center of it was old Tom Quartz a-goin' end over end, an' a-snorting' an' a-sneezin', an' a-clawin' an' a-reachin' for things like all possessed" (392). It is no wonder that, "al blacked up with powder an' smoke, an' all sloppy with mud 'n' slush f'm one end to the other," Tom Quartz becomes "prejudiced agin quartz-mining" and develops "his sagacity." Dick Baker's telling of the adventure and fond memories of the cat with which the slapstick account is framed subsume the farce, however. Mark Twain is left with the lasting impression not of the hyperbolic tale itself but of "the affection and the pride that lit up Baker's face when he delivered this tribute to the firmness of his humble friend of other days" (393).

Bibliography

PRIMARY

The Choice Humorous Works of Mark Twain. London: John Camden Hotten, 1873.

The Choice Humorous Works of Mark Twain. London: Chatto & Windus, 1877.

The Complete Short Stories of Mark Twain. Now Collected for the First Time. Edited by Charles Neider. Garden City, N.Y.: Hanover House, 1957.

Great Short Works of Mark Twain. Edited by Justin Kaplan. New York: Harper & Row, 1967.

"Mark's Letters to San Francisco *Call.*" Edited by A. E. Hutcheson. *Twainian* (March-April 1952): 4 and (May-June 1952):1.

Mark Twain in Eruption: Hitherto Unpublished Pages about Men and Events. Edited by Bernard DeVoto. New York: Harper & Brothers, 1940.

Mark Twain's Library of Humor. New York: Charles L. Webster, 1888.

Mark Twain's Library of Humor: The Primrose Way. New York: Harper & Brothers, 1906.

Mark Twain of the Enterprise: Newspaper Articles & Other Documents, 1862–1864. Edited by Henry Nash Smith. Berkeley and Los Angeles: University of California Press, 1957.

The Pattern of Mark Twain's 'Roughing It.' Edited by Franklin R. Rogers. Berkeley and Los Angeles: University of California Press, 1961.

Roughing It. Hartford and Chicago: American Publishing Co., 1872.

*Roughing It. Edited by Franklin R. Rogers and Paul Baender. Berkeley and Los Angeles: University of California Press, 1972.

Selections from American Humor. Leipzig, Germany: Tauchautz, 1888.

The Works of Mark Twain: Early Tales & Sketches. Vol. 2 (1864–1865). Edited by Edgar M. Branch and Robert H. Hirst. Vol. 15 of the Iowa-California edition of *The Works of Mark Twain.* Berkeley and Los Angeles: University of California Press, 1981.

SECONDARY

Baldanza, Frank. *Mark Twain: An Introduction and Interpretation.* New York: Holt, Rinehart & Winston, 1961.

Baldwin, David. "Humor in Mark Twain's 'Buck Fanshaw's Funeral.' " *Mark Twain Journal* 20, no. 2 (Summer 1981):16–18.

Beidler, Philip D. "Realistic Style and the Problem of Context in *The Innocents Abroad* and *Roughing It.*" *American Literature* 52 (1980–81):33–49.

Bellamy, Gladys C. *Mark Twain as Literary Artist.* Norman: University of Oklahoma Press, 1950.

Benson, Ivan. *Mark Twain's Western Years.* New York: Russell & Russell, 1966.

Budd, Louis J. *Mark Twain: Social Philosopher.* Bloomington: Indiana University Press, 1962.

Covici, Pascal, Jr. *Mark Twain's Humor: The Image of a World*. Dallas: Southern Methodist University Press, 1962.

Emerson, Everett. *The Authentic Mark Twain: A Literary Biography of Samuel L. Clemens*. Philadelphia: University of Pennsylvania Press, 1984.

Fatout, Paul. *Mark Twain in Virginia City*. Bloomington: Indiana University Press, 1964.

Feinstein, George. "Mark Twain's Idea of Story Structure." *American Literature* 18 (1946):160–63.

Fender, Stephen. " 'The Prodigal in a Far Country Chawing of Husks': Mark Twain's Search for a Style in the West." *Modern Language Review* 71 (1976):737–56.

Geismar, Maxwell. *Mark Twain: An American Prophet*. Boston: Houghton Mifflin, 1970.

Gerber, John C. "Mark Twain's Use of the Comic Pose." *PMLA* 77 (June 1962):297–304.

Gibson, William M. *The Art of Mark Twain*. New York: Oxford University Press, 1976.

Hill, Hamlin. *Mark Twain and Elisha Bliss*. Columbia: University of Missouri Press, 1964.

Hollenbach, John W. "Mark Twain, Story-Teller, at Work." *College English* 7 (March 1946):303–12.

Lynn, Kenneth. *Mark Twain and Southwestern Humor*. Boston: Little, Brown, 1959.

Mack, Effie Mona. *Mark Twain in Nevada*. New York: Scribner's, 1947.

Paine, Albert B. *Mark Twain: A Biography*. Vols. 1 and 2. New York: Harper & Brothers, 1912.

Rachal, John. "Scotty Briggs and the Minister: An Idea from Hooper's Simon Suggs?" *Mark Twain Journal* 17, no. 2 (Summer 1974):10–11.

Rogers, Franklin R. *Mark Twain's Burlesque Patterns*. Dallas: Southern Methodist University Press, 1960.

Rosen, Robert C. "Mark Twain's Jim Blaine and His Grandfather's Ram." *College Literature* 11 (Spring 1984):191–94.

Smith, Henry Nash. *Mark Twain: The Development of a Writer*. Cambridge, Mass.: Harvard University Press, 1962.

Spengemann, William C. *Mark Twain and the Backwoods Angel: The Matter of Innocence in the Works of Samuel L. Clemens*. Kent, Ohio: Kent State University Press, 1966.

Towers, Tom T. " 'Hateful Reality': The Failure of the Territory in *Roughing It*." *Western American Literature* 9 (1974):3–15.

21

The Five Boons of Life
A Fable
Little Bessie

Publication History

"The Five Boons of Life" appeared first in the December 1902 issue of *Harper's Magazine*, and was subsequently collected in book form in 1906. "A Fable" was published in *Harper's Magazine*, December 1909, then reprinted in the 1922 *Mysterious Stranger* volume.

"Little Bessie" is a series of dialogues, written in 1908–9 but unpublished in Mark Twain's lifetime because the author considered the satire too offensive for genteel tastes. The major part of chapter 1, "Little Bessie Would Assist Providence," was published in the appendix to Albert B. Paine's 1912 biography of Mark Twain. The entire piece, which includes six chapters, was not published until 1972 in *Mark Twain's Fables of Man*. Because Mark Twain apparently had not designated the ordering of chapters, editor John Tuckey arranged them "to provide the most logical literary progression" (33).

Circumstances of Composition, Sources, and Influences

"The Five Boons of Life" was written probably in the early spring 1902, while Mark Twain was living in New York, before his move to York Harbor, Maine, for the summer. At the time the author was greatly concerned with Olivia's failing health (she was to suffer a devastating attack in August), Jean's frequent bouts with epilepsy, Clara's romance with a young European pianist Ossip Gabrilowitsch, and problems disposing the Hartford, Connecticut, house, which, Hill reports, "was becoming a domestic albatross" (44). During this period, Joe Twichell revealed, Mark Twain "was ever profoundly affected with the feeling of the pathos of life. Contemplating its heritage of inevitable pain and tears, he would question if to any one it was a good gift" (*Mark Twain's Fables*, ed. Tuckey, 133).

Mark Twain's thoughts throughout 1902 drifted to the subject of death, occasioned in part, no doubt, by memories of his daughter Susy, almost daily confrontations with family illnesses, and his own advancing years. In June he traveled to Missouri to receive an honorary degree from the university at Columbia, and from there made a five-day excursion to Hannibal—his last visit to his boyhood home. Memories led him to rekindle a project he had first planned in an 1891 notebook entry: a reunion of Tom and Huck at age sixty, after "life has been a failure, all that was lovable, all that was beautiful is under the mound. They die together" (*Mark Twain's Hannibal* 17–18). He wrote some thirty-eight thousand words of this "final Huck Finn book," only to destroy the unfinished manuscript (Emerson 242–43; Hill 43). Later that summer, death becomes the subject of "Was It Heaven? or Hell?" Baetzhold reports that in his treatment of death in "The Five Boons of Life," Mark Twain drew heavily on W. E. H. Lecky's *History of European Morals* (1869), especially the discussion of the Stoic attitude toward death as "the end of all sorrow . . . the last and best boon of nature" (363, n. 13).

Mark Twain wrote "A Fable" in early June 1906 while living in Dublin, New Hampshire, for the summer. The preceding eighteen months Mark Twain had spent writing short pieces—usually letters—for magazines such as *Harper's;* extended, fragmentary fiction such as "Three Thousand Years among the Microbes," "No. 44, the Mysterious Stranger," "Eve's Diary"; or controversial philosophical essays like "As Concerns Interpreting the Deity." Emerson points out that the work of this period following Olivia's death reveals Mark Twain's vacillation of mood: at times he assumes the pose of detached "philosophical observer"; at other times he is a man "haunted by the past," the artist who attempts "to make sense out of life and to render his vision in an apt and extended fiction" (255). It is a time of pensive recollection and philosophical speculation and, as artist, Mark Twain became much more concerned with expressing or exploring an idea than in mastering literary form. In early 1906, spurred by his association with Albert Paine, Mark Twain focused his attention on his autobiography, giving blocks of time each day to long autobiographical dictations. In that work his interest lay primarily in assessing the significance of events in his life—chronology or exactitude of detail mattered little. As Paine points out, "these marvellous reminiscences bore only an atmospheric relation to history" (3:1268). In June his dictations turned to his reflections on religion, which, he wrote to William Dean Howells, "will get my heirs & assigns burnt alive" if published "this side of 2006 A.D." (Emerson 255–64). "A Fable," written at the same time, continues in this vein of philosophical speculation. It is, Hill argues, "a brief anecdote on the subjective nature of reality" (136).

Mark Twain began "Little Bessie" in early 1908, while on a yachting trip off the coast of Bermuda with his good friend and financial adviser, Henry H. Rogers. Apparently relaxed and in good spirits, he began the series of dialogues in a jocular mood. On the cover sheet of the typescript dated 22 February 1908 Mark Twain penned in ink, "It is dull, & I need wholesome excitement & distractions; so I will go lightly excursioning along the primrose path of theology" (*Mark Twain's Fables* 8). Mark Twain seemed to have written "Little Bessie" for his own amusement, never intending to publish the dialogues for fear his audience would consider them blasphemous. He returned to the story in the summer of 1909, while in residence at Stormfield (Long 253). At the same time he was arranging for the publication of "Captain Stormfield's Visit to Heaven," and met with Paine to discuss plans to complete *The Mysterious Stranger* (1916) (Emerson 269). In October of the same year he began "Letters from the Earth"— a series of thirteen letters, some seventeen thousand words of which were written in October or later but not published until 1962 (Emerson 269).

Mark Twain's decision to focus the story on the penetrating questions of an innocent young girl perhaps arose from his experiences with the "Angel Fish" club he established about the same time he started work on "Bessie." Stone argues that the club—a group of preteen adoring girls who gathered around the aging author to hear his stories—suggests that "his attachment to childhood and his special fondness for young maidens survived even the onslaught of his rage against the cosmos" (231). It is not difficult to imagine Mark Twain behind the Mr. Hollister of "Little Bessie," the adult friend who in reported conversation with the innocent girl fuels her irreverent speculations and thereby antagonizes the frustrated mother: "I wish that tiresome Hollister was in H——amburg! He is an ignorant, unreasoning, illogical ass, and I have told you over and over again to keep out of his poisonous company" (41). Echoing Philip Traum, that notorious corrupter of youth in *The Mysterious Stranger,* Hollister tells Bessie that "God is a murderer. . . . God can't make one moral law for man and another for Himself." Later Little Bessie reports that Hollister pointed out to her that "there never was a god yet that wasn't born of a Virgin . . . no virgin is safe where a god is. He says he wishes he was a god; he says he would make virgins so scarce that—" (44). Through the role of Hollister, Mark Twain in "Little Bessie" represents what Stone calls "the other side of his mind from the Angel Fish Club—the side that admired Jonathan Swift, wrote Colonel Sherburn's speech and *What Is Man?*, and created Philip Traum" (260).

Relationship to Other Mark Twain Works

"The Five Boons of Life" and "A Fable" are among several fables Mark Twain attempted in the early years of the twentieth century. Most of this writing was done for his own amusement, and much of it is fragmentary; virtually all of it is pessimistic, even bitter. The fable form accorded well with Mark Twain's determination in his later years to turn his attention to serious questions of profound moral, political, or spiritual import; as Tuckey writes, in these fables Mark Twain could "let his imagination rove freely over events that he saw as representative or symbolic of the nature and condition of man, past, present, or yet to be" (*Mark Twain's Fables* 3). Fragments from the period that are similar in form or tone to "The Five Boons of Life" include "The Bees," the Eddypus manuscripts, and "The Victims." The latter, also written in 1902 but not published until 1972 in *Mark Twain's Fables,* posits the true hierarchy of existence as the order of precedence in a universal cannibalism (Emerson 242). Similarly pessimistic is a fragmentary dialogue between the Master of the Universe and a mysterious stranger, entitled "If I Could Be There" (Paine 3:1162).

Of course Mark Twain also wrote a number of sentimental pieces about death—most notably "The Death Disk" (1901) and "The Californian's Tale" (1893). Fables such as "The Five Boons of Life," however, differ radically from these melodramatic stories that offer a more or less conventional climax that involves an escape from the implications or fact of death; as Bellamy notes, here death is a reprieve from life's agony—a treasured gift (370).

As a story about and involving animals with human characteristics, "A Fable" recalls "Jim Baker's Blue Jay Yarn" (1880). Gibson sees a strong thematic parallel between the two as well: both are concerned with the aesthetic problem of perspective. The owl and the jays in Baker's yarn see reality from radically different points of view. What is funny to the western jays fails to amuse the owl from Nova Scotia (71). The cat's "moral" in "A Fable" makes a similar point: "You can find in a text whatever you bring, if you stand between it and the mirror of your imagination" (599).

"Little Bessie" afforded Mark Twain an opportunity "to devise moral ideas," as he called them (Long 253), that became a recurring refrain in essays, stories, fables, and fragments written during the last decade of his life. The "moral ideas" take the form of satiric and often bitter attacks on conventional theological assumptions and hypocritical Christian practices. Like "Letters from the Earth"—written primarily in October 1909—and the *Mysterious Stranger* fragments, "Little Bessie" reflects the thinking "of a village agnostic grown old and bitter" (Stone 231).

In a June 1906 autobiographical dictation Mark Twain articulated the concept of Deity that governs the bulk of his later writings. It is, however, a theologically confused—even contradictory—concept born in bitterness and despair. On the one hand, God surfaces as a cold, aloof, impersonal force, unconcerned with human affairs, who simply sets the universe in motion according to unalterable natural law. On the other hand, he is a malicious "thug" who consciously and sadistically contrives unending miseries to plague powerless humans. According to both interpretations, God is unavailing, either because he is remote and indifferent or because he mettles maliciously to persecute (*Mark Twain's Fables* 4).

Such theological conceptions underlie "Little Bessie" as well as *The Mysterious Stranger* and "Letters from the Earth"—all considered by Mark Twain too potently satirical for publication in his lifetime. Tuckey points out that these themes are common to many of the unpublished fables and fragments he collects in his 1972 volume: "The Emperor-God Satire" stresses the absurdity of assuming that an aloof God is intimately involved with human affairs; "The Holy Children" and "The Second Advent," like "The Chronicle of Young Satan" and "The War Prayer," suggest that even if God were to be responsive to prayer, "his intervention would be catastrophic for human society"; and "In My Bitterness" and "The Synod of Praise"—like "Little Bessie"—directly indict God for his malevolence (4).

"Little Bessie" is among Mark Twain's many pieces that effectively use children as vehicles for social and religious satire. The little girl's innocent but pointed questions, prompted by the agnostic Hollister, expose the absurdity of her mother's conventional religious platitudes. Tuckey points out that this technique is a direct inversion of the device Mark Twain had used much earlier in "The Story of Mamie Grant, the Child Missionary" (written 1868) in which it is the child who defends and promotes Sunday school sentiments to a blasphemous adult who dares to question them (5). Both techniques are typical of Mark Twain's use of children: at times they are sentimental defenders of the faith whose courage, steadfast determination, and allegiance to principle serve as a rebuke to wavering or corrupted adults (e.g., Mamie Grant, Cathy Alison, or Joan of Arc); at other times their innocent skepticism and natural common sense pierce through adult sentimental nonsense and hypocrisy (e.g., Bessie, Huck Finn, or Theodor Fischer). Stone offers the fullest discussion of Mark Twain's use of childhood naiveté as fictional device. Among later works, "Little Bessie" like *The Mysterious Stranger* offers a radically different use of the child than does the maudlin "A Horse's Tale" (1906); but seen in the perspective of "a literary lifetime spent exploring childhood," Stone contends, "It was as natural for Mark Twain to imagine an improbable three-year-old like Bessie and to fill her mouth with amusing blasphemies as it was for him to create Cathy Alison, the *fin-de-siècle* cross between Joan of Arc and Elsie Dinsmore" (260–61).

Critical Studies

As both Paine (3:1162) and Gibson (95–96) point out, "The Five Boons of Life" assumes the form of the fairy tale. Compact, humorless, and never maudlin, the story relates an encounter between the good fairy and a youth. The fairy offers the impetuous young man his choice of five gifts in her basket—Fame, Love, Riches, Pleasure, Death—but cautions him to choose wisely, "for only one of them is valuable" (470).

Each of the first four sections of the story treats the youth's disillusionment with the gifts that in his vanity and ignorance he deems valuable. "There is no need to consider," he blithely responds initially, selecting first "the pleasures that youth delights in." After three "wasted" years exhausting pleasures that prove "short-lived and disappointing, vain and empty," the youth turns to love. This gift too disappoints, and after many years watching his loved ones pass from him, the now sobered man curses love from his "heart of hearts." Fame and wealth follow: the former, however, brings first "envy; then detraction; then calumny; then hate; then persecution. Then derision. . . . And last of all came pity, which is the funeral of fame" (471); the latter, because of his resolution to "spend, squander, dazzle," results in poverty. Through a lifetime of suffering at the hands of "gifts" he selected, the hero has learned a painful lesson: "They are not gifts, but merely lendings. Pleasure, Love, Fame, Riches: they are but temporary disguises for lasting realities: Pain, Grief, Shame, Poverty" (471).

This discovery throws into clear relief the value of the one gift he had persistently ignored, "that clear and sweet and kindly one, that steeps in dreamless and enduring sleep the pains that persecute the body, and the shames and griefs that eat the mind and heart" (471). But death is no longer available; the fairy has given it to a child who "trusted me, asking me to choose for it." The unfortunate hero is left, finally, with "what not even you have deserved: the wanton insult of old Age" (472).

The story is noteworthy for its controlled economy, restraint, and poetic expression of what is a classic sentiment—qualities lacking in the fragments from the period that lapse into bitter diatribes and uncontrolled expressions of personal frustration. Gibson contends that the story speaks for Mark Twain himself, a man who had known pleasure, wealth, fame, and love only to come to the realization in bitter old age that death is the most precious gift of all (95—96).

"A Fable" concerns itself with the question of aesthetic perception. Beginning with the fairy-tale opening "Once upon a time," it tells of an artist who after having "painted a small and very beautiful picture" places his work in front of a mirror (597). Viewing the art work through its reflection in the mirror, he thinks, "doubles the distance and softens it, and it is twice as lovely as it was before" (597). The "refined and civilized" housecat, who is "greatly admired" by the other animals of the forest because he "could tell so much which they didn't know before, and were not certain about afterward" (597), admires the artist's aesthetic effect and reports the phenomenon to the other animals. They, however, are puzzled and suspicious. Led by the jackass, they decide to see things for themselves. The problem is that the jackass does not know where to stand when looking in the mirror, and positions himself between the art work and the mirror: "the result was that the picture had no chance and didn't show up" (598). What the jackass sees in the mirror, of course, is his own reflection: "It was a handsome ass, and friendly," he reports to his colleagues, "but just an ass, and nothing more" (598). Then follow the bear, the tiger, the lion, the camel, and the elephant. Each positions himself between the picture and the mirror and as a result reports finding nothing but a reflection of its own image. The lesson of the tale, as the cat summarizes, is that "if you stand between it and the mirror of your imagination, you will find in a text whatever you bring. You may not see your ears, but they will be there" (599).

In the only published study of this story, Prince argues that "A Fable" satirizes traditional teaching methods, blasts "the age-old concept that a teacher's function is to interpret his subject in order to make it understandable for his students" (7). True learning, Prince argues, results from independent thinking and problem solving. But the fable has less to do with education than with art or literary criticism. Mark Twain calls into question any critical methodology that takes emphasis from the text and places it upon the perceiver or critic. None of the animals, save the cat, sees the "text," which is totally blocked from view by the intrusive presences of the various "critics" who see only their narcissistic reflection. Communication among them, or literary criticism, is futile—indeed impossible—because no two are talking about the same aesthetic experience. It is difficult to resist the temptation to draw analogies to contemporary, fashionable, literary theory, but I will.

Although Emerson contends that "Little Bessie" is "one of Mark Twain's best short pieces of his last years" (267), it has received very little critical attention—no doubt because the major portion of it remained unpublished until 1972. Stone, considering only the chapter published in the appendix to Paine's biography, labels the piece a fragment, "simply random jottings in conversational form" (260). The six chapters published in the Tuckey edition, however, form a coherent fiction with a unified theme and sufficient aesthetic integrity to qualify as a short story.

The opening of the first chapter introduces us to the precocious Bessie, "a good child, and not shallow, not frivolous, but meditative and thoughtful, and much given to thinking out the reasons of things and trying to make them harmonize with results," and presents the first in a series of dialogues between the girl and her mother: "Mamma, why is there so much pain and sorrow and suffering? What is it all for?" (34). Conflict arises in the story from the mother's inability to formulate cogent and plausible answers to her child's searching questions, which, touching upon such subjects as God's justice, the virgin birth, and the Trinity, frustrate conventional homiletic responses. A period of perhaps six months elapses in the course of the dialogues: the child is "nearly three years old" at the outset, "three and a half years old" at the end. The conclusion of the sixth chapter has a quality of closure that undercuts assumptions that "Little Bessie" is fragmentary. Totally frustrated, the mother dismisses Bessie with the admonition, "There, now, go along with you, and don't come near me again until you can interest yourself in some subject of a lower grade and less awful than theology"—to which the little girl innocently replies, "Mr. Hollister says there *ain't* any" (44).

It is, as Emerson points out, Bessie's "charming naiveté" that makes this story amusing (267), particularly in the discussions of virgin birth that fill out the last three chapters. Although Bessie employs scholastic logic to weave tight arguments her mother cannot refute, the presence of Mr. Hollister in the background, whose wry sarcasm and wit Bessie recounts to her mother, serves to make the child believable enough—at least for purposes of the fiction. The technique of filtering his pointed blasphemies through the child softens the harsh tone characteristic of other theological writing such as *The Mysterious Stranger* and *What Is Man?* (1906), and makes "Little Bessie" amusing and entertaining without blunting its serious thematic implications.

Bibliography

PRIMARY

The Complete Short Stories of Mark Twain. Now Collected for the First Time. Edited by Charles Neider. Garden City, N.Y.: Hanover House, 1957. ["The Five Boons of Life"; "A Fable."]

Mark Twain's Fables of Man. Edited by John C. Tuckey. Berkeley and Los Angeles: University of California Press, 1972. ["Little Bessie."]

Mark Twain's Hannibal, Huck & Tom. Edited by Walter Blair. Berkeley and Los Angeles: University of California Press, 1969.

The Mysterious Stranger and Other Stories. New York: Harper & Brothers, 1922.

The $30,000 Bequest and Other Stories. New York: Harper & Brothers, 1906.

SECONDARY

Baetzhold, Howard G. *Mark Twain and John Bull: The British Connection*. Bloomington: Indiana University Press, 1970.

Bellamy, Gladys C. *Mark Twain as a Literary Artist*. Norman: University of Oklahoma Press, 1950.

Emerson, Everett. *The Authentic Mark Twain: A Literary Biography of Samuel L. Clemens.* Philadelphia: University of Pennsylvania Press, 1984.

Gibson, William M. *The Art of Mark Twain.* New York: Oxford University Press, 1976.

Hill, Hamlin. *Mark Twain: God's Fool.* New York: Harper & Row, 1973.

Long, E. Hudson. *Mark Twain Handbook.* New York: Hendricks House, 1957.

Paine, Albert B. *Mark Twain: A Biography.* Vols. 3 and 4. New York: Harper & Brothers, 1912.

Prince, Gilbert. "Mark Twain's 'A Fable': The Teacher as Jackass." *Mark Twain Journal* 17, no. 4 (Winter 1974):7–8.

Stone, Albert E., Jr. *The Innocent Eye: Childhood in Mark Twain's Imagination.* New Haven: Yale University Press, 1961.

22

The Great Revolution in Pitcairn

Publication History

"The Great Revolution in Pitcairn" was written initially as a chapter for *A Tramp Abroad* (1880), but Mark Twain deleted the story from the book manuscript and published it instead in the March 1879 issue of the *Atlantic Monthly* (DeVoto 183; Baetzhold 44). The story is included in the 1882 *Stolen White Elephant* volume, and it is reprinted in the *Tom Sawyer Abroad* collection (1896).

Circumstances of Composition, Sources, and Influences

Mark Twain wrote "The Great Revolution in Pitcairn" in 1878, in the midst of a period (1876–79) marked by what Emerson calls "the strange disappearance of Mark Twain" (143). The beginnings of *Huckleberry Finn* (1885) lay gathering dust while Mark Twain devoted his attention to *A Tramp Abroad* and *The Prince and the Pauper* (1882), two books quite different from the earlier *Innocents Abroad* (1869) and *Roughing It* (1872) in that they abandon the characteristic western perspective that had earned his reputation. Mark Twain's humiliating "flop" at the 17 December 1877 Whittier birthday dinner, Emerson argues, triggered the author's "strange disappearance," for it emphasized his impossible professional dilemma and left him in many ways aesthetically paralyzed: "His very profitable career as a writer and as a lecturer had been founded on the literary personality he had created, and on that success he had built a life, complete with family, servants, an elegant home in a cultured New England city"; but that same literary personality caused him considerable personal embarrassment and, he feared, ostracized him from the eastern literary establishment to which he so desperately wanted to belong. "He would not or could not speak in the voice that had so humiliated him" (149–50).

DeVoto argues that despite professional uncertainties the mid to late 1870s was "the happiest period" of Mark Twain's personal life, for he enjoyed prosperity, fame, and domestic tranquility (56). He sought to bring his fiction in line with his aspirations to eastern respectability, to force his writing within the tight confines of genteel life; in short, he sought to bury

Mark Twain by severing the ties to his audacious past. The audience Mark Twain wanted to please was the conservative, upper middle-class readership of Howells's *Atlantic Monthly,* "the only audience that I sit down before in perfect serenity," Mark Twain wrote to Howells in December 1874, because it does not "require a 'humorist' to paint himself striped & stand on his head every fifteen minutes" (*Mark Twain-Howells Letters* 49).

The results of Mark Twain's conscious campaign for respectability are undistinguished. His two books *A Tramp Abroad* and *The Prince and the Pauper,* DeVoto writes, "are mediocre and nothing else written in the period rises so high." For the most part he wrote tame burlesques during this time—the unpublished "Simon Wheeler, Detective," "The Loves of Alonzo Fitz Clarence and Rosannah Ethelton" (1878), "The Stolen White Elephant" (1882), "Mrs. McWilliams and the Lightning" (1882)—that "are mostly painful reading now." Aesthetically, Mark Twain seemed to be drifting, "writing pleasurably but aimlessly, making money, enjoying life—and laying up trouble" (56).

The subject of "The Great Revolution in Pitcairn" is more serious than that characteristic of his light burlesques of the period and reveals, Baetzhold contends, "how deeply ingrained certain of its author's pessimistic attitudes had become during the late 1870's" (45). Written in Europe, while Mark Twain was still smarting from the Whittier dinner fiasco, "The Great Revolution in Pitcairn" reflects the author's 1876–77 reading of Carlyle, whose account of the French Revolution had established Mark Twain's "scorn for revolutionary mobs." The Missouri writer who had come to be identified with the western democratic spirit in America felt contempt for the ignorance and political incapacity of the masses. In a chapter intended for *A Tramp Abroad* but later omitted, he denounced "the awful curse of an unrestricted suffrage," and influenced by Carlyle, he emended the famous motto of the 1789 Revolution in a 21 March 1879 notebook entry: "Liberty (to rob . . . burn and butcher)—Equality (in bestiality)—Fraternity (of Devils)" (Baetzhold 42).

Relationship to Other Mark Twain Works

The story looks back to "The Curious Republic of Gondour," a utopian essay published anonymously at Mark Twain's request in the October 1875 *Atlantic.* In this essay Mark Twain denounced universal suffrage, which "had seemed to deliver all power into the hands of the ignorant and non-taxpaying classes." He offers for his readers' consideration the example of Gondour, a community that allocates votes on the basis of wealth and education; because learning is "more prevalent and more easily acquired than riches, educated men became a wholesome check upon wealthy men, since they could outvote them."

"The Great Revolution in Pitcairn" is no utopian fantasy, however. Rather, this "history of civilization in miniature" (Blair 184) focuses on the conditions that allow the tyrant to rise to power and bend the people's will to serve his own ends. It is, Baetzhold writes, "a condemnation of hypocritical piety and meanness of motive on the part of the mass of mankind which allows tyranny to prevail" (45). Scholars, therefore, have approached this story as an anticipation of *A Connecticut Yankee* (1889). Bellamy in particular notes the parallels between Butterworth Stavely and Hank Morgan: both are American Yankees who disrupt a simple, arcadian world with their technological improvements and in the process solidify their control; both eventually fall victim to a popular insurrection, and end by denouncing the masses in "Hitleresque oratory" for their "ingratitude" (315). Blair (183–84) and Baetzhold (44–45) see in this 1879 story the seeds of the pessimism that will control "The Man That Corrupted Hadleyburg" (1899) and *The Mysterious Stranger* (1916).

Critical Studies

"The Great Revolution in Pitcairn" is a tale of an American's rise to power in a remote South Sea island republic and his subsequent demise as a result of a popular insurrection. Pitcairn Island is a small community of farmers and fishermen whose "sole recreation" is religious devotion. Led by the reformed mutineer and homicide John Adams, the community had become "the purest and devoutest in Christendom." Its people "lived in a deep Sabbath tranquility, far from the world and its ambitions and vexations, and neither knowing nor caring what was going on in the mighty empires that lie beyond their limitless ocean solitudes" (191). Their innocence and ignorance make the inhabitants ripe for exploitation by the newly arrived American, Butterworth Stavely—"a doubtful acquisition" (193) to Pitcairn, which was at the time "an appanage of the British crown." Stavely works quickly "to ingratiate himself . . . by all the arts he could command": he sows "seeds of discontent," plots "to subvert the government," hatches a "coup d'état"—after explaining to the people what one was— and proclaims himself Emperor Butterworth I. Stavely institutes reforms that disrupt the simple, arcadian life on Pitcairn. Appealing to Italy and Germany as his models, he moves toward "Unification," builds an Army— taking "all the boys above the age of ten years away from their mothers" (201)—institutes class structure, introduces paper currency, and establishes taxes to fund his "improvements." Initially the islanders follow their demagogue like blind sheep, but eventually his outrages are more than their self-respect can bear and they overthrow him and once again hoist the British flag.

Mark Twain's satire takes aim in two directions. The first target is the American imperialist Stavely, who is, as Bellamy points out, "a palpable villain from the start" (315). Covici argues that through Stavely Mark Twain attacks the accoutrements of modern science and technology, for the American's "notion of progress is ridiculous, materialistic, and degrading"; Mark Twain "has nothing good to say about modern civilization's aims and proclivities" (93). The problem, however, lies not in the intrinsic quality of modern technology but in the absurdly inappropriate application of it to a rudimentary arcadian culture where it obviously has no place. Through Stavely, Mark Twain shatters the imperialist dream of imposing the framework of modern, Western culture in primitive, non-Western communities for the dubious purpose of securing power and influence.

The second target of Mark Twain's satire is the condition of ignorance that allows Stavely to rise to power in the first place. Baetzhold (45) and Blair (184) both see this as the central theme of Mark Twain's story. In its revelation of human vanity, gullibility, superstition, and moral cowardice, the story touches on more universal themes that reveal what Budd calls Mark Twain's "darkest musings" (64). Like those of medieval England (*Connecticut Yankee*), Dawson's Landing (*Pudd'nhead Wilson* [1894]), Hadleyburg, or Eseldorf (*Mysterious Stranger*), the citizens of Pitcairn are ripe for exploitation by a sophisticated stranger who manipulates them to serve his own ends. Stavely is Satan in Eden; he is, admittedly, the "palpable villain," but like Adam and Eve, the islanders are programmed by nature to be victims of his dangerous play.

Bibliography

PRIMARY

Mark Twain-Howells Letters: The Correspondence of Samuel L. Clemens and William D. Howells, 1872–1910. Edited by Henry Nash Smith and William M. Gibson. Vol. 1. Cambridge, Mass.: Harvard University Press, 1960.

The Stolen White Elephant Etc. By Mark Twain. Boston: James R. Osgood, 1882.

Tom Sawyer Abroad, Tom Sawyer, Detective and Other Stories Etc., Etc. By Mark Twain. New York: Harper & Brothers, 1896.

SECONDARY

Baetzhold, Howard G. *Mark Twain & John Bull: The British Connection.* Bloomington: Indiana University Press, 1970.

Bellamy, Gladys C. *Mark Twain as a Literary Artist.* Norman: University of Oklahoma Press, 1950.

Blair, Walter. *Mark Twain & Huck Finn*. Berkeley and Los Angeles: University of California Press, 1960.

Budd, Louis J. *Mark Twain: Social Philosopher*. Bloomington: Indiana University Press, 1962.

Covici, Pascal, Jr. *Mark Twain's Humor: The Image of a World*. Dallas: Southern Methodist University Press, 1962.

DeVoto, Bernard. *Mark Twain at Work*. Cambridge, Mass.: Harvard University Press, 1942.

Emerson, Everett. "The Strange Disappearance of Mark Twain." *Studies in American Fiction* 13 (Autumn 1985):143–55.

23

The Invalid's Story

Publication History

"The Invalid's Story," sometimes referred to as "The Limburger Cheese Story," was first published as a three-thousand-word addition to "Some Rambling Notes of an Idle Excursion" in the 1882 *Stolen White Elephant* volume (Brownell 2). It remained part of the excursion narrative in *Merry Tales* (1892). In its 1896 collected edition of Mark Twain's works, however, Harper and Brothers separated the two, printing "The Invalid's Story" and "Some Rambling Notes of an Idle Excursion" in different volumes. Subsequent editions sustained this separation, reprinting "The Invalid's Story" without indication of its original context (Horowitz 38–39). The Neider edition of *The Complete Short Stories* is based on the thirty-seven volume Stormfield edition (Harper and Brothers, 1922–29).

Circumstances of Composition, Sources, and Influences

"Some Rambling Notes of an Idle Excursion," a fictionalized account of Mark Twain's travel to Bermuda with Joe Twichell in May 1877, was originally published as a four-part serial in the *Atlantic Monthly* beginning October 1877, and in book form, *An Idle Excursion and Other Papers*, by London publishers Chatto and Windus in 1878. A study of the manuscript paper and ink suggests that "The Invalid's Story" was written in the late 1870s, probably 1877; Emerson contends that Mark Twain heard the story from Twichell during their Bermuda travels (103). The scholarly assumption, supported by Mark Twain-Howells correspondence, is that it was intended to be part of "An Idle Excursion" but was excised because William Dean Howells thought the piece to be indelicate (Horowitz 37–38). Manuscript evidence further indicates that Mark Twain had requested the story be inserted "at page 90" of *Punch, Brothers, Punch!* (1878), and later intended to include it as a separate chapter in *A Tramp Abroad* (1880); in both instances, however, the story was deleted prior to publication, again probably as a result of Howells's objections (Brownell 2; Hill 143–44; DeVoto 252) Evidently Mark Twain liked the story and was anxious to have it published; at the same time, it is equally evident that he valued highly the critical judgment of his good friend Howells, whose achievements as editor and author had made him for Mark Twain a representative of the genteel literary tastes and standards the western author believed he must satisfy.

DeVoto (252–53) and Blair (242) report that "The Invalid's Story" may have been based on an antebellum sketch by the southwestern humorist J. M. Field, "A Resurrectionist and His Freight." Field's sketch appeared in the Saint Louis *Reveille* (9 March 1846), was reprinted in *The Spirit of the Times* (21 March 1846), and appeared in books of 1847 and 1858. A similar story is printed in the 13 July 1865 issue of the Carson, Nevada, *Daily Appeal*. A more likely source is Artemus Ward, who included a variant of the story as part of his lecture program sometime between 1862 and 1864. Austin conjectures that Mark Twain heard Ward tell it during the "Babes in the Wood" lectures Mark Twain attended in Virginia City, Nevada, in December 1863, and that Ward's oral rendition was "evidently the 'germ' of Twain's" story written some fourteen years later (70–71).

Austin compares "The Invalid's Story" with a printed reconstruction of Ward's oral anecdote published by James F. Ryder in *Voigtlander and I* (1902). Such comparison reveals not only the generic differences between Yankee and southwestern humor but also Mark Twain's method of developing a story from scant source materials. Ward's anecdote, genteel in comparison to Mark Twain's lurid story, is a brief straightforward narrative with no dialogue until the climax; everything moves rapidly to a punch line that becomes justification for the whole tale. The prominent punch line of Ward's joke becomes merely a minor detail in Mark Twain's story, which is built on comic exaggeration. "The Invalid's Story" is much more substantially developed fiction than is the Ward source: additional plot details, extensive characterizing dialogue, and lurid, explicit description of odors push the story to over twenty-six hundred words; moreover, first-person point of view and substantial development of both the railway passenger, who serves as narrator, and Thompson the baggageman provide aesthetic interest and complexity to a story that makes a shambles of genteel sentimentality about death (Austin 70–73).

The Gothic fiction of Edgar Allan Poe, specifically "A Descent into the Maelstrom," is offered by Kemper as an influence on "The Invalid's Story." An "elaborate spoof" of Poe's fictional themes and characteristic techniques, Mark Twain's story takes "the Gothic tuck out of his predecessor" in its parody "of Poe's tone, character, and situation." The opening paragraphs of the two stories follow parallel paths as Mark Twain spoofs the overheated imagination of Poe's neurotic narrator: each refers rather vaguely to some traumatic, mysterious past event that the story will proceed to explain; moreover, the first-person engaged narrator—who has aged prematurely as a direct result of what he is about to rehearse—assures the reader that the fantastic tale to follow is true and hence, of course, all the more horrifying. The Poe protagonist characteristically narrates retrospectively, Kemper points out, informing us at the outset of the story's conclusion and thereby sacrificing suspense to heighten a psychological effect, usually terror. In "The Invalid's Story" Mark Twain employs this same technique, but he does so to generate a comic effect; indeed, if the reader were to believe that the obnoxious odors so vividly rendered actually emanated from a decaying corpse rather than from limburger cheese, he would be less amused than disgusted. The language and structure of Mark Twain's story, Kemper concludes, "undermines and mocks the gothic subject it describes" (13–14).

Relationship to Other Mark Twain Works

"The Invalid's Story" is among Mark Twain's "scatological" pieces, "immensely true," DeVoto writes, "to one kind of humor of the frontier and of Mark Twain" (253). Gibson links it to "1601," though he claims that more notorious piece is "formless and even mild" when read juxtaposed to "The Invalid's Story" (82). Additional parallels might be drawn to "Cannibalism in the Cars" (1868) and "The Great Prize Fight" (1863), sketches that depend for their effect on what Bellamy calls "the primitive humor of cruelty" (123). Horowitz sees in the story a preview of the cynicism characteristic of Mark Twain's later writings on institutionalized religion (39–40). The indelicate—some would say offensive—subject and tone of the story, written in 1877, should give pause to those who emphasize Mark Twain's overzealous desire to placate his wife's genteel tastes or his surrender to her heavy editorial hand in the decade following their marriage.

The most secure link to other Mark Twain writings, in fact, lies in the story's assault on genteel sensitivities, particularly as they govern our attitudes toward death. Its grotesque humor is reminiscent of "Cannibalism in the Cars," "Aurelia's Unfortunate Young Man"—the 1864 "condensed novel" that chronicles a young lady's wavering devotion to a lover who seems to disintegrate before her eyes—and "Lucretia Smith's Soldier" (1864), which exposes the sentimental excesses of a young woman who discovers she has "fooled away three mortal weeks here, snuffling and slobbering over the wrong soldier." In all four instances, reality intrudes to shatter genteel illusions and expectations that are comically inappropriate to the situation at hand. The story also provides an interesting counterpart to the Emmeline Grangerford section of *Huckleberry Finn* (1885); although the tone and language of the two differ, their satiric intentions are essentially the same; each employs irony to carry an extended joke at the expense of conventional attitudes toward death.

Critical Studies

Although Baldanza claims that in "The Invalid's Story" Mark Twain "rises to the heights of comic invention" (101), scholars generally condemn the story. Bellamy recoils from the "repulsive humor," arguing that by giving undue attention to the stench of corpses Mark Twain emphasizes "the indignity of human life" (123). Emerson flatly labels it a "disaster," its humor "unspeakable" (272). Most other Mark Twain scholars simply ignore the story that Howells thought would "challenge all literature for its like" (Bellamy 123).

Yet Mark Twain carefully structures the story to minimize the offense to his readers' sensibilities and to maximize comic effect. The dying narrator informs us at the outset that his fate is the result of a "prodigious mistake": planning to accompany the remains of his "dearest boyhood friend and schoolmate, John B. Hackett" by train from Cleveland, Ohio, to "his poor old father and mother in Wisconsin," the narrator in fact sits in a heated baggage car with a crate of rifles on which a stranger has placed "a package of peculiarly mature and capable limburger cheese" (188). The narrator tells of the obnoxious odors that emanated from what he thought was the apparently rotting corpse of Mr. Hackett; however, because the story is told retrospectively, we know the true contents of the box and that the actual source of the vile stench is the cheese. Part of the humor thus arises from dramatic irony: steps taken to defuse the smell of a corpse— pouring carbolic acid over it, making a fire of "chicken feathers, and dried apples, and leaf tobacco, and rags, and old shoes, and sulphur, and asafe-tida"—serve only to intensify the peculiar fragrance of the cheese (192).

The narrator is accompanied on his journey by the baggageman Thompson, whose "vernacular understatement" in describing the unmodifiable smell, Gibson argues, contributes largely to the story's comic effect (82). It is Thompson who first broaches the indelicate subject of the corpse's smell: "He's pretty ripe, *ain't* he!" (189). Trying to be as understanding as possible under the circumstances, Thompson attempts to comfort the narrator over the loss of his friend with the observation that "sometimes it's uncertain whether they're really gone or not"; yet before long he asserts,

"But *he* ain't in no trance!" (189). After spouting a few homiletic sentiments—"We've all got to go, they ain't no getting around it. Man that is born of woman is of few days and far between, as Scriptur' says"—Thompson succumbs to his overwhelming discomfort, disputing the narrator's claim that his friend had been dead only "two or three days" and giving "his views at considerable length upon the unwisdom of putting off burials too long" (189). When the smell of shared cigar smoke fails to "modify him worth a cent," serving only "to stir up his ambition," Thompson decides to take more forceful action (190). But his attempt to overpower the smell with carbolic acid proves futile: "It ain't no use. We can't buck agin *him*. He just utilizes everything we put up to modify him with, and gives it his own flavor and plays it back on us" (191). In utter desperation, Thompson builds the bonfire; its own odor proves so powerful that the narrator wonders "how even the corpse could stand it," yet "the original smell stood up out of it just as sublime as ever" (192). Thompson dejectedly surrenders: "We got to stay out here. . . . The Governor wants to travel alone, and he's fixed so he can outvote us." Ultimately death has triumphed over the living, leaving the two men "pisoned": "Yes, sir, we're elected, just as sure as you're born" (192).

Horowitz provides the most extensive and ingenious analysis of "The Invalid's Story," arguing that it is "a particularized symbolic commentary on the Church, a broad farce . . . of what has generally happened as the body of Christ . . . progresses through time." Germane to Horowitz's argument is the story's original context: it was positioned at the end of the Bermuda travel narratives that collectively develop an Easter motif introduced as the visitors arrive on Sunday, the third day of their voyage, at "the resurrection hour" when "the berths gave up their dead." Horowitz identifies the corpse in the story—on its way to reunion with its parents in the fictional city of "Bethlehem," Wisconsin—with Christ; as a result of the "prodigious mistake," of course, the corpse goes instead to the very real city of Peoria, Illinois, its place of honor usurped by a crate of rifles and packet of limburger cheese. Thompson, the baggageman who hums "Sweet By and By" while tending to the assumed coffin, is Saint Thomas Aquinas—the emissary of the church who tends to the bedrock of Christian faith. The railway car, "embodying a Christ, ministered by a Tom's son," symbolizes the church as the tale "takes on the form of an unorthodox trope." The Calvinistic language of the story's conclusion—"we're elected," the discovery of the truth about the cheese coming "too late to save *me*"—testifies to the pernicious, deadly hold of Mark Twain's early training in the Presbyterian church. The discovery of the fraudulent basis of church belief has come "too late to save" Mark Twain; hence the secular Bermuda experience, "with all its heavenly aspects," Horowitz concludes, "has proved insufficient balm" (39–44).

Bibliography

PRIMARY

The Complete Short Stories of Mark Twain. Now Collected for the First Time. Edited by Charles Neider. Garden City, N.Y.: Hanover House, 1957.

The Stolen White Elephant Etc. Boston: James R. Osgood, 1882.

SECONDARY

Austin, James C. "Artemus Ward, Mark Twain and the Limburger Cheese." *Midcontinent American Studies Journal* 4 (Fall 1963):70–73.

Baldanza, Frank. *Mark Twain: An Introduction and Interpretation.* New York: Holt, Rinehart & Winston, 1961.

Bellamy, Gladys C. *Mark Twain as a Literary Artist.* Norman: University of Oklahoma Press, 1950.

Blair, Walter. *Mark Twain and Huck Finn.* Berkeley and Los Angeles: University of California Press, 1960.

[Brownell, George Hiram.] "Twain's Writings Still Increase in Value." *Twainian* 4 (May 1945): 2–3.

DeVoto, Bernard. *Mark Twain's America.* Boston: Little, Brown, 1932.

Emerson, Everett. *The Authentic Mark Twain: A Literary Biography of Samuel L. Clemens.* Philadelphia: University of Pennsylvania Press, 1984.

Gibson, William M. *The Art of Mark Twain.* New York: Oxford University Press, 1976.

Hill, Hamlin. *Mark Twain and Elisha Bliss.* Columbia: University of Missouri Press, 1964.

Horowitz, Floyd R. " 'The Invalid's Story': An Early Mark Twain Commentary on Institutional Christianity." *Midcontinent American Studies Journal* 7 (Spring 1966): 37–44.

Kemper, Steven E. "Poe, Twain, and Limburger Cheese." *Mark Twain Journal* 21, no. 1 (Winter 1981–82):13–14.

24

Jim Baker's Blue Jay Yarn

Publication History

"Jim Baker's Blue Jay Yarn" first appeared in chapter 3 of *A Tramp Abroad,* published in March 1880. Among the "separatable stuff" of *A Tramp Abroad*—as Mark Twain wrote to William Dean Howells—the anecdote is a narrative digression, self-contained, and frequently reprinted in anthologies of southwestern humor and collections of Mark Twain's short fiction (DeVoto 247–53; *Humor of the Old Southwest* 402–5). It is sometimes given the title, "What Stumped the Bluejays."

Most anthologists and editors reprint the story as a self-contained unit. Gibson, however, argues that the yarn must be seen in its original context. In *A Tramp Abroad* Mark Twain introduces the tale in the second chapter as he describes his walk through the Black Forest. Evoking an atmosphere of "German legends and fairy tales" in a manner reminiscent of Washington Irving, Mark Twain encounters some ravens who seem to caw insults at him. Gradually he transforms the ravens from adversaries who "bandy words in raven" to masters of the western American art of the insult. He slips into the vernacular voice of Jim Baker, who tells the story of the American jay. Gibson contends that in reading the yarn out of context we overlook Mark Twain's masterful control of narrative technique: the story's "seamless narrative development, its easy passage through formal opening into a vernacular tale of real elegance, and its transmuting the atmosphere of German legend into the air of Western myth" (67–71).

"Jim Baker's Blue Jay Yarn" is the high point of a book that continually frustrated Mark Twain during its composition and, as Blair contends, was "not worth all the trouble it took to write it" (168; Paine 665). For all its aesthetic problems, however, *A Tramp Abroad* proved a commercial success: it sold sixty-two-thousand copies during the first year, far outstripping sales of Mark Twain's previous three books; in England, *A Tramp Abroad* achieved the best sales record of all Mark Twain's books during the author's lifetime (Kaplan, *Mr. Clemens* 350; Emerson 105).

Circumstances of Composition, Sources, and Influences

In early March 1878 Mark Twain signed a contract with Elisha Bliss to write for the American Publishing Company a subscription book about travel through Europe. The original idea was to produce another book like the enormously successful *Innocents Abroad* (1869). The contract with Bliss may have been the impetus for an extended trip to Germany, but more probably Mark Twain used the contract to justify a trip he had already decided was necessary to revitalize his sagging creative spirit. His humiliation at the Whittier birthday dinner in Boston 17 December 1877 had left him uncertain of his role in American letters. Acutely self-conscious, he had written to Howells a week after the dinner: "I feel that my misfortune has injured me all over the country; therefore it will be best that I retire from before the public at present" (*Mark Twain-Howells Letters* 212). Emerson hence suggests that Mark Twain left for Germany in mid-April 1878 largely to escape his embarrassment and the lethargy it engendered (98). In any event, upon his arrival in Germany, he began immediately writing material for *A Tramp Abroad*. But quickly a fundamental aesthetic problem arose: there was no focus to the project, no "narrative plank" to provide unity to the miscellaneous tales, sketches, short stories, and anecdotes he prepared. He wrote to Frank Bliss in July 1878: "I have written 800 pages of ms. . . . but it is in disconnected form & cannot be used until joined together by the writing of at least a dozen intermediate chapters" (Hill 133). A visit from his close friend Joe Twichell triggered an idea for a unifying thread. Mark Twain decided his book would be a burlesque account of a walking tour through Europe, undertaken by two American tramps—Mark Twain and a companion named Mr. Harris—who manage to do no walking at all. The strategy, however, proved unsuccessful. By this time Mark Twain was too sick of travel—of hotels, trains, museums, etc.—to bring the same freshness and ironic vision that had informed *Innocents Abroad*. *A Tramp Abroad* does indeed offer a series of chapters describing Mark Twain's adventures while traveling with Mr. Harris through Germany, Switzerland, and Italy—but there are frequent digressions, most of which, like the "Blue Jay Yarn," have nothing to do with Europe or the tour. What he could not fit even as a digression, Mark Twain stuffed into six appendices (Emerson 105; Rogers 80). The result is a disjointed work with occasionally brilliant digressions, the whole characterized by what Blair calls the "labored pursuit of humorous effects" (Mark Twain 168).

Throughout the composition of *A Tramp Abroad* Mark Twain knew he was having trouble and, in fact, looked for a pretext to abandon the project altogether (Kaplan, *Mr. Clemens,* 336). He wrote to Howells on 8 January 1880 that he had "been fighting a life-&-death battle with this infernal book & *hoping* to get it done some day. . . . A book which required 2600 pages of ms, & I have written nearer four thousand, first & last" (*Mark Twain-Howells Letters* 286–87). Hill points out that in writing *A Tramp Abroad* Mark Twain reversed the process he had followed in

Innocents Abroad. In the earlier book, the *Alta* letters had at the outset furnished a rudimentary structure, a "narrative plank"; in revising the letters for book publication he had only to flesh out his series of letters with appropriate anecdotes. In *A Tramp Abroad*, however, the digression became the basic structural unit, preceeding the flimsy unifying principle of the burlesque walking tour to which it bore scant resemblance (139).

The immediate source for "Jim Baker's Blue Jay Yarn" is a tale Mark Twain heard Jim Gillis tell while the author lived with Gillis at Jackass Hill in Calaveras County, California, during the winter 1864–65. Inclement weather forced Mark Twain to pass his time indoors, around the fire in Gillis's cabin or in the hotel saloon at nearby Angel's Camp. Here he heard Gillis and Ben Coon spin yarns from a vast storehouse of western American lore. Mark Twain remembered these tall tales, even jotted down notes about some of them, and used them later as the basis of such classic pieces as "Jim Smiley and His Jumping Frog" (1865) and the "Blue Jay Yarn." But he was struck as deeply by the tellers themselves and their deadpan manner of delivery (Bellamy 146; Benson 124). Long argues that behind Jim Baker or Simon Wheeler lies the narrator of the western tall tale—a real, vital person like Gillis or Coon who spins his fantastic yarn in an authentic idiom (133, 321).

The story belongs to the tradition of the bestiary, dating back to before Chaucer but surfacing in the antebellum South of Mark Twain's youth in the Negro slave narrative (DeVoto 251; Long 321). Mark Twain remembered fondly the stories he heard in childhood from the old Negro slave Uncle Dan'l and, as Lynn points out, later tended to conflate his memories of Uncle Dan'l with his response to Joel Chandler Harris's Uncle Remus tales (240). Harris supplied Mark Twain not an analogue for this particular story but the example of a method; as Arnold points out, the birds in the "Blue Jay Yarn" portray "frontier society just as Harris' creatures allegorize antebellum plantation life" (206). Mark Twain's 1881 correspondence with Harris reveals also that in the Uncle Remus tales Mark Twain found confirmation of his theory that the frame that encloses a story—the character of the narrator and his interaction with the auditor—rather than the actual yarn itself, is of paramount importance (Bellamy 149–50).

Like "Jim Smiley and His Jumping Frog," the "Blue Jay Yarn" bears strong affinities to the tradition of southwestern humor (Cohen and Dillingham 387–88). This genre, Arnold contends, involves two divergent strains of development, both of which leave their mark on Mark Twain's fiction. The first strain appears in the work of such ironic humorists as George Washington Harris, A. B. Longstreet, and Johnson Jones Hooper—essentially conservative satirists who use animals or metaphors featuring animals to expose the boorishness and cruelty of simple frontier people and hence assure an educated eastern audience of its inherent moral and cultural superiority. In the tales of Sut Luvingood or Simon Suggs, animals rarely achieve any autonomous personality for their function is either to illuminate human inadequacies or to provide occasion for slapstick humor at the expense of the country bumpkin. From Longstreet, Arnold contends, Mark Twain "learned his descriptive techniques," and the episode of the poodle and the pinch bug in *Tom Sawyer* (1876) testifies to his use of the slapstick tradition for humorous and satiric effect.

The second strain comes to Mark Twain from such "animal-admiring humorists" as Alexander McNutt and T. B. Thorpe. In McNutt's "Chunkey's Fight with the Panthers" the panther proves an awesome beast, a worthy and respected adversary in what becomes an epic conflict; in "The Big Bear of Arkansas," Thorpe creates a mythical bear, a creature he loves "like a brother," and in doing so demonstrates an affinity with what Arnold labels "the deeper rhythms of unity with the animal world which is central to Twain." Mark Twain, Arnold contends, fuses the two traditions of animal portraiture in southwestern humor, moving in the "Blue Jay Yarn" and later stories about the Indian crow to complete empathy with the animals and the natural realm they represent (196–202).

Relationship to Other Mark Twain Works

"Jim Baker's Blue Jay Yarn" shares much in common with "Jim Smiley and His Jumping Frog." Both are based on tall tales Mark Twain heard while living in Calaveras County, California, during the winter 1864–65, and both are rooted in regional folklore. Moreover, both tales are told in a frontier idiom by folk narrators who, as Hansen writes, "seem never to leave their rocking chairs" (420). Blair points out that the "Blue Jay Yarn" exploits the humorous effects resulting from the juxtaposition of realistic and fantastic passages, a technique that governs the "Jumping Frog" story and works well in Huck's account of the exploits of the duke and the dauphin in *Huckleberry Finn* (1885) ("Mark Twain's Other Masterpiece" 134–38).

The "Blue Jay Yarn" belongs to a long series of stories, sketches, and fragments about animals, virtually all of which are collected by Brashear and Rodney in *The Birds and Beasts of Mark Twain*. Animals of course play a significant role in Simon Wheeler's tale about Jim Smiley's gambling adventures and in *Tom Sawyer*, where their antics serve the purposes of burlesque humor. In Jim Baker's yarn, however, the jay becomes what Arnold calls a "full-fledged protagonist." Mercifully, Mark Twain here does not treat the jay in a vein of maudlin sentimentality, as he later treats the animal protagonists of "A Dog's Tale" (1903) and "A Horse's Tale" (1906). But he does identify with his animal protagonist, for like Jim Baker's frustrated jay Mark Twain knew well what it was like "to dump money, or the manuscript pages for a book, into holes which seemed too huge ever to fill" (Blair, *Mark Twain*, 176). Arnold contends that the jays manifest those qualities that made Mark Twain the celebrated spokesman for and chronicler of the American West: "his virtuosity at the profanity, bragging, posturing, exaggerating, and lying that constituted conversation in the frontier towns" (208).

Critical Studies

Mark Twain scholars generally regard "Jim Baker's Blue Jay Yarn" to be one of the author's most successful stories (Blair, "Mark Twain's Other Masterpiece," 132–33; Emerson 277). DeVoto calls it "a passage in pure humor" (252); Ferguson claims that it is "the most perfect example of the genuine Western tall story" of all Mark Twain's fiction (200). The story's successful blending of fantasy, realistic characterization of an individualized down-to-earth personality, and practical homespun commentary grounded in experience qualifies the "Blue Jay Yarn" as a sterling example of representative nineteenth-century humor (Blair, *Mark Twain*, 174).

Hansen subdivides American humor into two distinct categories: one, largely visual, is the humor of entropy, with an innate attraction to chaos and anarchy; the other, largely oral, is the humor of transformation, grounded in the creative power of language. Because one of the principal virtues of the "Blue Jay Yarn" is its language, the sure control of idiom and vernacular speech rhythms, Hansen cites the story as a prime example of transformational humor. Its narrator, like most of Mark Twain's imaginative liars, is a misanthropic loner: "Seven years ago, the last man in this region but one moved away," Jim Baker reports, and it has been thirteen years since he has had any contact with home in the states (140). His loneliness presents a challenge similar to the one the intriguing jay confronts in trying to fill with acorns the seemingly bottomless hole in the cabin roof; in effect, Hansen writes, "both Baker and the Jay are filling an emptiness—with language and acorns respectively." Through his transforming imaginative vision, his remarkable aesthetic capacity for empathy, Jim Baker creates "meaning, fellowship and delight, where little, if any, had existed." It is his language, Hansen concludes, that manifests his renovated life (419).

R. Galen Hanson also notes the resemblance of the jays to the human narrator who tells their story, arguing that the behavior of the birds illuminates not only "the language-inventing and language-learning nature of man" but also variations of human mood and feeling and the human capacity for abstract thought. To Hanson, the equation of animals and people puts our collective behavior in a humorous light and gently satirizes our capacity for self-deception: "There is always humor in it; it is hard to read without laughing aloud at one's own ways" (19). Blair, however, points to a dimension of "grimness" in the story generally overlooked by scholars. He grants that in its exaggeration of human foolishness, and in its rendition of the futile comic language and fantastic speculation of the harmlessly demented Jim Baker, the tale is amusing. At the same time Blair sees profound cynicism: Mark Twain defines the human being in "devastating terms" making "statements derogatory . . . of humanity in general." The "Blue Jay Yarn" testifies to Mark Twain's increasing pessimism that comes to fruition in *Huckleberry Finn* (Mark Twain 182).

One fundamental problem with the "Blue Jay Yarn," Blair complains, is that the story is based on an absurdity: "Baker's blue-jay . . . dumped acorns into his knot-hole for reasons that never were clarified" ("Mark Twain's Other Masterpiece" 139). Gervais responds to Blair's objection by calling attention to the context of the story within *A Tramp Abroad*. The story is one of cultural contrasts. In his travels through Germany, Mark Twain notes the "richly encultured landscape of Europe" that provides ample inspiration and materials for art; "the culturally empty landscape of the American West," by contrast, forces the artist to "create its dramas out of the rawest materials." Because of his nation's cultural impoverishment, the American artist must rely solely on language; the "Blue Jay Yarn," Gervais concludes, "shows a characteristic and continuing American concern for filling in with appropriate language the huge spaces of a newly settled continent" (12–13).

Another central critical problem in the story concerns the appropriateness of the last four lines, which introduce "an owl that come from Nova Scotia to visit the Yo Semite" who "took this thing in on his way back." Unlike the bluejays, the owl "said he couldn't see anything funny in it." But the owl is not necessarily an expert in matters of aesthetic judgment, for as Jim Baker informs us, "he was a good deal disappointed about Yo Semite, too" (143). DeVoto contends that the concluding four lines "mar the effect" of an otherwise perfectly unified story; "they are a blemish," he writes, because in straining toward a joke they depart "from the clear medium of the tale itself into burlesque" (252).

Shrell defends Mark Twain's story against DeVoto's objection, arguing that the introduction of the owl transforms the tale into a pointed defense of Mark Twain's narrative method. The jays represent a western or vernacular perspective on humor. Although impulsive and prone to foolish mistakes, they possess a quick, healthy sense of humor that encompasses the ability to laugh at themselves, as seen in this passage: "as each fellow lit on the door and took a glance, the whole absurdity of the contract that that first jay had tackled hit him home and he fell over backward, suffocating with laughter, and the next jay took his place and done the same. . . . It ain't any use to tell me a bluejay hasn't got a sense of humor, because I know better" (143). The owl, on the other hand, assumes a symbolic value opposite to that of the western jays. This wise but humorless easterner from Nova Scotia sees nothing amusing in the affair, just as he had found nothing of interest at "Yo Semite." "On the roof of the abandoned cabin," Shrell writes, "owl and bluejay—east and west—face each other" (285).

Shrell offers convincing evidence that this confrontation of eastern and western values dramatized in the last four sentences of the "Blue Jay Yarn" is in response to Mark Twain's humiliation at the December 1877 Whittier dinner sponsored by the *Atlantic Monthly*. Largely due to the influence of his friend and champion Howells, Mark Twain had become a regular contributor to the *Atlantic*, having published sixteen sketches or stories in its pages; yet both he and Howells sensed that Mark Twain's style and characteristically western humor had not received serious acceptance in the closed New England literary establishment (Emerson 97). The dinner was to have afforded Mark Twain his long sought opportunity to socialize with the pillars of that literary establishment as an equal, and Howells arranged for Mark Twain to address the guests; the occasion was, in a sense, his eastern debut. Mark Twain's speech was a western tall tale, an extravagant joke masterfully delivered, telling of his experience as a "callow and conceited" young writer just getting established in the West. Anxious to "try the virtue of my *nom de plume*," the fledgling artist identifies himself as Mark Twain to an old California miner in the hopes of gaining admittance to the man's cabin. The miner, however, is a bit suspicious of literary men, as the night before he had been victimized by "a rough lot" of three men who said they were Longfellow, Emerson, and Holmes—venerable fixtures of the eastern literary establishment who were honored guests at the dinner. The miner explains that the three had taken advantage of his hospitality— eaten his food, drank his liquor, stolen his boots, and perhaps worst of all, recited their poetry; when he protested, they threatened his life. Now with the arrival of another literary man, Mark Twain, the miner decides he'll have to leave the region: "I ain't suited to a literary atmosphere." Mark Twain assures the miner that the three "rough" men could not possibly have been "the gracious singers to whom we and the world pay loving reverence and homage": they must have been "imposters." To which the miner, upon reflection, responds, "Ah—imposters, were they? —are *you?*" Most of the dinner audience was entertained by Mark Twain's joke, despite what Emerson calls an implicit "element of hostility . . . a suggestion that the writers' gentility had an element of phoniness in it" (97–98). Howells, however, was not amused—and he was convinced, and convinced Mark Twain, that the audience found its humor offensive. Boston newspapers sharply attacked Mark Twain's crude "audacity," and he was devastated, sure that his "debut" had been a catastrophe and that he had been misunderstood.

There are, as Shrell points out, striking similarities between Jim Baker's yarn and the "Whittier Address": both are set in a California mining camp, narrated by a miner; both employ a combination of learned and vernacular language; in both the easterners are out West to see Yosemite; and both offer polarized eastern and western values. In dragging the humorless owl from the East into "Jim Baker's Blue Jay Yarn," Mark Twain is "able to re-create—with artistic detachment—another situation in which grotesque or audacious western humor failed to be understood." Hence the confrontation of the owl and the bluejays represents a clash of literary values; the humor of the story and the owl's inability to respond to it serve as a defense of the characteristic method of Mark Twain's fiction (287–90).

Bibliography

PRIMARY

The Birds and Beasts of Mark Twain. Edited by Minnie M. Brashear and Robert M. Rodney. Norman: University of Oklahoma Press, 1966.

*Great Short Works of Mark Twain. Edited by Justin Kaplan. New York: Harper & Row, 1967.

Humor of the Old Southwest. Edited by Hennig Cohen and William B. Dillingham. Boston: Houghton Mifflin, 1964.

Mark Twain-Howells Letters: The Correspondence of Samuel L. Clemens and William Dean Howells, 1872–1910. Edited by Henry Nash Smith and William M. Gibson. Vol. 1. Cambridge, Mass.: Harvard University Press, 1960.

A Tramp Abroad. Hartford: American Publishing Co., 1880.

SECONDARY

Arnold, St. George Tucker, Jr. "The Twain Bestiary: Mark Twain's Critters and the Tradition of Animal Portraiture in Humor of the Old Southwest." *Southern Folklore Quarterly* 40 (1977):195–211.

Bellamy, Gladys C. *Mark Twain as a Literary Artist.* Norman: University of Oklahoma Press, 1950.

Benson, Ivan. *Mark Twain's Western Years.* New York: Russell & Russell, 1966.

Blair, Walter. *Mark Twain & Huck Finn.* Berkeley and Los Angeles: University of California Press, 1960.

———. "Mark Twain's Other Masterpiece: 'Jim Baker's Blue Jay Yarn.' " *Studies in American Humor* 1 (1975):132–47.

DeVoto, Bernard. *Mark Twain's America.* Cambridge, Mass.: Harvard University Press, 1932.

Emerson, Everett. *The Authentic Mark Twain: A Literary Biography of Samuel L. Clemens.* Philadelphia: University of Pennsylvania Press, 1984.

Ferguson, Delancey. *Mark Twain: Man and Legend.* Indianapolis: Bobbs-Merrill, 1943.

Gervais, Ronald J. "What Remains When Everything Is Left Out: The Joke of 'Baker's Blue-Jay Yarn.' " *Mark Twain Journal* 21, no. 4 (Fall 1983):12–14.

Gibson, William M. *The Art of Mark Twain.* New York: Oxford University Press, 1976.

Hansen, Arlen J. "Entropy and Transformation: Two Types of American Humor." *American Scholar* 43 (Summer 1974):405–21.

Hanson, R. Galen. "Bluejays and Man: Twain's Exercise in Understanding." *Mark Twain Journal* 17, no. 1 (1973): 18–19.

Hill, Hamlin. *Mark Twain and Elisha Bliss.* Columbia: University of Missouri Press, 1964.

Kaplan, Justin. *Mr. Clemens and Mark Twain.* New York: Simon & Schuster, 1966.

Long, E. Hudson. *Mark Twain Handbook.* New York: Hendricks House, 1957.

Lynn, Kenneth. *Mark Twain and Southwestern Humor.* Boston: Little, Brown, 1960.

Paine, Albert B. *Mark Twain: A Biography.* Vol. 2. New York: Harper & Brothers, 1912.

Rogers, Franklin R. *Mark Twain's Burlesque Patterns.* Dallas: Southern Methodist University Press, 1960.

Shrell, Darwin H. "Twain's Owl and His Bluejays." In *Essays in Honor of Esmond Linworth Marilla,* edited by Thomas Austin Kirby and William John Olive, 283–90. Baton Rouge: Louisiana State University Press, 1970.

Smith, Henry Nash. *Mark Twain: The Development of a Writer.* Cambridge, Mass.: Harvard University Press, 1962.

25

Jim Smiley and His Jumping Frog

Publication History

First published as "Jim Smiley and His Jumping Frog" in the New York *Saturday Press* (18 November 1865), the story was reprinted ten times in the ten years following its initial publication. Branch and Hirst provide a thorough review of the various editions and revisions of the sketch (*Works* 577–81, 666–82) and conclude that the many authorial changes were designed, for the most part, to increase both the number and consistency of nonstandard spellings so as to enrich the regional flavor of the tale.

Bret Harte reprinted the story in the San Francisco *Californian* (16 December 1865) with a few alterations that Mark Twain probably authorized. Most notably, Mark Twain gave the story a new title, "The Celebrated Jumping Frog of Calaveras County," substituted the name of the place where he had originally heard the story—"Angel's Camp"—for the fictional "Boomerang," and changed the name Smiley to Greeley.

Mark Twain made additional revisions before including "The Celebrated Jumping Frog of Calaveras County" as the title sketch for his first book, published in late April 1867 by Charles Henry Webb (Emerson 38–39). Formerly editor of the *Californian*, Webb agreed to sponsor the book after George W. Carleton, New York Publishers of *Artemus Ward, His Travels,* had rejected it; information on Webb, his background and role in the publication of Mark Twain's first book, is provided by Kinnaird (124). The most significant change introduced in the text of the Webb edition is Mark Twain's abandonment of the frame letter to "Mr. A. Ward" that had enclosed the tale in the *Saturday Press* and *Californian* versions. Beginning "In compliance with the request of a friend of mine, who wrote me from the East," the Webb text replaces the references to A. Ward with one that more securely identifies the gentleman narrator's "eastern" connections.

An unauthorized reprinting of the Webb text appeared the same year (1867) in England, published by George Routledge and Sons. The plates for this printing were appropriated in two subsequent unauthorized British editions published by John Camden Hotten in 1870 and furnished printer's copy for a third in 1873; in these reprintings the story bears the title "The

Jumping Frog of Calaveras County." The first authorized text printed in England was published by George Routledge and Sons in 1870 with the title "The Celebrated Jumping Frog of Calaveras County," and reissued two years later with corrections and additional Mark Twain material. An author-revised text followed the same year. In 1874 Chatto and Windus published an authorized, revised, and corrected reissue of the pirated 1873 Hotten edition. Under the title "The Notorious Jumping Frog of Calaveras County," the story appeared in authorized American editions (*Mark Twain's Sketches*) in 1874 and 1875.

The "Jumping Frog" story appeared in a rather dubious French translation by Marie-Thèrese Blanc in the widely distributed and influential *Revue des deux mondes* (15 July 1872). Madame Blanc accompanied her translation with an assessment of Mark Twain's achievement and place in American letters in which she classified him with Josh Billings and Artemus Ward as purveyors of a crude, "western" humor that lacked the refinement of a regionalist like Bret Harte, whom Madame Blanc admired. Her article, with its "cultural condescension" and critical insensitivity to the possibility that persona and author are not identical, infuriated Mark Twain and, Wilson contends, contributed to his lifelong hatred of the French (537–56). More significantly, it occasioned Mark Twain's "retranslation" of "La Grenouille sauteuse du comte de Calaveras" back into the "civilized" English language. The French version and the English translation, dated Hartford, March 1875, follow the "Jumping Frog" story in the 1875 (*Mark Twain's Sketches*) edition, and are reprinted in Mark Twain's "Private History of the 'Jumping Frog' Story," published in the April 1894 issue of the *North American Review*. The text in *The Works of Mark Twain* (1981) is based on the original New York *Saturday Press* story.

Circumstances of Composition, Sources, and Influences

In July 1861 Mark Twain accompanied his brother Orion from Missouri to the Nevada Territory where, while working as a clerk in a government office, he submitted miscellaneous letters to the Virginia City *Territorial Enterprise*. Largely on the basis of his written burlesque of a speech by a Nevada chief justice that was admired by Dan De Quille, the city editor, the *Enterprise* hired him as a full-time staff writer. By 1863 the author had adopted the pen name Mark Twain and achieved regional notoriety as a result of his hoax "A Bloody Massacre near Carson" (October 1863) (Emerson 11–20). On 29 May 1864 Mark Twain moved to San Francisco where, working as a special correspondent for the *Enterprise*, he aggravated local police with a series of articles that exposed and denounced city corruption (Taylor 73–74). He thought it wise to leave San Francisco for a while, and on 4 December 1864 he traveled to Calaveras County, California, in the Sierra foothills. There he stayed with Jim Gillis at Jackass Hill and at nearby Angel's Camp until his return to San Francisco on 25 February 1865.

Inclement winter weather forced the author to stay indoors during his tenure in Calaveras County, either around the fire in Gillis's cabin or in the hotel bar at Angel's Camp. To pass the time, Gillis spun many a tall tale around the cabin stove, always relating his stories as if they were veracious history. But it was from Ben Coon, a derelict who hung out in the bar of the Angel's Camp hotel, that Mark Twain first heard the marvelous tale of the jumping frog (Emerson 25; Ferguson 103). Formerly a pilot on the Illinois River, Coon was a "solemn, fat-witted person, who dozed by the stove, or told slow, endless stories, without point or application" (Paine 271). Although Mark Twain liked the frog story well enough to record its details in his notebook—a fact that suggests he had neither heard the story before nor had read versions of it in newspapers (Benson 127)—it was Coon's masterful delivery of the oral anecdote that proved most influential on the young artist's development. Recalling Coon's rendition of the jumping frog tale, the author wrote in 1894: "in his mouth this episode was . . . the gravest sort of history . . . ; he was entirely serious, for he was dealing with what to him were austere facts, and . . . he saw no humor in his tale" ("Private History" 447). Mark Twain's fascination with the oral delivery of such mining camp raconteurs as Gillis and Coon surfaced in the first sketch published upon his return to San Francisco, "An Unbiased Criticism." Bellamy sees this piece as a rehearsal for "Jim Smiley and His Jumping Frog," for behind Mark Twain's creation of Simon Wheeler in the Jim Smiley story lies Ben Coon's "deadpan manner and vernacular language" (146; Branch, "Background Study," 592).

Immediately upon his return to San Francisco in late February 1865, Mark Twain discovered a letter from Artemus Ward requesting that he send something for inclusion in a book on Nevada Territory travels to be published by G. W. Carleton (Emerson 25–29; Branch, *Literary Apprenticeship,* 293–94). The Ward letter apparently inspired Mark Twain to put the frog tale into story form, as he wrote his mother and sister in a 20 January 1866 letter that the sketch was but "a squib which would have never been written but to please Artemus Ward" (*Mark Twain's Letters* 101). Yet the story did not come easily. Two surviving manuscript versions written between 1 September and 16 October 1865 (published for the first time in 1981 [*Works* 273–82])—"The Only Reliable Account of the Celebrated Jumping Frog of Calaveras County" and "Angel's Camp Constable"—together with earlier experiments with Ben Coon and Simon Wheeler published in the *Californian* "suggest that Clemens saw the humorous possibilities of his narrator more clearly than he saw how to bring that narrator and his frog story into conjunction" (*Works* 263–66). The third version, "Jim Smiley and His Jumping Frog," Mark Twain wrote during the week of 16–23 October 1865, but by that time he was too late to satisfy Carleton's deadline for the Ward book. The story was then funneled to Henry Clapp, Jr., publisher of the *Saturday Press,* who promptly released it on 18 November 1865 (Branch, *Literary Apprenticeship,* 293–94).

The established source of the story is the tale Mark Twain heard around the fire at Angel's Camp from Ben Coon, "a man," Mark Twain recalled, "who was not telling it to his hearers as a thing new to them, but as a thing which *they had witnessed and would remember*" ("Private History" 447). Branch and Hirst contend that the words "Only Reliable Account" and "Celebrated" in the title of the earlier manuscript version suggest that Mark Twain made no claims of originality for the basic story (*Works* 264). Coon's narrative, however, included only the skeleton tale of the shot-laden frog and emphasized the themes of human gullibility and conniving. Mark Twain embellished the story with the frame structure, the development of Smiley's uncontrollable and fantastic love of betting, and his exploitation of a variety of talented animals. The episodes of the fifteen-minute nag and Andrew Jackson, the dog, probably came from Mark Twain's experiences as a San Francisco reporter (Branch, "Background Study," 593).

The story itself had numerous analogues in American folk culture, for the theme of shrewdness outwitted was a common element of Negro, frontier, Yankee, and Indian lore. If Mark Twain had not heard any of these analogues before, they nevertheless lay behind Coon's oral tale (DeVoto 172–78; Cohen 17–18). Lewis surveys the various forms of the original joke and details Mark Twain's elaboration on them, and Morrissey offers a true story about grasshoppers in Virginia as a possible source (143–45). More easily documented possible sources are three published versions of the tale: "A Toad Story," *Sonora Herald,* 11 June 1853; Henry P. Leland, "Frogs Shot without Powder," New York *Spirit of the Times,* 26 May 1855; and Samuel Seabough, "Tricks and Defeats of Sporting Genius," *San Andreas Independent,* 11 December 1858. DeVoto claims that Mark Twain probably did read the Leland piece (173–74), and Cuff has compared Mark Twain's story to all three earlier printed versions before concluding, rather vaguely, that "to California folklore Mark Twain was in debt for the frog story" (155–58). The San Francisco *Times* (6 September 1867) was direct in its accusation of deliberate plagiarism: "we are told that his famous story 'The Jumping Frog of Calaveras,' was really written by Sam Seabough, now of the Sacramento *Union,* and by 'Mark' appropriated for his own" (*Works* 264, n. 5).

One influence on Mark Twain as he shaped the Jim Smiley story was Artemus Ward, whose letter triggered his efforts to convert the Ben Coon anecdote into a sketch suitable for publication in the Carleton collection and to whom the *Saturday Press* story is specifically addressed. By his success in the East as an author and his fame as a humorous speaker, Ward served as a standard against which Mark Twain could evaluate his own achievements. Blair points out that it has become "conventional" to assume that Ward's example taught Mark Twain both how to speak and how to write humorously (*Native Humor,* 149–50; Rowlette 14). Rodgers sees no evidence that Ward occasioned any specific alterations in Mark Twain's literary plans or narrative method, though unquestionably Ward, with his deadpan delivery, influenced Mark Twain's oral platform manner (278; Baender 193). It is probably Ward whom Mark Twain has in mind when in his 1895 essay "How to Tell a Story" he outlines the "American" technique: "the teller does his best to conceal the fact that he even dimly suspects that there is anything funny about it . . . . To string incongruities and absurdities together in a wandering and sometimes purposeless way, and seem innocently unaware that they are absurdities, is the basis of the American art" (*Great Short Works,* 182, 184–85). What Rodgers calls a "momentous step" in the composition of the "Jumping Frog" story occurred when the author furnished Simon Wheeler "with Ward's famous pose of comic innocence," making him "no mere purblind literalist like Ben Coon, but a past master of the oral art form perfected by Artemus Ward" (280–82). Throughout his "monotonous narrative" Wheeler "never smiled, he never frowned, he never changed his voice . . . he never betrayed the slightest suspicion of enthusiasm"; yet the "earnestness and sincerity" of his manner "showed . . . plainly that so far from his imagining that there was anything ridiculous or funny about his story, he regarded it as a really important matter, and admired its two heroes as men of transcendent genius in finesse" (*Works* 283).

The story as it originally appeared in the *Saturday Press* is an occasional piece, written at the request of Ward and intended to be published in his collection of Nevada Territory travels. It is thus appropriate that Ward furnishes the model for Wheeler's deadpan delivery. The letter to Ward, which provides the encompassing frame for the Wheeler-Smiley story, makes Mark Twain as character the butt of a practical joke perpetrated by his mentor who sends him in quest of Leonidas W. Smiley via "goodnatured, garrulous old Simon Wheeler" (Regan 38–39): "I have a lurking suspicion that your Leonidas W. Smiley is a myth—that you never knew such a personage, and that you only conjectured that if I asked old Wheeler about him it would remind him of his infamous *Jim* Smiley, and he would go to work and bore me nearly to death with some infernal reminiscence of him as long and tedious as it should be useless to me" (*Works* 282). In his condescending attitude and formal, elevated language, Mark Twain as narrator assumes one of what Gerber labels the author's "comic poses of superiority": that of the cultured "Gentleman" among the local country yokels. Such pose has its origins in the humor of the Old South and Southwest as practiced by such notable artists as T. B. Thorpe, A. B. Longstreet, Joseph Glover Baldwin, and Johnson Jones Hooper (297–99; Cox 26–27). Typically the detached narrator in this tradition is cool, amused, and at times sardonic as he reports to a civilized society the frontier antics of those whose dialect speech defines their moral as well as cultural inferiority (Holman 29–30).

Southwestern humor thus exerted the second major influence on Mark Twain's story. Having learned the value of the oral anecdote from Jim Gillis and Ben Coon at Angel's Camp, and having fashioned Simon Wheeler on the example of Artemus Ward, Mark Twain adopts for his story the narrative technique—the framework structure—characteristic of such masterpieces of southwestern humor as T. B. Thorpe's "Big Bear of Arkansas" and George Washington Harris's Sut Luvingood's yarns (Blair, *Native Humor,* 156; Branch, *Literary Apprenticeship,* 293–94). The use of two narrators—Mark Twain, the gentleman writing to Ward in the lofty language of the frame, and Simon Wheeler, who spins the yarns of Smiley's exploits in spoken dialect—generates the illusion that we are auditors to an oral tale rather than readers of a formal literary one (Cox 26). DeVoto claims that in offering "the life of America . . . refracted through a fine lens," the "Jumping Frog" story is "an accomplished masterpiece," a "culmination, not a beginning, of a distinct genre of American writing" (176–77); Baldanza concurs, labeling the story "the culminating jewel in the tradition of Southwest humor" (32).

Several scholars have noted that Mark Twain's story is significant not so much in its resemblance to southwestern humor as in its departure from that tradition. Wheeler's innocence, his total absorption in his own tale to the point that he is oblivious to his listener's attitude, marks a radical departure from the bragging, confident frontiersman of Thorpe's "Big Bear of Arkansas" (Cox 28–29). The fact that the gentleman-narrator tells a joke not at the expense of the yokel but on himself reverses the typical pattern in southwestern humor, for the obtuseness of Mark Twain as character disqualifies him as an authority who explicitly describes the real situation before him; instead, Mark Twain the author "lets the two speakers unconsciously suggest the real situation which they cannot perceive" (Spengemann 6; Lynn 275). The dialectic between the two narrators does more than merely provide the frame or occasion for Coon's tale of the shot-laden frog (Bellamy 149). It provides an innovation in point of view that raises the deceptively simple story above the limitations of its genre, furnishing the tale with its "inward moving structure" and "outward moving" dimensions of symbolic implication: like Wheeler's feigned naiveté, the apparent simplicity of the tale proves richly ironic; like Wheeler's story of

Jim Smiley's exploits and misadventures, the seemingly pointless and rambling story as a whole implies rather than asserts its insights into human nature and frontier culture (Krause 562–63).

Relationship to Other Mark Twain Works

"Jim Smiley and His Jumping Frog" is the most successful and aesthetically the most accomplished of Mark Twain's early sketches. DeVoto sees it as the culmination of Mark Twain's California writings, providing "pattern and direction" to the random currents of humor characteristic of his extravagant comic journalism (168). The identification of the tale with a specific, recognizable geographical area and social class is typical of Mark Twain's early writings (Baender 192), and links the "Jumping Frog" story to his first published piece, "The Dandy Frightening the Squatter," a humorous anecdote that appeared 1 May 1852 in the *Boston Carpet-Bag:* both are brief narratives that employ native themes—shrewdness outwitted, slick easterner confronting "poker-faced" westerner; each relates an anecdote in the tradition of southwestern humor, a tall tale grounded in American regional folklore and transmitted orally from one generation to the next (Branch, *Literary Apprenticeship*, 120–21).

Yet in scope, depth of characterization, complexity of point of view and structure, "Jim Smiley and His Jumping Frog" clearly surpasses anything Mark Twain had written to date, and marks a turning point in his literary development and career. Not only are the sharply defined Jim Smiley and Simon Wheeler Mark Twain's first vividly and fully realized characters (Emerson 104), but they secured for their creator an introduction to eastern audiences, established his national reputation, and fueled his plans to leave California for New York (Henry Nash Smith 11; Benson 129–31). The New York correspondent for the San Francisco *Alta California* reported back to his paper that "Mark Twain's story in the *Saturday Press* of November 18, called 'Jim Smiley and his Jumping Frog,' has set all New York in a roar, and he may be said to have made his mark" (Emerson 37–38). The "Jumping Frog" story is one of the rare occasions, Gerber contends, when the persona Mark Twain works with aesthetic force and consistency, controlling naturally the style, subject matter, and point of view of the tale (297, n. 1). His success with the persona in this story shattered any distinction between Samuel Clemens and Mark Twain the author may have wanted to maintain and earned him, Charles Henry Webb reports in his "Advertisement" to Mark Twain's first published book, "the *sobriquet* of The Wild Humorist of the Pacific Slope" (*Celebrated Jumping Frog*).

For a while Mark Twain seemed none too happy with the reputation as humorist the "Jumping Frog" story earned for him. In his 20 January

1866 letter to his mother and sister he dismisses the story as a "villainous backwoods sketch," and during his courtship of Olivia Langdon and in the early years of their marriage (1868–70), he seemed uncomfortable, if not disgusted, with the reductive role as humorist his public seemed to have cast for him. But gradually his opinion of the story and estimate of his achievements as humorist changed as he perceived that his role as "Wild Humorist of the Pacific Slope" was his greatest literary capital. Rogers writes: "In the period which saw the beginning of his friendship with Mrs. Fairbanks, his engagement and marriage to Livy, and his first association with the Reverend Mr. Twichell, he was sloughing off much of the pose of sophistication cultivated during his Bohemian days in San Francisco and beginning to capitalize upon his role as an 'old timer' in the 'wild' west" (165).

Although Baldanza notes that the stranger who fleeces Smiley by loading his frog Dan'l with lead foreshadows the duke and the dauphin in *Huckleberry Finn* (1885)—they are traveling confidence men who exploit ignorant, unsophisticated locals at circuses, fake shows, camp meetings, etc. (115)—it is the establishment of an appropriate and characteristic narrative voice that makes the "Jumping Frog" story so seminal in Mark Twain's development as artist (Blair, *Mark Twain*, 97). Simon Wheeler is charming and effective because he becomes the spokesman for what Henry Nash Smith calls the "vernacular" point of view. His natural habitat the barroom, Wheeler through language and implied values represents "gestures of escape from the pale negations and paler affirmations of the genteel tradition" (65). As the story's joke unfolds through the consciousness of Simon Wheeler, trivial and central incidents or episodes receive equal emphasis; Wheeler provides distance between author and story, and theme comes to us largely through devices of indirection. Like subsequent vernacular narrators such as Captain Stormfield or Huck Finn, Wheeler assumes importance in the story not so much because of his participation in events as because of his attitude toward what he witnesses (Cox 26; Covici 48–49).

Critical Studies

Most early scholarly discussions of "Jim Smiley and His Jumping Frog" stressed its origins in oral folklore, its place in the canon of Mark Twain's California/Nevada journalism, and its relationship to the southwestern humor school of T. B. Thorpe, George Washington Harris, etc. (Benson; Blair, *Native Humor;* Buckbee; DeVoto; Ferguson; Lewis). The first sustained critical analysis of the story appears in Branch's *Literary Apprenticeship* (1950) (120–29). Branch turns from discussion of the story's origins and background to focus on Simon Wheeler's method as storyteller, pointing out that Wheeler carefully and methodically builds up Smiley's character by providing three detailed episodes that demonstrate his love for betting: the stories of the "fifteen-minute nag," the "small bull-pup" Andrew Jackson, and the frog Dan'l Webster. Arranged in ascending order in terms of their "length, complexity, and human interest," these episodes serve finally to place emphasis in the story on Smiley, for it is he, not old Dan'l, who is fleeced. Branch then calls attention to what he terms the three levels of reality in the story: the commonsense realm of ordinary journalistic reality, represented by Mark Twain; the realm of human oddity represented by Simon Wheeler as perceived by Mark Twain; and the realm of the fantastic Jim Smiley and the stranger, who are creations of American folklore like Davy Crockett and Paul Bunyan. In a footnote, Branch notices that Mark Twain as character, with "his correct and self-deprecatory speech," stands in contrast to the westerners Wheeler and Smiley (294, n. 19).

The relationship of Mark Twain to Simon Wheeler has commanded considerable scholarly attention since Branch's pioneer analysis. Most of this attention has focused on the confrontation of East and West, genteel and vernacular values, implicit in the story's double frame structure: Mark Twain writing to Ward, his friend in the East, about his unsuccessful meeting with Simon Wheeler, the "garrulous" westerner who instead of giving information about the Rev. Leonidas W. Smiley tells him the story of how Jim Smiley, a fellow westerner, is fleeced by a stranger. Mark Twain enters Boomerang as the easterner inexperienced in the ways of the western frontier. Because of his genteel manner he allows himself to be imposed upon by Wheeler, the old westerner who "backed me into a corner and blockaded me there with his chair." Schmidt (271) and Covici (50–51) contend that we, as readers, perceive the gap between the author Mark Twain and his character of the same name who is oblivious to the humor of Wheeler's yarn, which is told ultimately at his expense; the sophisticated easterner, smug in his condescending local-colorist preconceptions, becomes the object of satire. Although Cox claims that it is not discernible from the story whether Wheeler is unconsciously funny or whether he is deliberately cajoling the green easterner (29–30), Wheeler's motive in corralling Mark Twain, according to Rodgers, is clear: "As a consummate practitioner of the art of sober-faced, tall-tale narration, he is playing upon Twain's seeming credulity, leading his victim through thickets of increasingly absurd detail to the point where truth must dawn and Twain discover himself the butt of an undeniably excellent joke" (277; Schmidt 272). The confrontation between East and West, Schmidt contends, becomes an attack on the genteel tradition as the story "ultimately asserts the superiority of vernacular brotherhood" (277).

Simon Wheeler's method of narration is one of the story's chief virtues

172 TWAIN'S SHORT STORIES

and delights. His poker-face delivery, his refusal or inability to distinguish between significant and trivial details or between the commonplace and the fabulous, and his utter disregard for his auditor's reaction are chief sources of humor in the story (Covici 50). What Mark Twain calls "the interminable narrative" begins with a summary of the range of Jim Smiley's betting activities—horse races, dog fights, cat fights, chicken fights, even the success of Parson Walker's exhortations at camp meetings—concluding with Smiley's preposterous offer: "Parson Walker's wife laid very sick, once, for a good while, and it seemed as if they weren't going to save her; but one morning he come in and Smiley asked him how she was, and he said she was considerable better—thank the Lord for his inf'nit mercy—and coming on so smart that with the blessing of Providence she'd get well yet—and Smiley, before he thought, says, "Well, I'll resk two-and-a-half that she don't, anyway' " (284). A man who "before he thought" would bet against the Lord's "inf'nit mercy . . . the blessing of Providence," is indeed a compulsive man who "would bet on *anything*." Already there is method to Wheeler's seemingly rambling tale: in concluding his introductory summary of Smiley's habitual wagering activities with the offense to Parson Walker and genteel piety, Wheeler puts the mannered easterner who comes inquiring after the Rev. Leonidas W. Smiley quite definitely in a subservient position. Wheeler's narrative then focuses on three specific, extended episodes—the nag, the bull-pup, the frog—each more detailed, complex, and fantastic than the last (Krause 565–68). The story concludes as Wheeler begins with yet another episode concerning Smiley and his "yaller one-eyed cow that didn't have no tail" only to be cut-off "good-naturedly" in mid-sentence by the utterly frustrated narrator: "O, curse Smiley and his afflicted cow!" (288). The ending, Cox points out, preserves the illusion that Wheeler digresses endlessly, that his ramblings have no point, when in fact he spins a yarn that "is a masterpiece of compression and economy" (32).

Wheeler's narrative method and the tale he tells mirror the structure of Mark Twain's story. Cox sees that the relationship of the stranger to Jim Smiley in the tale parallels the relationship of Simon Wheeler to Mark Twain within the frame: just as Smiley is duped by the deadpan stranger, so Wheeler's deadpan, colloquial style takes in the genteel literary language that precedes it; just as Smiley discovers the stranger's "secret act" of loading Dan'l Webster with lead pellets only after he has been fleeced, so the readers discover the story's "secret" structure only after they have been unwittingly lured into it (28–29). In the fullest discussion of the story's structure to date, Krause shows that "Jim Smiley and His Jumping Frog" is actually a complicated interfusion of several undercurrent stories that reveal the attitudes—of the narrator toward Ward, Simon Wheeler, Jim Smiley, his animals, and the stranger; of Wheeler toward Twain and easterners at large, toward Jim Smiley, his animals, and the stranger; of the western community who, through its embodiment Wheeler, finds Smiley's antics still entertaining; of the stranger; of Mark Twain the author toward all parties in the tale; of Jim Smiley; and of his animals, specifically the pup and the frog. The classical mold of the moral satire, Krause argues, shapes these undercurrent stories into a unified whole, largely through the interpenetration of tale and frame that Cox detected. In Wheeler's yarn Smiley's uncontrollable passion for gambling makes him vulnerable, for it causes him to abandon the xenophobia that normally insulates westerners against the guile of strangers; it is, however, this same xenophobia that motivates Wheeler in his relationship to Mark Twain as he narrates a story about the deception and trickery strangers—like Mark Twain—might attempt at the expense of seemingly simple westerners. The dimensions of the satire become clear once we see that Wheeler—as embodiment of the West—is taking his revenge "for the trick of an Easterner at the same time he plays an instructive joke on the fastidious Mark Twain, a Westerner trying to outgrow his background in exchange for eastern respectability" (563–66).

Krause's discussion of satire pertains not only to the structure of the story but also to its thematic implications. He provides a detailed analysis of the two historical figures for whom Jim Smiley's memorable animals are named: Andrew Jackson and Daniel Webster. The names of Smiley's pets suggest the sectional tensions or conflicting values underlying the various points of view that, according to Krause, the author implicitly reconciles: the ideal American is a composite of eastern and western values represented by Webster, "the Whiggish paragon of the self-made man," and Jackson, the actual realization of that paragon on the democratic frontier (568–76). Lawrence Smith too discusses the heroic ideal Mark Twain intimates in this "parable . . . of America." Though to the urban easterner Simon Wheeler may seem the harmless, stereotypical yokel—lazy, dim-witted, homely—he is in fact "an American Homer" who in native language celebrates heartland values that stand diametrically in opposition to the narrator's false genteel ones. Smiley's shrewdness and spirit of daring enterprise coupled with the stranger's "skeptical pragmatism" form an "American heroic ideal" (15–17).

Paul Smith provides a reading of the "Jumping Frog" story that furnishes more insight into the deficiencies of archetypal criticism than it does into the themes of Mark Twain's tale. The story, Smith argues, traces the tragic fall of American culture from its original lofty idealism and hence marks the beginning of Mark Twain's cynical acceptance of human depravity. The date of the story, "just seven short months after Appomatox," points explicitly to the theme of regional conflict, though Smith never quite makes clear how we as readers are to make the transposition from North/South to East/West. Mark Twain's colloquial references to Wheeler's "infernal reminiscence" Smith appears to take literally, for the story becomes an archetypal voyage into "the underworld of punishment and damnation": Mark Twain as narrator, like Aeneas or Dante the pilgrim, embarks on a quest for religious truth (information about the "mythic" Rev. Leonidas) that takes him beyond the comfortable, known world of the civilized East into the "enchanted wilderness" of the unknown West. Angel's Camp, or Boomerang as it was called in the 1865 version, becomes the Perilous Chapel of Jessie L. Weston's *From Ritual to Romance;* the narrator must plummet its inner recesses in his search for the truth concealed from him by the evil magus Simon Wheeler, the traditional enchanter who, like the Ancient Mariner or Simple Simon, spins an enticing web of deceptive magic (41–44). Published in the first volume of *Satire Newsletter,* Smith's essay may well be a parody of criticism that in its coy ingenuity calls more attention to itself than to what it ostensibly explicates or clarifies. In a deadpan manner that never suggests for a moment that there is anything absurd or humorous in the method followed or argument presented, Smith offers a reading of the story every bit as fantastic as Wheeler's yarn about Smiley's exploits with his humanized animals. Like Mark Twain the character in "Jim Smiley and His Jumping Frog," we as readers are taken in by the scholarly style and professional tone of the essay only to discover, ultimately, that we are the butt of an excellent joke.

Bibliography

PRIMARY

The Celebrated Jumping Frog of Calaveras County, and Other Sketches. Edited by John Paul. New York: Charles Henry Webb, 1867.

The Celebrated Jumping Frog of Calaveras County. And Other Sketches. London: George Routledge & Sons, 1870.

The Choice Humourous Works of Mark Twain. Now First Collected. London: John Camden Hotten, 1873.

The Choice Humorous Works of Mark Twain. Revised and Corrected by the Author. London: Chatto & Windus, 1874.

Great Short Works of Mark Twain. Edited by Justin Kaplan. New York: Harper & Row, 1967.

The Jumping Frog and Other Humourous Sketches. From the Original Edition. London: John Camden Hotten, 1870.

Mark Twain's Celebrated Jumping Frog of Calaveras County and Other Sketches. With the Burlesque Autobiography and First Romance. London: George Routledge & Sons, 1872.

Mark Twain's Letters. Edited by Albert B. Paine. Vol. 1. New York: Harper & Brothers, 1917.

Mark Twain's Sketches. Selected and Revised by the Author. London: George Routledge & Sons, 1872.

Mark Twain's Sketches, New and Old. Now First Published in Complete Form. Hartford and Chicago: American Publishing Co., 1875.

Mark Twain's Sketches, Number One. Authorized Edition. New York: American News Co., 1874.

"Private History of the 'Jumping Frog' Story." *North American Review* 158 (1894):446–53.

A 3rd Supply of Yankee Drolleries. London: John Camden Hotten, 1870.

The Works of Mark Twain: Early Tales and Sketches. Vol. 2 (1864–1865). Edited by Edgar M. Branch and Robert H. Hirst. Vol. 15 of the Iowa-California edition of *The Works of Mark Twain*. Berkeley and Los Angeles: University of California Press, 1981.

SECONDARY

Baldanza, Frank. *Mark Twain: An Introduction and Interpretation*. New York: Holt, Rinehart & Winston, 1961.

Baender, Paul. "The 'Jumping Frog' as a Comedian's First Virtue." *Modern Philology* 60 (February 1963):192–200.

Bellamy, Gladys C. *Mark Twain as a Literary Artist*. Norman: University of Oklahoma Press, 1950.

Benson, Ivan. *Mark Twain's Western Years*. Stanford, Calif.: Stanford University Press, 1938.

Blair, Walter. *Mark Twain & Huck Finn*. Berkeley and Los Angeles: University of California Press, 1960.

———. *Native American Humor, 1800–1900*. New York: American Book Co., 1937.

Branch, Edgar M. *The Literary Apprenticeship of Mark Twain, With Selections from His Apprentice Writing*. Urbana: University of Illinois Press, 1950.

———. " 'My Voice is Still for Setchell': A Background Study of 'Jim Smiley and His Jumping Frog.' " *PMLA* 82 (1967):591–601.

Buckbee, Edna Bryan. "Mark Twain's Treasure Pile." In *Pioneer Days of Angel's Camp*, 21–35. Angel's Camp, Calif.: Calaveras Californian, 1932.

Cohen, Hennig. "Twain's Jumping Frog: Folktale to Literature to Folktale." *Western Folklore* 22 (January 1963):17–18.

Covici, Pascal, Jr. *Mark Twain's Humor: The Image of a World*. Dallas: Southern Methodist University Press, 1962.

Cox, James M. *Mark Twain: The Fate of Humor*. Princeton, N.J.: Princeton University Press, 1966.

Cuff, Roger Penn. "Mark Twain's Use of California Folklore in His Jumping Frog Story." *Journal of American Folklore* 65 (April-June 1952):155–58.

Davis, Chestor L. "Jumping Frog and New York *Saturday Press;* Boston and New York Bohemians, W.D. Howells and 'Literary Friends.' " *Twainian* 18 (March-April 1959): 1–4.

DeVoto, Bernard. *Mark Twain's America*. Boston: Little, Brown, 1932.

Emerson, Everett. *The Authentic Mark Twain: A Literary Biography of Samuel L. Clemens*. Philadelphia: University of Pennsylvania Press, 1984.

Ferguson, Delancey. *Mark Twain: Man and Legend*. Indianapolis: Bobbs-Merrill, 1943.

Gerber, John C. "Mark Twain's Use of the Comic Pose." *PMLA* 77 (June 1962): 297–304.

Holman, C. Hugh. *Windows on the World: Essays on American Social Fiction*. Knoxville: University of Tennessee Press, 1979.

Kinnaird, Clark. "Mark Twain's First Book." *American Mercury* 60 (January 1945):124.

Krause, S. J. "The Art and Satire of Twain's 'Jumping Frog' Story." *American Quarterly* 16 (Winter 1964):562–76.

Lewis, Oscar. *The Origins of the Celebrated Jumping Frog of Calaveras County*. San Francisco: The Book Club of California, 1931.

Long, E. Hudson. *Mark Twain Handbook*. New York: Hendricks House, 1957.

Lynn, Kenneth. *Mark Twain and Southwestern Humor*. Boston: Little, Brown, 1959.

Morrissey, Frank R. "The Ancestor of the 'Jumping Frog.' " *Bookman* 53 (April 1921):143–45.

Paine, Albert B. *Mark Twain: A Biography*. Vol. 1. New York: Harper & Brothers, 1912.

Regan, Robert. *Unpromising Heroes: Mark Twain and His Characters*. Berkeley and Los Angeles: University of California Press, 1966.

Rodgers, Paul C., Jr. "Artemus Ward and Mark Twain's 'Jumping Frog.' " *Nineteenth Century Fiction* 28 (December 1973): 273–86.

Rogers, Franklin R. *Mark Twain's Burlesque Patterns*. Dallas: Southern Methodist University Press, 1960.

Rowlette, Robert. " 'Mark Ward on Artemus Twain': Twain's Literary Debt to Ward." *American Literary Realism* 6 (1973):13–25.

Schmidt, Paul. "The Deadpan on Simon Wheeler." *Southwest Review* 41 (Summer 1956):270–77.

Smith, Henry Nash. *Mark Twain: The Development of a Writer*. Cambridge, Mass.: Harvard University Press, 1962.

Smith, Lawrence R. "Mark Twain's 'Jumping Frog': Toward an American Heroic Ideal." *Mark Twain Journal* 20, no. 1 (1979):15–18.

Smith, Paul. "The Infernal Reminiscence: Mythic Patterns in Mark Twain's 'The Celebrated Jumping Frog of Calaveras County.' " *Satire Newsletter* 1 (Spring 1964):41–44.

Spengemann, William C. *Mark Twain and the Backwoods Angel: The Matter of Innocence in the Works of Samuel L. Clemens*. Kent, Ohio: Kent State University Press, 1966.

Taylor, J. Golden. "The Celebrated Jumping Frog of Calaveras County." *American West* 2 (Fall 1965):73–76.

Wilson, Mark K. "Mr. Clemens and Madame Blanc: Mark Twain's First French Critic." *American Literature* 45 (January 1974):537–56.

26

Legend of the Capitoline Venus
Is He Living or Is He Dead?

Publication History

The "Legend of the Capitoline Venus" is one of the earliest of the more than fifty pieces Mark Twain published in the Buffalo, New York, *Express* through the early 1870s, appearing on 23 October 1869. The title was shortened to "The Capitoline Venus" when the story was reprinted in the 1875 collection, *Sketches, New and Old.* This volume is included in the Author's National Edition of *The Writings of Mark Twain* (1917). Charles Neider includes the story in his one-volume edition of *The Complete Short Stories.*

"Is He Living or Is He Dead?" was written in 1893 and published in *Cosmopolitan* in September of the same year. The story is included in the *Hadleyburg* volume of 1900.

Circumstances of Composition, Sources, and Influences

Upon his return to the United States from the *Quaker City* excursion to Europe and the Holy Land, Mark Twain began a conscious attempt to gain respectability and acceptance as a bona fide man-of-letters. The impact of this "reformation" on his literary career centered largely on his revision of the *Alta* letters for publication as *The Innocents Abroad* (1869); Dickinson notes that in transforming these letters into cohesive book form, Mark Twain diligently pruned indelicacies, softened his slang, vulgarities, blasphemy, and attacks on European culture (139–57). Motivated by his love for Olivia Langdon, Mark Twain likewise sought a renovation of his personal life, hoping to prove to himself, his beloved, and her eminently respectable upper middle-class family that he was a worthy suitor with prospects for the future. Steinbrink reports that during the late 1860s Mark Twain "earnestly undertook a reformation of character that was intended to make him a conventionally 'better' person—more religious, more regular in his habits, more refined, more comprehensively civilized" (299). He wrote to Olivia's mother in early 1869 to ask that she recognize that the public personality Mark Twain and the private man Samuel Clemens were two distinct people; the latter, he assured her, had given up smoking, drinking, profanity, and, moreover, had become a Christian. Mrs. Langdon seems to have been duly impressed, for she wrote to Mrs. Fairbanks that "a great change has taken place in Mr. Clemens, and he seems to have entered upon a new manner of life, with higher and better purposes actuating his conduct" (*Mark Twain to Mrs. Fairbanks* 53).

Having won Olivia's heart and secured the blessing of her parents, Mark Twain decided it was time to establish roots before his scheduled 2 February 1870 wedding date. In the summer of 1869 he purchased one-third interest in the Buffalo *Express* with money advanced him by Jervis Langdon, his future father-in-law, and assumed a position as associate editor. His "Salutation," published in the 21 August 1869 *Express,* struck what was to serve as Mark Twain's characteristic pose in the more than fifty pieces written for the newspaper through the early 1870s: "I shall not make use of slang and vulgarity upon any occasion or under any circumstances, and shall never use profanity except when discussing house rent and taxes. . . . I shall not often meddle with politics, because we have a political Editor, who is already excellent and needs only a term or two in the penitentiary to be perfect" (Emerson 57). Steinbrink claims that by this time, "the basic terms of accommodation between writer and persona were at least provisionally established," and that Mark Twain had come to feel sufficiently at peace with himself "to satisfy his readers' expectations concerning Mark Twain's drollery and notoriety" (300, 315). By October he had begun a series of "Around the World" letters for the *Express.* The idea was for Mark Twain to write the letters while staying at home in Buffalo, using as his inspiration the reports of an actual traveler, Olivia's brother Charley Langdon. He wrote eight letters in the series; six of them, however, were based on his own earlier travels in the American West; they eventually found their way into the 1872 volume *Roughing It* (Emerson 57–58). The series is significant in that it signals Mark Twain's return to his western past for artistic materials—a further indication that he had achieved inner harmony and a clearer sense of professional direction. As Steinbrink writes, "Clemens could not have made imaginative use of this material while he was melodramatically declaring his unworthiness and repudiating his past during the last months of 1868. It was only after passing through that phase of his reformation and regaining his balance as a man and a writer that he was able to draw with increasing confidence upon the resources which that past contained" (315).

Part of the inspiration for the "Legend of the Capitoline Venus" is no doubt autobiographical. A story of an unappreciated, struggling artist who is denied the woman he loves until he raises fifty thousand dollars, it was written, Emerson reports, while Mark Twain felt "pressure to demonstrate his eligibility for Olivia's hand to her father" (57). The story also reflects

Mark Twain's recent experience in Europe, where antiquity seemed a more valuable quality in art than original genius or consummate craftsmanship. Such misguided aesthetic appreciation is not limited to Europe, however; Mark Twain concludes the story with the cautionary advice, "when you read about a gigantic Petrified Man being dug up near Syracuse, in the State of New York, or near any other place, keep your own counsel—and if the Barnum that buried him there offers to sell it to you at an enormous sum, don't you buy. Send him to the Pope!" The topical reference, he informs us in a note, is to "the famous swindle of the 'Petrified Man,' " which "was the sensation of the day in the United States" (273).

Mark Twain wrote "Is He Living or Is He Dead?" in 1893 while on an extended visit to New York. Like "The Esquimau Maiden's Romance" (1893), it was written quickly for money to cover living expenses while Mark Twain struggled to shore up sagging investments. The story was written for *Cosmopolitan,* whose editor had agreed to pay Mark Twain a total of five thousand dollars for twelve stories (Emerson 189). Mark Twain liked the story well enough to return to it in 1898 as the basis for a dramatic comedy, "Is He Dead?", a play Macnaughton claims was "certainly no worse than the popular drama of the United States" and "could have been . . . made into an entertaining, playable piece with some judicious cutting" (77–78).

Like the "Legend of the Capitoline Venus," this story reflects the contemporary frustrations of its author over the failure of his artistic productions to garner the public acclaim and financial return he thought they merited. Economic conditions and public aesthetic taste were such that the financially struggling artist seemed a more valuable commodity dead than alive.

Relationship to Other Mark Twain Works

In theme these two stories are similar to *Innocents Abroad* as they satirize the blind reverence for antiquity that seemed to characterize contemporary art criticism (Baldanza 101). In this context one remembers Mark Twain's untutored judgment at the Louvre that the imitations by art students were in many instances superior to the masters they copied, or his unabashed disappointment with Titian's "red"—badly faded through age but all the more reverenced by art critics who viewed reality through the colored perspective of tradition. Both the "Legend of the Capitoline Venus" and "Is He Living or Is He Dead?" revolve around elaborate artistic hoaxes and the public's gullible susceptibility to them. This theme recurs in *Huckleberry Finn* (1885) when those two irrepressible frauds, the duke and the dauphin, capitalize on the provinciality of their frontier audience by pretending to be Garrick and Kean performing scenes from Shakespeare.

The form of the "Legend of the Capitoline Venus," the condensed novel, is one Mark Twain has mastered in his early California journalistic sketches, such as "Aurelia's Unfortunate Young Man" (1864) and "Lucretia Smith's Soldier" (1864). Hence in some ways the piece is, as Emerson argues, "a continuation of the sketch writing he had begun in the west" (60). Rogers, however, links "The Capitoline Venus" to "An Awful, Terrible Medieval Romance"—also published in the *Express* (1 January 1870). Both employ the condensed novel format, but unlike the earlier California efforts, neither is what Rogers calls "a true burlesque." In these two *Express* pieces Mark Twain relies for his plot upon conventional situations and devices common to the contemporary popular literature he often parodied; his humor, however, derives not from the burlesque of such conventional fiction but from intrinsically comical ideas that previously would have taken the form of sketches or anecdotes. The condensed novel format simply serves as a vehicle to structure ideas. The method anticipates *Tom Sawyer* (1876), which uses the form of the burlesque novel to structure humorous episodes (100–101).

Critical Studies

The "Legend of the Capitoline Venus" is a six-chapter condensed novel set in Rome that tells the story of "a divinely gifted sculptor with nothing to eat" who must somehow earn fifty thousand dollars to secure the blessing of his beloved Mary's father and her hand in marriage. The old man is kindly disposed to the struggling artist, but in good conscience cannot allow his daughter to "marry a hash of love, art, and starvation." Fame, he tells the young artist, is "nothing—the market price of your marble scarecrow is the thing to look at. . . . Show me fifty thousand dollars and you can have my daughter—otherwise she marries young Simper" (266–67).

The artist's consummate aesthetic achievement is a "statue of America"; yet the tangible expression of his genius "has no sympathy for me in her cold marble countenance—so beautiful and so heartless." In his despair the artist turns to his friend John who, of a more practical cast of mind and with a sure command of the marketplace, initiates an ingenious plan: he smashes the statue with a hammer, rendering it a "battered and grotesque nightmare before him," then advertises the piece as an excavation. *Il Slangwhanger di Roma* reports: "Signor Smitthe unearthed the most remarkable ancient statue that has ever been added to the opulent art treasures of Rome." A Roman commission "decided unanimously that the statue is a Venus, and the work of some unknown but sublimely gifted artist of the third century before Christ. They consider it the most faultless work of art the world has any knowledge of" (271). With an established value of 10 million francs in gold, the statue returns the artist cum excavator one-half that sum and hence wins for him the hand of his beloved.

The story does indeed have autobiographical implications. Like the artist in the story, Mark Twain needed desperately to establish his prospects, to prove to his prospective father-in-law that he could earn a handsome living and support a family with his pen. To do so, he realized, might well involve certain aesthetic compromises, for his success depended on his ability to gauge the market; such, however, he felt is the price of domestic bliss. More generally the story suggests the plight of any artist who to survive must contend with the shallow values of a paying public led by fads and art critics who place a higher premium on antiquity and tradition than on brilliant, original creation. Significantly the pristine "Statue of America" is worthless, though critically acclaimed by "The Hon. Bellamy Foodle of Arkansas." Only after it is Europeanized, rendered a "battered and grotesque nightmare" to assume its identity as the "Capitoline Venus," does the art work attain commercial value. The humor of "The Capitoline Venus" rests largely in its satire of those who pretend to be guardians of culture but who in fact lack any true aesthetic sense. Restored "by the most noted Roman artists," the treasured "Capitoline Venus" is once again beautiful—though "nothing to what she was before that blessed John Smith broke her leg and battered her nose" (272–73).

"Is He Living or Is He Dead?" also concerns a hoax perpetrated by artists to inflate the commercial value of their work. The setting is Mentone, on the French Riviera, in March 1892. A brief frame introduces the main narrative: Mark Twain meets a wealthy gentleman in a hotel lobby who then tells a story from his youth, a tale of how as a struggling artist he conspired with three fellow painters to inflate the value of the work of one of their group—François Millet—by spreading the rumor he was dead.

The satire obviously is directed at public aesthetic taste and reveals the desperate plight of the artist in a capitalistic economy. Alive, Millet "hadn't any fame, even in his own village; and he was so poor that he hadn't anything to feed us on but turnips." His paintings are quite good, "of such great and high merit that, if an illustrious name were attached to them, they would sell at splendid prices" (310). The problem, thus, is one of marketing: how does one command a good price for a good product from customers unwilling to patronize a struggling, contemporary artist? The group understands well the shallow aesthetic values of its patrons: by spreading the rumor that Millet is dying, they immediately inflate the value of his existing work; once he is dead, the work, both finished and incomplete, becomes virtually priceless. The group even stages a mock funeral, with Millet acting as a pallbearer of the casket containing his wax likeness.

So anxious is the public to acquire Millet's paintings that all four artists profit enormously from the ruse.

Bibliography

PRIMARY

*The Complete Short Stories of Mark Twain. Now Collected for the First Time. Edited by Charles Neider. Garden City, N.Y.: Hanover House, 1957. ["Is He Living or Is He Dead?"]

The Man That Corrupted Hadleyburg and Other Stories and Essays. New York: Harper & Brothers, 1900.

Mark Twain Sketches, New and Old. Now First Published in Complete Form. Hartford and Chicago: American Publishing Co., 1875.

Mark Twain to Mrs. Fairbanks. Edited by Dixon Wecter. San Marino, Calif.: Huntington Library, 1949.

*The Writings of Mark Twain. Author's National Edition. Harper & Brothers Edition. Vol. 23. New York: P. F. Collier & Son, 1917. ["Legend of the Capitoline Venus."]

SECONDARY

Baldanza, Frank. Mark Twain: An Introduction and Interpretation. New York: Holt, Rinehart & Winston, 1961.

Dickinson, Leon T. "Mark Twain's Revisions in Writing The Innocents Abroad." American Literature 19 (1947):139–57.

Emerson, Everett. The Authentic Mark Twain: A Literary Biography of Samuel L. Clemens. Philadelphia: University of Pennsylvania Press, 1984.

Macnaughton, William R. Mark Twain's Last Years as a Writer. Columbia: University of Missouri Press, 1979.

Rogers, Franklin R. Mark Twain's Burlesque Patterns. Dallas: Southern Methodist University Press, 1960.

Steinbrink, Jeffrey. "How Mark Twain Survived Sam Clemens' Reformation." American Literature 55 (October 1983):299–315.

27

The Loves of Alonzo Fitz Clarence
and Rosannah Ethelton

Publication History

Written in late 1877, during what might be called the domestic period of Mark Twain's life, "The Loves of Alonzo Fitz Clarence and Rosannah Ethelton" was published in the *Atlantic Monthly* in the spring of 1878. It is picked up by James R. Osgood in his 1882 collection of Mark Twain pieces from the *Atlantic*, *The Stolen White Elephant*, a volume Emerson calls "the least distinguished" of all Mark Twain books (118).

Circumstances of Composition, Sources, and Influences

The story is a representative work from what is in many ways the bleakest and least productive period of Mark Twain's artistic career. After the completion of *Tom Sawyer* in 1875, the author entered a period of aesthetic decline and considerable professional frustration. Neither *Tom Sawyer* nor the best short stories of the period—"A True Story" (1874) and "Facts Concerning the Recent Carnival of Crime in Connecticut" (1876)—proved as commercially successful as he had hoped. He began in the summer of 1876 a sequel to *Tom Sawyer*, a first-person narrative he tentatively titled "Huck Finn's Autobiography," but wrote to William Dean Howells in August that he liked the piece "only tolerably well" and put it aside for three years. This was but one of at least five unfinished books initiated and then abandoned during the late 1870s. Committed to becoming a genuine man-of-letters, Mark Twain seems to have lost control of his career and enthusiasm for his art; attempts to break clear of patterns established in his successful early fiction produce uncertainty and disastrous attempts at new genres. In the fall of 1876 he began work with Bret Harte on a comic drama about a Chinese laundryman in the California mining country, *Ah Sin*—"that dreadful play," Mark Twain termed it, that opened in Washington D.C., in May 1877 but after a brief stint in New York and Saint Louis was retired in October of the same year. Another attempt at drama, *Simon Wheeler*, proved even more of an aesthetic disaster and Mark Twain could find no one to produce it (Emerson 92–96).

Ironically it is one of his finest efforts of the period that caused him the most frustration and self-doubt: a sketch he delivered orally at the Whittier birthday dinner in Boston 17 December 1877. Though a comic masterpiece in controlled vernacular dialect, the speech offended Howells and humiliated Mark Twain, causing him to reevaluate his career and position in American letters. He wrote to Howells asking that "The Loves of Alonzo Fitz Clarence and Rosannah Ethelton," already scheduled for publication in the *Atlantic,* be withdrawn so as not to damage the magazine's reputation (Hill 127). His plan, he informed Howells, was "to retire from before the country at present"; to his mother he wrote in February 1878, "I have about made up my mind to take my tribe & fly to some little corner of Europe & budge no more until I shall have completed one of the half dozen books that lie begun, upstairs" (Emerson 98–99).

Horowitz reports that the story responds to contemporary technological developments. The telephone that serves as the vehicle of the plot corresponds exactly to the first commercial telephone model introduced earlier in 1877. Always fascinated with gadgets and mechanical inventions, Mark Twain readily adapts this one to his burlesque purposes (16).

Relationship to Other Mark Twain Works

"The Loves of Alonzo Fitz Clarence and Rosannah Ethelton" looks backward rather than forward in terms of Mark Twain's development as an artist. The description of Aunt Susan's San Francisco apartment—"manifestly the private parlor of a refined and sensible lady"—anticipates the Grangerford parlor in *Huckleberry Finn* (1885):

> On a luxurious sofa, upholstered with some sort of soft Indian goods wrought in black and gold threads interwebbed with other threads not so pronounced in color, lay a great square of coarse white stuff, upon whose surface a rich bouquet of flowers was growing, under the deft cultivation of the crochet-needle. The household cat was asleep on this work of art. In a bay-window stood an easel with an unfinished picture on it, and a palette and brushes on a chair beside it. There were books everywhere: Robertson's Sermons, Tennyson, Moody and Sankey, Hawthorne, *Rab and his Friends,* cook-books, prayer-books, pattern-books—and books about all kinds of odious and exasperating pottery, of course. (131).

But the story is primarily a satire of romantic love fiction, and as such bears affinity to early journalistic pieces such as "Lucretia Smith's Soldier" (1864) and "Aurelia's Unfortunate Young Man" (1864). A great deal of the freshness, or spontaneity, of these earlier burlesques is missing from this tale, however; as Baldanza notes, Mark Twain handles his subject about "as gently as a steer in a slaughterhouse" (100). As in the earlier burlesques of female fiction, Mark Twain works within the conventions to attack them (Covici 207); yet the joke—of a romance conducted via telephone between two lovers who never see one another—is carried so far as to become tedious.

Critical Studies

The story has drawn scant critical commentary or analysis, largely because it is a light and airy piece detailing little of consequence. What comic joys there are in "The Loves of Alonzo Fitz Clarence and Rosannah Ethelton" result from the preposterous plot and from the language, which parodies the inflated language of popular romance fiction. Gibson notes that in its intermingling of the fashion parlance of women's literature with nautical diction, the story becomes one of Mark Twain's "early ventures into double talk" (14).

The story opens in Eastport, Maine, on a snowy December morning when "great white drifts banked themselves like graves across the streets" (127). Sitting alone "in his smug and elegant little parlor, in a lovely blue silk dressing-gown, with cuffs and facings of crimson satin, elaborately quilted," Alonzo Fitz Clarence longs for "a new interest, a fresh element, to whet the dull edge of captivity" (128). He telephones his Aunt Susan in San Francisco, ostensibly to learn the correct time so he can set his malfunctioning battery clock. While on the phone with Aunt Susan, Alonzo hears in the background a peculiarly flat rendition of "In the Sweet By-and-By" and immediately falls in love with the vocalist Rosannah Ethelton—"the daintiest thing these premises, within or without, could offer for contemplation"—who is in San Francisco, sitting in the ornate parlor of Aunt Susan's home. The extended description of Rosannah serves as the most striking example of Mark Twain's burlesque language: "delicately chiseled features, of Grecian cast; her complexion the pure snow of a japonica that is receiving a faint reflected enrichment from some scarlet neighbor of the garden; great, soft blue eyes fringed with long, curving lashes; an expression made up of the trustfulness of a child and the gentleness of a fawn; a beautiful head crowned with its own prodigal gold; a lithe and rounded figure, whose every attitude and movement was instinct with native grace" (132). After a two-hour conversation, the two young lovers initiate what promises to be a lasting romance.

Conflict in the story surfaces with the arrival of the antagonist Mr. Sidney Algernon Burley who, "with his empty head and his single little antic talent of mimicry," is likewise infatuated with the captivating Miss

Ethelton. Burley overhears Rosannah murmur, "All the day long, and all through my nightly dreams, one song sings itself, and its sweet burden is 'Alonzo Fitz Clarence, Alonzo Fitz Clarence, Eastport, state of Maine!' " Thus apprised of his foe's address, Burley resolves to thwart the budding romance: he "hissed through his teeth, in unconscious imitation of a popular favorite in melodrama, 'Him shall she never wed! I have sworn it! Ere great Nature shall have doffed her winter's ermine to don the emerald gauds of spring, she shall be mine!' " (136).

Posing as "a very prim and devout-looking Episcopal clergyman," Burley gains entrance to Clarence's home and his trust, and thereby learns to mimic his voice. On the telephone from Maine, posing as Alonzo, Burley asks Rosannah not to sing "Sweet By-and-By" any longer but to "try something modern." Her vanity wounded, Rosannah grows cold to her long-distance lover and their romance seems irrevocably blighted. By the time Alonzo discovers the hoax Burley has perpetrated, Rosannah has vanished: "So he took his carpet-sack and a portable telephone, and shook the snow of his native city from his artics, and went forth into the world. Time and again, strangers were astounded to see a wasted, pale, and woe-worn man laboriously climb a telegraph-pole in wintry and lonely places, perch sadly there an hour, with his ear at a little box, then come sighing down, and wander wearily away" (139).

Ultimately, of course, the two telephone lovers reestablish contact, clear up all misunderstandings, and take their revenge on Burley. Aunt Susan accompanies Rosannah from Hawaii across the United States to Eastport, "and had the happiness of witnessing the rapturous meeting between an adoring husband and wife who had never seen each other until that moment" (143).

Bibliography

PRIMARY

*The Complete Short Stories of Mark Twain. Now Collected for the First Time. Edited by Charles Neider. Garden City, N.Y.: Hanover House, 1957.

The Stolen White Elephant Etc. Boston: James R. Osgood, 1882.

SECONDARY

Baldanza, Frank. Mark Twain: An Introduction and Interpretation. New York: Holt, Rinehart & Winston, 1961.

Covici, Pascal, Jr. Mark Twain's Humor: The Image of a World. Dallas: Southern Methodist University Press, 1962.

Emerson, Everett. *The Authentic Mark Twain: A Literary Biography of Samuel L. Clemens.* Philadelphia: University of Pennsylvania Press, 1984.

Gibson, William M. *The Art of Mark Twain.* New York: Oxford University Press, 1976.

Hill, Hamlin. *Mark Twain and Elisha Bliss.* Columbia: University of Missouri Press, 1964.

Horowitz, Floyd R. "Mark Twain's Belle Lettre in 'The Loves of Alonzo Fitz Clarence and Rosannah Ethelton.' " *Mark Twain Journal* 13, no. 1 (Winter 1965):16.

28

Luck

Two Little Tales

Publication History

Mark Twain published "Luck" in the August 1891 issue of *Harper's Magazine*. The story was reprinted in *Merry Tales,* published by Charles Webster the following year. "Two Little Tales" first appeared in *Century,* November 1901, and then was included by Tauchnitz in its edition of *A Double-Barrelled Detective Story* published in Germany in 1902. First book publication in the United States came in 1903. The story is also included in *The $30,000 Bequest* volume published by Harper and Brothers in 1906.

Circumstances of Composition, Sources, and Influences

Mark Twain wrote "Luck" no later than 1886, since his daughter Susy recalled that her father read the story to members of the family in that year and that they had greatly enjoyed it. The author had heard the story from his good friend Joe Twichell and, Paine reports, followed his source almost verbatim. A footnote to the story supports Paine's supposition: "This is not a fancy sketch. I got it from a clergyman who was an instructor at Woolwich forty years ago, and who vouched for its truth" (*Complete Short Stories* 249). Although the story was purportedly based on fact, Mark Twain thought "it too improbable for literature" and placed it aside (Paine 842). In early spring 1891, however, Mark Twain faced severe financial pressures. His investment in the Paige typesetting machine was not turning out well and he was forced to borrow ten thousand dollars from Olivia's mother. To raise revenue he rifled his files for any material that might be publishable and in the process resurrected this "thin and unoriginal story," which he sent to *Harper's* (Emerson 170).

Mark Twain wrote "Two Little Tales" while living in London in the fall of 1900 and published it the following year in the British magazine *Century*. The story shows, Emerson writes, that the author's "disdain for writing for money was not complete" (230–31). Paine reports that the inspiration for "Two Little Tales" came directly from Mark Twain's experience with his investment in plasmon, a milk albumen he had adopted as his daily diet and with his partner J. Y. W. MacAlister hoped to market to the British War Office for troop use in South Africa. The obstacle confronting the business venture was governmental bureaucracy: how could Mark Twain or his partner cut through red tape to get the necessary interview with the medical director-general of the British army? MacAlister decided to use a personal approach, and worked through an acquaintance who was the director-general's close friend. The plan succeeded; on advice from his trusted friend, the chief medical officer agreed to experiment with plasmon and soon adopted it for his troops (Paine 1908–99).

Relationship to Other Mark Twain Works

"Luck" is what Baldanza calls a "gimmick story." Like "The Belated Russian Passport" (1902) and "The Californian's Tale" (1893) it carefully builds up reader expectations and then employs an O. Henry twist at the end to undercut those expectations (100). Justice or cosmic order would presumably dictate that "the supremest ass in the universe" (*Complete Short Stories* 253) would eventually come to an ignominious end. Instead his remarkable "luck" makes him a national hero. The idea that in an absurd or naturalistic universe coincidence plays a more important role than merit in determining one's fortune appears in early burlesques such as the "Story of the Bad Little Boy" (1865) and the "Story of the Good Little Boy Who Did Not Prosper" (1870) as well as in later satires like *The Mysterious Stranger* (1916).

Like "The Man Who Put Up at Gadsby's (1880), "Two Little Tales" satirizes governmental bureaucracy that results in gross inefficiency and perpetuates injustice (Baldanza 99). Like the naive claimant from Tennessee in the story from *A Tramp Abroad* (1880), the inventor's friend in "Two Little Tales" discovers that approaches through official governmental channels produce little result regardless of the justice or efficacy of the cause. But as in "The Belated Russian Passport," there emerges in "Two Little Tales" an effective alternative to the cumbersome inefficient official process: personal contact.

Critical Studies

The story "Luck" opens at a banquet in London to honor Lieutenant-General Lord Arthur Scoresby, "one of the two or three conspicuously illustrious English military names of this generation" (249). During the course of the ceremonies the narrator learns from a trusted friend, a clergyman, that Scoresby is in fact "an absolute fool." A few days later the narrator meets his friend again, who relates in detail the story behind Scoresby's rise to fame.

The clergyman reports that he had taught Scoresby in school. Although the boy was "evidently good, and sweet, and lovable, and guileless," he was also a dunce; his answers in class were "veritably miraculous for stupidity and ignorance" (250). Feeling sorry for the hopeless boy, the clergyman tutored him through his examinations, and as a result Scoresby gains a prominent position in the British army during the Crimean War—much to the dismay of his tutor: "Here was a wooden-head whom I had put in the way of glittering promotions and prodigious responsibilities" (251). As a captain in the war, Scoresby did nothing to erase his mentor's misgivings: "he never did anything *but* blunder." Others, however, mistook his blunders "for inspirations of genius." Scoresby's great triumph comes when mistaking his right hand for his left he inadvertently sends a small regiment over a hill to attack "an entire and unsuspected Russian army in reserve." The Russians, thinking no one would be so idiotic as to attack with a mere regiment, assumes the paltry force is the advance of an entire army and so flee in disarray. Thus the "lovable and unpretending" Scoresby, who "doesn't know enough to come in when it rains," becomes the nation's hero: "he has littered his whole military life with blunders, and yet has never committed one that didn't make him a knight or a baronet or a lord or something" (253).

Mark Twain's reservations about this story were well grounded. It is "too improbable for literature." Scoresby's "most phenomenal and astonishing luckiness" is not fiction, however; it is fact, Mark Twain assures us, and serves to undercut our propensity to make heroes of those whom chance propels to the forefront in the absurd world of war.

As the title suggests, "Two Little Tales" consists of two brief, interrelated narratives. The first, "The Man with a Message for the Director-General," establishes the conflict. An inventor has manufactured "a light and very cheap and durable boot, which would remain dry in wet weather" (400). He mentions his discovery to a friend, who immediately sees that the invention is ideal for British military use in South Africa and offers to bring the boot to the attention of the proper authorities. Unfortunately all attempts to reach the War Office through appropriate channels fail miserably; cold, impersonal bureaucracy renders inaccessible "the Director-General of the Shoe-Leather Department." A writer responds to his friend's dilemma that frustration is the predictable result of such a conventional but misguided approach. He offers as an exemplum a story he had written the night before—the second of the "Two Little Tales," entitled "How the Chimney-Sweep Got the Ear of the Emperor." Follow the example of this tale, the writer assures his friend, "then you will call on the Director-General at noon to-morrow and transact your business" (402).

The writer's tale is of a young chimney-sweep who knows a sure cure for an ailment that threatens the life of the emperor. The simple peasant boy thinks his only chance to reach the great emperor is to mail a letter, but as his friend Tommy explains, each night the trashman hauls away from the palace eighty thousand such letters, discarded unread. What is needed is a novel approach, one that will circumvent bureaucracy. Tommy proposes that he tell his closest friend of the cure, with the request that his friend in turn do the same with another, thus forming a "chain" of humanity leading to the emperor. Sure enough, by next evening news of the cure makes its way to the emperor, who is cured and who, in turn, works back down the chain to discover the boy who had saved his life.

Mark Twain then brings us back to the frame, or the first of the "Two Little Tales," to explain that, following the example of the chimney-sweep, the inventor's friend gets his interview with the director-general and the boot adopted for the military. Aided by art—the writer's tale—humanity triumphs over the deadening effects of a hopelessly cumbersome bureaucratic system.

Bibliography

PRIMARY

*The Complete Short Stories of Mark Twain. Now Collected for the First Time. Edited by Charles Neider. Garden City, N.Y.: Hanover House, 1957.

Merry Tales. New York: Charles L. Webster & Co., 1892.

My Debut as a Literary Person with Other Essays and Stories. Hartford: American Publishing Co., 1903.

The $30,000 Bequest and Other Stories. New York: Harper & Brothers, 1906.

SECONDARY

Baldanza, Frank. Mark Twain: An Introduction and Interpretation. New York: Holt, Rinehart & Winston, 1961.

Emerson, Everett. The Authentic Mark Twain: A Literary Biography of Samuel L. Clemens. Philadelphia: University of Pennsylvania Press, 1984.

Paine, Albert B. Mark Twain: A Biography. Vol. 3. New York: Harper & Brothers, 1912.

29

Lucretia Smith's Soldier

Publication History

"Lucretia Smith's Soldier" first appeared in the 3 December 1864 issue of the *Californian*, a San Francisco literary magazine established by Charles Henry Webb and Bret Harte earlier that year. The story was immediately popular and was reprinted by various newspapers in California and in New York, frequently without permission or acknowledgment of prior publication. The 15 January 1865 reprinting in the *California Sunday Mercury* so angered Charles Henry Webb that he felt compelled to protest publicly in the *Californian* on 4 February 1865 (*Works* 127).

The story is included in the 1867 *Jumping Frog* collection, with some minor changes in diction and punctuation and a rather substantial revision of the opening paragraph. Probably the work of the publisher Webb, this revision transforms the "Note from the Author" to "Mr. Editor" into a more condensed, less topical, introduction designed for a national rather than a local audience: the reference to "stories in *Harper's Weekly*" that inspired the sketch becomes the more general "stories which have lately been so popular"; the allusion to "the Hon. T. G. Phelps, who has so long and ably represented this State [California] in Congress" disappears, as does specific mention of local publishing firms "Roman & Co. and Bancroft & Co.," and reference to the "excellent beer" supplied by a San Francisco brewery (*Works* 616). Virtually all the revisions in the Webb text are sustained in subsequent reprintings.

The Webb text is appropriated and printed unaltered in numerous unauthorized British editions published over the next five years (by George Routledge and Sons in 1867, 1870, and 1872 [the latter as *Mark Twain's Celebrated Jumping Frog*], and by John Camden Hotten in 1870). For the authorized British edition of *Mark Twain's Sketches* published in 1872, the author revised the story slightly: he deleted Lucretia's internal monologue—" 'Drat it!' The words were in her bosom, but she locked them there"—and dropped the words, "and slobbering," from a later speech. These changes are sustained in the Chatto and Windus edition of 1874. Initially Mark Twain intended to include "Lucretia Smith's Soldier" in his *Mark Twain's Sketches, New and Old* (1875), but either he or Elisha Bliss decided to delete the story prior to publication. A detailed discussion of all textual emendations is provided by Branch and Hirst (*Works* 615–21). The Iowa-California edition of *The Works of Mark Twain* (1981) bases its text on the original publication in the *Californian*.

Circumstances of Composition, Sources, and Influences

When Mark Twain arrived in San Francisco on 29 May 1864 he was already well known. His sketches, articles, and hoaxes published in the Virginia City, Nevada, *Enterprise* during the preceding twenty-two months had earned him notoriety and gained for him access to the city's literary circles. He quickly secured a position as the only full-time reporter for the *Morning Call*, but was almost immediately dissatisfied. In Nevada he had been a columnist and feature writer, with the liberty to pursue his interests; with the *Call*, however, he chafed under tight editorial supervision and found that the detail work involved in covering court cases, fires, and accidents, coupled with his duties as dramatic critic, enforced upon him a daily routine that he found debilitating and demoralizing (Ferguson 96–98; Benson 118–21). This is a period in his life when, as Mark Twain writes in *Roughing It* (1872), he "felt meaner, and lowlier and more despicable than the worms," a time when he struggled "lest the consciousness coming strong upon me that I was *entirely* penniless, might suggest suicide" (380–81; *Works* 126).

Free-lance writing afforded Mark Twain some release from the constraints imposed by his position with the *Call*. Soon after his arrival in San Francisco, Mark Twain sold two sketches to the *Golden Era*, California's first literary magazine. Established in 1852, its offices attracted the city's bohemian literati—Bret Harte, Charles Stoddard, Fitzhugh Ludlow, Orpheus C. Kerr, and Prentice Mulford. The first of Mark Twain's sketches, "Evidence in the Case of Smith vs. Jones" (26 June 1864), is a burlesque of the court trials he attended daily for the *Call*; the second, "Early Rising, as Regards Excursions to the Cliff House," mocks Ben Franklin's admonition "early to bed, early to rise, makes a man healthy, wealthy, and wise" (Benson 114–21). Rogers reports that the connection with the *Golden Era* and association with the bohemians who frequented its offices fueled Mark Twain's interest in "the dominant form of nineteenth-century British and American humor, the burlesque novel," the genre of "Lucretia Smith's Soldier." Perfected by Thackeray in England, the burlesque or condensed novel proved popular with Bret Harte who, under the pseudonym "J. Keyser," had published a series of them in the *Golden Era* from January 1861 to March 1863 (Rogers 14–18). From the *Golden Era* Mark Twain soon switched his loyalty to the newly established *Californian*, a literary magazine published by Harte and Charles Henry Webb that Mark Twain thought the best in the country. For the rather lavish sum of fifty dollars a month, Mark Twain agreed to supply the *Californian* one article a week. Although still employed by the *Call* on a reduced work load—an assistant was hired to assume the reporter's night duties—Mark Twain directed his intellectual energies and aesthetic interests toward his new post (Ferguson 98–99).

The close work with Harte and Webb proved a major influence on Mark Twain's development as literary artist. As early as 1863 he had begun writing in the burlesque mode, largely in imitation of John Phoenix, and his "Original Novelette"—published in the *Call,* 4 July 1864—is an initial attempt at the "condensed novel" form popularized by Harte and Webb (*Works* 31–33). Harte exerted what Ferguson calls a "refining influence" on Mark Twain's burlesque style; it was Harte, Mark Twain revealed to Thomas Bailey Aldrich in 1871, who transformed him "from an awkward utterer of coarse grotesqueness to a writer of paragraphs and chapters that have a certain favor in the eyes of some of the decentest people in the land" (Ferguson 98–99).

As a burlesque condensed novel, "Lucretia Smith's Soldier" obviously is indebted to the popular Civil War romances that inspired it, "those nice, sickly war stories in *Harper's Weekly.*" The introduction to the story ridicules by parody the formal style and pomposity of the prefaces and acknowledgments characteristic of sentimental fiction (Branch, *Literary Apprenticeship,* 118–19). Other specific targets of Mark Twain's satire, Branch and Hirst contend, are the platitudinous sentiments of Pierce Egan's *Such Is Life,* serialized in the *Golden Era* in 1864 and alluded to in the sketch's final paragraph; and Mary Elizabeth Braddon's *Trail of the Serpent,* a sentimental novel of extraordinary trial and tribulation serialized in the *Golden Era* from December 1863 to February 1864 (*Works* 126).

Relationship to Other Mark Twain Works

"Lucretia Smith's Soldier" belongs to Mark Twain's San Francisco bohemian period (1863–71). During this time of literary apprenticeship the author's talents turned primarily to burlesque and parody, often in imitation of or in tribute to other writers in the bohemian group; in fact, in a January 1866 letter to the Gold Hill *News* rival journalist Albert S. Evans disdainfully referred to Mark Twain as a "sage-brush Bohemian" (Rogers 18–19).

Branch groups the story with "The Killing of Julius Caesar Localized" (1864) and "Still Further Concerning that Conundrum" (1864) as "burlesques of literary fashions and manners" (*Literary Apprenticeship* 118–19). Into that same category fall "Aurelia's Unfortunate Young Man" (1864), "Story of the Bad Little Boy" (1865), "The Story of the Good Little

Boy Who Did Not Prosper" (1870), and "The Boy's Manuscript" (ca. 1870)—condensed novels that parody popular sentimental fiction. To these may be added several unpublished burlesque sketches composed during the same period: "Burlesque I1 Trovatore" (1866), "Who Was He?" (1867), "The Story of Mamie Grant, the Child Missionary" (1868), and "Burlesque l'Homme Qui Rit" (ca. 1869). Taken collectively, these sketches, fragments, and stories testify to what Emerson calls "the antiromantic and skeptical frame of mind Clemens had developed" (24–25). Such virulent antiromantic sentiments were characteristic of the bohemians as a group, and Mark Twain's preoccupation with the subject may have resulted in part from his desire to impress an audience with what he knew they would enjoy.

Critical Studies

"Lucretia Smith's Soldier" is among those early comic pieces that are critically flawed, Cox contends, because they "fail to go beyond the mechanism of burlesque" (24). Although most elements of the short story are present—character development, conflict, rising action, etc.—the plot of "Lucretia Smith's Soldier" is basically a single extended joke at the expense of sentimental illusions. Its humor results largely from its clever parody of the conventions and language of "those nice, sickly war stories in *Harper's Weekly*" and its ironic deflation of the characters' romantic reveries and expectations.

The "Note From the Author" to "Mr. Editor" establishes the tone and satiric method the story will follow. Mark Twain thanks the "Hon. T. G. Phelps" for gaining him access to "the official records in the War Department at Washington," which supplied the "facts" of the case; the publishing firms "Roman & Co. and Bancroft & Co." for loaning him "sundry maps and military works, so necessary for reference in building a novel like this," and "the accommodating Directors of the Overland Telegraph Company . . . for tendering me the use of their wires at the customary rates" (128). The acknowledgments, with all their pompous diction, are pointless, for in no way do the services mentioned prove germane to the story that follows. The crowning irony, however, comes from the author's confession that "the inspiration which enabled me in this production to soar so happily into the realms of sentiment and soft emotion" proceeds directly "from the excellent beer manufactured at the New York Brewery, in Sutter Street, between Montgomery and Kearny" (128). Despite the polite style and inflated diction, the point is obvious and serves to deflate the pompous tone: one would have to be drunk to take seriously the sentimental illusions that motivate the story's central characters.

Each of the condensed novel's four miniature chapters follows a consistent structural pattern: the characters' sentimental illusions, nursed and
fed by an overactive imagination, confront the bitter facts of life that serve
to render those illusions ridiculously inappropriate. The story opens in May
1861 on a small New England village that "lay wrapped in the splendor
of the newly-risen sun" (129). Reginald de Whittaker, Clerk for Bushrod
& Ferguson—"general dry goods and grocery dealers, and keepers of the
Post-office"—falls into reverie while sweeping the floor, thinking of how
pleased his love will be when she learns he is to be a soldier: "He pictured
himself in all manner of warlike situations; the hero of a thousand extraordinary adventures; . . . and beheld himself, finally, returning to his old
home, a bronzed and scarred Brigadier-General, to cast his honors and his
matured and perfect love at the feet of his Lucretia Borgia Smith." Just as
the "thrill of joy and pride suffused his system," however, Reginald glanced
at his broom and "came toppling down from the clouds," for he "was an
obscure clerk again, on a salary of two dollars and a half a week" (129).

Chapter 2 chronicles the last meeting of Reginald and Lucretia. Anxious to reveal to his beloved his decision to enlist, Reginald is stunned by
Lucretia's "chilling demeanor" as she draws back "like an offended queen."
Ironically she is disgusted that her young man has not responded to the
call of martial duty, and before he has a chance to announce the news that
would thrill her, she orders him "back to your pitiful junk-shop and grab
your pitiful yard-stick." No longer "an effeminate dry-goods student," Reginald surrenders to his "warrior soul" and refuses to plead his case. The
next day he marches solemnly off to war, stripped of the illusions that
motivated his enlistment.

When in chapter 3 Lucretia learns of her mistake, she is grief-stricken.
Her sorrow, however, focuses on her own loss: "Alas! other maidens would
have soldiers in those glorious fields, and be entitled to the sweet pain of
feeling a tender solicitude for them, but she would be unrepresented. No
soldier in all the vast armies would breathe her name as he breasted the
crimson tide of war!" (131). Her remorse, predicated on a romanticized
view of war, turns to resolution as she learns from the grim "long list of
maimed and killed" that "R. D. Whittaker, private soldier" has been "desperately wounded!" The poor Lucretia now has an object for her sentimental, and selfish, illusions.

Chapter 4 details Lucretia's patient and tender care for her heavily
bandaged soldier, as with "happy face" she ministers to his needs, "feeling
that when he did get well again she would hear that which would more
than reward her for all her devotion" (132). But again, the harsh facts of
life shatter romantic expectations. As the surgeons unravel the bandages
from the healing young man, Lucretia, "with beaming eyes and a fluttering
heart" discovers an awful truth: "O confound my cats if I haven't gone

and fooled away three mortal weeks here, snuffling and slobbering over the wrong soldier!" (132–33). The wounded proves to be Richard Delworthy Whittaker of Wisconsin, "the soldier of dear little Eugenie Le Mulligan." "Such is life," Mark Twain concludes, "and the trail of the serpent is over us all" (133).

Bibliography

PRIMARY

The Celebrated Jumping Frog of Calaveras County, And Other Sketches. Edited by John Paul. New York: Charles Henry Webb, 1867.

The Celebrated Jumping Frog of Calaveras County. And Other Sketches. Edited by John Paul. London: George Routledge & Sons, 1867.

The Celebrated Jumping Frog of Calaveras County. And Other Sketches. London: George Routledge & Sons, 1870.

The Choice Humorous Works of Mark Twain. Revised and Corrected by the Author. London: Chatto & Windus, 1874.

The Jumping Frog and Other Humorous Sketches. From the Original Edition. London: John Camden Hotten, 1870.

Mark Twain's Celebrated Jumping Frog of Calaveras County And Other Sketches. With the Burlesque Autobiography and First Romance. London: George Routledge & Sons, 1872.

Mark Twain's Sketches. Selected and Revised by the Author. London: George Routledge & Sons, 1872.

Roughing It. Edited by Franklin R. Rogers and Paul Baender. Berkeley and Los Angeles: University of California Press, 1972.

The Works of Mark Twain: Early Tales & Sketches. Vol. 2 (1864–1865). Edited by Edgar M. Branch and Robert H. Hirst. Vol. 15 of the Iowa-California edition of *The Works of Mark Twain.* Berkeley and Los Angeles: University of California Press, 1981.

SECONDARY

Benson, Ivan. *Mark Twain's Western Years.* Stanford, Calif.: Stanford University Press, 1938.

Branch, Edgar M. *The Literary Apprenticeship of Mark Twain, With Selections from His Apprentice Writings.* Urbana: University of Illinois Press, 1950.

Cox, James M. *Mark Twain: The Fate of Humor.* Princeton, N.J.: Princeton University Press, 1966.

Emerson, Everett. *The Authentic Mark Twain: A Literary Biography of Samuel L. Clemens.* Philadelphia: University of Pennsylvania Press, 1984.

Ferguson, Delancey. *Mark Twain: Man and Legend.* Indianapolis: Bobbs-Merrill, 1943.

Rogers, Franklin R. *Mark Twain's Burlesque Patterns.* Dallas: Southern Methodist University Press, 1960.

30

The Man That Corrupted Hadleyburg

Publication History

"The Man That Corrupted Hadleyburg" was written in Vienna, Austria, in December 1898. The autograph manuscript housed in the Pierpont Morgan Library (New York) shows that virtually the entire text was written on paper from the Metropole Hotel, Vienna (McKeithen 476). The story first appeared in print in the December 1899 issue of *Harper's Magazine* and was published in book form in June of the following year. Editions were published in England and in Germany later in 1900. Emerson reports that the story proved profitable, netting Mark Twain about two thousand dollars (222–24).

The story is among the most widely reprinted of Mark Twain's works and appears in virtually every anthology of nineteenth-century American literature.

Circumstances of Composition, Sources, and Influences

Two signal events in the late 1890s profoundly affected Mark Twain's temperament and consequently colored the tone and shape of his literary activity until his death in 1910. The failure of the Paige typesetting machine and the Webster Publishing Company culminated a series of bad investments that left the once wealthy Mark Twain bankrupt in 1895 and forced the proud author to embark on a world lecture tour to pay off his debts—one hundred cents on the dollar (Clark 1; Chard 595). Yet the resilient author seems to have recovered from this initial setback. He wrote to his close friend and financial adviser, Henry H. Rogers, that he had "begun life on a new and not altogether unpromising basis" (*Correspondence with Rogers* 100). In fact, Mark Twain seemed almost anxious to begin his career anew, and to give particular attention to establishing his reputation as a serious writer. Macnaughton argues that he was somewhat encouraged that his new life "would probably be similar to the life he had led just after his marriage" (10).

If Clemens responded to his 1895 bankruptcy as something of an exciting challenge, he was devastated by the death of his daughter Susy, of spinal meningitis in August of the following year. He wrote to Howells of Susy's death: "What a ghastly tragedy it was; how cruel it was; how exactly & precisely it was planned; & how remorselessly every detail of the dispensation was carried out . . . . Will healing ever come, or life have value again?" (*Mark Twain-Howells Letters* 663). Mark Twain engaged in several desperate ploys to evade the shocking fact of Susy's death: he longed to believe that all life was but a nightmare from which he would eventually awake; he turned his home in Connecticut into a virtual shrine to the dead daughter; and with Olivia, Clemens made several pathetic attempts to communicate with Susy through a spiritual medium (in May 1900 and in March 1901). But always he was forced back upon the undeniable fact of her mortality, which left him grief-stricken, guilt-laden, and bitter. On the first anniversary of Susy's death he wrote: "there you lie poor abused slave, set free from the unspeakable insult of life, and by the same Hand that flung it in your face in the beginning. But I lie: you have still nothing to be thankful for; for you have not been freed out of pity for you, but to drive one more knife into my heart. . . . [God] never does a kindness. When He seems to do one, it is a trap which He is setting" (*Mark Twain's Fables* 131–32).

Profoundly shaken as he was by the death of Susy, Mark Twain had also to confront the increasingly severe attacks of epilepsy suffered by his youngest daughter, Jean, and the rapidly deteriorating health of his wife, Olivia—a largely nervous condition aggravated if not caused, doctors suggested and Mark Twain suspected, by her husband's vocal despair and bitterness. Intense psychological pressure left the author the victim of wild fluctuations of mood that manifested themselves, on the one hand, in sentimental effusions over young girls and innocent fictional heroines in whom he saw Susy's image and, on the other hand, in vitriolic attacks on the "damned human race," the cosmic injustices under which it labored but, paradoxically, he thought it deserved, and the Deity he held responsible for the whole wretched mess.

Scholars traditionally have turned to these biographical facts to explain Mark Twain's failings as artist during the last years of his career. In what is perhaps the most provocative and controversial study of Mark Twain since Van Wyck Brooks's *Ordeal of Mark Twain* (1920), Hamlin Hill's *Mark Twain: God's Fool* (1973) argues that the author lost psychological control during the last ten years of his life. With frequent use of terms like "obsession" and "despair" Hill pens a bleak portrait of a pathetic, desperate man incapable of sustained literary achievement. Hill's reading of these last years predictably has received attack. In a review of Hill's book Tuckey counters that "despite the tensions of his last years, he [Mark Twain] remained appreciably sane as well as creative" (117). Kahn insists that the "total effect" of Mark Twain's later work, especially *The*

Mysterious Stranger (1916), is "one of mature mastery and control" (7). And most recently, Macnaughton focuses on Mark Twain's renewed sense of vocation and his achievements as "a professional writer," arguing that his failures are best explained not in terms of his assumed despair (which Macnaughton calls into question) but in terms of his problems as a professional writer trying to appeal to a diverse, though still largely genteel, audience. Mark Twain's notebook entries, Macnaughton asserts, "suggest a man preoccupied with grief. But they also suggest a writer who hopes to use dimensions of his experience—his guilt regarding his relationship with his daughters, his fears about old age, the frustration created by his memories of an irrecoverable past—as sources for a new kind of publishable fiction" (16–17).

Whether or not Mark Twain was able to retain his sanity during his later years, without question he perceived himself outside the main drift of American society. In a letter to his friend Joe Twichell written in January 1897—some five months after Susy's death—Mark Twain wrote: "You have seen us go to sea, a cloud of sail, and the flag at the peak; and you see us now, chartless, adrift—derelicts; battered, water-logged, our sails a ruck of rags, our pride gone" (*Mark Twain's Letters* 640). The image of himself as a "derelict" captures well Mark Twain's sense of alienation from the American society whose values and aspirations he had embodied to the world for more than a generation. Coming to maturity in the years just before the Civil War, Mark Twain achieved fame, stature, and wealth in the boom times of Reconstruction. His early writing demonstrates his faith in America, his hope if not confidence that its industrial might and democratic principles (now freed from the stigma of Negro slavery) could bring new vitality to a world still emerging from the shackles of a feudal order. But by the mid-1880s Mark Twain had come to share with Howells an uneasy conviction that American civilization was "coming out all wrong in the end" (Howells 417). Stung by a series of bad investments, Mark Twain retreated to Europe, where he lived for nine years in an attempt to economize and struggle clear of debt. Never quite an expatriate, Mark Twain nevertheless felt himself separated from the drift of a nation he could no longer understand or celebrate. He wrote to Howells from Vienna in January 1898: "We *are* a pair of old derelicts drifting around, now, with some of our passengers gone and the sunniness of the other in eclipse" (*Mark Twain-Howells Letters* 656).

Mark Twain's new pose as derelict or drifter linked him, as artist, to the strangers or outsiders omnipresent in his fiction after 1890: David Wilson, the "man" who corrupted Hadleyburg, or the satanic visitor in such works as "The War Prayer" (1923) and the various *Mysterious Stranger* manuscripts. Such strangers harken back to Colonel Sherburn in *Huckleberry Finn* (1885) in that they typically use their vantage point as outsiders to direct abusive criticism toward a social order that had become closed or self-contained, thereby eliminating the possibility that such criticism could emerge from its own ranks. This new pose also comported well with Mark Twain's hope to be accepted as a "serious" writer. Hill notes that "the most important single fact in Mark Twain's life in 1900 was his tentative, exploratory removal of his fictional disguise" (16). Indirect satire, blunted by humor and nostalgia, seemed no longer sufficient to counter the world's manifold abuses; instead, Mark Twain determined to confront these abuses head-on.

In casting his persona Mark Twain as a "derelict," the author gave the outsider once associated with the roguish Tom Sawyer or orphan Huck a decidedly demonic coloring (Ziff 71). Laboring in a spiritual agony that led him to engage in a sustained vendetta against a God he held personally responsible for human misery, Mark Twain became obsessed with the desire to vent his frustration in art. He confided to Howells in 1899: "What I have been wanting is a chance to write a book without reserves. . . . I believe I can make it tell what I think of man, & how he is constructed, & what a shabby poor ridiculous thing he is, & how mistaken he is in his estimate of his character & powers & qualities & his place among the animals" (*Mark Twain-Howells Letters* 698–99). The book he apparently wanted to write turned out to be *The Mysterious Stranger*—a hodgepodge of manuscripts and false starts that DeVoto argues afforded the author an opportunity to purge his guilt by portraying a meaningless, naturalistic world in which human choice and moral responsibility are delusion (105–27). The deterministic themes of *The Mysterious Stranger,* however, dominate the bulk of Mark Twain's literary activity at the turn of the century. Prompted and sustained by an inner rage seeking release, much of this activity proved fragmentary and incoherent; little of it earned him any money. In the eighteen months prior to the composition of "The Man That Corrupted Hadleyburg," Mark Twain's writing took myriad forms—a play, philosophical essays, autobiography, translations, and a variety of serious and commercial fiction. He began work on *What Is Man?* (1906), *The Mysterious Stranger* (1916), *The Great Dark* (1942), "My Platonic Sweetheart" (1898), and "Concerning the Jews" (1898); plans were formulated for a sustained attack on Mary Baker Eddy and Christian Science (Emerson 223). Macnaughton speculated that Mark Twain turned to "The Man That Corrupted Hadleyburg" in December 1898 largely because his work during the summer had been financially inconsequential and aesthetically frustrating (100).

The major literary influences on the story seem to come from Milton. Clark (3), Scherting (18), and Covici (190–92) see "The Man That Corrupted Hadleyburg" as a demonstration of Milton's theme in "Areopagitica": "I cannot praise a fugitive and cloistered virtue, unexercised and unbreathed." Because the story recounts the fall of Hadleyburg's citizens from Eden-like conditions as a result of an intruder's appeal to their vanity and greed, some (Rule, for example) see the story as an ironic rendition of the biblical account of the Fall in Genesis. Scharnhorst, however, argues that the stronger influence is *Paradise Lost*. Mark Twain had often expressed his disappointment that Satan had fared ignominiously at Milton's hands, and in 1898 he confessed a desire to "rehabilitate Satan's reputation." The result is "The Man That Corrupted Hadleyburg"; Mark Twain recasts major sections of Milton's epic "to fashion a modern, though no less paradoxical, parable of the Fortunate Fall" (60). When Mark Twain's stranger resolves, "That is the thing to do—I will corrupt the town," he parallels Milton's Arch-Fiend who, "Stirred up with envy and revenge," retaliates for his expulsion from heaven. For Milton, of course, the Fall proves fortunate because it permits the full redemptive power of God's grace to come into play; in Mark Twain's story, the moral corruption of the town likewise proves fortunate, Scharnhorst argues, for it occasions deliverance from moral blindness (63).

Three other suggested literary sources or influences deserve mention. While Scherting acknowledges that the basic theme of "cloistered virtue" comes from Milton, he argues that the story's structural similarities to "The Cask of Amontillado" suggest Poe's story to be the "stronger and more immediate influence" (18). In each story, mottoes appear to complement theme; both outsiders defer vengeance until the appropriate moment for exacting it arises; and both exploit the vanity and challenge the pure reputations of their victims (18–19). On the other hand, Marshall argues that the "matrix for understanding Hadleyburg" is the classical myth of Baucis and Philemon. Mark Twain's adaptation of the myth proves ironic, however, since his characters lack the "positive qualities" displayed by heroes of the classical tale (4–7). Finally, Werge sees an echo of Dante's *Inferno*, book 23, in Mark Twain's exploration of the sin of hypocrisy. Two specific parallels—gilded lead as symbol or image of the sin, and "a pervasive tone and imagery of weight, weariness, and oppressiveness to dramatize the external and inner life of the hypocrite"—reinforce the more general similarity in theme. For both Dante and Mark Twain, hypocrisy is a form of theft and fraud, and Hadleyburg's citizens, like their counterparts in the eighth circle of Dante's hell, assume grotesque, morally perverted forms (17).

Several critics have read "The Man That Corrupted Hadleyburg" as an exposé of the evil festering beneath the placid façade of the small American villages that in the popular mythology of the period were usually seen as the source of indigenous national virtue (Bellamy 287; Stone 191). Such a reading leads naturally to the desire to locate a specific model for Mark Twain's fictional village. Nye (69–73) offers Oberlin, Ohio, a claim rejected by Cardwell (257–64). More recently, Chard suggests that Hadley-burg is but a thinly disguised portrait of Fredonia, New York—a village forty-five miles from Buffalo with which the author was familiar and one whose smugness he found offensive (595). In fact, however, Hadleyburg bears generic resemblances to the many villages that provide the setting for Mark Twain's later fiction—Dawson's Landing (*Pudd'nhead Wilson* [1894]) or Eseldorf *(The Mysterious Stranger)*, for example—and to read the story as a satiric exposé of one specific village seems unnecessarily reductive.

Relationship to Other Mark Twain Works

Most scholars agree that "The Man That Corrupted Hadleyburg" of-fers a deterministic vision of human behavior consistent with the pessimis-tic tone of Mark Twain's later writing in general (Laing 35–48; Bennett 10; Long 228–29; Baldanza 135). Like *What Is Man?* and *The Mysterious Stranger*—extended projects on which Mark Twain was working at the time he wrote "Hadleyburg"—the story demonstrates, DeVoto writes, "man's complete helplessness in the grip of the inexorable forces of the universe" as well as his "essential cowardice, pettiness and evil" (115; Briden and Prescott 383). Gribben points out that the story dramatizes the theme of mental entrapment in "suffering married couples," and links the story to similar portraits of marriage in the McWilliams stories (1875; 1882), and "The $30,000 Bequest" (1904) (189). The failure of Mark Twain's investments and death of Susy in the mid-1890s are generally cited as pre-cipitating causes of the author's "increasing misanthropy," but as Gibson points out, evidence suggests that these biographical facts "merely inten-sified an outlook that had already turned bleak": the same outrage at hu-man folly that governs "The Man That Corrupted Hadleyburg"—the pessimistic depiction of an avaricious struggle for position and wealth, and the naturalistic concern with the shaping forces of social training and he-redity—surfaces earlier in *A Connecticut Yankee* (1889), *Pudd'nhead Wil-son*, "The Great Revolution in Pitcairn" (1879), and "Captain Stormfield's Visit to Heaven" (1907–8) (163; Smith 172; Bellamy 315–16).

In "Hadleyburg," while trying to remember a service he had rendered Barclay Goodson that might justify his claim to the money, Edward Rich-ards recalls that he had saved Goodson from marrying a "very sweet and pretty girl" who "carried a teaspoon of negro blood in her veins." Such moral hypocrisy grounded in absurd racial prejudice is typical of Mark Twain's earlier ironic handling of racial themes in both *Huckleberry Finn* and *Pudd'nhead Wilson* (Gibson 91–92; Park 508–10). The fact that the story demonstrates "that all men have their price," Spangler contends, places "Hadleyburg" in a long series of attacks on Gilded Age America, with its criticism directed toward "a plutocratic elite"—the nineteen leading citizens—rather than toward common humanity represented by Jack Halliday (20).

In documenting "how we damned humans come to damn ourselves," the story assumes a psychological focus that, Covici contends, renders any consideration of the aging author's personal "despair" essentially irrelevant (189). The real villain, as in *Huckleberry Finn* and *The Mysterious Stranger*, may well be the moral sense—a conscience that haunts its victims, inflicting often unwarranted mental agony for imaginary transgressions (Allen 259). Emerson, however, argues that the mental agony suffered by Hadleyburg's guilt-ridden citizens is warranted indeed. Quite unlike *What Is Man?*, this story is a moral fable that holds individuals strictly accountable for their actions. It studies, with clinical precision, the citizens' pitiful attempts at rationalization to avoid the psychological and practical consequences of their misdeeds and, in a courtroom scene parallel to those of *Pudd'nhead Wilson* and *The Mysterious Stranger*, exposes them all to profound and justified embarrassment—a technique Mark Twain had used earlier in *Roughing It* (1872), *Old Times on the Mississippi* (1874–75), and *Huckleberry Finn* (223).

Structurally, "The Man That Corrupted Hadleyburg" bears strong affinities to *The Mysterious Stranger*. Eseldorf and Hadleyburg are similarly smug, sleepy villages; Frau Brandt and Barclay Goodson are essentially decent human beings who prove exceptions to the general depravity of the townspeople. Moreover, the central situation is parallel in the two stories. In *The Mysterious Stranger*, the essentially honest Father Peter finds a wallet of gold coins and, sorely in need, is tempted. He is subsequently defended by Satan in a public trial against charges brought by a wicked astrologer. In "Hadleyburg," the financially distraught Richards couple is tempted by gold coins deposited in their care by another mysterious stranger, who uses the coins to expose the depravity of the town's citizens in a public assembly that resembles a courtroom scene (Clark 1–4). The satanic figure hence dominates the central scene of each story; and like the ironic strangers in "The £1,000,000 Bank-Note" (1893) and "The $30,000 Bequest," he intrudes into a complacent village with money to subvert the entire social order by laying bare an ugly truth about the human condition (Cox 265).

Satan, as character, appears in many of Mark Twain's later writings, developing out of what Brodwin labels "a persistent Mark Twain character type, the sometimes 'innocent,' sometimes devious stranger striving either to 'con' or to 'reform' the people and society around him." Satan assumes a variety of poses or "masks" in the later fiction. In "Sold to Satan" (1904), "That Day in Eden" (1900), and "Eve Speaks" (1900), he is a "sympathetic commentator on the tragedy of man's fall" who unfortunately fails in his attempt to enlighten Adam and Eve and thus enable them to avoid the Fall.

In "Letters from the Earth" (1962), Satan is the "mischievous, sarcastic questioner of God's ways," while in *The Mysterious Stranger* he proves to be a force of amoral " 'innocence' charged with divine-like creative power." The "vengeful Stranger" Stephenson in "The Man That Corrupted Hadleyburg" assumes a more conventional satanic role—he is the tempter and "Father of Lies" (207–8).

Critical Studies

"The Man That Corrupted Hadleyburg" is the most critically acclaimed of all Mark Twain's short fiction, "a tale," Paine claims, "that in its own way takes its place with the half-dozen great English short stories of the world" (1068). Although maintaining that as a general proposition the genre of the short story was not Mark Twain's "metier," Ferguson grants that this one is nearly perfect (278). The story may lack the tragic grandeur of *Pudd'nhead Wilson*—the chilling, irremediable evil of a Tom Driscoll or "the vivid thrust of Roxy's passion"—but critics like Smith are quick to praise its formal qualities: tight construction, even tone, language control, etc. (184). The most recent biographer of Mark Twain concurs: "The Man That Corrupted Hadleyburg," Emerson writes, is Mark Twain's "most effectively plotted story, highly economical and suspenseful, rich in implications" (232).

The implications of the story drew immediate response from contemporary reviewers who, for the most part, praised the story's serious tone and philosophical dimensions as signaling the emergence of a "new" Mark Twain, one prepared to assume the role as "critic and censor" of late nineteenth-century American life (Archer 414–15; Hill 222). Subsequently the story has been read as an exposé of the moral depravity festering beneath the innocuous facade of village life and as an attack on "the spiritual integrity of industrial America" (Brooks 146). The philosophical bases and moral didacticism of the fable, however, suggest that Mark Twain was less concerned with provincial sociological analysis of a specifically American condition than with probing and dramatizing the more universal problems of human nature, guilt, free will, and conscience.

Whether Mark Twain was able to channel his ideas and observations into aesthetically satisfying fiction that makes a cohesive philosophical statement has become a matter of some dispute. Wagenknecht asserts that "there never was a more effective parable of the corrupting effects of greed on human character" (156), and Covici labels the story one of "the most important works" of Mark Twain's later life (189). Yet Mark Twain's new, more direct, approach to his art was not without its drawbacks. Among the litany of high praise that characterized contemporary critical response to the story, the *Blackwood's Magazine* reviewer voiced a discordant note, criticizing Mark Twain for his blatant didacticism, his habit "of pointing morals, of drawing lessons" (Hill 21). Related to the *Blackwood's* reviewer's objection is the indisputable fact that after *Personal Recollections of Joan of Arc* (1896) Mark Twain was unable to bring any sustained fiction to a satisfactory conclusion. Never a master of form, the earlier Mark Twain could nevertheless sustain a novel because, like *The Innocents Abroad, Roughing It, Tom Sawyer, Huckleberry Finn,* or *A Connecticut Yankee,* it grew from episodes and situations, most of which were intrinsically comic; the themes, or ideological constructs, emerged almost in passing. But, during the last fifteen years of his life, the "serious" Mark Twain tried desperately in his fiction to embody particular ideas; these preconceived notions, born in rage and neither carefully thought out nor intellectually consistent, determined the form of the fable, sketch, or aborted novel. As a result, Mark Twain tried repeatedly to give form to the same intellectual complex of ideas—starting, abandoning, then beginning anew projects that are essentially ideological clones. In an attempt to explain his numerous unfinished projects, Mark Twain wrote in a 1906 autobiographical dictation: "As long as a book would write itself I was a faithful and interested amanuensis and my industry did not flag, but the minute that the book tried to shift to *my* head the labor of contriving its characters, inventing its adventures and conducting its situations, I put it away and dropped it out of my mind" (*Mark Twain in Eruption* 196)

"The Man That Corrupted Hadleyburg" is, however, finished and receives praise as a tightly written, polished work of art. Varisco suggests that the presence of a neutral narrator, one who objectively reports the story without overtly moralizing, helps to explain why this story succeeds as fiction while others from the period fail (130). Other critics, however, argue that "Hadleyburg" too suffers aesthetically from the author's attempt to make it a vehicle for the demonstration of his intrinsically contradictory philosophy (Bellamy 308–9). Macnaughton complains that the wooden characters in the story become merely "mouthpieces in what was really a disguised essay designed to promote Mark Twain's ideas" (100).

"The Man That Corrupted Hadleyburg" exposes the hypocrisy of a small, isolated village whose self-righteous citizens take inordinate pride in their honesty, which, they believe, separates them from the rest of humanity. The town motto—"Lead Us Not into Temptation"—suggests that the moral incorruptibility upon which Hadleyburg claims its fame as the "most honest and upright town in all the region" results not from the superior moral fiber of its citizens but from the fact that theirs is a "cloistered virtue": "throughout the formative years temptations were kept out of the way of the young people, so that their honesty could have every chance to harden and solidify" (231). As the character Mary Richards shrewdly notes, however, untested honesty is *"artificial . . .* and weak as water when temptation comes" (*Great Short Works* 241). What hardens and solidifies is not the town's assumed virtue but its inhumanity: "it is a mean town, a hard, stingy town, and hasn't a virtue in the world but this honesty it is so celebrated for and so conceited about" (241). Retreating behind its well-publicized moral façade, the town ostracizes those who tarnish its carefully cultivated image or fail to share its smug estimate of itself: the "loafing, good-natured, no account" Jack Halliday or the victimized Reverend Burgess, "the best-hated man among us" (243).

Another whose humanity had been denied or abused by an unidentified Hadleyburg citizen is the ironic stranger who, apparently motivated by a desire to avenge an undisclosed offense, orchestrates the elaborate hoax that will expose the town for what it is (Covici 190–92). As Male points out, the stranger operates on the periphery of this "inside narrative" of the town's moral undoing (283–88). By dropping the sack of fraudulent gold coins in the Richardses' parlor, then giving them the responsibility of finding the legitimate claimant, the stranger becomes a catalyst who simply triggers the experiment that, given human nature, will inevitably bring to the surface the avarice and hypocrisy lurking in every citizen's heart (Bellamy 308). The stranger's coins thus serve as an objective correlative of the town's virtue: glittering gold on the outside—the façade offered to the world; worthless lead discs underneath—the reality that ties Hadleyburg's citizens to a common humanity enslaved by greed.

As the story's title indicates, the stranger is ostensibly a satanic figure—the tempter in Eden—who occasions the corruption of a town. The fact that all nineteen of Hadleyburg's leading citizens fall prey to the stranger's hoax leads most commentators to see the story as a satiric dramatization of Mark Twain's pessimism (Emerson 232; Howard 219; Long 228–29). Smith contends that the stranger's motive—vengeance for an undisclosed offense—and his mysterious air link him to the Deity as he is frequently characterized in Mark Twain's later writings; the working out of his hoax reveals "the theme of human bondage in an almost algebraic fashion" (183). For Nebeker, the stranger is the Calvinist Deity, a villain who so orchestrates environmental conditions and programs human nature that he condemns humanity to a "corrupt, mortal life"; the protagonists of the fable, the "morally bankrupt" Richardses, are weak "but essentially guiltless" victims of God's vengeance (635–37). God's vengeance succeeds, Baldanza argues, because human beings are powerless to deny their essentially depraved natures. Considered rational analysis convinces Hadleyburg's prominent citizens that they have no legitimate moral claim to the money, but the irresistible force of self-interest renders free moral choice an illusion; all succumb to the temptation, Baldanza writes, because "their wills were powerless to renounce the wealth." The story thus serves to dramatize the philosophical determinism of *What Is Man?:* the human is "an exteriorly determined machine, with no originality of idea and no freedom of will" (133–37).

Rucker and Emerson approach the story's pessimism from a perspective opposite to that of Nebeker and Baldanza. The Richardses, the town's representative couple, fall not because they are doomed by cosmic forces beyond their control but because they fail to make "the morally correct choices . . . to act consciously and deliberately for primarily moral ends" (Rucker 52). Indeed, Emerson contends that a "presupposition of freedom" is the basis of the story; despite Richards' plea that his action "was ordered. *All* things are" ordered (*Great Short Works* 271), he and his wife "are thoroughly reprehensible" in a story that dramatizes human responsibility for moral choices (Emerson 222–23).

A major defect of "The Man That Corrupted Hadleyburg," according to Bellamy, is that its philosophical inconsistencies permit—even encourage—these radically different reader responses. Mark Twain sets his story within a deterministic framework, introducing the stranger who, consistent with the principles of literary naturalism "devises almost laboratory conditions for the testing of human behavior" (308). The stranger sets what Ferguson calls a "tragedy trap" (279) to which Hadleyburg's elite respond as a single entity; all predictably are helpless, for none can govern a programmed, universal human nature. The townspeople are "essentially duplicates, in psychology and action, of one another and . . . thus participate in a collective identity" (Briden and Prescott 383). Even the readers are victim, for as they watch the demise of the pathetic Richards couple they see mirrored their own likely fate in similar circumstances: "there, with or without the grace of God, go I" (Ferguson 279). Yet Mark Twain proves unable to sustain the amoral objectivity demanded of the naturalist in Zola's *Roman experimental,* for he holds his characters morally responsible for their actions. The incongruous theme of divine justice, operating through the conscience of the protagonists to punish hypocrisy and moral weakness, destroys the unity of a story predicated on determinist assumptions that would, presumably, posit behavior beyond the control and responsibility of human will; as a result, "Hadleyburg settles itself on a philosophic quicksand" (Bellamy 308–9).

Burhans disagrees with Bellamy, however, perceiving instead a logical and aesthetic consistency operative in Mark Twain's exploration of the tension between determinism and moral vales; in fact, Burhans contends, the author's "moralism functions . . . in terms of his determinism" (376). Like *Huckleberry Finn,* "Hadleyburg" treats the relationship between conscience and the heart. It offers two distinct types of moral values—those that are abstract, posited unchecked by a cloistered social order, and those that are empirically verified, arising from concrete human situations; it also provides two types of conscience—a prescriptive one, shaped by environmental training and removed from the demands of daily life, and one that develops amorally as an emotion of self-approval generated by psychological necessity (376–82). In each instance, the story dramatizes the movement from the former to the latter, taking on the quality of what Gibson calls "high moral comedy" as the citizens come to recognize "that a 'fugitive and cloister'd virtue' cannot compare to virtue tried and hardened through resistence to temptation" (90). The town's citizens succumb to the stranger's hoax because, shielded from temptations, they are "unpracticed in recognizing and resisting them." But they learn a painful lesson from their experience: in confronting temptation, their moral values—heretofore abstract and meaningless—are tested empirically and adapted to fit genuine human emotions. Hence the story, Burhans argues, is neither philosophically inconsistent nor unduly pessimistic. Mark Twain reconciles the antithetical visions of morality and conscience to achieve a formal unity that finally suggests, through the transformation of Hadleyburg into "an honest town once more," that "the experience of living can determine man to his salvation as well as to his perdition" (384).

Two other critics have read the story as a celebration of the town's moral regeneration. Rule contends that at the outset Hadleyburg is an "ironic Eden"; consequently, the stranger assumes "the role of savior rather than corrupter," for he initiates a process that culminates in the unmasking of the town's debilitating hypocrisy (619–29). Covici undermines those critics who traditionally have viewed the story as a scornful attack on the entire village. For one thing, Covici argues, the whole town is not guilty of avarice and hypocrisy: the late Mr. Goodson, the "no account" Jack Halliday, and the Reverend Burgess all prove to be exceptions for they are neither penurious, nor vain, nor naive. Moreover, the story's focus is less moral than psychological: Mark Twain scrutinizes "the psychological defenses of the citizens with a precision almost clinical"; in this way he captures, Macnaughton writes, the *"feel* of the process of rationalization" (102–3). The public meeting at which the town, subconsciously aware of its past iniquity, revels in its degradation serves as a mass confessional. In nominating Halliday, the habitual debunker who "always noticed everything, and always made fun of it, too, no matter what it was" (*Great Short Works* 243), as the appropriate one to reward the presumed virtue of the Richards couple, Hadleyburg satirizes itself in a mood "of almost joyful acceptance of the disillusioning truth." As they abandon their fraudulent reputation, the citizens "achieve a moral victory" for they have awakened to a mature, healthy awareness of human limitation (Covici 189–204).

But the tale of Hadleyburg's fortunate fall and "moral victory" is but one of two narratives in Mark Twain's story; it is, Harris argues, "an umbrella, or cover, tale" that provides a context for the darker narrative concerning the Richards couple. The apparent philosophical inconsistencies that Bellamy notes—the conflict of moralism and determinism—result from the fact that the Richards narrative differs in theme and tone from the enveloping story of Hadleyburg's liberating moral progression. Aware that his readers might find his bleakly deterministic vision unpalatable and pressed to produce commercially successful fiction, Mark Twain softens the Calvinistic despair implicit in his account of the protagonists' demise with a morally reassuring account of the town's reformation as "a ploy," Harris contends, "to make his ideas publishable." The thematic tension between the two narratives makes "The Man That Corrupted Hadleyburg" a subtle attack on the popular banal fiction published in *Harper's,* the *Atlantic Monthly,* and in the newspapers of the time, for Mark Twain expects the sophisticated reader to see through the literary stereotype controlling the umbrella tale to confront the more disturbing implications of the Richards narrative: that "little seems to have been learned by any of the characters concerned" and hence there is no reassuring moral "message" to what is finally a bleakly naturalistic tale (241).

Harris rests her argument on the assumption that Edward and Mary Richards are Hadleyburg's "most corrupt characters" and hence not representative of its leading citizens. Here Harris follows the lead of Rucker, who condemns the Richardses for "not making the morally correct choices" (53). Male seems closer to the mark, however, labeling the Richardses "a receptive intelligence" standing between the stranger and the town (287). Of all Hadleyburg's citizens, they are the ones singled out for scrutiny; as readers, we are led to assume that their rationalization, plotting, jaundiced view of others, and inherent greed mirror the thoughts and behavior of all nineteen as they succumb to the stranger's temptation. Admittedly they do not make "morally correct choices," but, finally, who does? Indeed, the story documents rather graphically that humans do not make moral choices at all but behave as they must according to nature, conditioning, and circumstance. Briden and Prescott write that "the paradox of identity at the story's center is that the Hadleyburgians, though driven by an imperative of self-satisfaction, exhibit nothing in thought or action that points to a truly individualized self whose satisfaction is sought" (385). The Richardses differ from the other eighteen but not in the degree of their corruption; rather, they are the only ones spared public exposure at the town meeting. The mechanics of the plot, not moral choices, isolate the Richards couple, for they are the only ones who have the opportunity to sustain their hypocrisy. To assume that their silence proves them the "most corrupt" assumes as well that any of the other eighteen would have acted differently in their position.

Indeed, because the Richardses are typical or representative the story serves as an attack on "banal theology and banal literature." If we assume with Harris and Rucker that they are atypical, then the story would seem to suggest that moral rejuvenation is possible for most but not all people, that the overwhelming majority of us (eighteen of nineteen) can learn from our mistakes, become enlightened, and change our natures. If, however, the Richardses are representative, then the story calls into question the reassuring moral lesson of the "umbrella tale" and offers a final vision consistent with the often articulated philosophical determinism of Mark Twain's later writing. Edward and Mary Richards are the only ones in Hadleyburg whom we see confronted with a moral choice after the town's assumed transformation. That this representative couple chooses unwisely or immorally and continues to be the slave of greed and hypocrisy, suggests that Hadleyburg's rejuvenation is but illusion, that no fundamental change in human nature is possible. The irony of the story's concluding sentence supports such a reading: "It is an honest town once more, and the man will have to rise early that catches it napping again" (277). The first clause is patently absurd, for Hadleyburg was never an honest town; furthermore, the syntax suggests a restoration, not a transformation—a return to pride in a deceptive, misconceived self-concept. The second clause is likewise fraught with irony, for it implies not that Hadleyburg has changed morally but that it is simply cleverer, less naive—no one will catch "it napping again." "The Man That Corrupted Hadleyburg" lays bare human nature, and the lessons it teaches are naturalistic ones. The story demonstrates that human behavior is controlled absolutely by perceived self-interest, social training, and circumstances beyond our control. Attempts to alter human nature produce illusory results, but an acceptance of our limitations can enable us to survive, and an understanding of what we are positions us to manipulate ourselves and others to achieve wealth and status (Brodwin 212). Conscience, or the moral sense, occasions no change in moral behavior, but it does have profound psychological impact: it weakens us, and eventually insures our demise in a Darwinistic struggle for survival.

Bibliography

PRIMARY

*Great Short Works of Mark Twain. Edited by Justin Kaplan. New York: Harper & Row, 1967.

The Man That Corrupted Hadleyburg and Other Stories and Essays. New York: Harper & Brothers, 1900.

Mark Twain in Eruption: Hitherto Unpublished Pages about Men and Events. Edited by Bernard DeVoto. New York: Harper & Brothers, 1940.

Mark Twain's Correspondence with Henry Huttleston Rogers, 1893–1909. Edited by Lewis Leary. Berkeley and Los Angeles: University of California Press, 1969.

Mark Twain's Fables of Man. Edited by John S. Tuckey. Berkeley and Los Angeles: University of California Press, 1972.

Mark Twain-Howells Letters: The Correspondence of Samuel L. Clemens and William Dean Howells, 1872–1910. Edited by Henry Nash Smith and William M. Gibson. Vol. 2. Cambridge, Mass.: Harvard University Press, 1960.

Mark Twain's Letters. Vol. 2. New York: Harper & Brothers, 1917.

SECONDARY

Allen, Charles A. "Mark Twain and Conscience." *Literature and Psychology* 7 (May 1957):17–21. Reprint in *Mark Twain's Wound: A Casebook,* edited by Lewis Leary, 257–68. New York: Thomas Y. Crowell, 1962.

Archer, William. "*The Man That Corrupted Hadleyburg—a* New Parable." *Critic* 37 (November 1900):414–15.

Baldanza, Frank. *Mark Twain: An Introduction and Interpretation.* New York: Holt, Rinehart & Winston, 1961.

Bellamy, Gladys C. *Mark Twain as a Literary Artist.* Norman: University of Oklahoma Press, 1950.

Bennett, Fordyce Richard. "The Moral Obliquity of 'The Man That Corrupted Hadleyburg.' " *Mark Twain Journal* 21, no. 3 (Spring 1983):10–11.

Bertolotti, D. S., Jr. "Structural Unity in 'The Man That Corrupted Hadleyburg.' " *Mark Twain Journal* 14, no. 1 (Winter 1967):19–21.

Briden, Earl F. and Mary Prescott. "The Lie That I Am I: Paradoxes of Identity in Mark Twain's 'Hadleyburg.' " *Studies in Short Fiction* 21 (Fall 1984):383–391.

Brodwin, Stanley. "Mark Twain's Masks of Satan: The Final Phase." *American Literature* 45 (1973):206–27.

Brooks, Van Wyck. *The Ordeal of Mark Twain.* 1920. Rev. ed. New York: E. P. Dutton, 1933.

Burhans, Clinton S., Jr. "The Sober Affirmation of Mark Twain's Hadleyburg." *American Literature* 34 (November 1962):375–84.

Cardwell, Guy A. "Mark Twain's Hadleyburg." *Ohio State Archeological and Historical Quarterly* 60 (1951):257–64.

Chard, Leslie F., II. "Mark Twain's 'Hadleyburg' and Fredonia, New York." *American Quarterly* 16 (Winter 1964):595–601.

Clark, George P. "The Devil That Corrupted Hadleyburg." *Mark Twain Journal* 10, no. 1 (Winter 1956):1–4.

Covici, Pascal, Jr. *Mark Twain's Humor: The Image of a World.* Dallas: Southern Methodist University Press, 1962.

Cox, James M. *Mark Twain: The Fate of Humor.* Princeton, N.J.: Princeton University Press, 1964. 265.

DeVoto, Bernard. *Mark Twain at Work.* Cambridge, Mass.: Harvard University Press, 1942.

Emerson, Everett. *The Authentic Mark Twain: A Literary Biography of Samuel L. Clemens.* Philadelphia: University of Pennsylvania Press, 1984.

Ferguson, Delancey. *Mark Twain: Man and Legend.* Indianapolis: Bobbs-Merrill, 1943.

Foner, Philip S. *Mark Twain: Social Critic.* New York: International Publishers, 1958.

Gibson, William M. *The Art of Mark Twain.* New York: Oxford University Press, 1976.

Gribben, Alan. "Those Other Thematic Patterns in Mark Twain's Writings." *Studies in American Fiction* 13 (Autumn 1985):185–200.

Harris, Susan K. " 'Hadleyburg': Mark Twain's Dual Attack on Banal Theology and Banal Literature." *American Literary Realism* 16 (Autumn 1983):240–52.

Hill, Hamlin. *Mark Twain: God's Fool.* New York: Harper & Row, 1973.

Howard, Leon. *Literature and the American Tradition.* New York: Doubleday, 1960.

Howells, William D. *Life and Letters.* Edited by Mildred Howells. Vol. 1. Garden City, N.Y.: Doubleday, 1928.

Kahn, Sholom. *Mark Twain's "Mysterious Stranger": A Study of the Manuscript Texts.* Columbia: University of Missouri Press, 1978.

Laing, Nita. "The Later Satire of Mark Twain." *Midwest Quarterly* 2 (Autumn 1960):35–48.

Long, E. Hudson. *Mark Twain Handbook.* New York: Hendricks House, 1957.

Macnaughton, William R. *Mark Twain's Last Years as a Writer.* Columbia: University of Missouri Press, 1979.

Male, Roy R. "The Story of the Mysterious Stranger in American Literature." *Criticism* 3 (Fall 1961):281–94.

Malin, Irving. "Mark Twain: The Boy as Artist." *Literature and Psychology* 6 (Summer 1961):78–84.

Marshall, W. Gerald. "Mark Twain's 'The Man That Corrupted Hadleyburg' and the Myth of Baucis and Philemon." *Mark Twain Journal* 20, no. 2 (1979):4–7.

McKeithan, Daniel M. "The Morgan Manuscript of *The Man That Corrupted Hadleyburg*." *Texas Studies in Literature and Language* 2 (Winter 1961):476–80.

Nebeker, Helen E. "The Great Corrupter or Satan Rehabilitated." *Studies in Short Fiction* 8 (Fall 1971):635–37.

Nye, Russel B. "Mark Twain in Oberlin." *Ohio State Archeological and Historical Quarterly* 47 (1938):69–73.

Paine, Albert B. *Mark Twain: A Biography.* Vol. 3. New York: Harper & Brothers, 1912.

Park, Martha M. "Mark Twain's Hadleyburg: A House Built on Sand." *College Language Association Journal* 16 (1972):508–13.

Rucker, Mary E. "Moralism and Determinism in 'The Man That Corrupted Hadleyburg.' " *Studies in Short Fiction* 14 (Winter 1977):49–54.

Rule, Henry B. "The Role of Satan in 'The Man That Corrupted Hadleyburg.' " *Studies in Short Fiction* 6 (Fall 1969):619–29.

Scharnhorst, Gary. "Paradise Revisited: Twain's 'The Man That Corrupted Hadleyburg.'" *Studies in Short Fiction* 18 (Winter 1981):59–64.

Scherting, Jack. "Poe's 'The Cask of Amontillado': A Source for Twain's 'The Man That Corrupted Hadleyburg.'" *Mark Twain Journal* 16 (Summer 1972):18–19.

Smith, Henry Nash. *Mark Twain: The Development of a Writer*. Cambridge, Mass.: Harvard University Press, 1962.

Spangler, George M. "Locating Hadleyburg." *Mark Twain Journal* 14 (Summer 1969):20.

Stone, Albert E., Jr. *The Innocent Eye: Childhood in Mark Twain's Imagination*. New Haven: Yale University Press, 1961.

Tuckey, John S. Review of *Mark Twain: God's Fool* by Hamlin Hill. *American Literature* 46 (1974):117.

Varisco, Raymond. "A Militant Voice: Mark Twain's 'The Man That Corrupted Hadleyburg.'" *Revista/Review InterAmericana* 8 (Spring 1978):129–37.

Wagenkencht, Edward. *Mark Twain: The Man and His Work*. New Haven: Yale University Press, 1935.

Werge, Thomas. "The Sin of Hypocrisy in 'The Man That Corrupted Hadleyburg' and *Inferno* XXIII." *Mark Twain Journal* 18, no. 1 (1976):17–18.

Ziff, Larzer. *The American 1890s: Life and Times of a Lost Generation*. Lincoln: University of Nebraska Press, 1966.

31

The Man Who Put Up at Gadsby's

Publication History

"The Man Who Put Up at Gadsby's" appeared as a letter to the Virginia City, Nevada, *Territorial Enterprise*, 8 February 1868 (Emerson 46). Mark Twain subsequently revised and expanded the initial sketch and included it as a chapter in *A Tramp Abroad* (1880). Charles Neider prints this revised version as a self-contained unit in *The Complete Short Stories*.

Circumstances of Composition, Sources, and Influences

Upon his return to New York on 19 November 1867 from the *Quaker City* excursion to Europe and the Holy Land, Mark Twain moved to Washington, D.C., to assume a position as secretary to Nevada senator William Stewart. He spent the winter 1867–68 in the nation's capital, using as his headquarters the offices of the New York *Tribune*. Such an arrangement proved a rather common means of support for literary people during the period: Walt Whitman was at the same time a clerk in the attorney general's office, and Mark Twain's close friend James H. Riley was in Washington working as a clerk to a congressional committee on mining and as a political correspondent for the *Alta*. Senator Stewart hired Mark Twain, Kaplan reports, for "the satisfaction of playing Maecenas to a literary celebrity and the use of Clemens' popularity with the Western press to advance his own reputation" (88). Their relationship, however, was stormy and unsatisfactory: Stewart thought Mark Twain "disreputable," his demeanor coarse and offensive; the author had difficulty taking either his position or the senator very seriously and soon burlesqued both in print. After two months Mark Twain quit, under threat of a thrashing from his physically imposing employer (88–89).

Most of Mark Twain's literary activity during the period was journalistic. He furnished sketches and letters to the *Alta*, the *Herald*, the Chicago *Republican*, and a literary magazine, the *Galaxy*. In December he initiated a new series of letters for the Virginia City *Territorial Enterprise*, eleven in all from 4 December 1867 to 2 March 1868.

"The Man Who Put Up at Gadsby's" was among the *Enterprise* letters and reflects Mark Twain's disenchantment with Washington, its chronic inefficiency and rampant political corruption. He wrote to his brother Orion, "There are more pitiful intellects in this Congress! . . . I am most infernally tired of Washington," and discouraged his brother from seeking government employment in the nation's capital: "I hope you will set type till you complete that invention, for surely government pap must be nauseating food for a *man*—a man whom God has enabled to saw wood and be independent" (Bellamy 101).

Mark Twain returned to the sketch during his extended tour of Europe in 1878–79. When pressed to fill out *A Tramp Abroad*—a lengthy subscription book he had contracted to write—he expanded the story and inserted it as an "interpolated American tale" at the end of volume 1 (Baldanza 62). Frustrated with the entire project, and dispirited over the humiliating response to his address at the Whittier birthday dinner, Mark Twain never seemed to gain control over *A Tramp Abroad*. Until he discovered an idea for the "narrative plank" that would furnish some cohesion to the book—i.e., the burlesque walking tour—Mark Twain spent his time writing or revising miscellaneous sketches, stories, and anecdotes he hoped he would somehow be able to use to satisfy the insatiable demands of subscription book publication; as Hill writes, "the digressive tale actually became the unit of composition, with the unifying principle of a burlesque walking tour added later" (136). "The Man Who Put Up at Gadsby's" is a relatively self-contained digression in a book whose joys lie primarily in digressive tales such as "Jim Baker's Blue Jay Yarn" (1880) and "Nicodemus Dodge and the Skeleton" (1880). All three are, as Kaplan notes, "outcroppings of [Mark Twain's] native vein" in a book ostensibly about European travel (353). The critical consensus is that these interpolated American stories are the best features of "a manufactured piece of work, turned out for trade, uninspired, and holding no more interest for the reader than it held for its reluctant author" (Long 202).

Relationship to Other Mark Twain Works

As a political satire, the story shares affinities with *The Gilded Age* (1873) and several shorter pieces that burlesque governmental incompetence. Incapacitating bureaucracy is the subject of both "The Facts in the Great Beef Contract" (1869) and "The Belated Russian Passport" (1902) (Baldanza 99). "Facts concerning the Recent Resignation" (1868) relates Mark Twain's unappreciated efforts to reform inefficient and financially irresponsible governmental agencies during his brief stint in Washington (Bellamy 101).

Structurally, the place of "The Man Who Put Up at Gadsby's" within the context of *A Tramp Abroad* reflects the method characteristic of Mark Twain's travel writing in general. *Innocents Abroad* (1869), *Roughing It* (1872), *Life on the Mississippi* (1883), and *Following the Equator* (1897) are all, as Baldanza calls *A Tramp Abroad,* "a melange of facts, history, curious personalities, and rather elaborate humorous stories" (62). This is not to say that all these works are as uninspired or so structurally flawed as *A Tramp Abroad;* indeed, the first three rank among Mark Twain's finest achievements, largely because of his control of a narrative persona. In each of them, however, the author's most distinguished writing often surfaces in digressive short fiction.

Critical Studies

"The Man Who Put Up at Gadsby's" is a short, gently but clearly satirical narrative that has occasioned no substantial critical commentary. A frame introduces the story: walking the streets of Washington at midnight during a fierce snowstorm, Mark Twain and his friend Riley encounter a man named Lykins—a teacher from San Francisco who has come to the nation's capital to secure a vacant postmastership. The vernacular character's intention is to "rush this thing through and get along home," expecting to leave Washington for New York the next evening and then proceed back to San Francisco the following morning: "I ain't the talking kind, I'm the *doing* kind!" (149). The remainder of the story is essentially a joke at the expense of the green westerner's naiveté.

The chief interest of the tale lies in the characterization of Riley who, "in a voice which had nothing mocking in it—to an unaccustomed ear," plays upon Lykins's simplistic expectations regarding the operation of government bureaucracy. In a sense the story is a reverse of the "Jumping Frog" tale, for here it is the vernacular westerner who is duped by the deadpan, sophisticated veteran of eastern institutional structures and held captive to a rambling narrative he sees as irrelevant to the business at hand. Riley, like Simon Wheeler, corners his unsuspecting prey, "backed Mr. Lykins against an iron fence, buttonholed him, fastened him with his eye, like the Ancient Mariner, and proceeded to unfold his narrative as placidly and peacefully as if we were all stretched comfortably in a blossomy summer meadow instead of being persecuted by a winter midnight tempest" (150). The illustrative story he tells is about a similar yokel, a man from Tennessee, who arrived in Washington on 3 January 1834 to collect a "little claim against the government." Expecting to settle his business in a few minutes, he instructs his Negro coachman to wait for him in front of Gadsby's hotel. Delay after delay ensues, causing the Tennessee claimant slowly to divest himself of earthly possessions while awaiting settlement.

His optimism, however, remains unabated; more than thirty years have passed, and he is still waiting: "I'm great friends with that old patriarch. He comes every evening to tell me good-by. I saw him an hour ago—he's off for Tennessee early tomorrow evening—as usual; said he calculated to get his claim through and be off before night-owls like me have turned out of bed" (152). The impatient Lykins fails to see the point of the long-winded story. Riley grants him it may seem irrelevant, but adds, "if you are not in *too* much of a hurry to rush off to San Francisco with that post-office appointment . . . I'd advise you to *'put up at Gadsby's'* for a spell, and take it easy" (156). The story ends with Mark Twain's revelation that Lykins "never got that post-office."

The satire is aimed in two directions. Gently and humorously, the story exposes the gross inefficiency of government bureaucracy that makes a shambles of human lives; at the same time, it ridicules those foolish or inexperienced enough to assume that it would function otherwise.

Bibliography

PRIMARY

The Complete Short Stories of Mark Twain. Now Collected for the First Time. Edited by Charles Neider. Garden City, N.Y.: Hanover House, 1957.

A Tramp Abroad. Hartford: American Publishing Co., 1880.

SECONDARY

Baldanza, Frank. *Mark Twain: An Introduction and Interpretation*. New York: Holt, Rinehart & Winston, 1961.

Bellamy, Gladys C. *Mark Twain as a Literary Artist*. Norman: University of Oklahoma Press, 1950.

Emerson, Everett. *The Authentic Mark Twain: A Literary Biography of Samuel L. Clemens*. Philadelphia: University of Pennsylvania Press, 1984.

Hill, Hamlin. *Mark Twain and Elisha Bliss*. Columbia: University of Missouri Press, 1964.

Kaplan, Justin. *Mr. Clemens and Mark Twain*. New York: Simon & Schuster, 1966.

Long, E. Hudson. *Mark Twain Handbook*. New York: Hendricks House, 1957.

32

A Medieval Romance

Publication History

Under the title "An Awful Terrible Medieval Romance," this story was first published in the Buffalo *Express* on 1 January 1870. Book publication the following year by Sheldon and Company violated Mark Twain's contract with Elisha Bliss, which stipulated that the author was to publish no book with another firm until *Roughing It* (1872) was completed and in circulation (Hill 42). Paine reports that the 1871 book "was not important, from any standpoint"; soon after its publication Mark Twain acquired the plates and destroyed them (433). Routledge and Sons appended the story to an 1872 British edition of Mark Twain stories and sketches. Retitled "A Medieval Romance," the story resurfaced in the 1875 edition of *Mark Twain's Sketches, New and Old*.

Circumstances of Composition, Sources, and Influences

The story was written during a period that Mark Twain described in 1906 as "among the blackest, the gloomiest, the most wretched of my long life" (Kaplan 188). Having completed his revisions of *Innocents Abroad* (1869), engaged in his courtship of Olivia Langdon, and frustrated in his attempts to cultivate an orthodox religious faith, Mark Twain chafed under the stigma of his reputation as a "mere" humorist. He feared his humble origins and raw western background ill suited his newfound ambitions to become a gentleman and a writer who could earn the respect of the legitimate eastern literary establishment. In his early thirties, unmarried, his career seemingly adrift, Mark Twain feared the well of his creativity had gone dry. Such insecurities surface in the *Burlesque Autobiography*, which is, Kaplan writes, a "single-minded" exercise in "hostility and self-hatred—nakedly displayed" (189).

In "Awful Terrible Medieval Romance" Mark Twain reverts to a formula that had served him well in his days as a San Francisco journalist—the condensed novel. Shaped by Bret Harte and Charles Henry Webb, this form gave full rein in the mid-1860s to Mark Twain's talent for the burlesque hoax and produced such comic gems as "Aurelia's Unfortunate Young

Man" (1864) and "Lucretia Smith's Soldier" (1864). Moreover, the ostensible subject of the story's burlesque attack was that favorite whipping boy of the San Francisco bohemian literati, the romance. But the freshness of the form that had inspired Mark Twain five years earlier had apparently dissipated; "A Medieval Romance," Kaplan reports, is a "dull burlesque," mechanical and uninspired. The story is interesting primarily as an indication of the author's sense of aesthetic failure, his inability to manage story form, for "the point of this story is that the author doesn't know how to end it" (189–90).

Relationship to Other Mark Twain Works

Kaplan overstates his argument that "A Medieval Romance" testifies to Mark Twain's despair over a loss of aesthetic control. Admittedly the author suggests that his failure to conclude "A Medieval Romance" is a personal inability to control his story: "The truth is, I have got my hero (or heroine) into such a particularly close place that I do not see how I am ever going to get him (or her) out of it again, and therefore I will wash my hands of the whole business" (*Complete Short Stories* 56). In fact, however, the absence of an ending is a logical outcome dictated by the absurdities of the genre burlesqued, the romance. "A *reductio ad absurdum* of narrative methods of the middle ages" (Baldanza 99), the story teases its readers as it leads its characters into complicated predicaments from which they cannot be rescued, only to conclude, "The remainder of this thrilling and eventful story will *not* be found in this or any other publication, either now or at any future time" (56). Like "Jim Blaine and His Grandfather's Ram" (1872), "A Medieval Romance" is "purposely unresolved"; that is the fulcrum of its hoax as the story burlesques a popular literary form and the conventional expectations of nineteenth-century readers who patronize it (Covici 143–44). Hence it is inappropriate to link this story to the fragments and false starts that characterize Mark Twain's declining creativity and artistic control during the last decade of his life.

More germane is the relationship the story bears to other stories that burlesque the inherent deficiencies of popular fiction. This list of such stories is long, and spans Mark Twain's literary career: from early condensed novels such as "Aurelia's Unfortunate Young Man," "Lucretia Smith's Soldier," and the "Story of the Bad Little Boy" (1865), through such parodies as "The Loves of Alonzo Fitz Clarence and Rosannah Ethelton" (1878) and "The Esquimau Maiden's Romance" (1893), to his burlesques of detective fiction, "The Stolen White Elephant" (1882) and "The Double-Barreled Detective Story" (1902). Rogers argues that as a condensed novel, "A Medieval Romance" is not a pure burlesque; rather, like the "Legend of the Capitoline Venus" (1869), the story utilizes the burlesque form to structure a single humorous idea that earlier in his career might well have assumed the form of a sketch or anecdote. Rogers offers the story as an anticipation of *Tom Sawyer* (1876) in its extended burlesque of a mode of popular fiction (100–101).

Critical Studies

The story plays upon a common theme of romance, that of sexual masquerade. The complications that ensue, however, defy the neat, carefully structured endings of Shakespearean comic romances. Indeed, the story assumes the form of a classic tragedy, for human attempts to manipulate providence insure the dreadful fate they are intended to foil.

The plot of "A Medieval Romance" turns upon a hoax perpetrated by the lord of Klugenstein against his brother Ulrich, duke of Brandenburgh, to guarantee that the line of succession should pass to his own house. The rules of the game, so to speak, are established by their father who "on his death bed, decried that if no son were born to Ulrich the succession should pass to my house, provided a *son* were born to me. And further, in case no son were born to either, but only daughters, then the succession should pass to Ulrich's daughter if she proved stainless; if she did not, my daughter should succeed if she retained a blameless name" (51). When a daughter is born to the lord of Klugenstein he promptly murders "the leech, the nurse, and six waiting women" who know her sex and proclaims to the world he has been blessed with a son. The charade becomes all the more crucial as the years pass since the only child of his fraternal rival is female.

When the child Conrad has reached the age of twenty-eight, she is sent to Brandenburgh to claim the right of succession. Her father cautions his daughter not to "sit for a single instant in the great ducal chair before she hath been absolutely crowned in presence of the people" because "a law as old as Germany" specifies death as the penalty for any woman who sits on the throne before she is formally crowned. To further protect his interests, the lord sends the "shrewd and handsome Count Detzin" to tamper with the affections of his brother's eighteen-year-old daughter so as to insure that she not be "stainless" should the sex of his own child come to light before formal coronation ceremonies. All goes awry, however, when Ulrich's daughter—pregnant with Detzin's child and then abandoned—falls in love with Conrad, her female cousin who in male disguise is the pretender to the throne of Brandenburgh. Spurned in her love a second time, Ulrich's daughter must face the additional humiliation of public trial because she has given birth out of wedlock. Conrad, the heir apparent, must preside over the trial and, though she has not yet been crowned, is required to do so from the ducal throne since a member of the royal family stands accused. Ulrich's distraught daughter takes her revenge when she publicly identifies Conrad as the father of her illegitimate child. Conrad thus is trapped in an impossible dilemma: "To disprove the charge he must reveal that he was a woman, and for an uncrowned woman to sit in the ducal chair was death!" (56).

The hoax around which the plot of "A Medieval Romance" revolves having proved disastrous for all parties concerned, Mark Twain makes the reader the victim of an even more elaborate hoax. He abandons his story at the height of its dramatic intensity, making the whole a burlesque of the narrative methods and conventional devices of the genre. Covici writes that Mark Twain simultaneously involves his heroine in a complicated tangle of events from which she cannot plausibly escape yet encourages the reader to hope that somehow all will end happily; the hoax thus works to expose the insurmountable aesthetic inconsistencies of the romance form (144).

Bibliography

PRIMARY

*The Complete Short Stories of Mark Twain. Now Collected for the First Time. Edited by Charles Neider. Garden City, N.Y.: Hanover House, 1957.

Mark Twain's (Burlesque) Autobiography and First Romance. New York: Sheldon & Co., 1871.

Mark Twain's Celebrated Jumping Frog of Calaveras County and Other Sketches. With the Burlesque Autobiography and First Romance. London: George Routledge & Sons, 1872.

Mark Twain's Sketches, New and Old. Now First Published in Complete Form. Hartford and Chicago: American Publishing Co., 1875.

SECONDARY

Baldanza, Frank. Mark Twain: An Introduction and Interpretation. New York: Holt, Rinehart & Winston, 1961.

Covici, Pascal, Jr. Mark Twain's Humor: The Image of a World. Dallas: Southern Methodist University Press, 1962.

Hill, Hamlin. Mark Twain and Elisha Bliss. Columbia: University of Missouri Press, 1962.

Kaplan, Justin. Mr. Clemens and Mark Twain. New York: Simon & Schuster, 1966.

Paine, Albert B. Mark Twain: A Biography. Vol. 2. New York: Harper & Brothers, 1912.

Rogers, Franklin R. Mark Twain's Burlesque Patterns. Dallas: Southern Methodist University Press, 1962.

33

The £1,000,000 Bank-Note

Publication History

Written in autumn 1892, "The £1,000,000 Bank-Note" first appeared in the January 1893 issue of *Century Magazine*. Charles L. Webster and Company then published it as the title piece of a collection of "new stories" in February 1893. The entire contents of this 1893 volume is reprinted in *The American Claimant, etc.* (1917). Harper and Brothers also published "The £1,000,000 Bank-Note" as a separate pamphlet in 1917.

Circumstances of Composition, Sources, and Influences

Although he had planned the story years earlier, Mark Twain wrote "The £1,000,000 Bank-Note" in late 1892 while living in Florence, Italy, at the Villa Viviani (Paine 957). The last six months of 1892 were for Mark Twain a period of considerable literary activity. He revised *Tom Sawyer Abroad* (1894), began work on "Those Extraordinary Twins" (1894), and by late fall started transforming the latter into *Pudd'nhead Wilson* (1894). In the meantime, Mark Twain wrote nine essays and five short stories, including "The Californian's Tale," "The Esquimau Maiden's Romance," and "Is He Living or Is He Dead?" (all 1893).

Mark Twain's worries about money fueled this flurry of activity. Revenue from the Webster Publishing Company had about dried up. Debts were accumulating and living expenses abroad were higher than Mark Twain had anticipated. Emerson reports that "The £1,000,000 Bank-Note" reflects "the author's need for credit as he was facing bankruptcy" (188). Budd writes that the story "appeals to fantasies about windfalls of money" (2363). It is, Covici contends, "patently a dream of wish-fulfillment" (207).

Relationship to Other Mark Twain Works

An "ironic parable of unexpected (and undeserved) wealth," this story, Geismar contends, concerns "the central folk myth of the period," and is related in theme to "many other stories by Mark Twain in the early nineties" (130–31). Admittedly, both "The Esquimau Maiden's Romance" and

"Is He Living or Is He Dead?" concern money and its relationship to happiness, but "The £1,000,000 Bank-Note" shares stronger affinities to "The Man That Corrupted Hadleyburg" (1899) and "The $30,000 Bequest" (1904), stories written and published around the turn of the century, after Mark Twain's total financial collapse in the mid-1890s. Morgan specifically compares "The £1,000,000 Bank-Note" with "The $30,000 Bequest," but emphasizes the radical differences between the two. Both are concerned with sudden acquisition of vast wealth that is chimerical, but the former is a "fairy tale romance," while the latter is a naturalistic study of an inevitable decline to "total annihilation and death" (6). Henry Adams, the Adamic hero of "The £1,000,000 Bank-Note," successfully withstands the temptation of money; he achieves prominence, Morgan writes, "not through his own greed and money worship, but through the greed and money worship of the society surrounding him." Saladin and Electra Foster, the couple in "The $30,000 Bequest," are neither so virtuous nor so fortunate. They fall victim to the lure of wealth, sacrificing their piety, virtue, human relationships, and general contentment to their fantasies and greed. As in "The Man That Corrupted Hadleyburg," the promise of wealth in each story is in fact a test of moral virtue. In this earlier story, Adams proves up to the challenge; in the later one, the Fosters do not (Morgan 8–10).

Critical Studies

"The £1,000,000 Bank-Note" is a first-person narrative of Henry Adams, a twenty-seven-year-old mining-broker's clerk in San Francisco who, "alone in the world, and . . . nothing to depend on but my wits and clean reputation," arrives in London "ragged and shabby" with one dollar in his pocket (315–16). His adventure begins when two wealthy old gentlemen select him to settle a wager: he is given a million-pound bank-note as an interest free loan for thirty days. Of course he cannot cash the note, for he could never explain how he came to possess it; he cannot even give it away: it was "useless to me, as useless as a handful of ashes." But the "monster" serves our hero well, for the appearance of wealth earns him special consideration from all around him. People give him housing, clothes, meals, even force loans on him: "I drifted naturally into buying whatever I wanted, and asking for change. Within a week I was sumptuously equipped with all needful comforts and luxuries" (321). Newspapers make him a celebrity. Aristocracy opens doors for him. In a short time he rises to social prominence, gains prosperity, and wins the love of a beautiful heiress—all without cashing the note. At the end of thirty days he returns the note to the two brothers, one of whom happens to be the stepfather of Adams's beloved. As reward for passing his test, the hero is granted his wish—to become the benefactor's son-in-law.

Covici sees the story as "a romance that offends no one because the combination of love and dollars" is so clearly a fantasy (207). Others, however, see a more serious side to the story. Foner argues that there is a strong element of social satire in "The £1,000,000 Bank-Note." The story presents Mark Twain's "acid comments on a society that treats people according to how much money they have"; it is not Adams's character but his appearance of wealth that secures his standing in a capitalistic society (160–61). Geismar too sees the story as an exposé of the abuses of a capitalistic society based on money (131).

Morgan, however, stresses not the social but the moral dimensions of Mark Twain's romance. Adams prospers precisely because of his character and ingenuity, his only possessions at the beginning of the tale. He successfully resists the temptations that the skeptical brother thought would do him in. He uses his wits to manipulate others, those prone to avarice, to serve his interests, but at the end he returns the money intact and asks only that he be allowed to wed the woman he truly loves. The story is, Morgan contends, another of Mark Twain's fictional versions of Adam's temptation; in this one, however, Adam(s), because of his character and ingenuity, resists the satanic temptation to win his Eve and paradise too (6–10). Unlike the Fosters in "The $30,000 Bequest" or the Richardses in "The Man That Corrupted Hadleyburg," Adams never loves the money. And it is the love of money, not money itself, that is the proverbial root of all evil.

Bibliography

PRIMARY

The American Claimant, etc. New York: Harper & Brothers, 1917.

The Complete Short Stories of Mark Twain. Now Collected for the First Time. Edited by Charles Neider. Garden City, N.Y.: Hanover House, 1957.

The £1,000,000 Bank-Note and Other New Stories. New York: Charles L. Webster & Co., 1893.

The £1,000,000 Bank-Note. New York: Harper & Brothers, 1917.

SECONDARY

Budd, Louis J. "Mark Twain." *Critical Survey of Short Fiction.* Edited by Frank MaGill. Vol. 6. Englewood Cliffs, N.J.: Salem Press, 1981.

Covici, Pascal, Jr. *Mark Twain's Humor: The Image of a World.* Dallas: Southern Methodist University Press, 1962.

Emerson, Everett. *The Authentic Mark Twain: A Literary Biography of Samuel L. Clemens.* Philadelphia: University of Pennsylvania Press, 1984.

Foner, Philip S. *Mark Twain: Social Critic.* New York: International Publishers, 1958.

Geismar, Maxwell. *Mark Twain: An American Prophet.* Boston: Houghton Mifflin, 1970.

Morgan, Ricki. "Mark Twain's Money Imagery in 'The £1,000,000 Bank-Note' and 'The $30,000 Bequest.' " *The Mark Twain Journal* 19, no. 1 (1977–78):6–10.

Paine, Albert B. *Mark Twain: A Biography.* Vol. 3. New York: Harper & Brothers, 1912.

34

Political Economy

Publication History

"Political Economy" first appeared in *Galaxy*, September 1870, a literary periodical edited by Francis P. Church. The story is collected in the 1875 volume of *Mark Twain's Sketches, New and Old*.

Circumstances of Composition, Sources, and Influences

Shortly after his marriage to Olivia Langdon in early February 1870, Mark Twain decided to supplement his work on the Buffalo *Express* by contributing a series of sketches, stories, articles, imaginary letters and reviews to the *Galaxy*. His motivation was in part financial, in part a desire to gain wider distribution for his work. The agreement with editor Francis Church called for ten pages of printed matter for each monthly issue. In all Mark Twain contributed eighty-seven pieces to the magazine, most of them nondescript. In Mark Twain's own words, he was "periodical dancing before the public" (Emerson 58–60). "Political Economy," which chronicles the comic frustration of the literary protagonist who finds it virtually impossible to continue his writing in the face of constant interruption from a local peddler, no doubt reflects the pressures Mark Twain felt in adjusting to the rigors of genteel life in a respectable middle-class household.

Relationship to Other Mark Twain Works

Although Emerson contends that the *Galaxy* contributions represent "no new developments in the writer's career" (60), "Political Economy" in fact introduces a new genre to Mark Twain's comic repertoire: the domestic farce. The story's subject matter, tone, and burlesque method anticipate the more polished McWilliams stories written in the late 1870s and early 1880s, "The Canvasser's Tale" (1876), and the newspaper sketch, "Playing Courier" (New York *Sun*, 8 January 1892). These satires of genteel domestic life portray an "absent-minded husband . . . at hilarious disadvantage" in their focus on "life's little exasperations" (Baldanza 99).

Critical Studies

"Political Economy" is a succinct and amusing burlesque account of a writer's confrontation with a zealous lightning rod salesman. The first-person narrator is in the midst of composing an essay on the subject of "political economy" when he is interrupted by a peddler at the door. "Struggling all the time to keep a tight rein on my seething political-economy ideas," the narrator impatiently listens to the loquacious salesman's pitch before directing him to "make any kind of a job he pleased out of it, but let me get back to my work" (60). The story then moves back and forth, with the writer struggling in his study to sustain his essay but being called to the door intermittently to discuss lightning rods and the difficulties of this particular project: "I hurried off, boiling and surging with prodigious thoughts wombed in words of such majesty that each one of them was in itself a straggling procession of syllables that might be fifteen minutes passing a given point, and once more I confronted him—he so calm and sweet, I so hot and frenzied" (61). After numerous such interruptions, and an expenditure of nine hundred dollars, his house is equipped with such a prodigious display of lightning rods—never before "such a stack of them on one establishment"—that it is the principal attraction in town: "Our street was blocked night and day with spectators, and among them were many who came from the country to see" (63). The story reaches its climax when a thunderstorm finally comes and provides a spectacle worthy of the crowd's attention: "for all the falling stars and Fourth-of-July fireworks of a generation, put together and rained down simultaneously out of heaven in one brilliant shower upon one helpless roof, would not have any advantage of the pyrotechnic display that was making my house so magnificently conspicuous in the general gloom of the storm. . . . For one whole day and night not a member of my family stuck his head out of the window but he got the hair snatched off it as smooth as a billiard-ball" (63–64).

Burlesque exaggeration carries the story and provides its principal delight. The relationships between the writer and the peddler, however, also prove interesting. The story is structured as a series of confrontations between the reclusive writer and the aggressive salesman. Ironically the expert on "political economy" is taken by the smooth-talking peddler at the very time he is struggling with language to share his "expertise" with the world. Gibson points out that writer and peddler are akin in their use of nonsense language to cloak fundamental ignorance: the former, while writing on "international confraternity and biological deviation," proves no match for the latter who persuades him that sufficient lightning rods will render harmless the "recalcitrant and dephlogistic messenger of heaven" and make "its further progress apocryphal" (14). So impressed with the loquacious salesman is the writer that he asks, "if he learned to talk out of a book, and if I could borrow it anywhere?" (61).

Bibliography

PRIMARY

The Complete Short Stories of Mark Twain. Now Collected for the First Time. Edited by Charles Neider. Garden City, N.Y.: Hanover House, 1957.

Mark Twain's Sketches, New and Old. Now First Published in Complete Form. Hartford and Chicago: American Publishing Co., 1875.

SECONDARY

Baldanza, Frank. *Mark Twain: An Introduction and Interpretation.* New York: Holt, Rinehart & Winston, 1961.

Emerson, Everett. *The Authentic Mark Twain: A Literary Biography of Samuel L. Clemens.* Philadelphia: University of Pennsylvania Press, 1984.

Gibson, William M. *The Art of Mark Twain.* New York: Oxford University Press, 1976.

35

The Second Advent
The International Lightning Trust
Randall's Jew Story

Publication History

Unpublished during Mark Twain's lifetime, these three essentially complete short stories appear only in John Tuckey's 1972 edition of *Mark Twain's Fables of Man*. A brief critical commentary precedes each story in the Tuckey edition; a discussion of textual history and listing of manuscript revisions are included in the "Textual Apparatus" section at the end of the book. Tuckey's notes provide the most complete and substantive information and analysis available for each of the stories: "The Second Advent" (50–52, 493–503); "The International Lightning Trust" (78–79, 511–33); "Randall's Jew Story" (283, 634–37).

Circumstances of Composition, Sources, and Influences

Although Paine speculates that "The Second Advent" was written "probably in 1871" (2:561), more recent scholarship dates its composition in the early 1880s. Long conjectures that the story was written in 1883. As evidence Long points to some notes Mark Twain made regarding the story in that year: "Write the Second Advent, with full details—lots of Irish disciples—Paddy Ryan for Judas and other disciples. Star in the East. People want to know how wise men could see it move while sober. John interviewed" (29). Tuckey, however, accepts the last line of the story as establishing the date of composition in 1881, and points out that the surviving manuscript is essentially a complete first draft. Twenty-two of the eighty-four manuscript pages were appropriated from "The Holy Children," a fragment from the 1870s (50–52). The 1883 note to which Long refers suggests that Mark Twain intended to revise or expand the story. Paine writes that Mark Twain had intended to develop the story into a novel (2:561). None of these contemplated revisions was carried out. In a note on the title page of the manuscript, Paine calls the story a "semi-burlesque of a new Christ, born in Arkansas" and judges it "hardly usable" (Tuckey 50–51).

The initial idea for the story came during Mark Twain's excursion to Europe and the Holy Land aboard the *Quaker City* in 1867 (Tuckey 6). Sloane points out that the story applies "the same realistic test to senti-mentalized religion" characteristic of Mark Twain's satire of the Old Masters and skepticism toward the Holy Land in *Innocents Abroad* (1869) (96). The "holy Talmage" of "The Second Advent" is the Reverend T. DeWitt Talmage, a prominent Brooklyn clergyman and distinguished orator who was a target of Mark Twain's satire in the 1870s for his complaint about the "smell" of his working-class parishioners.

Mark Twain wrote "The International Lightning Trust" in 1909 and sent it to Harper and Brothers for what he hoped would be immediate publication (Paine 4:1684). After Mark Twain's death in 1910, however, his literary executor Albert Paine recalled the manuscript on the pretense that it did not meet the author's usual standard of excellence. Actually both Paine and Clara, Mark Twain's daughter, objected to the story's satire of conventional religious piety and its attack on corporate trusts (Tuckey 78–79). Their decision to suppress the manuscript was part of a concerted effort to sanitize Mark Twain's image after his death.

Although he did not get around to writing "The International Lightning Trust" until 1909, Mark Twain conceived the basic idea for the story a decade earlier when he considered including a "lightning lottery" in his novella *Which Was It?* (1899–1903) (Tuckey 79). The story shows some influence from one of Mark Twain's favorite books, W. E. H. Lecky's *History of European Morals,* as protagonist Jasper Hackett cites Lecky as the inspiration for his profitable scheme (Baetzhold 363, n. 13).

"Randall's Jew Story" was written sometime in the late 1890s. Tuckey notes that the manuscript paper is the same as that of Mark Twain's correspondence in 1894 but that the ink type is that used as late as 1898 (283). The story reflects Mark Twain's sustained interest in Jews and develops more fully the sympathetic portrayal of the Jewish personality initiated in "Newhouse's Jew Story," a sketch discarded from *Following the Equator* (1897) (Emerson 208).

Relationship to Other Mark Twain Works

These three stories are related in that they ridicule or expose conventional Christian beliefs and practices: the first two satirize sentimental pieties and superstition; the last one undercuts stereotypical assumptions behind the anti-Semitism widespread in nineteenth-century Protestant America.

Although "The Second Advent" pokes fun at several elements of the biblical account of the nativity story—including the virgin birth, the star in the East, the wise men—the central target of its satire is the concept of "special providence." The idea that the general laws of the universe would permit exceptions for a particular group of people Mark Twain thought sentimental, implausible, and egotistical, and he lambasted it throughout his career. Tuckey sees the story as closely parallel to "The Man That Corrupted Hadleyburg" (1899), since "the events of each story prompt a reversal of religious values, and the outcomes of both are formal resolutions inverting the previous moral stances of the villagers." Just as Hadleyburg's elite learn that their esteemed cloistered virtue is a dangerous sham and revise their motto to read "Lead Us into Temptation," so the citizens of Black Jack, Arkansas, learn that their prayers for special providences have disastrous consequences and henceforth permit only those petitions that specify, "Lord, Thy will, not mine, be done!" (52). In tone and subject matter, "The Second Advent" resembles other unpublished religious satires like "Little Bessie" and *Letters from the Earth* as it turns sacred tenets of Christian faith into fodder for humorous burlesque.

The concept of special providence also receives satiric treatment in "The International Lightning Trust," for the two entrepreneurs Jasper Hackett and Stephen Spaulding build a lucrative business upon their "trust in providence." Tuckey writes, "Their lightning trust amounts to a partnership in a divine lottery that dispenses just enough prizes to insure that all of the dupes will play the game" (79). If Mark Twain believed, as he writes in an 1886 notebook entry, that "these myriads of globes are merely the blood-corpuscles ebbing & flowing through the arteries of God, & we but animalculae that infest them, disease them, pollute them: & God does not know we are there, & would not care if He did" (Tuckey 51), he was nevertheless fascinated if not haunted by the idea of sudden death providentially decreed. Gribben writes, "Twain invariably associates the lightning stroke and its attendant thunderclap . . . with a divine Providence that angrily exacts an awesome vengeance for petty misconduct" (192). "Captain Stormfield's Visit to Heaven" (1907–08) and *The Mysterious Stranger* (1916) are the most notable of those works that reinforce the sentiments of the 1886 notebook entry, as they expose the blind egotism of our assumption that we occupy a special and closely observed place in a benevolent God's carefully ordered universe. At the same time, Mark Twain's *Autobiography* testifies to a nagging Presbyterian conscience that sees personal and communal catastrophes as the result of divine intervention intended to chasten, punish, or instruct wayward followers. At the end of "The International Lightning Trust" Jasper Hackett witnesses two men struck by lightning while fishing on the Sabbath. Chance or Providence? Gribben comments: "This odd, almost childish linking of lightning with deserved punishment, specifically retaliation for religious lapses, and with the Mississippi, somehow signified more for Twain's psyche than he could ever state fully on the printed page" (192).

"The International Lightning Trust" is also a satire on nineteenth-century business practices, but as is the case with its satire of special providences, there is some ambiguity. Tuckey reports that the attack on business trusts was the major reason Paine and Clara suppressed the manuscript. Yet, despite his attack on business in *The Gilded Age* (1873), Mark Twain was himself a speculator and entrepreneur; moreover, he felt great admiration for and gratitude toward H. H. Rogers, the Standard Oil executive who had saved him from financial ruin in the 1890s. Jager argues that Mark Twain was fascinated by the capitalistic entrepreneur whose enterprise he considered a form of art: "For Twain, successful capitalization was a creative achievement"; he "was simply intrigued by business, . . . the novelty it offered and the excitement of turning an idea into cash through commercial artistry" (10). This story is not bitter in tone; instead, Hackett and Spaulding display "an almost amiable roguishness" (Tuckey 78–79). In this "rather amusing satire on business practices," Emerson notes, greed receives sympathetic treatment (268).

Mark Twain wrote a number of essays, letters, and stories in the 1890s concerned with Jews and the problem of anti-Semitism in American society: a letter "To the Editor of the American Hebrew" (1889 or 1890); an essay, "Concerning the Jews" (1898); a sketch, "Newhouse's Jew Story," discarded from *Following the Equator* (Emerson 208); and the unpublished, untitled, short story that Tuckey labeled "Randall's Jew Story." Because it "avoids the patronizing tone, the didacticism, and the simplistic analyses of social attitudes" that mar the nonfictional writing of the Jewish question, "Randall's Jew Story" is Mark Twain's most effective tribute to the Jew (Tuckey 283).

The motif of the duel links "Randall's Jew Story" to other Mark Twain stories and sketches that turn upon a recurring thematic pattern Gribben calls "The Waiting Grave." *A Tramp Abroad* (1880), *Life on the Mississippi* (1883), and *Pudd'nhead Wilson* (1894) all contain dueling episodes that force us as readers to confront the very real possibility of sudden, violent death (191). The duel, however, receives more sympathetic treatment than the senseless frontier feud of the Shepherdsons and Grangerfords satirized in *Huckleberry Finn*, for the code invoked permits demonstration of courage and virtue in the face of palpable danger. Both "Randall's Jew Story" and the "Newhouse Jew Story" depict the shrewdness and courage of Jewish gentlemen who use "the dueling code to defeat lecherous gamblers" (Gribben 191).

Critical Studies

"The Second Advent" is an elaborate burlesque of the Christ story, generally amusing in its cleverness but no doubt offensive to Christians sensitive to liberties taken with essential elements of their faith. Paine saw little merit in a story whose heavy-handed satire, he claims, "leads only to grotesquery and literary disorder" (2:561).

The setting for "The Second Advent" is a rural nineteenth-century hamlet that resembles the medieval towns of *A Connecticut Yankee* (1889) and *The Mysterious Stranger*. Black Jack, Arkansas, is a remote, decrepit village where "ignorance, sloth and drowsiness prevail": there is but one church, no school, and "no newspapers, no railways, no factories, no library." Hogs sunning themselves in public places and "the loafing savage" are characteristic of this village "far removed from the busy world and the interests which animate it" (53). When young Nancy Hopkins discovers she is pregnant as the result of an immaculate conception, Black Jack serves as the site for a farcical reenactment of the nativity story.

Mark Twain's satirical method is essentially dialectical: the claims of a small group of believers are juxtaposed to the rational objections of hard-headed skeptics. When Jackson Barnes, the village blacksmith to whom Nancy is engaged, explains to the gossiping townspeople—"rude gross pioneers" who "coarsely joked about it over their whisky in the village grocery"—that "God has honored her, God has overshadowed her, and to Him she will bear this child," he is greeted with derision and bombarded with questions designed to expose the implausibility of his story. Barnes, however, remains steadfast: "This is merely the Second Advent. . . . He is to be again born of an obscure Virgin, because the world cannot help but believe and be convinced by that circumstance, since it has been convinced by it before" (57). When "certain wise men from the far east," this time "editors from New York and other great cities, and presidents of Yale and Princeton and Andover and other great colleges," determine to follow "a star shining in the east—it was Venus," they are countered by skeptical astronomers who insist "that a star could not be followed." The wise men themselves fall into two factions: the "religious faction" accepts the testimony of Nancy and Barnes as "clear, coherent, cogent, and without flaw, discrepancy, or doubtful feature"; the "editorial faction," however, strongly dissents and warns of a sinister "ecclesiastical interest" at work. The cautious skeptics lose out to the emotional fury of the believers, whose most convincing appeal is to precedent, "the fact that all these things have happened before, in exactly the same way." Led by Talmage, the wise men bestow gifts—not frankincense, gold, and myrrh but "a History of the Church's Dominion During the First Fourteen Centuries; a History of the Presbyterian Dominion in Scotland; a History of Catholic Dominion in

England; a History of Salem Witchcraft; a History of the Holy Inquisition; in addition, certain toys for the child to play with—these being tiny models of the Inquisition's instruments of torture; and a little Holy Bible with the decent passages printed in red ink" (60–61).

The story concludes with a satirical account of Christ's ministry, when after thirty years of oblivion He begins "to teach in the Churches, and to do miracles" and appoints twelve disciples. Most prominent among the disciples is St. Talmage, who at the beck and call of the believers of Black Rock, calls forth miracles at their bidding. But the miracles produce so many disastrous consequences that "restrictions came to be placed upon the disciples' prayers, by public demand" (67). Experience teaches the villagers that special providence is dangerous and they resolve henceforth to rely solely upon God's wisdom; all petitions must "begin and end with the words, 'Lord, thy will, not mine, be done' " (68). So severe is the chaos engendered by special petitions that the community pursues and crucifies Christ and eleven of the disciples. Only Talmage is spared for he, like Judas, betrayed the others for thirty pieces of silver.

"The International Lightning Trust," Emerson writes, demonstrates that even in his last year of life Mark Twain "was still capable of turning out perfectly competent, if undistinguished, commercial fiction" (268). The story charts the rise to prosperity of two young printers who, out of work and destitute, devise a brilliant scheme that not only brings them riches but eventually enables then to win the love of two women who had abandoned them for a plumber and a carpenter.

The scheme involves the formation of a trust company that insures anyone against the possibility of death by lightning. Hackett and Spaulding succeed because they understand human nature: "I perceive we are going to trade on the assfulness of the human race" (85). Although their motto is "In Providence We Trust," the two entrepreneurs carefully calculate their success on three factors: 1) a universal, if irrational, human fear of lightning; 2) the lure of a large return on a minimal investment ($1 brings $5,000, $5 brings $35,000, $10 brings $100,000); and 3) the odds, which show that only twenty-eight of some ninety million Americans are killed by lightning in a given year. They actually want victims (beneficiaries), for the news of a large payoff brings many additional policyholders whose premiums more than offset the benefit payment; in fact, the occasional benefit payment is their best advertising.

Despite their prosperity, Hackett and Spaulding are not content while they remain "unmarried to the idols of their young hearts." The young women, however, "stood steadfastly upon principle" and would not marry them "while the carpenter and the plumber remained undead"; moreover, they do not want to appear "golddiggers" by marrying billionaires while they themselves remain penniless. Again the two entrepreneurs must trust in Providence, and their faith is rewarded: the carpenter and the plumber, after fishing on the Sabbath, are struck by lightning and killed. Providentially, Jasper Hackett happens to be present and slips a hundred-thousand-dollar ticket into the pocket of each dead man; the money, of course, goes to the two young women, who thus are no longer penniless and are free to marry. All ends happily: "By humble faith, virtue, and brave self-sacrifice" Hackett and Spaulding achieve "sublime heights." Their story, Mark Twain concludes, "is a lesson for us all" (104).

"Randall's Jew Story" is a tale told by an elderly gentleman to a group of the same designed to dispel the group's virulent anti-Semitism. The account details the heroic action of a "handsome, courteous, intelligent, alert, good-hearted" young Jew who risks his fortune and his life to rescue a young mulatto woman from a vicious slavetrader aboard a Mississippi Riverboat in 1850. The slavetrader wins the girl in a poker game with a naive, outmatched planter. Although public sentiment runs high and is unanimously against the trader, only the Jew intervenes and offers to buy the girl for the money owed the trader by the planter: "All those men present there, felt a deep pity for that young slave girl and a sincere desire to save her; but the Jew went further—he *materialized* his pity—put up his money to try to save her; he had a bigger heart than those others" (288). When the trader refuses the generous offer, the Jew strikes the trader "a sounding blow on the mouth with the back of his hand," thus forcing him into a duel in which the trader is killed. Since "there was no bill of sale to tell tales," the girl remains safely with the planter, whose own daughter regards her as a sister. Only the Jew, the narrator informs us, "was bright enough to think of" the duel, and only he had the courage to risk his life to save a helpless victim: "And the finest thing of all was his risking his life out of pure humanity on such unequal terms: his life—a man's life—against a mere animal's life, a mere brute's life" (289). The experience teaches the gentleman-narrator a lesson that has lasted into old age: "I have weighed his people ever since in scales which are not loaded."

Bibliography

PRIMARY

Mark Twain's Fables of Man. Edited with an introduction by John S. Tuckey. Berkeley and Los Angeles: University of California Press, 1972.

SECONDARY

Baetzhold, Howard G. *Mark Twain and John Bull: The British Connection*. Bloomington: Indiana University Press, 1970.

Emerson, Everett. *The Authentic Mark Twain: A Literary Biography of Samuel L. Clemens.* Philadelphia: University of Pennsylvania Press, 1984.

Gribben, Alan. "Those Other Thematic Patterns in Mark Twain's Writings." *Studies in American Fiction* 13 (Autumn 1985): 185–200.

Jager, Ronald B. "Mark Twain and the Robber Barons: A View of the Gilded Age Businessman." *Mark Twain Journal* 17, no. 3 (1975):8–12.

Long, E. Hudson. *Mark Twain Handbook.* New York: Hendricks House, 1957.

Paine, Albert B. *Mark Twain: A Biography.* Vols. 2 and 4. New York: Harper & Brothers, 1912.

Sloane, David E. E. *Mark Twain as a Literary Comedian.* Baton Rouge: Louisiana State University Press, 1979.

36

Some Learned Fables
for Good Old Boys and Girls

Publication History

Mark Twain wrote this story in 1874 and sent it to William Dean Howells for publication in the *Atlantic Monthly*. Howells rejected it in September 1874. Mark Twain revised the story for publication the following year in his volume *Mark Twain's Sketches, New and Old*, where it appears with the title, "Some Fables for Good Old Boys and Girls: Part First, Part Second, Part Third." The story is the longest of the seven new sketches appearing in the 1875 collection (Hill, *Mark Twain*, 89–90; Emerson 88).

Circumstances of Composition, Sources, and Influences

Preparing the manuscript for *Sketches, New and Old* afforded Mark Twain an opportunity to review his achievement in the early years of his career. As Emerson contends, the volume "represented his past" (88); fifty-six of the sixty-three sketches were reprinted from previously published work, which Mark Twain had come to see as largely apprentice writing.

The author's attitude toward his past was ambivalent. He was anxious to shed his reputation as a mere humorist and to enter the mainstream of the eastern literary establishment. To Howells, who in a review of the 1875 volume had noted "a growing seriousness of meaning" in these sketches of a "subtile humorist," Mark Twain wrote a letter expressing his wife's gratitude: "the thing that gravels her is that I am so persistently glorified as a mere buffoon" (Emerson 89). At the same time Mark Twain had come to realize that his commercial and aesthetic success as a writer depended largely on his ability to use his western past, and he turned to that past as inspiration for two of his finest achievements: *Tom Sawyer* (1876) and "Old Times on the Mississippi," which he began publishing serially in the *Atlantic* in 1874. In assembling the manuscript for *Sketches, New and Old*, Mark Twain developed a renewed interest in sketch writing. One of the original contributions, "Experience of the McWilliamses with Membranous Croup," is a successful domestic farce that pointedly focuses its attention on Mark

Twain's life as an eastern gentleman in a genteel family setting. "Some Learned Fables," however, is more "western" in its outlook and method; about Tumble-Bug, a roguish skeptic who exposes the pompous absurdity of the eastern scientific community led by Dr. Bull-Frog and Professor Snail, the story shows "that Mark Twain still had a good word to say for the values he had adopted in the West" (Emerson 88).

A major influence on "Some Learned Fables" comes from Mark Twain's reading about science. Brashear (244) and Cummings (245–61) call attention to Mark Twain's familiarity with Thomas Paine and the English empiricists Thomas Hobbes, John Locke, and David Hume. Waggoner reveals that Mark Twain also knew well the scientific thought of his own time, and that his imagination was stimulated by recent discoveries in anthropology, evolution, and geology; moreover, Waggoner argues, Mark Twain had come to share the naturalistic concept of humans and nature formulated by Charles Darwin and Thomas Huxley (359–61). If during the nineteenth century science and religion became competing, dichotomous approaches to truth, then Mark Twain, at first glance, seems clearly on the side of science. Deism, Darwinism, and his boyhood training in the Presbyterian church were, Cummings writes, "the foundation ideas of his life" ("Mark Twain's Theory" 213). Even after presenting two lectures by Mark Twain that satirize paleontology, Hamlin Hill insists that "Twain, underneath the humorist's mask, was aware of and to some extent sympathetic with the problems and methods of science" ("Mark Twain's 'Brace' " 239).

If the concern for science reflects Mark Twain's reading of Darwin, Huxley, and others, his approach to the subject shows the influence of Jonathan Swift. Paine was the first to note the parallel to *Gulliver's Travels* (551), a parallel more fully developed by Baetzhold. The deflation of human intellectual pretension, he argues, comes directly from Swift: "The learned bugs, reptiles, and rodents . . . with their proclivities for building 'a mountain of facts out of a spoonful of supposition' reflect the various attacks on 'projectors' in *Gulliver's*" (*Mark Twain* 267).

Relationship to Other Mark Twain Works

Largely because of its title, "Some Learned Fables for Good Old Boys and Girls" is often linked to the "Story of the Bad Little Boy" (1865) and the "Story of the Good Little Boy Who Did Not Prosper" (1870). Bellamy argues that in its attack on didacticism the story is a burlesque of sentimental fiction for children (111). Baldanza calls it "a less successful satire" than the two condensed novels (99), and indeed as a burlesque of a genre the story does not succeed for it bears only tangential relation to the type of fiction parodied.

Gibson sees in the language of "Some Learned Fables" a parallel to Mark Twain's 1878 story "The Loves of Alonzo Fitz Clarence and Rosannah Ethelton." The scientific expedition rests its findings on Professor Snail's "perlustration and perscontation" of an "isoperimetrical protuberance." As in the 1878 story Mark Twain uses nonsense language, or double talk, to define the absurd pretensions of his characters (14).

The story may be most profitably compared to other Mark Twain writings that satirize science or pseudosciences that seek authenticity by appropriating the methodology of legitimate sciences. Of some relevance is "The Great Revolution in Pitcairn" (1879), a story that anticipates *A Connecticut Yankee* (1889) in its exposé of the dangers when science and technology are introduced into a world not ready for them (Bellamy 314–15). More directly germane is Mark Twain's satiric treatment of paleontology in a series of 1871 articles that appeared in the Buffalo *Express* (Hill, "Mark Twain's 'Brace,' " 228–39). The basic problem with paleontology is that it draws deductions that are not logically or conclusively demonstrated by hard evidence. Like the reptiles, bugs, and rodents of "Some Learned Fables," the paleontologist builds "a mountain of facts out of a spoonful of supposition": "it is a precious privilege to live in an epoch of paleontologists, for the uneducated investigator would not be able to tell a primeval graveyard from a primeval restaurant" (Hill, "Mark Twain's 'Brace,' " 232). In *Christian Science* (1907), Mark Twain attacks Mary Baker Eddy and her followers for using the same dubious approach to truth; the "scientific precepts" of Eddy's book *Science and Health* savor of the dogmatic assertions of the medieval church: "without ever presenting anything which may rightfully be called by the strong name of Evidence, and sometimes without ever mentioning a reason for a deduction at all, it thunders out the startling words, "I have Proved' so and so" (*Christian Science* 31).

The 1871 *Express* articles seem to belie Waggoner's claim that Mark Twain wholeheartedly adopted Darwin's theory of evolution, for Darwin's 1859 *Origin of Species* bases its deductions on evidence like that which Mark Twain devastates in his "Brace of Brief Lectures on Science." Perhaps here—and in "Some Learned Fables"—the author is merely exploiting science for comic purposes and, as Hill argues, does not really believe the criticism he hurls at geology. Cummings would agree with Hill: the "outrageous burlesque on scientists" is consistent with the antirealistic tone and subject matter characteristic of much of Mark Twain's sketch writing in the 1870s ("Mark Twain's Theory" 209). Poole reports that popular magazines as well as scientific journals carried Darwinian debate throughout the 1870s, and that Mark Twain was well aware of the controversy (202). Hence perhaps we can conclude that in the early 1870s Mark Twain shared the popular objection to Darwin's thesis: that it was merely a theory based on questionable and ultimately unverifiable documentation. Although several of Mark Twain's fictional heroes are empirical in their approach to human experience—notably Huck Finn and David Wilson—Mark Twain's reservations about the methodology of science resurface later in his discussion of Priestly in *The Secret History of Eddypus* (written 1901–02; published 1972) (Wilson 72–82). During this last phase of Mark Twain's life, Poole reports, Darwinian theories serve as usable metaphors to express the author's personal vision of the human condition in an alien universe; but, Poole concludes, "Mark Twain neither accepted Darwinian evolution as fully as many critics have assumed nor found in it any absolute theory of man's condition" (203).

Critical Studies

"Some Learned Fables" is actually a single extended beast fable that details the antics of a group of insects, reptiles, and rodents on a scientific expedition into "the unknown and unexplored world" with the purpose of verifying "the truth of the matters already taught in their schools and colleges" (*Complete Short Stories* 105). Although the story is "too long and unfocused," as Emerson writes (88), it is an amusing and generally effective burlesque of science.

Members of the expedition fall into three general categories: the scientists, an intellectual, pretentious, and self-centered group that includes Professors Bull-Frog, Snail, Angle-Worm, Fieldmouse, Mud-Turtle, and Woodlouse; the aristocracy, represented by Lord Grand-Daddy-Longlegs; and the common laborers, like the profane, earthly, and skeptical Tumble-Bug, who are not allowed to voice their opinions on august scientific matters. In the course of his burlesque account of their professional debate, Mark Twain manages to lampoon much of contemporary science: paleontology, astronomy, philology, Darwinism, even the very idea of a scientific expedition (Baetzhold, "Mark Twain on Scientific Investigations," 128–54). The scientists, predictably, misread evidence, draw preposterous conclusions, exaggerate the importance of their findings. They conclude their "official" report of the expedition, "All honor to the mystery-dispelling eye of godlike Science!" (121). The "vulgar, ignorant carpers," like the "obscene Tumble-Bug," are not convinced by the pompous official report. And it is the Tumble-Bug who is allowed the final word: "He said that all he had learned by his travels was that science only needed a spoonful of supposition to build a mountain of demonstrated fact out of; and that for the future he meant to be content with the knowledge that nature had made free to all creatures and not go prying into the august secrets of the Deity" (121).

Bibliography

PRIMARY

Christian Science, with Notes Containing Corrections to Date. New York: Harper & Brothers, 1907.

*The Complete Short Stories of Mark Twain. Now Collected for the First Time. Edited by Charles Neider. Garden City, N.Y.: Hanover House, 1957.

Mark Twain's Sketches, New and Old. Now First Published in Complete Form. Hartford and Chicago: American Publishing Co., 1875.

SECONDARY

Baetzhold, Howard G. *Mark Twain & John Bull: The British Connection.* Bloomington: Indiana University Press, 1970.

————. "Mark Twain on Scientific Investigation: Contemporary Allusions in 'Some Learned Fables for Good Old Boys and Girls.' " In *Literature and Ideas in America: Essays in Memory of Harry Hayden Clark,* edited by Robert Falk, 128–54. Athens: Ohio University Press, 1975.

Baldanza, Frank. *Mark Twain: An Introduction and Interpretation.* New York: Holt, Rinehart & Winston, 1961.

Bellamy, Gladys C. *Mark Twain as a Literary Artist.* Norman: University of Oklahoma Press, 1950.

Brashear, Minnie. *Mark Twain: Son of Missouri.* Chapel Hill: University of North Carolina Press, 1934.

Cummings, Sherwood. "Mark Twain's Acceptance of Science." *Centennial Review* 6 (1962):245–61.

————. "Mark Twain's Theory of Realism; or, The Science of Piloting." *Studies in American Humor* 2 (January 1976):209–21.

Emerson, Everett. *The Authentic Mark Twain: A Literary Biography of Samuel L. Clemens.* Philadelphia: University of Pennsylvania Press, 1984.

Gibson, William M. *The Art of Mark Twain.* New York: Oxford University Press, 1976.

Hill, Hamlin. *Mark Twain and Elisha Bliss.* Columbia: University of Missouri Press, 1964.

————. "Mark Twain's 'Brace of Brief Lectures on Science.' " *New England Quarterly* 34 (June 1961):221–39.

Paine, Albert B. *Mark Twain: A Biography.* Vol. 2. New York: Harper & Brothers, 1912.

Poole, Stan. "In Search of the Missing Link: Mark Twain and Darwinism." *Studies in American Fiction* 13 (Autumn 1985):201–15.

Waggoner, Hyatt. "Science in the Thought of Mark Twain." *American Literature* 8 (January 1937):359–61.

Wilson, James D. " 'Monumental Sarcasm of the Ages': Science and Pseudoscience in the Thought of Mark Twain." *South Atlantic Bulletin* 40 (May 1975):72–82.

37

The Stolen White Elephant

Publication History

"The Stolen White Elephant" was the title piece of a collection of Mark Twain stories and sketches published by James R. Osgood in 1882. Subsequently the story was included in the *Tom Sawyer Abroad* volume.

Circumstances of Composition, Sources, and Influences

Mark Twain wrote "The Stolen White Elephant" in late November or early December 1878, intending it originally to be a chapter of *A Tramp Abroad* (1880). The story was inspired by sensational newspaper coverage of an extraordinary grave robbery—the theft of the corpse of dry-goods merchant Alexander T. Stewart from the family crypt—and the subsequent attempts of New York detectives to locate Stewart's remains. News stories broke on 8 November 1878, and as Baetzhold shows, details of the case and the detectives' antics are no less bizarre and absurd than those recounted in "The Stolen White Elephant" (183–90). Mark Twain wrote to Howells from Munich on 21 January 1879: "When the detectives were nosing around after Stewart's loud remains, I threw a chapter into my present book in which I have very extravagantly burlesqued the detective business—if it *is* possible to burlesque that business extravagantly" (*Mark Twain-Howells Letters* 246).

The specific target of Mark Twain's burlesque is Allan Pinkerton, founder of the National Detective Agency, whose operation and methods Mark Twain had parodied earlier in *Cap'n Simon Wheeler, Amateur Detective* (1877). The Pinkerton agency's pretensions of infallibility—evident in its badge, motto, and Pinkerton's self-serving detective fiction—become the primary object of burlesque deflation in Mark Twain's story. "The Stolen White Elephant" is, Baldanza writes, "a brutal attack on the detectives' pretensions to certainty" (100).

Baetzhold suggests two possible sources for details pertaining to the culture of Siam. The first is a book, Frank Vincent's *Land of the Elephants: Sights and Scenes in South-Eastern Asia* (1874), given to Mark Twain in 1877 by the author. The second and more pervasive source is a widely

248 TWAIN'S SHORT STORIES

copied newspaper item from the *Times of India,* March 1878, which was entitled "Funeral of a Siamese God" in a *New York Times* reprint (194).

Relationship to Other Mark Twain Works

"The Stolen White Elephant" is an extravagant burlesque not so much of detective fiction like the later "A Double-Barreled Detective Story" (1902) as of detectives themselves, their pompous assumption of infallibility and ridiculously inappropriate procedures. It is, as Paine writes, "an amazingly good take-off on what might be called the spectacular detective" (734). It is thus related in subject and tone to both the dramatic and prose fiction versions of *Cap'n Simon Wheeler, Amateur Detective,* which likewise parody Pinkerton and his agency's extravagant methods. Later in his career Mark Twain put the conventions of detective fiction to more serious purposes: courtroom revelations and trial scenes play prominent dramatic roles in *Pudd'nhead Wilson* (1894), *Personal Recollections of Joan of Arc* (1896), *Tom Sawyer, Detective* (1896), "The Man That Corrupted Hadleyburg" (1899), and "The Chronicle of Young Satan" (1916). But in "A Double-Barreled Detective Story" Mark Twain again burlesques detectives, this time the famous Sherlock Holmes, and broadens his satire to include the whole genre of detective fiction.

Bellamy sees in this story an early sign of the philosophical nihilism that comes to control much of Mark Twain's later writing (331). The tone of the piece, however, is light and links it more clearly to the good-natured burlesques of his early journalistic period.

Critical Studies

Baetzhold's 1976 article is the only sustained consideration of the story in print, and he focuses his attention almost exclusively on sources. "The Stolen White Elephant" is clearly extravagant burlesque at the expense of detectives and their unwavering reliance on inflexible methods of scientific investigation even when circumstances render those methods absurd. Comic effect depends upon hyperbole and incongruity. As Baetzhold writes, "Clemens obviously read his papers with an eye to the ridiculous" (184).

A brief frame introduces the story. Its purpose is to establish plausibility for a tale that taxes credulity. Mark Twain, as character, is the passive auditor to a "curious history" told to him by "a chance railway acquaintance," a "gentleman more than seventy years of age" whose "thoroughly good and gentle face and earnest and sincere manner imprinted the unmistakable stamp of truth upon every statement" (199).

The gentleman then narrates the extraordinary series of events that have left him "a ruined man and a wanderer on the earth" (216). He turns out to have been in the Indian civil service, given the responsibility of conveying a "transcendently royal" gift—a white elephant—from the king of Siam to the queen of England. Disaster strikes in transit when the elephant is stolen in Jersey City. Anarchic madness ensues when responsibility for locating the prized elephant falls to "the celebrated Inspector Blunt."

Neither the gentleman narrator nor Inspector Blunt sees anything unusual about the case. News of the pilfered white elephant "had no more visible effect upon [Blunt's] iron self-possession than if I had told him somebody had stolen my dog." "Nothing," Blunt responds, "can be accomplished in this trade of mine without strict and minute method" (200). The method is absurdly inappropriate, however, and yields disastrous results. Virtually no one, least of all the deadpan narrator, seems aware of the incongruity of the situation and the hyperbolic procedures. The only discordant note is struck by a single "contemptible" newspaper: "Great is the detective! He may be a little slow in finding a little thing like a mislaid elephant—he may hunt him all day and sleep with his rotting carcass all night for three weeks, but he will find him at last—if he can get the man who mislaid him to show him the place!" (216). Ruined as he is by the whole ordeal, the narrator remains convinced of Blunt's prodigious skills: "my admiration for that man, whom I believe to be the greatest detective the world has ever produced, remains undimmed to this day, and will so unto the end" (216).

Bibliography

PRIMARY

The Complete Short Stories of Mark Twain. Now Collected for the First Time. Edited by Charles Neider. Garden City, N.Y.: Hanover House, 1957.

Mark Twain-Howells Letters: The Literary Correspondence of Samuel L. Clemens and William Dean Howells, 1872–1910. Edited by Henry Nash Smith and William M. Gibson. Vol. 1. Cambridge, Mass.: Harvard University Press, 1960.

The Stolen White Elephant Etc. Boston: James R. Osgood, 1882.

Tom Sawyer Abroad, Tom Sawyer Detective and Other Stories, Etc. Etc. New York: Harper & Brothers, 1896.

SECONDARY

Baetzhold, Howard G. "Of Detectives and Their Derring-Do: The Genesis of Mark Twain's 'The Stolen White Elephant.'" *Studies in American Humor* 2 (January 1976):183–95.

Baldanza, Frank. *Mark Twain: An Introduction and Interpretation.* New York: Holt, Rinehart & Winston, 1961.

Bellamy, Gladys C. *Mark Twain as a Literary Artist*. Norman: University of Oklahoma Press, 1950.

Paine, Albert B. *Mark Twain: A Biography*. Vol. 2. New York: Harper & Brothers, 1912.

38

Story of the Bad Little Boy
Story of the Good Little Boy
Who Did Not Prosper

Publication History

"Story of the Bad Little Boy" was first published 23 December 1865 in the San Francisco *Californian*. It was initially entitled "The Christmas Fireside For Good Little Boys and Girls. By Grandfather Twain. The Story of the Bad Little Boy That Bore a Charmed Life." The story was the first of two original Mark Twain sketches published by Bret Harte in the *Californian*. Mark Twain then submitted the piece to the *Atlantic*, but the young assistant editor, William Dean Howells, rejected it: "A little fable like yours," Howells explained, "wouldn't leave it [the *Atlantic*] a single Presbyterian, Baptist, Unitarian, Episcopalian, Methodist or Millerite *paying* subscriber—all the dead-heads would stick to it and abuse it in the denominational newspapers" (191). It is interesting that Howells, who was to become Mark Twain's literary mentor and one of his most trusted friends, initiated his relationship with Mark Twain by warning him "that his Western sketches were too strong for Eastern tastes" (Stone 34).

The story was reprinted in Mark Twain's first book *The Celebrated Jumping Frog of Calaveras County* (1867), unchanged except for its new title, "The Story of the Bad Little Boy Who Didn't Come to Grief." It was reprinted, textually unaltered, in numerous unauthorized British editions of Mark Twain's sketches published between 1867 and 1872; in one of these, the John Camden Hotten *Screamers* edition (1871), the title was shortened to "Story of the Bad Little Boy." The abbreviated title served for the 1872 Routledge edition, which incorporated four minor authorial revisions, and for the authorized 1875 American edition, *Mark Twain's Sketches, New and Old*, in which four additional changes were made in proof. A summary of textual emendations appears in the Branch and Hirst edition (*Works* 715–18). The editors base their text on the original publication in the *Californian*.

"Story of the Good Little Boy Who Did Not Prosper" appeared first in the May 1870 issue of *Galaxy*. It was reprinted in *Piccadilly Annual*

(1870) and in *Nast's Almanac* (1873). The first authorized book publication appears in the 1875 *Sketches, New and Old.*

Circumstances of Composition, Sources, and Influences

The "Story of the Bad Little Boy" was written some ten months after Mark Twain's return to San Francisco from Calaveras County and just prior to his trip to the "Sandwich Islands" (Hawaii) aboard the *Ajax* as a correspondent for the Sacramento *Daily Union*. Although published some five years later, "Story of the Good Little Boy Who Did Not Prosper" is a companion piece, for like its predecessor it too makes "laborious fun of the pious and, to Twain, misleading morality of Sunday School tracts" (Stone 34). In style and tone both stories are typical of Mark Twain's California journalism: like the major portion of his apprentice writing, these stories depend for their humor upon burlesque and parody; both reflect the urbane attitudes of the San Francisco bohemian society with which Mark Twain associated; and both seem intended to satisfy the perceived demands of that society for light-hearted parody that in its assumption of people's inherently selfish nature debunks the conventional optimism of the age (Rogers 19; Branch, *Literary Apprenticeship,* 150).

The two stories follow in the same genre as "Whereas" (1864) and "Lucretia Smith's Soldier" (1864): the condensed novel that burlesques the popular sentimental fiction of the period. The genre proved fashionable among San Francisco's bohemian literati, and Bret Harte's earlier experiments with the form probably inspired Mark Twain's efforts. Harte in fact published a volume of such condensed novels in 1867. Mark Twain's first attempt in the genre, "Original Novelette," appeared in the 4 July 1864 issue of the *Call* (Emerson 30–31). The stories of the "Bad Little Boy" and "Good Little Boy" foreshadow the development of what Sloane identifies as the characteristic mode of Mark Twain's humor in the early 1870s: "Twain's genius lies in the ability to refocus humor on the broader philosophical aspects of culture and social relationships. Twain's own ethics were firmly fixed in a 'new' mode combining a liberated Presbyterianism with the practical roughness of a rising professional in a democratic society." (148).

The specific object of satire in these two stories is the simplistic juvenile fiction that inundated the nineteenth-century American book market. Such fiction accompanied blatantly didactic plots that invariably rewarded virtue and punished vice or bad habits with moralistic authorial commentary (Blair, "Structure," 76–77). A typical example is Mrs. E.D.E.N. Southworth's sentimental novel *Self-Made, or Out of the Depths,* published serially in the New York *Ledger* (1863–64). Mrs. Southworth offers her young hero as an example to us all of the rise to "earthly honors" and "eternal glory" that follows inevitably from the practice of "virtue, energy, and perseverance." Cawelti surveys the range of this jejune fiction, noting in particular the popularity of Horatio Alger's "juvenile phantasies of mobility in America." Such books reinforced the facile optimism characteristic of genteel society (125–30). So thoroughly had these books permeated the consciousness of the American people that Henry Ward Beecher, in the 1860s, saw fit to attack from the pulpit the fictional portraits of "impossible boys, with incredible goodness" (Blair, *Mark Twain,* 65–66).

In his parody of these adolescent conduct books, Mark Twain had ample precedent in the literature of the mid-century humorists. Blair reports that as early as the 1840s there surfaced a tradition in American humor that ridiculed the unrealistic expectations of youth generated by sentimental fiction by offering more honest or balanced portraits of naturally mischievous boys who eventually matured into responsible adults. Some, such as Johnson Jones Hooper in his creation of Simon Suggs, fascinated readers with "amoral portraits of unregenerate boys" that subverted the moral vision of genteel tales about well-behaved children who invariably prospered (*Mark Twain* 65; "Structure" 77).

Baetzhold suggests a possible link between "Story of the Good Little Boy" and Wordsworth's "Ode: Intimations of Immortality." Mark Twain's story not only lampoons "the fatuous moralism of the Sunday School tale" but also attacks "the romantic idea of the divine innocence of unspoiled childhood" (280). Jacob Blivens, the hero of Mark Twain's 1870 story, seems an "ironic counterpart" to Wordsworth's child in the "Intimations" ode who comes into this world "trailing clouds of glory": blown through a factory roof in the aftermath of a nitroglycerin explosion, Blivens "soared away toward the sun, with the fragments of . . . fifteen dogs stringing after him like the tail of a kite" (*Complete Short Stories* 70).

Relationship to Other Mark Twain Works

These two condensed novels are among a series of Mark Twain pieces that direct a satiric attack on moralistic juvenile fiction. Precedent for them is established in earlier newspaper sketches, specifically Mark Twain's "Advice for Good Little Boys" published 1 July 1865 in the San Francisco *Youths' Companion* (*Works* 405). In his "Advice for Good Little Girls," published in the *Territorial Enterprise* (1863), Mark Twain admonished youngsters with regard to their parents "to respect their little prejudices, and humor their little whims, and put up with their little foibles until they go to crowding you too much" (Branch, *Literary Apprenticeship* 150). "The Story of Mamie Grant, the Child Missionary," written in July 1868 but left unpublished, anticipates the theme of "Story of the Good Little Boy." This is the story of a nine-year-old girl, a devout and enthusiastic Sunday school student, who tries to save the souls of the various business people who visit her uncle's home. Unfortunately her efforts have disastrous consequences for the uncle: she stops his newspaper subscription, antagonizes the tax collector, and endangers his homestead when she prevents the return of the thousand dollars needed to forestall mortgage foreclosure. Yet Mamie is immensely pleased with her day's work: "I have saved a paper carrier, a census bureau, a creditor & a debtor, & they will bless me forever. . . . I may yet see my poor little name in a beautiful Sunday School book" (Emerson 49). The May 1870 *Galaxy* sketch, "Story of the Good Little Boy Who Did Not Prosper," begins with a specific reference to "a moral sketch which I published five or six years ago" (*Works* 406) and, because it too plays upon the experiential contradictions of genteel reward and punishment theory, is often treated as a companion piece to "Story of the Bad Little Boy" (Baldanza 99).

Blair sees the "Story of the Bad Little Boy" and "The Story of the Good Little Boy Who Did Not Prosper" as "germinal" to *Tom Sawyer* (1876), a novel that develops out of Mark Twain's "antipathy to the conventional plot structure of juvenile tales" ("Structure" 79). Certainly Tom's actions in the opening chapters of the novel—playing hooky from school, cheating to amass Sunday school tickets for Bible verses he never read, lying to his aunt, fighting with and bullying other children, associating with the town pariah Huck Finn—prove him to be what Mrs. Southworth and her genteel readers would call a "bad boy"; yet, as Blair points out, Tom enjoys the approval of Mark Twain, who clearly admires him more than he does the "good," well-behaved brother Sid (*Mark Twain* 66–67).

The two companion pieces, however, contain bleaker implications than the classic novel they foreshadow. In his roguish behavior, Tom Sawyer is a normal boy with an essentially good heart, a boy who calls back for most of us memories of our own childhood; his pranks are amusing in large part because they frustrate the meaningless, constricting proprieties of would-be guardians of decency who intrude into areas where moral dicta are simply inappropriate and who themselves often lack humanity and compassion. Tom succeeds, as in the fence whitewashing episode, because he can play to his advantage natural human foibles, a quality that should insure his success as a respectable adult in capitalistic America. The bad little boy, Jim, on the other hand, moves from his childhood pranks— stealing jam from the pantry, apples from Farmer Acorn's tree, a penknife from his teacher, and then framing "poor Widow Wilson's son, the moral boy"—to become as an adult an absolute moral terror: "And he grew up, and married, and raised a large family, and brained them all with an axe one night, and got wealthy by all manner of cheating and rascality, and now he is the infernalist wickedest scoundrel in his native village, and is universally respected, and belongs to the Legislature" (*Works* 410). Bellamy sees that the satire here is broadly based: its target "is the perversity of the human race . . . which makes material success, however acquired, a sufficient endowment for universal respect and a seat in the legislature." The story, she contends, foreshadows *The Gilded Age* (1873), where we have "a full-blown rascal with a seat in the national Congress" (111–12). Branch notes that underneath both these burlesque sketches lies an ironic sense of life ungoverned by moral law, and an acceptance of human beings as gullible, perverse, incorrigibly selfish creatures. Such conceptions serve here as the basis for comic parody; later, however, they govern the tragic vision of such works as *Pudd'nhead Wilson* (1894) and *The Mysterious Stranger* (1916) (*Literary Apprenticeship* 150–51).

Critical Studies

Both stories have occasioned very little sustained critical commentary and analysis, in large part because they are so transparent in their inversion of the conventional moralistic children's fable. Both are, Stone complains, "simply extended jokes. The humor is forced, the style banal, and no effort is made to delineate character or develop situation for any purpose except to provoke laughs" (35). Cox argues that a lack of richness or complexity results from the limitations of their mode—the burlesque—which concerns itself more with inverting the parent form than with generating a new plot (128). Branch sees the tales as among many early pieces that "dissipated into secondary comic effect," primarily because Mark Twain, in his strong emotional involvement with his subject, turns to invective and moralizing and sacrifices the detachment that satiric indirection and subtlety might have afforded him (*Literary Apprenticeship* 156).

The fullest discussions of the stories are provided by Blair ("Structure" 75–88) and Cawelti (125–67). Blair's concern is to trace connections of these stories to the structure and method of *Tom Sawyer*. Cawelti sees the story as part of Mark Twain's ambivalent critique of American capitalism. Finally, Cawelti argues, Mark Twain never quite manages to separate the meaning of American democracy from the Algerine ideal of self-improvement; yet at the same time he becomes painfully aware that his century had made a mockery of that ideal: "the young are told that merit consists in following the injunctions of narrow-minded teachers, while in practice they soon learn to emulate the corruption and chicanery of those who manage to amass large sums of money" (151–52).

Bibliography

PRIMARY

The Celebrated Jumping Frog of Calaveras County, and Other Sketches. Edited by John Paul. New York: Charles Henry Webb, 1867.

*The Complete Short Stories of Mark Twain. Now Collected for the First Time. Edited by Charles Neider. Garden City, N.Y.: Hanover House, 1957. ["Story of the Good Little Boy Who Did Not Prosper."]

Mark Twain's Sketches. Selected and Revised by the Author. London: George Routledge & Sons, 1872.

Mark Twain's Sketches, New and Old. Now First Published in Complete Form. Hartford and Chicago: American Publishing Co., 1875.

Screamers: A Gathering of Scraps of Humour, Delicious Bits, & Short Stories. London: John Camden Hotten, 1871.

*The Works of Mark Twain: Early Tales & Sketches, Vol. 2 (1864–1865). Edited by Edgar M. Branch and Robert H. Hirst. Vol. 15 of the Iowa-California edition of *The Works of Mark Twain.* Berkeley and Los Angeles: University of California Press, 1981. ["Story of the Bad Little Boy."]

SECONDARY

Baetzhold, Howard G. *Mark Twain & John Bull: The British Connection.* Bloomington: Indiana University Press, 1970.

Baldanza, Frank. *Mark Twain: An Introduction and Interpretation.* New York: Holt, Rinehart & Winston, 1961.

Bellamy, Gladys C. *Mark Twain as a Literary Artist.* Norman: University of Oklahoma Press, 1950.

Blair, Walter. *Mark Twain & Huck Finn.* Berkeley and Los Angeles: University of California Press, 1960.

———. "On the Structure of *Tom Sawyer.*" *Modern Philology* 37 (August 1939):75–88.

Branch, Edgar M. *The Literary Apprenticeship of Mark Twain, With Selections from His Apprentice Writings.* Urbana: University of Illinois Press, 1950.

Cawelti, John G. *Apostles of the Self-Made Man.* Chicago: University of Chicago Press, 1965.

Cox, James M. *Mark Twain: The Fate of Humor.* Princeton, N.J.: Princeton University Press, 1966.

Emerson, Everett. *The Authentic Mark Twain: A Literary Biography of Samuel L. Clemens.* Philadelphia: University of Pennsylvania Press, 1984.

Howells, Mildred, ed. *Life and Letters of William Dean Howells.* Vol. 1. Garden City, N.Y.: Doubleday, 1928.

Rogers, Franklin R. *Mark Twain's Burlesque Patterns.* Dallas: Southern Methodist University Press, 1960.

Sloane, David E. E. "Mark Twain's Comedy: the 1870s." *Studies in American Humor* 2 (January 1976):146–56.

Stone, Albert E., Jr. *The Innocent Eye: Childhood in Mark Twain's Imagination.* New Haven: Yale University Press, 1961.

39

The $30,000 Bequest

Publication History

Mark Twain wrote "The $30,000 Bequest" while living at the Villa Quarto in Florence, Italy, during the winter of 1903–4. The story appeared first in *Harper's Weekly*, 10 December 1904, and then served as the title story for a book of sketches published in 1906.

Circumstances of Composition, Sources, and Influences

The summer of 1903, which Mark Twain spent at Quarry Farm near Elmira, New York, was not an especially productive time. He did manage to write a sentimental, antivivisection story, "A Dog's Tale" (1903), for his daughter Jean, but most of his time was spent in preparation for the move to Florence necessitated by Olivia's declining health. Before leaving the United States, however, Mark Twain entered an agreement with Harpers—a "sort of half promise" as he wrote to Joe Twichell in 1904—to grind out thirty thousand words annually to supplement his income from the collected edition Harpers was publishing at the time (Emerson 245; Paine 1212). The last substantial fiction Mark Twain was to complete and publish during his lifetime, "The $30,000 Bequest" was one of several sketches he wrote during the fall 1903-winter 1904 to allay Olivia's anxieties over the expenses in Italy. He had hopes that the story and other miscellaneous magazine writing would generate some seventy-five hundred dollars to improve the couple's financial situation.

A preoccupation with money had been a fairly constant factor in Mark Twain's personal and professional life; indeed, as Hill notes, "he speculated, suffered, and sued as instinctively as he wrote" (80). A series of unfortunate investments made in the expectation of quick, easy, and substantial returns had brought Mark Twain to the point of bankruptcy by the mid-1890s, and subsequently much of his artistic effort sprang from his desperation to satisfy creditors. Scholars see Mark Twain's anxieties about money as the inspiration for "The $30,000 Bequest," a thinly veiled autobiographical story in which he accepts responsibility for the catastrophes that resulted from his fascination with dreams of wealth in the late

1880s (Emerson 244–45; Geismar 249–50; Morgan 6). On his deathbed, Saladin Foster articulates the lesson he has learned and voices hope that his fate might serve as a cautionary tale to others who share his pursuit of illusory wealth: "Vast wealth, acquired by sudden and unwholesome means, is a snare. It did us no good, transient were its feverish pleasures; yet for its sake we threw away our sweet and simple and happy life—let others take warning by us" (522). Hill argues that Foster's dying words "might almost serve as the epigraph for the Clemens' marriage and life together." Like Mark Twain, Saladin Foster is rash, ill-tempered, and eventually dishonest; like Olivia, Electra is a conventional Christian obsessed with money and speculation who is injured by her insensitive husband's "untimely and ill-chosen playfulness" about Christian missionaries. Both couples have daughters who lose suitors because the pretentious parents think the men have not achieved a proper financial and social position. In short, the fictional family like its real model has sacrificed "a sweet and simple and happy life" to its pride, ostentation, vanity, and dreams of wealth (79; Emerson 244–45).

A more direct and, it seems to me, plausible inspiration for the story is Mark Twain's memory of his family's illusory hopes of fortune from inherited land in Tennessee. As a young man, John Clemens—Mark Twain's father—invested five hundred dollars in seventy-five thousand acres of land situated midway between the Cumberland and Tennessee rivers. Rich in mineral deposits and heavily timbered, the land would eventually yield, John Clemens thought, a fortune to secure his family's future. His dream and the children's deferred hopes, however, never materialized; some forty years later, the disillusioned family surrendered the land for unpaid taxes. Mark Twain describes the experience in his *Autobiography:* the Tennessee land "kept us hoping and hoping during forty years, and forsook us at last. It put our energies to sleep and made visionaries out of all of us—dreamers and indolent. . . . It is good to begin life poor; it is good to begin life rich—these are wholesome; but to begin it poor and *prospectively* rich! The man who has not experienced it cannot imagine the curse of it" (94). "The $30,000 Bequest," McMahan contends, is Mark Twain's "artistic delineation of this curse" (23).

Relationship to Other Mark Twain Works

"The $30,000 Bequest" is among a series of sketches and stories concerned with the effects of money on the human spirit and interpersonal relationships. These stories, written between 1893–1903, fall roughly into two categories: those, like "The £1,000,000 Bank-Note" (1893) and "You've Been a Dam Fool, Mary. You Always Was!" (completed 1904), that are essentially reassuring in their demonstration of people's ability to resist the temptations of easy money and to treasure character, human relationships, and compassion more than financial gain; and those like "The Man That Corrupted Hadleyburg" (1899), "Sold to Satan" (1903), and "The $30,000 Bequest," that remain bleaker testimonies to the malignant, corrupting influence of wealth or dreams of wealth, bringing to the surface avaricious instincts that doom people to moral ruin and psychological disintegration (Macnaughton 196–98).

Morgan analyzes money imagery in "The £1,000,000 Bank-Note" and "The $30,000 Bequest" to demonstrate that the stories, though they offer radically different conclusions, provide a thematically consistent statement (6–10). In each story, as in "Hadleyburg," an outsider or stranger intrudes into a morally complacent, closed social order and tempts with illusory promises of wealth (Cox 265). The protagonists of the two stories, however, differ radically—in their character, their response to the temptation of easy money, and their ultimate fate. Henry Adams, the hero of "The £1,000,000 Bank-Note," is essentially innocent and honest, less affected by the sudden promise of quick riches than are his neighbors, and is finally rewarded by Providence for his strength of character. Saladin and Electra Foster, on the other hand, prove "morally deficient." Initially honest, having prospered as a result of hard work, clean living, and thrifty habits, the Fosters nevertheless fall victim to their dreams of "comrading with kings and princes and stately lords and ladies." When they learn of their impending fortune bequeathed by an uncle "not for love, but because money had given him most of his troubles and exasperations" (499), their dreams of money become the focus of their attention and, as a result, their piety, moral virtue, thrifty habits, and human relationships all crumble. The story does indeed demonstrate, as Saladin recognizes, that "vast wealth acquired by sudden and unwholesome means" brings destruction; but, as Morgan points out, the problem is not the "vast wealth" but the "sudden and unwholesome means" of acquisition. The promise of money in both stories is a test, a challenge to virtue: Adams passes, and is rewarded; the Fosters do not, and are destroyed (6–10).

Which of the two perspectives more clearly reflects Mark Twain's attitudes toward human nature? Covici thinks that "The Man That Corrupted Hadleyburg" and "The $30,000 Bequest" are more powerful and convincing because they are more realistic. "The £1,000,000 Bank-Note" is a romance, Covici argues, and for Mark Twain "only in a dream world can money and compassionate idealism or love go together." The union of love and dollars in the earlier romance is an illusion, "a dream of wish-fulfillment"; in "Hadleyburg" and "The $30,000 Bequest" realistic observation of actual, plausible human behavior transforms dream into nightmare with the discovery that money—that object of the fabled "American

262 TWAIN'S SHORT STORIES

dream"—and love are incompatible (207–8). In fact, Long argues, "The $30,000 Bequest" exposes the dangers of falling prey to a fantasy world, for it is their escape into the realm of dream that dooms the Fosters to utter destruction. The story hence becomes another of Mark Twain's attacks on romanticism, akin to "A Curious Experience" (1881)—a tale that portrays a boy so infatuated with the romance of dime novels that he can neither perceive nor function in the real world. The romance may serve us well when it offers a vision of the possibility of heroic action, calls us to exercise the best in our nature and so transcend the naturalistic forces that doom most of us to cowardice and simple greed. Yet when our romantic vision envelops the world in "a deceptive haze," when it distorts moral values and perverts human relationships—as it does with the Grangerfords in *Huckleberry Finn* (1885) or with the characters in "Hadleyburg," *The Mysterious Stranger* (1916), and "The $30,000 Bequest"—then it is the responsibility of the "serious" writer to devastate that vision with an unflinching depiction of our real nature and the forces that shape it (Long 258). Mark Twain confided to Howells in an 1899 letter: "What I have been wanting is a chance to write a book without reserves. . . . I believe I can make it tell what I think of man, & how he is constructed, & what a shabby poor ridiculous thing he is, & how mistaken he is in his estimate of his character & powers & qualities & his place among the animals" (*Mark Twain-Howells Letters* 698–99).

Critical Studies

"The $30,000 Bequest" dramatizes the corrupting effects of greed and the consequences of an obsession with dreams of wealth. Since the pursuit of riches is an integral part of our national myth, the story questions certain fundamental values of American life: money is not a blessing providing access to an enhanced life but a curse that saps the soul's vitality and devastates human relationships. "For its sake," Saladin comes to realize, "we threw away our sweet and simple and happy life" (522). In this story Mark Twain avoids the diffusiveness generally characteristic of his attacks on American culture by focusing exclusively on the dreams, obsessions, and demise of two characters—Saladin and Electra Foster—who, by implication, are representative of American society at large (Macnaughton 196–98). The initial introduction to the couple provides little to distinguish Sally and Aleck from other Americans of their class: we learn Sally's profession (bookkeeper), his age (thirty-five, mid-life), his salary, and a brief history of its gradual, steady increase over the years; we learn that the couple's hard work, thrift, clean living, and Aleck's management of their assets have afforded them moderate prosperity and a happy, conventional middle-class life.

But we also learn that the Eden they have created for themselves fails to satisfy. Although Aleck is "happy in her husband, happy in her children, and the husband and the children were happy in her" (498), she like her spouse is "a dreamer of dreams and a private dabbler in romance." The tragic flaw to which the couple will succumb has been identified: in the private sanctuary of their parlor, the Fosters dream of an upward mobility made possible only by a vast increase in fortune, of "comrading with kings and princes and stately lords and ladies." The apparent opportunity to realize their insatiable dreams seems imminent, for the couple learns that Tilbury Foster, "a sort of vague and indefinite uncle or second or third cousin," intends to bequeath to them thirty thousand dollars in cash—"not for love, but because money had given him most of his troubles . . . and he wished to place it where there was good hope that it would continue its malignant work" (499). The couple pays no heed to the warning explicit in Tilbury's bequest, "for both were dreaming"—Sally of ways to spend it, Aleck of investments to secure its increase.

The expectations of fabulous riches, however, does not alter character so much as it brings to the surface destructive forces latent within us all. As Covici notes, the recurring gambling metaphor—specifically poker—accentuates the universality of the central character, establishing him as a rather ordinary, unpretentious man while at the same time revealing his grasp of his own limitations, which eventually occasion his demise: it "both vivifies him and foreshadows his actions" (24). After censuring his wife for being "immorally pious" in her hypocritical albeit conventional expression of joy that Uncle Tilbury apparently continues to live, Sally retreats and apologizes, aware that in his impatience he had blundered: "Then, musingly, he apologized to himself. 'I certainly held threes—I *know* it—but I drew and didn't fill. That's where I'm so often weak in the game. If I had stood pat—but I didn't. I never do. I don't know enough' " (504). Sally's lament here is two-fold. On the one hand, he regrets his failure to "fill"; such failure, however, lies beyond Sally's control for, as Covici points out, no one in poker controls the fall of the cards and, indeed, the story revolves around the couple's doomed hopes for a fortune that never falls their way. On the other hand, Sally laments his own inadequacy in the game—his inability to stand pat, to pass, and to bluff successfully. It is this character weakness that eventually blights his marriage and creates his misery. As Sally surrenders to fantasies of wealth, he engages vicariously in all sorts of debauched behavior. The transgressions are as imaginary as his wealth, but their effect on human relationships is real: Aleck notes the glazed eyes and slack face that testify to his fantasies; he cannot "bluff" her, and their "happy" life together is irretrievably lost (Covici 24–25).

Another character flaw that the promise of riches accentuates but does not cause is Saladin's failure to take control of the household. That the reversal of sex roles preexists the illusory hope of wealth is suggested by the couple's "pet names. Saladin's was a curious and unsexing one—Sally; and so was Electra's—Aleck" (498–99). The reversal of sex roles manifests itself primarily in the couple's attitude toward money: "From her marriage-day forth, Aleck's grip had been upon the purse, and Sally had seldom known what it was to be privileged to squander a dime on non-necessities" (500). News of the bequest intensifies, or brings to the surface, the preex-istent condition: Sally dreams of spending the imaginary inheritance, begs Aleck for her permission to indulge his frivolous materialism; Aleck, on the other hand, calculates means of investing and increasing their wealth and disciplines and dominates her weaker husband's lack of control. McMahan argues that Aleck's calculating mind and obsession with invest-ments, her "drive for wealth and power," is for Mark Twain "a perversion of the natural social order" (24).

Other perversions surface as well. Family life deteriorates as soon as the Fosters learn of their imminent fortune. Absorbed in thoughts of their prospective wealth and what to do with it, Sally and Aleck become obli-vious to their children, who "took themselves away early, for the parents were silent, distraught, and strangely unentertaining. The good-night kisses might as well have been impressed upon vacancy, for all the response they got; the parents were not aware of the kisses, and the children had been gone an hour before their absence was noticed" (500). What thoughts Sally and Aleck do have of their daughters are subsumed by their fantasies of wealth: Gwendolen and Clytemnestra become pawns to enhance the fam-ily's social position as their parents consider appropriate suitors, rejecting real ones like Adelbert and Hosannah—"the changed financial conditions had raised up a social bar between their daughters and the young mechan-ics" as well as a succession of imaginary ones of decidedly more elevated social standing. Their final choices are, in Aleck's words, assets rather than liabilities: a prince with "a gambling-hall, and a graveyard, and a bishop, and a cathedral—all his very own . . . the tidiest little property in Eu-rope"; and "His Royal Highness Sigismund-Siegfried-Lauenfeld-Denkel-spiel-Schwartzenberg Blutwurst, Hereditary Grand Duke of Katzenyammer" (518–19).

Friendships and long-held values likewise fall victim to the Fosters' reveries. When Mrs. Eversly Bennett, the parson's wife, calls to discuss a charity, she finds the formerly affable couple rude hosts indeed, for they "were not hearing a word she was saying; so she got up, wondering and indignant, and went away" (503). Despite the fact that both had been staunch supporters of temperance, "with all that implies of boiler-iron vir-tue and unendurable holiness," the couple introduces champagne at din-ner—"not real champagne, but plenty real enough for the amount of imagination expended on it." The narrator sees their action as demonstration of a "sad truth": "whereas principle is a great and noble protection against showy and degrading vanities and vices, poverty is worth six of it" (511). With poverty seemingly no longer an obstacle to degrading vanities, the couple succumbs, hence calling into question the moral validity of any principle they had heretofore espoused.

The most damning perversion brought to light by the Fosters' obsession with wealth concerns the couple's religious views and attitudes. Both are at the outset conventionally religious: Aleck, McMahan surmises, "was a Christian from the cradle, and duty and the force of habit required her to go through the motions"; Sally, less devout than his wife, nevertheless subscribes to Christian faith and practice "as a kind of fire insurance" (24–25). As the story unfolds, however, the couple comes to conflate their spiritual and economic objectives, revealing, as Morgan points out, their "cash-nexus view of God and of religion" (9). "As diligently all the week as she studied her Bible Sundays," Aleck peruses "with an eye single to finance" the *Wall Street Pointer* and the Chicago paper. Gradually she is unable to distinguish between spiritual and monetary "investments." Sally, for his part, stands in awe of his wife's manipulation of her "worldly stocks" as much as of her "conservative caution in working her spiritual deals." When the couple begins to break the Sabbath, abandoning church to devote their time first to planning and managing their investments and then to directing their expenditures, it becomes apparent that their true god is money. For Mark Twain, however, they are not alone; their action is merely a logical extension of a kind of religion "long popular in American society—the love-God-and-He-will-make-you-prosperous variety" (McMahan 25). The Fosters have simply eliminated the middleman; the bequest makes God expendable.

Macnaughton notes the "moral toughness" of Mark Twain's tale (198). The recognition that for the sake of wealth "we threw away our sweet and simple and happy life" comes too late to the deluded and foolish couple, who "lived yet two years, in mental night, always brooding, steeped in vague regrets and melancholy dreams, never speaking" (522). Most disturbing is not that the couple suffers from their greed and vanity, nor even that there is no motive save malignity in Tilbury's scheme, but that, finally, the Fosters fail to learn from their experience. Theirs is no fortunate fall; for Mark Twain suffering is not necessarily redemptive. Although Saladin recognizes that "transient were . . . [the] feverish pleasures" of vast wealth and hopes "others take warning by us," his dying words testify to his unregenerate condition: "with base and cunning calculation he [Tilbury] left us but thirty thousand, knowing we would try to increase it, and ruin our life and break our hearts. Without added expense he could have left us far above desire of increase, far above the temptation to speculate" (522). Macnaughton mistakenly attributes this concluding expression of persistent greed to Aleck; certainly it would not have been out of character. But the fact that this lament comes from Sally serves to undercut his conventional sermonizing about the evils of greed, which immediately precedes it.

Bibliography

PRIMARY

*The Complete Short Stories of Mark Twain. Now Collected for the First Time. Edited by Charles Neider. Garden City, N.Y.: Hanover House, 1957.

Autobiography. Edited by A. B. Paine. Vol. 2. New York: Harper & Brothers, 1924.

Mark Twain-Howells Letters: The Correspondence of Samuel L. Clemens and William Dean Howells, 1872–1910. Edited by Henry Nash Smith and William M. Gibson. Vol. 2. Cambridge, Mass.: Harvard University Press, 1960.

The $30,000 Bequest and Other Stories. New York: Harper & Brothers, 1906.

SECONDARY

Covici, Pascal, Jr. Mark Twain's Humor: The Image of a World. Dallas: Southern Methodist University Press, 1962.

Cox, James M. Mark Twain: The Fate of Humor. Princeton, N.J.: Princeton University Press, 1966.

Emerson, Everett. The Authentic Mark Twain: A Literary Biography of Samuel L. Clemens. Philadelphia: University of Pennsylvania Press, 1984.

Geismar, Maxwell. Mark Twain: An American Prophet. Boston: Houghton Mifflin, 1970.

Hill, Hamlin. Mark Twain: God's Fool. New York: Harper & Row, 1973.

Long, E. Hudson. Mark Twain Handbook. New York: Hendricks House, 1957.

Macnaughton, William R. Mark Twain's Last Years as a Writer. Columbia: University of Missouri Press, 1979.

McMahan, Elizabeth. "Finance and Fantasy as Destroyers in Twain's 'The $30,000 Bequest.'" Mark Twain Journal 21, no. 2 (Summer 1982):23–26.

Morgan, Ricki. "Mark Twain's Money Imagery in 'The £1,000,000 Bank-Note' and 'The $30,000 Bequest.'" Mark Twain Journal 19, no. 1 (1977):6–10.

Paine, Albert B. Mark Twain: A Biography. Vol. 3. New York: Harper & Brothers, 1912.

40

A True Story

Publication History

Although a note in the Author's National Edition of *The Writings of Mark Twain* dates the composition of "A True Story" as "about 1876" (265), actually the sketch was written in the summer 1874 during Mark Twain's stay at Quarry Farm near Elmira, New York (Emerson 77). Kaplan reports that Mark Twain "reticently and apologetically" sent the piece to Howells, who published it in the November 1874 issue of the *Atlantic Monthly*. The story bore the subtitle, "Repeated Word for Word as I Heard It," and though the first of Mark Twain's many contributions to the *Atlantic*, it earned him the highest rate the magazine had ever paid its contributors, twenty dollars a page (Kaplan 276–77; Long 183).

"A True Story" appeared in the 1875 American Publishing Company edition of *Sketches, New and Old*, and was printed with "The Recent Carnival of Crime" in 1877. It is included in several popular and readily accessible anthologies of Mark Twain's short fiction.

Circumstances of Composition, Sources, and Influences

During the summer of 1874 Mark Twain lived at Quarry Farm devoting most of his time to *The Adventures of Tom Sawyer* (1876). Olivia's sister, Mrs. Sue Crane, had a Negro cook—Auntie Cord—who had been a slave for more than forty years (Bellamy 299). Auntie Cord told Mark Twain of her experiences while in bondage and he, in turn, told her story to some friends, whose enthusiastic response prompted him to write it as "A True Story. Repeated Word for Word as I Heard It" (Gibson 76). Wisbey reports that the story is indeed faithful to factual details from Auntie Cord's life (1, 3–4).

Mark Twain had wanted for some time to crack the pages of the *Atlantic*, a "high brow" eastern literary magazine that symbolized to him the respectability he sought as a serious man-of-letters: its audience, he wrote to Howells, "is the only audience that I sit down before in perfect serenity (for the simple reason that it don't require a 'humorist' to paint himself striped & stand on his head every fifteen minutes)" (*Mark Twain-*

Howells Letters 49). A bit unsure whether his serious tale of pathos and human dignity would prove suitable for the *Atlantic,* Mark Twain sent the piece to Howells with an apologetic note: "I enclose also a 'True Story' which has no humor in it. You can pay me as lightly as you choose for that, for it is rather out of my line" (*Mark Twain-Howells Letters* 22). More in his "line" at the time, Gibson reports, were domestic farces drawn from the frustrating but gently amusing hassles of his bourgeois life in Hartford—e.g., the numerous McWilliamses stories (1875; 1882) (80). But Howells liked "A True Story" very much. Not only did he think it "extremely good and touching with the best and reallest kind of black talk in it" and accept it for immediate publication in the *Atlantic* at the maximum twenty-dollars-per-page rate (*Mark Twain-Howells Letters* 24), but in a December 1875 review of *Sketches, New and Old* he singled it out for lavish praise: "The rugged truth of the sketch leaves all other stories of slave life infinitely far behind, and reveals a gift in the author for the simple, dramatic report of reality which we have seen equalled in no other American writer" (Kaplan, *Mr. Clemens,* 277).

Mark Twain labored consciously to sustain the realistic qualities of the story that Howells so greatly admired. He explained to Howells that he had written "A True Story" exactly as he had heard it from Auntie Cord, "only starting with the beginning rather than the middle as she did" (Paine 514). He changes the order of events largely to improve narrative cogency and to accommodate the frame—the pleasantries exchanged by "Misto C——" and Aunt Rachel—that encloses the narrative. The title and subtitle obviously lend the aura of history rather than fiction to the tale and serve, Gibson suggests, "to warn the reader not to expect humor as its central feature" (77). It is, however, his concern for language that reveals Mark Twain's care in composing and revising this story to give it authenticity. He copied as exactly as he could the speech and demeanor of Auntie Cord and carefully revised the dialect in proof (Bellamy 299–300). His plan, he told Howells, was to polish Aunt Rachel's speech by reading it aloud from galleys because Auntie Cord had pronounced (and hence he would have to spell) the same word variously depending upon its place in a sentence (Gibson 19).

Relationship to Other Mark Twain Works

In its use of the frame story, "A True Story" structurally resembles several of Mark Twain's most successful early tales: "Jim Smiley and His Jumping Frog" (1865), "Jim Baker's Blue Jay Yarn" (1880), and "Jim Blaine and His Grandfather's Ram" (1872). Such a structure introduces a brief interplay between the persona Mark Twain and a vernacular narrator before permitting the vernacular character to tell a tale in an authentic colloquial voice. Just as Mark Twain allows the West to express itself—its prejudices, values, and unique world view—through representative spokesmen such as Simon Wheeler, Jim Blaine, and Jim Baker, so in "A True Story" he permits another minority point of view full and poignant expression—that of the American black. Moreover, as in the "Jumping Frog" and "Grandfather's Ram" stories, the character Mark Twain is once again the butt of a joke. This time Aunt Rachel's story makes him appear stupid and insensitive in his patronizing assumption that in her sixty years she had "never had any trouble."

The story is one of several Mark Twain works to focus on the customs, behavior, and psychology of black people in the antebellum South. In *The Gilded Age* (1873), Mark Twain had in Uncle Dan'l created a black character of some depth and complexity; moreover, in Dan'l's dialect speech— "the rising and falling inflections, the oratorial climaxes of the old Negro"—he had achieved a significant advance over previous literary efforts to mimic black talk (Bellamy 299). In "A True Story" Mark Twain comes much closer to realizing and sustaining the full emotional power of what Kaplan calls "impeccably nuanced but never obscure dialect" (*Mr. Clemens* 276–77). His explicit sympathy for the Negro and profound vision of the evil and inhumanity of slaveholding foreshadow fuller treatment of the same subject in *Huckleberry Finn* (1885) and *Pudd'nhead Wilson* (1894). Aunt Rachel is like Jim and Roxy a realistically drawn and fully realized character whose suffering at the hands of a white social order affords Mark Twain ample opportunity for satire and cultural analysis that deflates common racist misconceptions about blacks (Kellner 18–19).

Mark Twain also discovers in "A True Story" the potential of humor as a vehicle for pathos. Although characteristically Mark Twain generates his humor from false or excessive pathos (e.g., Emmeline Grangerford's sentimental effusions over the recent dead, or Tom Sawyer's self-pity at his own funeral), genuinely pathetic situations such as those that envelop his black characters might also fall within the purview of his comic vision (Gibson 124). Mark Twain shows a remarkable ability to place characters in comic situations or to have them respond comically in tragic ones without sacrificing their essential dignity. Minstrel elements surface in the behavior and speech of Rachel, Jim, and Roxy—but they are not minstrel characters. Humor serves to lighten or make bearable incredibly bleak circumstances, and in itself reflects the balanced vision, the equanimity of spirit, in the face of a hostile universe that constitutes his black characters' heroism.

"A True Story" served another, albeit indirect, function in Mark Twain's development as a writer. During the decade that preceded it, Mark Twain found most of his materials for fiction in either his experiences abroad or in his western adventures. Although such materials inspired comic masterpieces like *Innocents Abroad* (1869), "Jim Smiley and His Jumping Frog," and *Roughing It* (1872), he had almost exhausted them, as the aesthetic failure of *A Tramp Abroad* (1880) and his focus on domestic farces suggest. Howells was so taken with "A True Story" that in the fall of 1874 he requested a sequel for the *Atlantic*. Mark Twain initially responded that he had nothing to offer, but his concern for the language and the personality of the Negro in writing "A True Story"—composed just as he was bringing *Tom Sawyer* to a conclusion—had brought back to Mark Twain the aura of the antebellum South and memories of his childhood on the river and with slaves on the nearby plantations. He then responded to Howells's request with "Old Times on the Mississippi"; shortly afterwards he began work on *Huckleberry Finn* (Emerson 84–87).

Critical Studies

The realism and pathos of "A True Story" has made it one of the most admired of Mark Twain's sketches. Howells cited it as an example of the author's "serious" fiction (Long 189) and praised its "simple, dramatic report of reality." Kaplan calls it "a moving story, one of Mark Twain's best" (*Mr. Clemens* 276), a judgment that echoes the opinion of J. W. De Forest, author of *Miss Ravenal's Conversion* (1867), who wrote to Howells that "the story of the negress,—was a really great thing, amazingly natural & humorous, & touching even to the drawing of tears" (*Mark Twain-Howells Letters* 25).

The story overcomes its potential for melodrama and maudlin sentimentality through sheer force of Aunt Rachel, who is, as Fenger points out, one of Mark Twain's most balanced and fully developed characters (41). Her biblical name automatically lends her poignancy, and Mark Twain quickly transforms her from conventional Negro cook, "sitting respectfully below our level . . . for she was colored," to an awesome heroic personality: as she "warmed to her subject," ready to tell about the slave auction that splintered her family, Aunt Rachel "towered above us, black against the stars" (*Writings of Mark Twain* 267). A woman "of mighty frame and stature . . . her eye . . . undimmed and her strength unabated," Aunt Rachel "knows all 'bout slavery, 'case I ben one of 'em my own se'f" (266). Courageous and resilient, she is nevertheless "unsentimentally drawn"; as Gibson points out she is "a recognizably flawed human being" (79–80). She is vain of her Maryland ancestry ("I's one o' de ole Blue Hen's chickens, I is!" [267]) and position as officers' cook ("my place was wid de officers, an' it rasp me to have dem common sojers cavortin' roun' my kitchen like dat"), and she is contemptuous of Negroes she considers "trash" (270).

These human flaws furnish the humor in the story: her spirited defense of her kitchen during the "big sojer ball"; her contempt before "a spruce young nigger a-sailin' down de room wid a yaller wench roun' de wais' "; her response to the "nigger ridgment" that laughs at her, "Well, I jist march' on dem niggers—so, lookin' like a gen'l—an' dey jist cave' away befo' me an' out at de do!" (270–71). The humor, however, is inextricably bound to pathos, for it arises from the incongruity of action and situation. She is proud of her ancestral origins, her "blue hen" stock, yet the helpless victim of a social system that has its cruel way with her solely because of her race; she struggles to maintain the illusion of position and control in a world where finally she has neither. Her heroism arises from this same incongruity and is reflected in her demeanor and narrative method. Despite her chilling tale of suffering and abuse, she remains "a cheerful, hearty soul," refuses to surrender her dignity in the face of incredible affronts to it, and is still open to "joy" in what is an exceedingly hostile society.

Aunt Rachel's heroic affirmation of her dignity is evident in the brief frame that introduces her tale. Mark Twain, the white gentleman accustomed to a life of comfort and ease, witnesses Rachel's abundant good spirit: "She would let off peal after peal of laughter, and then sit with her face in her hands and shake with throes of enjoyment which she could no longer get breath enough to express" (265). He approaches her with customary racist condescension, assuming that she is a "happy-go-lucky" black without a care in the world: "Aunt Rachel, how is it that you've lived sixty years and never had any trouble?" Rachel's immediate response—"without even a smile in her voice" she asks "Misto C——" if he is "in 'arnest"— catches the unreflective Mark Twain off guard and, as he admits, "sobered my manner and my speech, too." As she begins her tale, Aunt Rachel explodes Mark Twain's racist assumptions of superiority by establishing their common humanity: "Well, sah, my ole man—dat's my husband'— he was lovin' an' kind to me, jist as kind as you is to yo' own wife. An' we had chil'en—seven chil'en—an' we loved dem chil'en jist de same as you loves yo' chil'en. Dey was black, but de Lord can't make no chil'en so black but what dey mother loves 'em an' wouldn't give 'em up, no, not for anything dat's in dis whole world" (266). From then on the story belongs to Aunt Rachel, and a poignant tale it is—of "trouble" Mark Twain in his sheltered bourgeois world never imagined. The effect is to leave him stunned and speechless. Bellamy (49–50) writes that it is a tribute to the artist's "restraint" that he closes "A True Story" with Rachel's ironic words, "Oh no, Misto C——, I hain't had no trouble. An' no *joy!*" (272).

The story is a remarkably succinct and realistic account of black life in the antebellum South. It celebrates the courage and dignity of the black woman and dramatizes the love and integrity of Negro families despite the splintering effects of chattel slavery. It exposes the hideous nature of the

South's "peculiar institution" and documents the chaos that ensued once slaveholders deserted their plantations leaving blacks to fend for themselves. Too, the story devastates numerous racist stereotypes while avoiding overt didacticism. Blacks are hardly carefree children with no problems of consequence. And, *Gone with the Wind* to the contrary, neither did they stand with their masters to oppose the invading Union armies; rather, Aunt Rachel's story presents the Union army as a liberating force. Slaves prove eager to assist Union soldiers, and many blacks play significant roles in the liberation of their brothers by participating in conflict as U.S. soldiers. As Foner writes, "In but a few pages, Twain tells us more about the Negro people, the true nature of slavery, the Civil War, the role of the Negro people in that conflict, than is achieved in many volumes" (202–4; Budd 92).

Bibliography

PRIMARY

The Complete Short Stories of Mark Twain. Now Collected for the First Time. Edited by Charles Neider. Garden City, N.Y.: Hanover House, 1957.

Great Short Works of Mark Twain. Edited by Justin Kaplan. New York: Harper & Row, 1967.

Mark Twain-Howells Letters. The Correspondence of Samuel L. Clemens and William Dean Howells, 1872–1910. Edited by Henry Nash Smith and William M. Gibson. Vol. 1. Cambridge, Mass.: Harvard Unversity Press, 1960.

Mark Twain's Sketches, New and Old. Hartford: American Publishing Co., 1875.

"A True Story." *Atlantic Monthly,* 4 November 1874, 591–94.

A True Story and The Recent Carnival of Crime. Boston: James R. Osgood, 1877.

*The Writings of Mark Twain. Author's National Edition. Vol. 19. New York: Harper & Brothers, 1915.

SECONDARY

Bellamy, Gladys C. *Mark Twain as a Literary Artist.* Norman: University of Oklahoma Press, 1950.

Budd, Louis J. *Mark Twain: Social Philosopher.* Bloomington: Indiana Unversity Press, 1962.

Emerson, Everett. *The Authentic Mark Twain: A Literary Biography of Samuel L. Clemens.* Philadelphia: University of Pennsylvania Press, 1984.

Fenger, Gerald J. *Perspectives of Satire in Mark Twain's Short Stories.* Ph.D. dissertation, Texas Christian University, 1974. Reprint in *Critical Approaches to Mark Twain's Short Stories,* edited by Elizabeth McMahan, 39–42. Port Washington, N.Y.: Kennikat Press, 1981.

Foner, Philip. *Mark Twain: Social Critic.* New York: International Publishers, 1958.

Gibson, William M. *The Art of Mark Twain.* New York: Oxford University Press, 1976.

Kaplan, Justin. *Mr. Clemens and Mark Twain.* New York: Simon & Schuster, 1966.

Kellner, Robert Scott. "Mark Twain and the Mental Cripple: The Challenge of Myth." *Mark Twain Journal* 21, no. 4 (Fall 1983):18–20.

Long, E. Hudson. *Mark Twain Handbook.* New York: Hendricks House, 1957.

Paine, Albert B. *Mark Twain: A Biography.* Vol. 2. New York: Harper & Brothers, 1912.

Smith, Henry Nash. *Mark Twain: The Development of a Writer.* Cambridge, Mass.: Harvard University Press, 1962.

Wisbey, Herbert A., Jr. "The True Story of Auntie Cord." *Mark Twain Society Bulletin* 4 (June 1981):1, 3–4.

41

Was It Heaven? or Hell?

Publication History

Mark Twain wrote "Was It Heaven? or Hell?" in late summer 1902 and published the story in the Christmas issue of *Harper's Magazine* that same year (Ferguson 293; Hill 52). The story was collected in *The $30,000 Bequest and Other Stories* (1906) and in the Author's National Edition.

Circumstances of Composition, Sources, and Influences

During the summer 1902 while Mark Twain and his family resided at York Harbor, Maine, William Dean Howells was a frequent visitor to their rented cottage, "The Pines." One evening on the verandah, Howells told Mark Twain a story concerning some former occupants of the cottage: a tale of two elderly women who shielded their dying niece from the knowledge that her daughter was afflicted with the same fatal illness that was claiming her own life (Paine 1177). Later in the summer Mark Twain used Howell's story as the basis for "Was It Heaven? or Hell?"

The story draws emotional poignancy from Mark Twain's memories of his wife's numerous convalescences and his daughter Susy's death in the mid-1890s, and the moral dilemma it dramatizes—the necessity of sinning for benevolent reasons—was one with which Mark Twain could readily identify (Hill 52; Baldanza 137). Baetzhold points out that Mark Twain had marked in his copy of W. E. H. Lecky's *History of European Morals* a quotation from Cardinal Newman's *Anglican Difficulties* citing the official church doctrine that it is morally better to endure dire calamities than to commit "one single venial sin." Mark Twain's story, Baetzhold contends, dramatizes "the moral quandary that such a principle could create" (364).

Events in the Mark Twain household in late 1902 rendered "Was It Heaven? or Hell?" eery prophecy. In August Olivia suffered a severe heart attack that left her bedridden. When in December daughter Jean contracted an extremely serious case of pneumonia, the family struggled to keep news of the daughter's illness and deteriorating condition from her mother. Clara assumed the role of censor, deciding what her mother should see and hear;

she was especially concerned to keep Mark Twain away from Olivia for fear that he might leak information about Jean's problems. Not surprisingly, Clara complained that "Was It Heaven? or Hell?" was too personal (Hill 52–56; Emerson 243). In a notebook entry, 27 December 1902, Mark Twain too noted the uncanny resemblance between his story and personal predicament: "For 6 days now my story in the Christmas *Harper's*—"Was It Heaven? or Hell?"—has been enacted in this household. Everyday Clara & the nurse have lied about Jean to her mother" (Paine 1190).

Relationship to Other Mark Twain Works

The story is among the many sentimental pieces of Mark Twain's later years, akin in tone to "The Californian's Tale" (1892), "The Death Disk" (1901), and "A Dog's Tale" (1903). Its serious thematic concerns, however, link the story to some of his more distinguished work. Like "The Man That Corrupted Hadleyburg" (1899), the story examines the problem of honesty and what Baldanza calls "the corroding psychological effects of conscience" (137). The conflict between inflexible moral codes and genuine human needs recalls similar conflicts dramatized in *Huckleberry Finn* (1885) (Wilson 80–94); again, Mark Twain clearly advocates moral action based not on abstract principle but on compassionate responses to individual human situations.

Critical Studies

The story opens with a simple statement of a moral transgression: "You told a lie? You confess it—you actually confess it—you told a lie!" (472). The culprit is the adored young niece, Helen Lester; the accusers, her doting aunts whose religious training "in the matter of morals and conduct . . . had been so uncompromisingly strict that it had made them exteriorly austere." Committed to "absolute truth, iron-bound truth, implacable and uncompromising truth, let the resulting consequences be what they might" (472–73), the aunts force young Helen to confront her dying mother with a confession of her sin. The local doctor soon arrives, censures the aunts for their hypocrisy and moral inflexibility, and announces that both mother and daughter have typhoid. "Impressionable, impulsive, emotional," the doctor "knew nothing about etiquette"; townspeople, some in reverence, some derisively, refer to him as "The *Only* Christian" (474). He orders the aunts not to disturb the mother with news of her daughter's fatal illness, for compassion dictates that she be allowed to die in peace. The aunts, however, are determined to tell the truth at all cost, but when actually confronted with the mother's pathetic solicitations about her daughter's condition, they prove weak and lie. The mother eventually dies, spared the agony of knowing her daughter too had succumbed to the fever. At the end of the story the two aunts must answer to "the angel of the Lord" for their deceit. They admit that their "sin is great" and confess they are incapable of "perfect and final repentance," because "we know that if we were in those hard straits again our hearts would fail again, and we should sin as before." Their honesty here is striking and ironic: the women refuse to lie about their repentance to the angel of the Lord, even though they believe that the truth will cost them their souls. Their final disposition is left to the reader to discern: "Was It Heaven? or Hell?" (488). The paradox of the story resembles that of *Huckleberry Finn:* the action they think endangers their immortal souls actually saves them; their weakness is strength.

"Was It Heaven? or Hell?" so exaggerates the moral dilemma confronted by the two "utterly dear and lovable and good" old aunts that it assumes the qualities of a fable. It is, Paine argues, "next to 'Hadleyburg,' . . . Mark Twain's greatest fictional sermon" (1177). Unlike "Hadleyburg," however, the story is excessively sentimental—Paine labels it "a heartbreaking history which probes the very depths of the human soul," and reports that the story brought an avalanche of letters from grateful readers who had faced a dilemma identical to the one depicted in the story (1190). Archibald Henderson, writing in 1909, cited the story as testimony to Mark Twain's moralistic nature, one of several of his "vindications of the moral principle" (210). Today, Mark Twain's story is not so highly regarded, perhaps because as Wagenknecht writes, "we can no longer conceive the possibility of any sane person wishing to debate the subject against him" (213). The characters are too stereotyped, the moral alternatives too clear-cut, the author's bias too apparent for effective fiction.

Bibliography

PRIMARY

The Complete Short Stories of Mark Twain. Now Collected for the First Time. Edited by Charles Neider. Garden City, N.Y.: Hanover House, 1957.

The $30,000 Bequest and Other Stories. New York: Harper & Brothers, 1906.

The Writings of Mark Twain. Author's National Edition. Harper & Brothers edition. Vol. 6. New York: P. F. Collier & Son, 1917.

SECONDARY

Baetzhold, Howard G. *Mark Twain and John Bull: The British Connection.* Bloomington: Indiana University Press, 1970.

Baldanza, Frank. *Mark Twain: An Introduction and Interpretation.* New York: Holt, Rinehart, & Winston, 1961.

Emerson, Everett. *The Authentic Mark Twain: A Literary Biography of Samuel L. Clemens.* Philadelphia: University of Pennsylvania Press, 1984.

Ferguson, Delancey. *Mark Twain: Man and Legend.* Indianapolis: Bobbs-Merrill, 1943.

Hill, Hamlin. *Mark Twain: God's Fool.* New York: Harper & Row, 1973.

Henderson, Archibald. "Mark Twain." *Harper's Monthly,* May 1909, 948–55. Reprint in *Critical Essays on Mark Twain,* edited by Louis J. Budd, 205–12. Boston: G. K. Hall, 1982.

Paine, Albert B. *Mark Twain: A Biography.* Vol. 3. New York: Harper & Brothers, 1912.

Wagenknecht, Edward. *Mark Twain: The Man and His Work.* New Haven: Yale University Press, 1935.

Wilson, James D. *"Adventures of Huckleberry Finn:* From Abstraction to Humanity." *Southern Review* 10 (January 1974):80–94.

42

You've Been a Dam Fool, Mary. You Always Was!

Publication History

Mark Twain completed "You've Been a Dam Fool, Mary. You Always Was!" in January 1904, while in residence at the Villa di Quarto in Florence, Italy. In February Mark Twain sent the story to F. A. Duneka at Harper and Brothers, who rejected it largely because he found the title objectionable. Although Mark Twain indicated his willingness to make minor modifications to satisfy Duneka, the story remained unpublished until 1972 (Hill 76–77). Tuckey's edition of *Mark Twain's Fables of Man* includes the only published version of the story.

Circumstances of Composition, Sources, and Influences

The idea for the story came to Mark Twain in the spring of 1895. Mark Twain records in his notebook in May of that year the details of his confrontation with a man on board a steamer who had been "abusing Southern honesty." To the stranger's derogatory remarks, Mark Twain counters with an anecdote that later serves as the germ of the story. A Mr. Hand, who was a Northerner living in South Carolina before the war, was the business partner of a Southern gentleman. While on a trip north, the war erupted and Hand was unable to return. His former partner moved from South Carolina to another part of the South, and with their mutual money, speculated in cotton and amassed a fortune. When he finally locates Hand, he presents him with six hundred thousand dollars, his half of the fortune.

Mark Twain did not return to his idea for the story until 1903 when, while living in Florence for reasons of Olivia's health, he shaped his initial notebook entry into short fiction. He wrote to Duneka on 30 December 1903 that he had written a draft of "The Midsummer Story" and that Olivia was "editing the hellfire out of" it. Tuckey reports, however, that there is no evidence that Olivia exerted any editorial supervision over "You've Been a Dam Fool, Mary"; rather, Mark Twain himself continued to tinker with the manuscript into January of the following year (*Mark Twain's Fables* 249).

Relationship to Other Mark Twain Works

"You've Been a Dam Fool, Mary. You Always Was!" forms part of what Tuckey calls a "minority report" amidst the wealth of pessimistic writing characteristic of the last decade of Mark Twain's life. A story of an "honest rebel" who remains loyal to his former Northern partner when it would have been easy and profitable to exploit him, "You've Been a Dam Fool, Mary," like *Personal Recollections of Joan of Arc* (1896) and "Newhouse's Jew Story," testifies to people's capacity for altruistic action (*Mark Twain's Fables* 16). Macnaughton links the story to "The $30,000 Bequest" (1904) and the sketch "Sold to Satan" (written 1904), for all three "focus on the uses and abuses of money and the desire for gain" (197). "You've Been a Dam Fool, Mary" differs from the other two pieces, however, for it is an account of money put to good use, of friendship and kindness overcoming self-interest. For that reason, Macnaughton calls it the "weakest of the three" works, a "sentimental, moralistic story" (197).

Gribben sees in the story Mark Twain's desperate hope for an escape from environmental pressures that enslave, and links the story to "The £1,000,000 Bank-Note" (1893), "The $30,000 Bequest" and *Following the Equator* (1897). All present "eccentric benefactors" whose unexpected bequest offers the opportunity for freedom to "their fortunate beneficiaries" (197). Preoccupied with financial pressures through much of his later life, Mark Twain repeatedly in his fiction explores the effects of sudden, vast, unexpected wealth upon those trapped in desperate straits. Often the scenario takes a tragic turn, as in "The Man That Corrupted Hadleyburg" (1899) or "The $30,000 Bequest," when the illusion of unmerited riches brings to the surface people's base instincts and shatters any hope of contentment with a simple life. But at other times, as in this story and in "The £1,000,000 Bank-Note," money accentuates the best in human nature as it brings freedom "from the anxieties and images that haunted [Mark Twain's] dreams and his fiction" (Gribben 197).

Critical Studies

Although the story treats the theme of money and testifies to the human capacity for altruistic action, it is also a parable that provides a prescription for reconciliation of sectional differences after the war. Thomas Hill, the Northerner, and James Marsh, the Southerner, are representatives of their regions; separated they are, like their respective regions, incomplete and floundering; united, having dispelled suspicion and distrust, they, like the Union, can become strong and prosperous.

Hill and Marsh complement one another, each possessing the virtues and deficiencies of their regions. The industrial strength and skilled, conscientious labor of the North are reflected in Hill and his smithy, masters of the iron trade and dedicated hard workers; Marsh, having made his fortune in cotton through his charismatic personality and shrewd management of money, represents the social graces and pioneering spirit of the South: "The Southerner was full of energy and business shrewdness, the Northerner was untiringly industrious, faithful, and valuable, but he had no faculty for business, nor for planning and pushing" (252). Each lacks an ingredient essential for economic prosperity: Marsh has the shrewdness and imagination indispensable for business success, but lacks the capital represented by Hill's eight hundred dollars; Hill, having obtained capital through hard work and thrift, lacks business skills, for he is hopelessly inept at collecting debts.

But the link between the two men is more than economic. The two are psychologically dependent on one another. Without Marsh, Hill withers. Separated from his friend, Marsh puts their mutual investment to good use and prospers, but he is fragmented and discontented until he finds his partner and repays a debt of honor. Marsh never wavers in his search for Hill, and feels whole and redeemed with the public confirmation of his friend's unwavering belief in him. Personal relationships overcome sectional differences. Honor and faith are more important than money in securing the welfare of the united men.

Bibliography

PRIMARY

Mark Twain's Fables of Man. Edited by John S. Tuckey. Berkeley and Los Angeles: University of California Press, 1972.

SECONDARY

Gribben, Alan. "Those Other Thematic Patterns in Mark Twain's Writings." *Studies in American Fiction* 13 (Autumn 1985):185–200.

Hill, Hamlin. *Mark Twain: God's Fool*. New York: Harper & Row, 1973.

Macnaughton, William R. *Mark Twain's Last Years as a Writer*. Columbia: University of Missouri Press, 1979.

Appendix

Publication History of Mark Twain's Short Stories

1882	"Mrs. McWilliams and the Lightning"
	"The McWilliamses and the Burglar Alarm"
	"The Invalid's Story"
	"The Stolen White Elephant"
1883	"A Dying Man's Confession"
	"The Professor's Yarn"
	"A Burning Brand"
1891	"Luck"
1893	"The Californian's Tale"
	"The Esquimau Maiden's Romance"
	"Extracts from Adam's Diary"
	"Is He Living or Is He Dead?"
	"The £1,000,000 Bank-Note"
1897	"Cecil Rhodes and the Shark"
	"The Joke That Made Ed's Fortune"
	"A Story without End"
1899	"The Man That Corrupted Hadleyburg"
1901	"The Death Disk"
	"Two Little Tales"
1902	"The Five Boons of Life"
	"The Belated Russian Passport"
	"A Double-Barreled Detective Story"
	"Was It Heaven? or Hell?"
1903	"A Dog's Tale"
1904	"The $30,000 Bequest"
1905	"Eve's Diary"
1906	"A Horse's Tale"
1907–8	"Extracts from Captain Stormfield's Visit to Heaven"
1909	"A Fable"
1972	"Little Bessie"
	"The Second Advent"
	"The International Lightning Trust"
	"Randall's Jew Story"
	"You've Been a Dam Fool, Mary. You Always Was!"

Index